A Primer on Partial Least Squares Structural Equation Modeling (PLS-SEM)

Second Edition

SAGE was founded in 1965 by Sara Miller McCune to support the dissemination of usable knowledge by publishing innovative and high-quality research and teaching content. Today, we publish over 900 journals, including those of more than 400 learned societies, more than 800 new books per year, and a growing range of library products including archives, data, case studies, reports, and video. SAGE remains majority-owned by our founder, and after Sara's lifetime will become owned by a charitable trust that secures our continued independence.

Los Angeles | London | New Delhi | Singapore | Washington DC | Melbourne

A Primer on Partial Least Squares Structural Equation Modeling (PLS-SEM)

Second Edition

Joseph F. Hair, Jr.
Kennesaw State University

G. Tomas M. Hult
Michigan State University

Christian M. Ringle
Hamburg University of Technology, Germany, and
The University of Newcastle, Australia

Marko Sarstedt
Otto-von-Guericke University, Magdeburg, Germany, and
The University of Newcastle, Australia

Los Angeles | London | New Delhi
Singapore | Washington DC | Melbourne

FOR INFORMATION:

SAGE Publications, Inc.

2455 Teller Road

Thousand Oaks, California 91320

E-mail: order@sagepub.com

SAGE Publications Ltd.

1 Oliver's Yard

55 City Road

London, EC1Y 1SP

United Kingdom

SAGE Publications India Pvt. Ltd.

B 1/I 1 Mohan Cooperative Industrial Area

Mathura Road, New Delhi 110 044

India

SAGE Publications Asia-Pacific Pte. Ltd.

3 Church Street

#10-04 Samsung Hub

Singapore 049483

Acquistions Editor: Leah Fargotstein

Editorial Assistant: Yvonne McDuffee

eLearning Editor: Katie Ancheta

Production Editor: Kelly DeRosa

Copy Editor: Gillian Dickens

Typesetter: Hurix Systems Pvt. Ltd.

Proofreader: Scott Oney

Indexer: Will Ragsdale

Cover Designer: Michael Dubowe

Marketing Manager: Susannah Goldes

Printed in the United States of America

Library of Congress Cataloging-in-Publication Data

Names: Hair, Joseph F.

Title: A primer on partial least squares structural equation modeling (PLS-SEM) / Joseph F. Hair, Jr., Kennesaw State University, USA [and three others].

Description: Second edition. | Los Angeles : Sage, [2017] | Includes bibliographical references and index.

Identifiers: LCCN 2016005380 | ISBN 9781483377445 (pbk.)

Subjects: LCSH: Least squares. | Structural equation modeling.

Classification: LCC QA275 .P88 2017 | DDC 511/.42—dc23 LC record available at http://lccn.loc.gov/2016005380

This book is printed on acid-free paper.

16 17 18 19 20 10 9 8 7 6 5 4 3 2 1

Brief Contents

Visit the companion site for this book at http://study.sagepub.com/
hairprimer2e.

Detailed Contents

Visit the companion site for this book at http://study.sagepub.com/ hairprimer2e.

Preface

The first edition of our book was published just two years ago, in 2014. Why the need for a new edition when the first edition has been out only 2 years?

At the time we wrote the first edition, we were confident the interest in partial least squares structural equation modeling (PLS-SEM) was increasing, but even we did not anticipate hot interest in the method would explode! Applications of PLS-SEM have grown exponentially in the past few years, and two journal articles we published before the first edition provide clear evidence of the popularity of PLS-SEM. The two articles have been the most widely cited in those journals since their publication—our 2012 article in the *Journal of Academy of Marketing Science*, "An Assessment of the Use of Partial Least Squares Structural Equation Modeling in Marketing Research," cited more than 800 times according to Google Scholar, has been the number one highest impact article published in the top 20 marketing journals, according to Shugan's list of most cited marketing articles (http://www.marketingscience.org; e.g., Volume 2, Issue 3). It has also been awarded the 2015 *Emerald Citations of Excellence* award. Moreover, our 2011 article in the *Journal of Marketing Theory and Practice*, "PLS-SEM: Indeed a Silver Bullet," has surpassed more than 1,500 Google Scholar citations.

During this same timeframe, PLS-SEM has gained widespread interest among methods researchers as evidenced in a multitude of recent research papers that offer novel perspectives on the method. Very prominent examples include the rejoinders to Edward E. Rigdon's (2012) *Long Range Planning* article by Bentler and Huang (2014); Dijkstra (2014); Sarstedt, Ringle, Henseler, and Hair (2014); and Rigdon (2014b) himself. Under the general theme "rethinking partial least squares path modeling," this exchange of thoughts represents the point of departure of the most important PLS-SEM developments we expect to see in the next few years. Moreover, Rönkkö and Evermann's (2013) paper in *Organizational Research Methods* offered an excellent opportunity to show how uninformed and blind criticism of the PLS-SEM method leads to misleading, incorrect, and false conclusions (see the rejoinder by Henseler et al., 2014). While this debate also nurtured some advances of PLS-SEM—such as the new heterotrait-monotrait (HTMT) criterion to assess discriminant validity (Henseler, Ringle, & Sarstedt, 2015)—we believe that it is important to reemphasize our previous call: "Any extreme position that (often systematically) neglects the beneficial features of the other technique and may result in prejudiced boycott calls, is not good research practice and does not help to truly advance our understanding of methods and any other research subject" (Hair, Ringle, & Sarstedt, 2012, p. 313).

Research has also brought forward methodological extensions of the original PLS-SEM method, for example, to uncover unobserved heterogeneity or to assess measurement model invariance. These developments have been accompanied by the release of SmartPLS 3, which implements many of these latest extensions in highly user-friendly software. This new release is much more than just a simple revision. It incorporates a broad range of new algorithms and major new features that previously had to be executed manually. For example, SmartPLS 3 runs on both Microsoft Windows and Mac OSX and includes the new consistent PLS algorithm, advanced bootstrapping features, the importance-performance map analysis, multigroup analysis options, confirmatory tetrad analysis to empirically assess the mode of measurement model, and additional segmentation techniques. Furthermore, new features augment data handling (e.g., use of weighted data) and the graphical user interface, which also includes many new options that support users running their analyses and documenting the results. In light of the developments in terms of PLS-SEM use, further enhancements, and extensions of the method and software support, a new edition of the book is clearly timely and warranted.

As noted in our first edition, the global explosion of data, often referred to as the "Age of Big Data," is pushing the world toward data-driven discovery and decision making. The abundance of data presents both opportunities and challenges for scholars, industry, and government. While more data are available, there are not enough individuals with the analytical skills to probe and understand the data. Analysis requires a rigorous scientific approach dependent on knowledge of statistics, mathematics, measurement, logic, theory, experience, intuition, and many other variables affecting the situational context. Statistical analysis is perhaps the most important skill. While the other areas facilitate better understanding of data patterns, statistics provides additional substantiation in the knowledge-developing process. User-friendly software makes the application of statistics in the process efficient and cost-effective, in both time and money.

The increasing reliance on and acceptance of statistical analysis as well as the advent of powerful computer systems have facilitated the analysis of large amounts of data and created the opportunity for the application of more advanced next-generation analysis techniques. SEM is among the most useful advanced statistical analysis techniques that have emerged in the social sciences in recent decades. SEM is a class of multivariate techniques that combines aspects of factor analysis and regression, enabling the researcher to simultaneously examine relationships among measured variables and latent variables (assessment of measurement theory) as well as between latent variables (assessment of structural theory).

Considering the ever-increasing importance of understanding latent phenomena, such as consumer perceptions, expectations, attitudes, or intentions, and their influence on organizational performance measures (e.g., stock prices), it is not surprising that SEM has become one of the most prominent statistical analysis techniques today. While there are many approaches to conducting SEM, the most widely applied method since the late 1970s has been covariance-based SEM (CB-SEM). Since its introduction by Karl Jöreskog in 1973, CB-SEM has received considerable interest among empirical researchers across virtually all social sciences disciplines. For many years, the predominance of LISREL, EQS, and AMOS, among the most well-known software tools to perform this kind of analysis, led to a lack of awareness of the composite-based PLS-SEM approach as a very useful alternative approach to SEM. Originated in the 1960s by the econometrician Herman Wold (1966) and further developed in the years after (e.g., Wold, 1975, 1982, 1985), PLS-SEM has become an increasingly visible method in the social science disciplines.

Figure 1 summarizes the application of PLS-SEM in the top journals in the marketing and strategic management disciplines, as well as *MIS Quarterly,* the flagship journal in management information systems research. PLS-SEM use has increased exponentially in a variety of disciplines with the recognition that PLS-SEM's distinctive methodological features make it an excellent alternative to the previously more popular CB-SEM approach. Specifically, PLS-SEM has several advantages over CB-SEM in many situations commonly encountered in social sciences research such as when sample sizes are small or

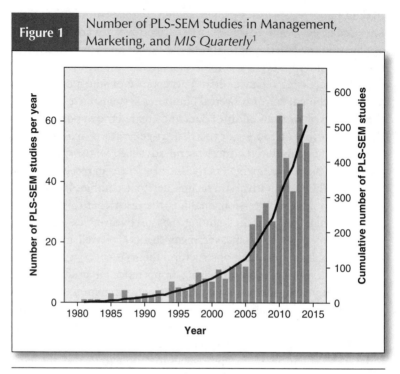

| **Figure 1** | Number of PLS-SEM Studies in Management, Marketing, and *MIS Quarterly*[1] |

Note: PLS-SEM studies published in *MIS Quarterly* were only considered from 1992 on.

[1]For the selection of journals and details on the use of PLS-SEM in the three disciplines, see Hair, Sarstedt, Ringle, and Mena (2012); Hair, Sarstedt, Pieper, and Ringle (2012a); and Ringle, Sarstedt, and Straub (2012). Results for the most recent years have been added to the figure for the same selection of journals.

when complex models with many indicators and model relationships are estimated. However, PLS-SEM should not be viewed simply as a less stringent alternative to CB-SEM but rather as a complementary modeling approach to SEM. If correctly applied, PLS-SEM indeed can be a silver bullet in many research situations.

PLS-SEM is evolving as a statistical modeling technique, and while there are several published articles on the method, until our first edition, there was no comprehensive book that explained the fundamental aspects of the method, particularly in a way that could be comprehended by individuals with limited statistical and mathematical training. This second edition of our book updates and extends the coverage of PLS-SEM for social sciences researchers and creates awareness of the most recent developments in a tool that will enable them to pursue research opportunities in new and different ways.

The approach of this book is based on the authors' many years of conducting and teaching research, as well as the desire to communicate the fundamentals of the PLS-SEM method to a much broader audience. To accomplish this goal, we have limited the emphasis on equations, formulas, Greek symbols, and so forth that are typical of most books and articles. Instead, we explain in detail the basic fundamentals of PLS-SEM and provide rules of thumb that can be used as general guidelines for understanding and evaluating the results of applying the method. We also rely on a single software package (SmartPLS 3; http://www.smartpls.com) that can be used not only to complete the exercises in this book but also in the reader's own research.

As a further effort to facilitate learning, we use a single case study throughout the book. The case is drawn from a published study on corporate reputation and we believe is general enough to be understood by many different areas of social science research, thus further facilitating comprehension of the method. Review and critical thinking questions are posed at the end of the chapters, and key terms are defined to better understand the concepts. Finally, suggested readings and extensive references are provided to enhance more advanced coverage of the topic.

We are excited to share with you the many new topics we have included in this edition. These include the following:

- An overview of the latest research on composite-based modeling (e.g., distinction between composite and causal indicators), which is the conceptual foundation for PLS-SEM

- Consideration of the recent discussion of PLS-SEM as a composite-based method to SEM

- More on the distinction between PLS-SEM and CB-SEM and the model constellations, which favor the use of PLS-SEM

- Introduction of a new criterion for discriminant validity assessment: the HTMT ratio of correlations

- Discussion of the concept of model fit in a PLS-SEM context, including an introduction of the following model fit measures: standardized root mean square residual (SRMR), root mean square residual covariance (RMS_{theta}), and the exact fit test

- Introduction of several methods for constructing bootstrap confidence intervals: percentile, studentized, bias corrected and accelerated, and two double bootstrap methods

- Revision and extension of the chapter on mediation, which now covers more types of mediation, including multiple mediation

- Extended description of moderation (e.g., orthogonalizing approach for creating the interaction term, measurement model evaluation)

- Inclusion of moderated mediation and mediated moderation

- Brief introduction of advanced techniques: importance-performance map analysis, hierarchical component models, confirmatory tetrad analysis, multigroup analysis, latent class techniques (FIMIX-PLS, REBUS-PLS, PLS-POS, PLS-GAS, PLS-IRRS), measurement invariance testing in PLS-SEM (MICOM), and consistent PLS

- Consideration of the latest literature on PLS-SEM

All examples in the edition are updated using the newest version of the most widely applied PLS-SEM software—SmartPLS 3. The book chapters and learning support supplements are organized around the learning outcomes shown at the beginning of each chapter. Moreover, instead of a single summary at the end of each chapter, we present a separate topical summary for each learning outcome. This approach makes the book more understandable and usable for both students and teachers. The SAGE website for the book also includes other support materials to facilitate learning and applying the PLS-SEM method.

We would like to acknowledge the many insights and suggestions provided by the reviewers: Maxwell K. Hsu (University of Wisconsin), Toni M. Somers (Wayne State University), and Lea Witta (University of Central Florida), as well as a number of our colleagues and students. Most notably, we thank Jan-Michael Becker (University of Cologne), Adamantios Diamantopoulos (University of Vienna), Theo Dijkstra (University of Groningen), Markus Eberl (TNS Infratest), Anne Gottfried (University of Southern Mississippi), Verena Gruber (University of Vienna), Siegfried P. Gudergan (University of Newcastle), Karl-Werner Hansmann (University of Hamburg), Jörg Henseler (University of Twente), Lucas Hopkins (Florida State University), Ida Rosnita Ismail (Universiti

Kebangsaan Malaysia), Marcel Lichters (Harz University of Applied Sciences), David Ketchen (Auburn University), Gabriel Cepeda Carrión (University of Seville), José Luis Roldán (University of Seville), Lucy Matthews (Middle Tennessee State University), Roger Calantone (Michigan State University), Arthur Money (Henley Business School), Christian Nitzl (Universität der Bundeswehr München), Arun Rai (Georgia State University), Sascha Raithel (Freie Universität Berlin), Edward E. Rigdon (Georgia State University), Phillip Samouel (University of Kingston), Rainer Schlittgen (University of Hamburg), Manfred Schwaiger (Ludwig-Maxmillians University, Munich), Donna Smith (Ryerson University), Detmar W. Straub (Georgia State University), Sven Wende (SmartPLS GmbH), and Anita Whiting (Clayton State University) for their helpful remarks.

Also, we thank the team of doctoral student and research fellows at Hamburg University of Technology and Otto-von-Guericke-University Magdeburg—namely, Kathi Barth, Doreen Neubert, Sebastian Lehmann, Victor Schliwa, Katrin Engelke, Andreas Fischer, Nicole Richter, Jana Rosenbusch, Sandra Schubring, Kai Oliver Thiele, and Tabea Tressin—for their kind support. In addition, at SAGE we thank Vicki Knight, Leah Fargotstein, Yvonne McDuffee, and Kelly DeRosa. We hope this book will expand knowledge of the capabilities and benefits of PLS-SEM to a much broader group of researchers and practitioners. Last, if you have any remarks, suggestions, or ideas to improve this book, please get in touch with us. We appreciate any feedback on the book's concept and contents!

Joseph F. Hair, Jr.
Kennesaw State University

G. Tomas M. Hult
Michigan State University

Christian M. Ringle
Hamburg University of Technology, Germany,
and The University of Newcastle, Australia

Marko Sarstedt
Otto-von-Guericke University, Magdeburg, Germany,
and The University of Newcastle, Australia

Visit the companion site for this book at http://study.sagepub.com/hairprimer2e.

To the Academy of Marketing Science (AMS) and its members

About the Authors

 **Joseph F. Hair, Jr.** is Founder and Senior Scholar of the Doctoral Degree in Business Administration, Coles College, Kennesaw State University. He previously held the Copeland Endowed Chair of Entrepreneurship and was Director, Entrepreneurship Institute, Ourso College of Business Administration, Louisiana State University. He has authored more than 50 books, including *Multivariate Data Analysis* (7th edition, 2010) (cited 140,000+ times), *MKTG* (9th edition, 2015), *Essentials of Business Research Methods* (2016), and *Essentials of Marketing Research* (3rd edition, 2013). He also has published numerous articles in scholarly journals and was recognized as the Academy of Marketing Science Marketing Educator of the Year. A popular guest speaker, Professor Hair often presents seminars on research techniques, multivariate data analysis, and marketing issues for organizations in Europe, Australia, China, India, and South America.

 **G. Tomas M. Hult** is Professor and Byington Endowed Chair in International Business and Director of the International Business Center in the Eli Broad College of Business at Michigan State University. He has been Executive Director of the Academy of International Business and President of the AIB Foundation since 2004, was Editor-in-Chief of the *Journal of the Academy of Marketing Science* from 2009 to 2015, and has been on the U.S. Department of Commerce's District Export Council since 2012. Professor Hult is one of some 80 elected Fellows of the Academy of International Business. He is one of the world's leading authorities in global strategy, with a particular focus on topics dealing with the intersection of global strategy and supply chain management. In various ranking studies, Hult is listed as one of the top-cited authors in business and economics (e.g., Thomson Reuters). He regularly teaches doctoral seminars on multivariate statistics, structural equation modeling, and hierarchical linear modeling worldwide. Dr. Hult is a dual citizen of Sweden and the United States. More information about Tomas Hult can be found at http://www.tomashult.com.

Christian M. Ringle is a Chaired Professor of Management at the Hamburg University of Technology (Germany) and Conjoint Professor at the Faculty of Business and Law at the University of Newcastle (Australia). He holds a master's degree in business administration from the University of Kansas and received his doctor of philosophy from the University of Hamburg (Germany). His widely published research addresses the management of organizations, strategic and human resource management, marketing, and quantitative methods for business and market research. He is cofounder and the Managing Director of SmartPLS (http://www.smartpls.com), a software tool with a graphical user interface for the application of the partial least squares structural equation modeling (PLS-SEM) method. Besides supporting consultancies and international corporations, he regularly teaches doctoral seminars on multivariate statistics, the PLS-SEM method, and the use of SmartPLS worldwide. More information about Christian Ringle can be found at http://www.tuhh.de/hrmo/team/prof-dr-c-m-ringle.html.

 Marko Sarstedt is Chaired Professor of Marketing at the Otto-von-Guericke University, Magdeburg (Germany) and Conjoint Professor to the Faculty of Business and Law at the University of Newcastle (Australia). He previously was an Assistant Professor of Quantitative Methods in Marketing and Management at the Ludwig-Maximilians-University Munich (Germany). His main research is in the application and advancement of structural equation modeling methods to further the understanding of consumer behavior and to improve marketing decision making. His research has been published in journals such as *Journal of Marketing Research, Journal of the Academy of Marketing Science, Organizational Research Methods, MIS Quarterly, International Journal of Research in Marketing, Long Range Planning, Journal of World Business,* and *Journal of Business Research.* According to the Handelsblatt ranking, Marko Sarstedt is among the top three young academic marketing researchers in Germany, Austria, and Switzerland. He regularly teaches doctoral seminars on multivariate statistics, structural equation modeling, and measurement worldwide.

CHAPTER 1

An Introduction to Structural Equation Modeling

LEARNING OUTCOMES

1. Understand the meaning of structural equation modeling (SEM) and its relationship to multivariate data analysis.

2. Describe the basic considerations in applying multivariate data analysis.

3. Comprehend the basic concepts of partial least squares structural equation modeling (PLS-SEM).

4. Explain the differences between covariance-based structural equation modeling (CB-SEM) and PLS-SEM and when to use each.

CHAPTER PREVIEW

Social science researchers have been using statistical analysis tools for many years to extend their ability to develop, explore, and confirm research findings. Application of first-generation statistical methods such as factor analysis and regression analysis dominated the research landscape through the 1980s. But since the early 1990s, second-generation methods have expanded rapidly and, in some disciplines, represent almost 50% of the statistical tools applied in empirical research. In this chapter, we explain the fundamentals of second-generation statistical methods and establish a foundation that will enable you to understand and apply one of the emerging second-generation tools, referred to as **partial least squares structural equation modeling (PLS-SEM)**.

WHAT IS STRUCTURAL EQUATION MODELING?

Statistical analysis has been an essential tool for social science researchers for more than a century. Applications of statistical methods have expanded dramatically with the advent of computer hardware and software, particularly in recent years with widespread access to many more methods due to user-friendly interfaces with technology-delivered knowledge. Researchers initially relied on univariate and bivariate analysis to understand data and relationships. To comprehend more complex relationships associated with current research directions in the social science disciplines, it is increasingly necessary to apply more sophisticated multivariate data analysis methods.

Multivariate analysis involves the application of statistical methods that simultaneously analyze multiple variables. The variables typically represent measurements associated with individuals, companies, events, activities, situations, and so forth. The measurements are often obtained from surveys or observations that are used to collect primary data, but they may also be obtained from databases consisting of secondary data. Exhibit 1.1 displays some of the major types of statistical methods associated with multivariate data analysis.

Exhibit 1.1	Organization of Multivariate Methods	
	Primarily Exploratory	**Primarily Confirmatory**
First-generation techniques	• Cluster analysis • Exploratory factor analysis • Multidimensional scaling	• Analysis of variance • Logistic regression • Multiple regression • Confirmatory factor analysis
Second-generation techniques	• Partial least squares structural equation modeling (PLS-SEM)	• Covariance-based structural equation modeling (CB-SEM)

The statistical methods often used by social scientists are typically called **first-generation techniques** (Fornell, 1982, 1987). These techniques, shown in the upper part of Exhibit 1.1, include regression-based approaches such as multiple regression, logistic regression, and analysis of variance but also techniques such as exploratory and confirmatory factor analysis, cluster analysis, and multidimensional scaling. When applied to a research question, these methods can be used to either confirm a priori established theories or identify data patterns and relationships. Specifically, they are **confirmatory** when testing the hypotheses of existing theories and concepts and **exploratory** when they search for patterns in the data in case there is no or only little prior knowledge on how the variables are related.

It is important to note that the distinction between confirmatory and exploratory is not always as clear-cut as it seems. For example, when running a regression analysis, researchers usually select the dependent and independent variables based on a priori established theories and concepts. The goal of the regression analysis is then to test these theories and concepts. However, the technique can also be used to explore whether additional independent variables prove valuable for extending the concept being tested. The findings typically focus first on which independent variables are statistically significant predictors of the single dependent variable (more confirmatory) and then which independent variables are, relatively speaking, better predictors of the dependent variable (more exploratory). In a similar fashion, when exploratory factor analysis is applied to a data set, the method searches for relationships between the variables in an effort to reduce a large number of variables to a smaller set of composite factors (i.e., combinations of variables). The final set of composite factors is a result of exploring relationships in the data and reporting the relationships that are found (if any). Nevertheless, while the technique is exploratory in nature (as the name already suggests), researchers often have a priori knowledge that may, for example, guide their decision on how many composite factors to extract from the data (Sarstedt & Mooi, 2014). In contrast, the confirmatory factor analysis allows testing and substantiating an a priori determined factor and its assigned indicators.

First-generation techniques have been widely applied by social science researchers. However, for the past 20 years, many researchers have increasingly been turning to **second-generation techniques** to overcome the weaknesses of first-generation methods (Exhibit 1.1).

These methods, referred to as **structural equation modeling (SEM)**, enable researchers to incorporate unobservable variables measured indirectly by indicator variables. They also facilitate accounting for **measurement** error in observed variables (Chin, 1998).

There are two types of SEM: **covariance-based SEM (CB-SEM)** and **partial least squares SEM (PLS-SEM;** also called **PLS path modeling**). CB-SEM is primarily used to confirm (or reject) theories (i.e., a set of systematic relationships between multiple variables that can be tested empirically). It does this by determining how well a proposed theoretical model can estimate the covariance matrix for a **sample** data set. In contrast, PLS-SEM is primarily used to develop theories in exploratory research. It does this by focusing on explaining the variance in the dependent variables when examining the model. We explain this difference in more detail later in the chapter.

PLS-SEM is evolving as a statistical modeling technique, and while there are numerous introductory articles on the method (e.g., Chin, 1998; Chin, 2010; Haenlein & Kaplan, 2004; Hair, Ringle, & Sarstedt, 2011; Henseler, Ringle, & Sarstedt, 2012; Henseler, Ringle, & Sinkovics, 2009; Mateos-Aparicio, 2011; Rigdon, 2013; Roldán & Sánchez-Franco, 2012; Tenenhaus et al., 2005; Wold, 1985) and its use across a variety of disciplines (do Valle & Assaker, in press; Hair, Sarstedt, Pieper, & Ringle, 2012; Hair, Sarstedt, Ringle, & Mena, 2012; Lee et al., 2011; Nitzl, 2016; Peng & Lai, 2012; Richter, Sinkovics, Ringle, & Schlägel, in press; Ringle, Sarstedt, & Straub, 2012; Sarstedt, Ringle, Smith, Reams, & Hair, 2014), until the first edition of this book, there was no comprehensive textbook that explains the fundamental aspects of the method, particularly in a way that can be comprehended by the nonstatistician. This second edition of our book expands and clarifies the nature and role of PLS-SEM in social sciences research and hopefully makes researchers aware of a tool that will enable them to pursue research opportunities in new and different ways.

CONSIDERATIONS IN USING STRUCTURAL EQUATION MODELING

Depending on the underlying research question and the empirical data available, researchers must select an appropriate multivariate analysis method. Regardless of whether a researcher is using first- or second-generation multivariate analysis methods, several considerations are necessary in deciding to use multivariate analysis, particularly SEM. Among the most important are the following five elements: (1) composite variables, (2) measurement, (3) measurement scales, (4) coding, and (5) data distributions.

Composite Variables

A **composite variable** (also referred to as a **variate**) is a linear combination of several variables that are chosen based on the research problem at hand (Hair, Black, Babin, & Anderson, 2010). The process for combining the variables involves calculating a set of weights, multiplying the weights (e.g., w_1 and w_2) times the associated data observations for the variables (e.g., x_1 and x_2), and summing them. The mathematical formula for this linear combination with five variables is shown as follows (note that the composite value can be calculated for any number of variables):

$$Composite\ value = w_1 \cdot x_1 + w_2 \cdot x_2 + \ldots + w_5 \cdot x_5,$$

where x stands for the individual variables and w represents the weights. All x variables (e.g., questions in a questionnaire) have responses from many respondents that can be arranged in a data matrix. Exhibit 1.2 shows such a data matrix, where i is an index that stands for the number of responses (i.e., cases). A composite value is calculated for each of the i respondents in the sample.

Measurement

Measurement is a fundamental concept in conducting social science research. When we think of measurement, the first thing that comes to mind is often a ruler, which could be used to measure someone's height or the length of a piece of furniture. But there are many other examples of measurement in life. When you drive, you use a

Exhibit 1.2	Data Matrix				
Case	x_1	x_2	$\ldots$	x_5	**Composite Value**
1	x_{11}	x_{21}	$\ldots$	x_{51}	v_1
$\ldots$	$\ldots$	$\ldots$	$\ldots$	$\ldots$	$\ldots$
i	x_{1i}	x_{2i}	$\ldots$	x_{5i}	v_i

speedometer to measure the speed of your vehicle, a heat gauge to measure the temperature of the engine, and a gauge to determine how much fuel remains in your tank. If you are sick, you use a thermometer to measure your temperature, and when you go on a diet, you measure your weight on a bathroom scale.

Measurement is the process of assigning numbers to a variable based on a set of rules (Hair, Celsi, Money, Samouel, & Page, 2016). The rules are used to assign the numbers to the variable in a way that accurately represents the variable. With some variables, the rules are easy to follow, while with other variables, the rules are much more difficult to apply. For example, if the variable is gender, then it is easy to assign a 1 for females and a 0 for males. Similarly, if the variable is age or height, it is again easy to assign a number. But what if the variable is satisfaction or trust? Measurement in these situations is much more difficult because the phenomenon that is supposed to be measured is abstract, complex, and not directly observable. We therefore talk about the measurement of **latent** (i.e., unobservable) **variables** or **constructs.**

We cannot directly measure abstract concepts such as satisfaction or trust. However, we can measure indicators or manifestations of what we have agreed to call satisfaction or trust, for example, in a brand, product, or company. Specifically, when concepts are difficult to measure, one approach is to measure them indirectly with a set of **indicators** that serve as proxy variables. Each item represents a single separate aspect of a larger abstract concept. For example, if the concept is restaurant satisfaction, then the several proxy variables that could be used to measure this might be the following:

1. The taste of the food was excellent.

2. The speed of service met my expectations.

3. The wait staff was very knowledgeable about the menu items.

4. The background music in the restaurant was pleasant.

5. The meal was a good value compared with the price.

By combining several **items** to form a scale (or index), we can indirectly measure the overall concept of restaurant satisfaction. Usually, researchers use several items to form a multi-item scale, which indirectly measures a concept, as in the restaurant satisfaction example above. The several measures are combined to form a single composite score (i.e., the score of the variate). In some instances, the composite score is a simple summation of the several measures. In other instances, the scores of the individual measures are combined to form a composite score using a linear weighting process for the several individual measures. The logic of using several individual variables to measure an abstract concept such as restaurant satisfaction is that the measure will be more accurate. The anticipated improved accuracy is based on the assumption that using several items to measure a single concept is more likely to represent all the different aspects of the concept. This involves reducing **measurement error,** which is the difference between the true value of a variable and the value obtained by a measurement. There are many sources of measurement error, including poorly worded questions on a survey, misunderstanding of the scaling approach, and incorrect application of a statistical method. Indeed, all measurements used in multivariate analysis are likely to contain some measurement error. The objective, therefore, is to reduce the measurement error as much as possible.

Rather than using multiple items, researchers sometimes opt for the use of **single-item constructs** to measure concepts such as satisfaction or purchase intention. For example, we may use only "Overall, I'm satisfied with this restaurant" to measure restaurant satisfaction instead of all five items described above. While this is a good way to make the questionnaire shorter, it also reduces the quality of your measurement. We are going to discuss the fundamentals of measurement and measurement evaluation in the following chapters.

Measurement Scales

A **measurement scale** is a tool with a predetermined number of closed-ended responses that can be used to obtain an answer to a question. There are four types of measurement scales, each representing a different level of measurement—nominal, ordinal, interval, and ratio. Nominal scales are the lowest level of scales because they are the most restrictive in terms of the type of analysis that can be carried out. A **nominal scale** assigns numbers that can be used to identify and classify objects (e.g., people, companies, products, etc.) and is also referred to as a categorical scale. For example, if a survey asked a respondent to identify his or her profession and the categories are doctor, lawyer, teacher, engineer, and so forth, the question has a nominal scale. Nominal scales can have two or more categories, but each category must be mutually exclusive, and all possible categories must be included. A number could be assigned to identify each category, and the numbers could be used to count the number of responses in each category, or the modal response or percentage in each category.

The next higher level of scale is called ordinal. If we have a variable measured on an **ordinal scale,** we know that if the value of that variable increases or decreases, this gives meaningful information. For example, if we code customers' use of a product as nonuser = 0, light user = 1, and heavy user = 2, we know that if the value of the use variable increases, the level of use also increases. Therefore, something measured on an ordinal scale provides information about the order of our observations. However, we cannot assume that the differences in the order are equally spaced. That is, we do not know if the difference between "nonuser" and "light user" is the same as between "light user" and "heavy user," even though the differences in the values (i.e., 0 – 1 and 1 – 2) are equal. Therefore, it is not appropriate to calculate arithmetic means or variances for ordinal data.

If something is measured with an **interval scale,** we have precise information on the rank order at which something is measured and, in addition, we can interpret the magnitude of the differences in values directly. For example, if the temperature is 80°F, we know that if it drops to 75°F, the difference is exactly 5°F. This difference of 5°F is the same as the increase from 80°F to 85°F. This exact "spacing" is called **equidistance,** and equidistant scales are necessary for certain analysis techniques, such as SEM. What the interval scale does not give us is an absolute zero point. If the temperature is 0°F, it may feel cold, but the temperature can drop further. The value of 0 therefore does not mean that there is no temperature at all (Sarstedt & Mooi, 2014). The value of interval scales is that almost any type of mathematical computations can be carried out, including the mean and standard deviation. Moreover, you can convert and extend interval scales to alternative interval scales. For example, instead of degrees Fahrenheit (°F), many countries use degrees Celsius (°C) to measure the temperature. While 0°C marks the freezing point, 100°C depicts the boiling point of water. You can convert temperature from Fahrenheit into Celsius by using the following equation: Degrees Celsius (°C) = (degrees Fahrenheit (°F) – 32) · 5 / 9. In a similar way, you can convert data (via rescaling) on a scale from 1 to 5 into data on a scale from 0 to 100: ([data point on the scale from 1 to 5] – 1) / 4 · 100.

The **ratio scale** provides the most information. If something is measured on a ratio scale, we know that a value of 0 means that a particular characteristic for a variable is not present. For example, if a customer buys no products (value = 0), then he or she really buys no products. Or, if we spend no money on advertising a new product (value = 0), we really spend no money. Therefore, the zero point or origin of the variable is equal to 0. The measurement of length, mass, and volume as well as time elapsed uses **ratio scales**. With ratio scales, all types of mathematical computations are possible.

Coding

The assignment of numbers to categories in a manner that facilitates measurement is referred to as **coding**. In survey research, data are often precoded. Precoding is assigning numbers ahead of time to answers (e.g., scale points) that are specified on a questionnaire. For example, a 10-point agree-disagree scale typically would assign the number 10 to the highest endpoint "agree" and a 1 to the lowest endpoint "disagree," and the points between would be coded 2 to 9. Postcoding is assigning numbers to categories of responses after data are collected. The responses might be to an open-ended question on a quantitative survey or to an interview response in a qualitative study.

Coding is very important in the application of multivariate analysis because it determines when and how various types of scales can be used. For example, variables measured with interval and ratio scales can always be used with multivariate analysis. However, when using ordinal scales such as Likert scales (which is common within an SEM context), researchers have to pay special attention to the coding to fulfill the requirement of equidistance. For example, when using a typical 5-point Likert scale with the categories (1) *strongly disagree*, (2) *disagree*, (3) *neither agree nor disagree*, (4) *agree*, and (5) *strongly agree*, the inference is that the "distance" between categories 1 and 2 is the same as between categories 3 and 4. In contrast, the same type of Likert scale but using the categories (1) *disagree*, (2) *neither agree nor disagree*, (3) *somewhat agree*, (4) *agree*, and (5) *strongly agree* is unlikely to be equidistant as only one item can receive a rating below the neutral category "neither agree nor disagree." This would clearly bias any result in favor of a better outcome. A good Likert scale, as above, will present symmetry of Likert items about a middle category that have clearly defined linguistic qualifiers for each category. In such symmetric scaling, equidistant attributes will typically be more clearly observed or, at least, inferred. When a Likert scale is perceived as symmetric and equidistant, it will behave more like an interval scale. So while a Likert scale is ordinal, if it is well presented, then it is likely the Likert scale can approximate an interval-level measurement, and the corresponding variables can be used in SEM.

Data Distributions

When researchers collect quantitative data, the answers to the questions asked are reported as a distribution across the available (predefined) response categories. For example, if responses are requested using a 9-point agree-disagree scale, then a distribution of the answers in each of the possible response categories $(1, 2, 3, \ldots, 9)$ can be calculated and displayed in a table or chart. Exhibit 1.3 shows an example of the frequencies of a corresponding variable x. As can be seen, most

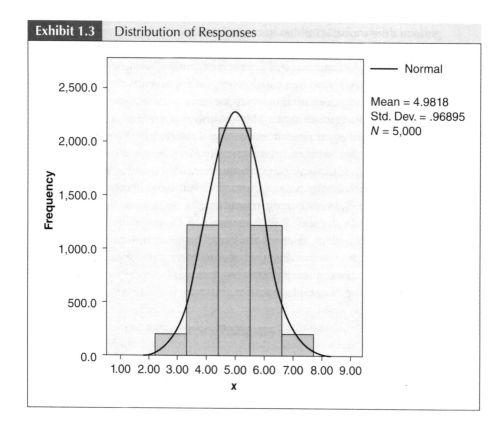

Exhibit 1.3   Distribution of Responses

respondents indicated a 5 on the 9-point scale, followed by 4 and 6, as well as 3 and 7, and so on. Overall, the frequency count approximately follows a bell-shaped, symmetric curve around the mean value of 5. This bell-shaped curve is the normal distribution, which many analysis techniques require to render correct results.

While many different types of distributions exist (e.g., normal, binomial, Poisson), researchers working with SEM generally only need to distinguish normal from nonnormal distributions. Normal distributions are usually desirable, especially when working with CB-SEM. In contrast, PLS-SEM generally makes no assumptions about the data distributions. However, for reasons discussed in later chapters, it is nevertheless worthwhile to consider the distribution when working with PLS-SEM. To assess whether the data follow a normal distribution, researchers can apply statistical tests such as the Kolmogorov-Smirnov test and Shapiro-Wilk test (Sarstedt & Mooi, 2014). In addition, researchers can examine two measures of distributions—skewness and kurtosis (Chapter 2)—which allow assessing to what extent the data deviate from normality (Hair et al., 2010).

STRUCTURAL EQUATION MODELING WITH PARTIAL LEAST SQUARES PATH MODELING

Path Models With Latent Variables

Path models are diagrams used to visually display the hypotheses and variable relationships that are examined when SEM is applied (Hair et al., 2011; Hair, Celsi, Money, Samouel, & Page, 2016). An example of a path model is shown in Exhibit 1.4.

Constructs (i.e., variables that are not directly measured) are represented in path models as circles or ovals (Y_1 to Y_4). The **indicators,** also called **items** or **manifest variables,** are the directly measured proxy variables that contain the raw data. They are represented in path models as rectangles (x_1 to x_{10}). Relationships between constructs as well as between constructs and their assigned indicators are shown as arrows. In PLS-SEM, the arrows are always single-headed, thus representing directional relationships. Single-headed arrows are considered predictive relationships and, with strong theoretical support, can be interpreted as causal relationships.

A PLS path model consists of two elements. First, there is a **structural model** (also called the **inner model** in the context of PLS-SEM)

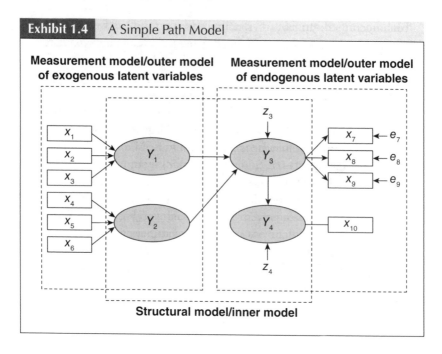

Exhibit 1.4   A Simple Path Model

that represents the constructs (circles or ovals). The structural model also displays the relationships (paths) between the constructs. Second, there are the **measurement models** (also referred to as the **outer models** in PLS-SEM) of the constructs that display the relationships between the constructs and the indicator variables (rectangles). In Exhibit 1.4, there are two types of measurement models: one for the **exogenous latent variables** (i.e., those constructs that explain other constructs in the model) and one for the **endogenous latent variables** (i.e., those constructs that are being explained in the model). Rather than referring to measurement models of exogenous and endogenous latent variables, researchers often refer to the measurement model of one specific latent variable. For example, x_1 to x_3 are the indicators used in the measurement model of Y_1 while Y_4 has only the x_{10} indicator in the measurement model.

The **error terms** (e.g., e_7 or e_8; Exhibit 1.4) are connected to the (endogenous) constructs and (reflectively) measured variables by single-headed arrows. Error terms represent the unexplained variance when path models are estimated. In Exhibit 1.4, error terms e_7 to e_9 are on those indicators whose relationships go from the construct to the indicator (i.e., reflectively measured indicators). In contrast, the formatively measured indicators x_1 to x_6, where the relationship goes from the indicator to the construct, do not have error terms Finally, for the single-item construct Y_4, the direction of the relationships between the construct and the indicator doesn't matter as construct and item are equivalent. For the same reason, there is no error term connected to x_{10}. The structural model also contains error terms. In Exhibit 1.4, z_3 and z_4 are associated with the endogenous latent variables Y_3 and Y_4 (note that error terms on constructs and measured variables are labeled differently). In contrast, the exogenous latent variables that only explain other latent variables in the structural model do not have an error term.

Path models are developed based on theory. **Theory** is a set of systematically related hypotheses developed following the scientific method that can be used to explain and predict outcomes. Thus, hypotheses are individual conjectures, whereas theories are multiple hypotheses that are logically linked together and can be tested empirically. Two types of theory are required to develop path models: **measurement theory** and **structural theory**. The latter specifies how the constructs are related to each other in the structural model, while measurement theory specifies how each construct is measured.

Measurement Theory

Measurement theory specifies how the latent variables (constructs) are measured. Generally, there are two different ways to measure unobservable variables. One approach is referred to as reflective measurement, and the other is a formative measurement. Constructs Y_1 and Y_2 in Exhibit 1.4 are modeled based on a **formative measurement model.** Note that the directional arrows are pointing from the indicator variables (x_1 to x_3 for Y_1 and x_4 to x_6 for Y_2) to the construct, indicating a causal (predictive) relationship in that direction.

In contrast, Y_3 in the exhibit is modeled based on a **reflective measurement model.** With reflective indicators, the direction of the arrows is from the construct to the indicator variables, indicating the assumption that the construct causes the measurement (more precisely, the covariation) of the indicator variables. As indicated in Exhibit 1.4, reflective measures have an error term associated with each indicator, which is not the case with formative measures. The latter are assumed to be error free (Diamantopoulos, 2011). Last, note that Y_4 is measured using a single item rather than multi-item measures. Therefore, the relationship between construct and indicator is undirected.

The approach to modeling constructs (i.e., formative vs. reflective and multi-items vs. single items) is an important consideration in developing path models. These approaches to modeling constructs as well as their variations are explained in more detail in Chapter 2.

Structural Theory

Structural theory shows how the latent variables are related to each other (i.e., it shows the constructs and the path relationships between them in the structural model). The location and sequence of the constructs are based on theory or the researcher's experience and accumulated knowledge. When path models are developed, the sequence is from left to right. The variables on the left side of the path model are independent variables, and any variable on the right side is the dependent variable. Moreover, variables on the left are shown as sequentially preceding and predicting the variables on the right. However, variables may also serve as both the independent and dependent variable.

When latent variables serve only as independent variables, they are called **exogenous latent variables** (Y_1 and Y_2). When latent variables serve only as dependent variables (Y_4) or as both independent and dependent variables (Y_3), they are called **endogenous latent variables.** Any latent variable that has only single-headed arrows going out of it is an exogenous latent variable. In contrast, endogenous latent variables can have either single-headed arrows going both into and out of them (Y_3) or only going into them (Y_4). Note that the exogenous latent variables Y_1 and Y_2 do not have error terms since these constructs are the entities (independent variables) that are explaining the dependent variables in the path model.

PLS-SEM, CB-SEM, AND REGRESSIONS BASED ON SUM SCORES

There are two main approaches to estimating the relationships in a structural equation model (Hair et al., 2010; Hair et al., 2011). One is the more widely applied CB-SEM approach. The other is PLS-SEM, which is the focus of this book. Each is appropriate for a different research context, and researchers need to understand the differences in order to apply the correct method. Finally, some researchers have argued for using regressions based on **sum scores,** instead of some type of indicator weighting as done by PLS-SEM. The latter approach offers practically no value beyond PLS-SEM.

For this reason, we discuss sum scores only in brief and focus on the PLS-SEM and CB-SEM methods.

To answer the question of when to use PLS-SEM versus CB-SEM, researchers should focus on the characteristics and objectives that distinguish the two methods (Hair, Sarstedt, Ringle, et al., 2012). In situations where theory is less developed, researchers should consider the use of PLS-SEM as an alternative approach to CB-SEM. This is particularly true if the primary objective of applying structural modeling is prediction and explanation of target constructs (Rigdon, 2012).

A crucial conceptual difference between PLS-SEM and CB-SEM relates to the way each method treats the latent variables included in the model. CB-SEM considers the constructs as common factors that explain the covariation between its associated indicators. The scores of these common factors are neither known nor needed in the estimation of model parameters. PLS-SEM, on the other hand, uses proxies to represent the constructs of interest, which are weighted composites of indicator variables for a particular construct. For this reason, PLS-SEM constitutes a composite-based approach to SEM, which relaxes the strong assumptions of CB-SEM that all the covariation between sets of indicators is explained by a common factor (Henseler et al., 2014; Rigdon, 2012; Rigdon et al., 2014). At the same time, using weighted composites of indicator variables facilitates accounting for measurement error, thus making PLS-SEM superior compared with multiple regression using **sum scores.** In the latter case, the researcher assumes an equal weighting of indicators, which means that each indicator contributes equally to forming the composite (Henseler et al., 2014). Referring to our descriptions on composite variables at the very beginning of this chapter, this would imply that all weights w are set to 1. The resulting mathematical formula for a linear combination with five variables would be as follows:

$$\textit{Composite value} = 1 \cdot x_1 + 1 \cdot x_2 + \ldots + 1 \cdot x_5.$$

For example, if a respondent has the scores 4, 5, 4, 6, and 7 on the five variables, the corresponding composite value would be 26. While easy to apply, regressions using sum scores equalize any differences in the individual item weights. Such differences are, however, common in research reality, and ignoring them entails substantial biases in the parameter estimates (e.g., Thiele, Sarstedt, & Ringle, 2015). Furthermore, learning about individual item weights offers important insights as the researcher learns about each item's importance for forming the composite in a certain context (i.e., its relationships with other composites in the structural model). When measuring, for example, customer satisfaction, the researcher learns which aspects covered by the individual items are of particular importance for the shaping of satisfaction.

It is important to note that the proxies produced by PLS-SEM are not assumed to be identical to the constructs, which they replace. They are explicitly recognized as approximations (Rigdon, 2012). As a consequence, some scholars view CB-SEM as a more direct and precise method to empirically measure theoretical concepts, while PLS-SEM provides approximations. Other scholars contend, however, that such a view is quite shortsighted as common factors derived in CB-SEM are also not necessarily equivalent to the theoretical concepts that are the focus of research. In fact, there is always a large validity gap between the concept a researcher intends to measure and the concrete construct used to measure a particular concept (e.g., Rigdon, 2012; Rossiter, 2011).

In social sciences research, viewing measurement as an approximation seems more realistic (e.g., Rigdon, 2014b), making the distinction between PLS-SEM and CB-SEM in terms of their treatment of constructs questionable. This view is also supported by the way CB-SEM is applied in research practice. When using CB-SEM, initially hypothesized models almost always exhibit inadequate fit. In response, researchers should reject the model and reconsider the study (which usually requires gathering new data), particularly when many variables must be deleted to achieve fit (Hair et al., 2010). Alternatively, they frequently respecify the original theoretically developed model in an effort to improve fit indices beyond the suggested threshold levels. By doing so, researchers arrive at a model with acceptable fit, which they conclude theory supports. Unfortunately, the latter is a best-case scenario that almost never applies in reality. Rather, researchers engage in exploratory specification searches in which model subsets are modified with the aim of arriving at a satisfactory model fit. However, models that are the product of such modifications often do not correspond particularly well to the true models and tend to be overly simplistic (Sarstedt, Ringle, Henseler, & Hair, 2014).

Apart from differences in the philosophy of measurement, the differing treatment of latent variables and, more specifically, the availability of latent variable scores also has consequences for the methods' areas of application. Specifically, while it is possible to estimate latent variable scores within a CB-SEM framework, these estimated scores are not unique. That is, an infinite number of different sets of latent variable scores that will fit the model equally well are possible. A crucial consequence of this **factor (score) indeterminacy** is that the correlations between a common factor and any variable outside the factor model are themselves indeterminate. That is, they may be high or low, depending on which set of factor scores one chooses. As a result, this limitation makes CB-SEM extremely unsuitable for prediction (e.g., Dijkstra, 2014). In contrast, a major advantage of PLS-SEM is that it always produces a single specific (i.e., determinate) score for each composite for each observation, once the weights are established. These determinate scores are proxies of the concepts being measured, just as factors are proxies for the conceptual variables in CB-SEM (Becker, Rai, & Rigdon, 2013). Using these proxies as input, PLS-SEM applies ordinary least squares (OLS) regression with the objective of minimizing the error terms (i.e., the residual variance) of the endogenous constructs. In short, PLS-SEM estimates coefficients (i.e., path model relationships) that maximize the R^2 values of the (target) endogenous constructs. This feature achieves the prediction objective of PLS-SEM. PLS-SEM is therefore the preferred method when the research objective is theory development and explanation of variance (prediction of the constructs). For this reason, PLS-SEM is regarded as a **variance-based** approach to SEM.

Note that PLS-SEM is similar but not equivalent to **PLS regression,** another popular multivariate data analysis technique. PLS regression is a regression-based approach that explores the linear relationships between multiple independent variables and a single or multiple dependent variable(s). PLS regression differs from regular regression, however, because in developing the regression model, it constructs composite factors from both the multiple independent variables and the dependent variable(s) by means of principal component analysis. PLS-SEM, on the other hand, relies on prespecified networks of relationships between constructs as well as between constructs and their measures (see Mateos-Aparicio, 2011, for a more detailed comparison between PLS-SEM and PLS regression).

Several considerations are important when deciding whether or not to apply PLS-SEM. These considerations also have their roots in the method's characteristics. The statistical properties of the PLS-SEM algorithm have important features associated with the characteristics of the data and model used. Moreover, the properties of the PLS-SEM method also affect the evaluation of the results. There are four critical issues relevant to the application of PLS-SEM (Hair et al., 2011; Hair, Sarstedt, Ringle, et al., 2012; Ringle et al., 2012): (1) the data, (2) model properties, (3) the PLS-SEM algorithm, and (4) model evaluation issues. Exhibit 1.5 summarizes the key characteristics of PLS-SEM. An initial overview of these issues is provided in this chapter, and a more detailed explanation is provided in later sections of the book, particularly as they relate to the PLS-SEM algorithm and evaluation of results.

PLS-SEM works efficiently with small sample sizes and complex models and makes practically no assumptions about the underlying data (Cassel, Hackl, & Westlund, 1999). For example, different from maximum likelihood–based CB-SEM, which requires normally distributed data and regression using sum scores, which assume normally distributed residuals, PLS-SEM makes no distributional assumptions (i.e., it is nonparametric). In addition, PLS-SEM can easily handle reflective and formative measurement models, as well as single-item constructs, with no identification problems. It can therefore be applied in a wide variety of research situations. When applying PLS-SEM, researchers also benefit from high efficiency in parameter estimation, which is manifested in the method's greater **statistical power** than that of CB-SEM. Greater statistical power means that PLS-SEM is more likely to render a specific relationship significant when it is in fact significant in the population. The very same holds for regressions based on sum scores, which lag behind PLS-SEM in terms of statistical power (Thiele et al., 2015).

There are, however, several limitations of PLS-SEM. In its basic form, the technique cannot be applied when structural models contain causal loops or circular relationships between the latent variables. Early extensions of the basic PLS-SEM algorithm that have not yet been implemented in standard PLS-SEM software packages, however, enable handling of circular relationships (Lohmöller, 1989). Furthermore, since PLS-SEM does not have an established global goodness-of-fit measure, its use for theory testing and confirmation is generally limited. Recent research, however, has started developing goodness-of-fit measures within a PLS-SEM framework, therefore broadening the method's applicability (e.g., Bentler & Huang, 2014). For example, Henseler et al. (2014) introduced the standardized root mean square residual (SRMR), which measures the squared discrepancy between the observed correlations and the model-implied correlations, as a means to validate a model. This measure has also been

Exhibit 1.5	Key Characteristics of PLS-SEM
Data Characteristics	
Sample size	• No identification issues with small sample sizes • Generally achieves high levels of statistical power with small sample sizes • Larger sample sizes increase the precision (i.e., consistency) of PLS-SEM estimations
Distribution	• No distributional assumptions; PLS-SEM is a nonparametric method
Missing values	• Highly robust as long as missing values are below a reasonable level
Scale of measurement	• Works with metric data, quasi-metric (ordinal) scaled data, and binary coded variables (with certain restrictions) • Some limitations when using categorical data to measure endogenous latent variables
Model Characteristics	
Number of items in each construct measurement model	• Handles constructs measured with single- and multi-item measures
Relationships between constructs and their indicators	• Easily incorporates reflective and formative measurement models
Model complexity	• Handles complex models with many structural model relations
Model setup	• No causal loops (no circular relationships) are allowed in the structural model
PLS-SEM Algorithm Properties	
Objective	• Minimizes the amount of unexplained variance (i.e., maximizes the R^2 values)
Efficiency	• Converges after a few iterations (even in situations with complex models and/or large sets of data) to the optimum solution; efficient algorithm

(Continued)

Exhibit 1.5	(Continued)
Nature of constructs	• Viewed as proxies of the latent concept under investigation, represented by composite variables
Construct scores	• Estimated as linear combinations of their indicators • Are determinate • Used for predictive purposes • Can be used as input for subsequent analyses • Not affected by data inadequacies
Parameter estimates	• Structural model relationships are generally underestimated and measurement model relationships are generally overestimated when estimating data from common factor models • Consistency at large • High levels of statistical power
Model Evaluation Issues	
Evaluation of the overall model	• No established global goodness-of-fit criterion
Evaluation of the measurement models	• Reflective measurement models: reliability and validity assessments by multiple criteria • Formative measurement models: validity assessment, significance and relevance of indicator weights, indicator collinearity
Evaluation of the structural model	• Collinearity among sets of constructs, significance of path coefficients, criteria to assess the model's predictive capabilities
Additional analyses	• Impact-performance matrix analysis • Mediating effects • Hierarchical component models • Multigroup analysis • Uncovering and treating unobserved heterogeneity • Measurement model invariance • Moderating effects

Source: Adapted from Hair JF, Ringle CM and Sarstedt M (2011) PLS-SEM: Indeed a Silver Bullet. *Journal of Marketing Theory and Practice* 19: 139–151 Copyright © 2011 by M.E. Sharpe, Inc. reprinted by permission of the publisher (Taylor & Francis Ltd., http://www.tandfonline.com).

implemented in the SmartPLS 3 software and will be discussed in the context of structural model evaluation in Chapter 6.

Other characteristics of PLS-SEM are that the parameter estimates are not optimal regarding consistency—a characteristic often incorrectly referred to as PLS-SEM bias (Chapter 3). Although CB-SEM advocates strongly emphasize this difference in the two methods, simulation studies show that the differences between PLS-SEM and CB-SEM estimates are very small when measurement models meet minimum recommended standards in terms of number of indicators and indicator loadings. Specifically, when the measurement models have four or more indicators and indicator loadings meet the common standards (≥ 0.70), there is practically no difference between the two methods in terms of parameter accuracy (e.g., Reinartz, Haenlein, & Henseler, 2009; Thiele et al., 2015). Thus, the extensively discussed PLS-SEM bias is of no practical relevance for the vast majority of applications (e.g., Binz Astrachan, Patel, & Wanzenried, 2014). More importantly, the divergence of parameter estimates of PLS-SEM should not be considered a bias but a difference resulting from the methods' differing treatment of the construct measures (common factors vs. composites). Furthermore, recent research has developed modifications of the original PLS-SEM algorithm, which correct for the PLS-SEM differences. Most notably, Dijkstra and Henseler's (2015a, 2015b) consistent PLS (PLSc) approach provides corrected model estimates while maintaining all of the PLS method's strengths, such as the ability to handle complex models when the sample size is limited, formatively measured constructs, and nonlinear relationships (for an alternative approach, see Bentler & Huang, 2014). At https://www.smartpls.com/documentation/pls-sem-compared-with-cb-sem, we offer a comparative estimation of the highly popular technology acceptance model (TAM; Davis, 1989) using PLS, PLSc, and various CB-SEM–based estimators such as maximum likelihood. The comparison shows that PLS, PLSc, and maximum likelihood–based CB-SEM are in close correspondence, whereas alternative CB-SEM–based estimators yield much different results.

In certain cases, particularly when there is little a priori knowledge of structural model relationships or the measurement characteristics of the constructs, or when the emphasis is more on exploration than confirmation, PLS-SEM is superior to CB-SEM. Furthermore, when CB-SEM assumptions are violated with regard to normality of distributions, **minimum sample size,** and maximum model complexity, or related methodological anomalies occur in the process of model estimation, PLS-SEM is a good methodological alternative for theory testing.

Exhibit 1.6 displays the rules of thumb that can be applied when deciding whether to use CB-SEM or PLS-SEM. As can be seen, PLS-SEM is not recommended as a universal alternative to CB-SEM. Both methods differ from a statistical point of view, are designed to achieve different objectives, and rely on different philosophies of measurement. Neither of the techniques is generally superior to the other, and neither of them is appropriate for all situations. In general, the strengths of PLS-SEM are CB-SEM's limitations and vice versa. It is important that researchers understand the different applications each approach was developed for and use them accordingly. Researchers need to apply the SEM technique that best suits their research objective, data characteristics, and model setup (see Roldán & Sánchez-Franco, 2012, for a more detailed discussion).

Data Characteristics

Minimum Sample Size Requirements

Data characteristics such as **minimum sample size,** nonnormal data, and scale of measurement (i.e., the use of different scale types) are among the most often stated reasons for applying PLS-SEM (Hair, Sarstedt, Ringle, et al., 2012; Henseler et al., 2009). While some of the arguments are consistent with the method's capabilities, others are not. For example, small sample size is probably the most often abused argument with some researchers using PLS-SEM with unacceptably low sample sizes (Goodhue, Lewis, & Thompson, 2012; Marcoulides & Saunders, 2006). These researchers oftentimes believe that there is some "magic" in the PLS-SEM approach that allows them to use a very small sample (e.g., less than 100) to obtain results representing the effects that exist in a population of several million elements or individuals. No multivariate analysis technique, including PLS-SEM, has this kind of "magic" capabilities. However, the result of these misrepresentations has led to skepticism in general about the use of PLS-SEM.

A **sample** is a selection of elements or individuals from a larger body or population. The individuals are specifically selected in the sampling process to represent the population as a whole. A good sample should reflect the similarities and differences found in the population so that it is possible to make inferences from the (small)

Exhibit 1.6	Rules of Thumb for Choosing Between PLS-SEM and CB-SEM

Use PLS-SEM when

- The goal is predicting key target constructs or identifying key "driver" constructs.
- Formatively measured constructs are part of the structural model. Note that formative measures can also be used with CB-SEM, but doing so requires construct specification modifications (e.g., the construct must include both formative and reflective indicators to meet identification requirements).
- The structural model is complex (many constructs and many indicators).
- The sample size is small and/or the data are nonnormally distributed.
- The plan is to use latent variable scores in subsequent analyses.

Use CB-SEM when

- The goal is theory testing, theory confirmation, or the comparison of alternative theories.
- Error terms require additional specification, such as the covariation.
- The structural model has circular relationships.
- The research requires a global goodness-of-fit criterion.

Source: Adapted from Hair JF, Ringle CM and Sarstedt M (2011) PLS-SEM: Indeed a Silver Bullet. *Journal of Marketing Theory and Practice* 19: 139–151 Copyright © 2011 by M.E. Sharpe, Inc. reprinted by permission of the publisher (Taylor & Francis Ltd., http://www.tandfonline.com).

sample about the (large) population. Hence, the size of the population and particularly the variation of the variables under research affects the sample size required in the sampling process. In addition, when applying multivariate analysis techniques, the technical dimension of the sample size becomes relevant. The minimum sample size shall safeguard that the results of the statistical method such as PLS-SEM have adequate statistical power. In these regards, an insufficient sample size may not reveal a significant effect that exists in the underlying population (which results in committing a Type II error). Moreover, the minimum sample size shall ensure that the results of the statistical method are robust and the model is generalizable. An insufficient sample size may lead to PLS-SEM results that highly differ from those of another sample. In the following, we focus on the PLS-SEM method and its technical requirements of the minimum sample size.

The overall complexity of a structural model has little influence on the sample size requirements for PLS-SEM. The reason is the algorithm does not compute all relationships in the structural model at the same time. Instead, it uses OLS regressions to estimate the model's partial regression relationships. Two early studies systematically evaluated the performance of PLS-SEM with small sample sizes and concluded it performed well (e.g., Chin & Newsted, 1999; Hui & Wold, 1982). More recently, a simulation study by Reinartz et al. (2009) indicated that PLS-SEM is a good choice when the sample size is small. Moreover, compared with its covariance-based counterpart, PLS-SEM has higher levels of statistical power in situations with complex model structures or smaller sample sizes. Similarly, Henseler et al. (2014) show that solutions can be obtained with PLS-SEM when other methods do not converge or provide inadmissible solutions. For example, problems often are encountered when using CB-SEM on complex models, especially when the sample size is limited. Similarly, CB-SEM suffers from identification and convergence issues when formative measures are involved (e.g., Diamantopoulos & Riefler, 2011).

Unfortunately, some researchers believe that sample size considerations do not play a role in the application of PLS-SEM. This idea is fostered by the often-cited 10 times rule (Barclay, Higgins, & Thompson, 1995), which indicates the sample size should be equal to the larger of

1. 10 times the largest number of formative indicators used to measure a single construct, or

2. 10 times the largest number of structural paths directed at a particular construct in the structural model.

This rule of thumb is equivalent to saying that the minimum sample size should be 10 times the maximum number of arrowheads pointing at a latent variable anywhere in the PLS path model. While the 10 times rule offers a rough guideline for minimum sample size requirements, PLS-SEM—like any statistical technique—requires researchers to consider the sample size against the background of the model and data characteristics (Hair et al., 2011; Marcoulides &

Chin, 2013). Specifically, the required sample size should be determined by means of power analyses based on the part of the model with the largest number of predictors.

Since sample size recommendations in PLS-SEM essentially build on the properties of OLS regression, researchers can rely on rules of thumb such as those provided by Cohen (1992) in his statistical power analyses for multiple regression models, provided that the measurement models have an acceptable quality in terms of outer loadings (i.e., loadings should be above the common threshold of 0.70). Alternatively, researchers can use programs such as G*Power (which is available free of charge at http://www.gpower.hhu.de/) to carry out power analyses specific to model setups.

Exhibit 1.7 shows the minimum sample size requirements necessary to detect minimum R^2 values of 0.10, 0.25, 0.50, and 0.75 in any of the endogenous constructs in the structural model for significance levels of 1%, 5%, and 10%, assuming the commonly used level of statistical power of 80% and a specific level of complexity of the PLS path model (i.e., the maximum number of arrows pointing at a construct in the PLS path model). For instance, when the maximum number of independent variables in the measurement and structural models is five, one would need 45 observations to achieve a statistical power of 80% for detecting R^2 values of at least 0.25 (with a 5% probability of error).

Data Characteristics

As with other statistical analyses, missing values should be dealt with when using PLS-SEM. For reasonable limits (i.e., less than 5% values missing per indicator), **missing value treatment** options such as mean replacement, EM (expectation-maximization algorithm), and nearest neighbor (e.g., Hair et al., 2010) generally result in only slightly different PLS-SEM estimations. Alternatively, researchers can opt for deleting all observations with missing values, which decreases variation in the data and may introduce biases when certain groups of observations have been deleted systematically.

The use of PLS-SEM has two other key advantages related to data characteristics (i.e., distribution and scales). In situations where it is difficult or impossible to meet the stricter requirements of more traditional multivariate techniques (e.g., normal data distribution), PLS-SEM is the preferred method. PLS-SEM's greater flexibility is described by the label "soft modeling," coined by Wold (1982), who

Exhibit 1.7 Sample Size Recommendation in PLS-SEM for a Statistical Power of 80%

Maximum Number of Arrows Pointing at a Construct (Number of Independent Variables)	Significance Level											
	10%				5%				1%			
	Minimum R^2				Minimum R^2				Minimum R^2			
	0.10	0.25	0.50	0.75	0.10	0.25	0.50	0.75	0.10	0.25	0.50	0.75
2	72	26	11	7	90	33	14	8	130	47	19	10
3	83	30	13	8	103	37	16	9	145	53	22	12
4	92	34	15	9	113	41	18	11	158	58	24	14
5	99	37	17	10	122	45	20	12	169	62	26	15
6	106	40	18	12	130	48	21	13	179	66	28	16
7	112	42	20	13	137	51	23	14	188	69	30	18
8	118	45	21	14	144	54	24	15	196	73	32	19
9	124	47	22	15	150	56	26	16	204	76	34	20
10	129	49	24	16	156	59	27	18	212	79	35	21

Source: Cohen (1992): A Power Primer. Psychological Bulletin 112: 155–159.

developed the method. It should be noted, however, that "soft" is attributed only to the distributional assumptions and not to the concepts, models, or estimation techniques (Lohmöller, 1989). PLS-SEM's statistical properties provide very robust model estimations with data that have normal as well as extremely nonnormal (i.e., skewness and/ or kurtosis) distributional properties (Reinartz et al., 2009; Ringle, Götz, Wetzels, & Wilson, 2009). It must be remembered, however, that influential outliers and collinearity do influence the OLS regressions in PLS-SEM, and researchers should evaluate the data and results for these issues (Hair et al., 2010).

The PLS-SEM algorithm generally requires **metric data** on a ratio or interval scale for the measurement model indicators. But the method also works well with ordinal scales with equidistant data points (i.e., quasi-metric scales; Sarstedt & Mooi, 2014) and with binary coded data. The use of binary coded data is often a means of including categorical control variables or moderators in PLS-SEM models. In short, dummy-coded indicators can be included in PLS-SEM models but require special attention (see some note of caution by Hair, Sarstedt, Ringle, et al., 2012) and should not be used as the ultimate dependent variable. Exhibit 1.8 summarizes key considerations related to data characteristics.

Model Characteristics

PLS-SEM is very flexible in its modeling properties. In its basic form, the PLS-SEM algorithm requires all models to be without circular relationships or loops of relationships between the latent variables in the structural model. While models with causal loops are seldom specified in business research, this characteristic does limit the applicability of PLS-SEM if such models are required. Note, however, that Lohmöller's (1989) extensions of the basic PLS-SEM algorithm allow for handling such model types. Other model specification requirements that constrain the use of CB-SEM, such as distribution assumptions, are not relevant with PLS-SEM.

Measurement model difficulties are one of the major obstacles to obtaining a solution with CB-SEM. For instance, estimation of complex models with many latent variables and/or indicators is often impossible with CB-SEM. In contrast, PLS-SEM can be used in such situations since it is not constrained by identification and other technical issues. Consideration of reflective and formative measurement

| **Exhibit 1.8** | Data Considerations When Applying PLS-SEM |

- As a *rough* guideline, the minimum sample size in a PLS-SEM analysis should be equal to the larger of the following (10 times rule): (1) 10 times the largest number of formative indicators used to measure one construct or (2) 10 times the largest number of structural paths directed at a particular construct in the structural model. Researchers should, however, follow more elaborate recommendations such as those provided by Cohen (1992) that also take statistical power and effect sizes into account. Alternatively, researchers should run individual power analyses, using programs such as G*Power.

- With larger data sets ($N = 250$ and larger), CB-SEM and PLS-SEM results are very similar when an appropriate number of indicator variables (four or more) are used to measure each construct (consistency at large).

- PLS-SEM can handle extremely nonnormal data (e.g., high levels of skewness).

- Most missing value treatment procedures (e.g., mean replacement, pairwise deletion, EM, and nearest neighbor) can be used for reasonable levels of missing data (less than 5% missing per indicator) with limited effect on the analysis results.

- PLS-SEM works with metric, quasi-metric, and categorical (i.e., dummy-coded) scaled data, albeit with certain limitations.

models is a key issue in the application of SEM. PLS-SEM can easily handle both formative and reflective measurement models and is considered the primary approach when the hypothesized model incorporates formative measures. CB-SEM can accommodate formative indicators, but to ensure model identification, they must follow distinct specification rules (Diamantopoulos & Riefler, 2011). In fact, the requirements often prevent running the analysis as originally planned. In contrast, PLS-SEM does not have such requirements and handles formative measurement models without any limitation. This also applies to model settings in which endogenous constructs are measured formatively. The applicability of CB-SEM to such model settings has been subject to considerable debate (Cadogan & Lee, 2013; Rigdon, 2014a), but due to PLS-SEM's multistage estimation process (Chapter 3), which separates measurement from structural model estimation, the inclusion of formatively measured endogenous

Exhibit 1.9	Model Considerations When Choosing PLS-SEM

- Measurement model requirements are quite flexible. PLS-SEM can handle reflective and formative measurement models as well as single-item measures without additional requirements or constraints.
- Model complexity is generally not an issue for PLS-SEM. As long as appropriate data meet minimum sample size requirements, the complexity of the structural model is virtually unrestricted.

constructs is not an issue in PLS-SEM (Rigdon et al., 2014). The only problematic issue is when a high level of collinearity exists between the indicator variables of a formative measurement model.

Finally, PLS-SEM is capable of estimating very complex models. For example, if theoretical or conceptual assumptions support large models and sufficient data are available (i.e., meeting minimum sample size requirements), PLS-SEM can handle models of almost any size, including those with dozens of constructs and hundreds of indicator variables. As noted by Wold (1985), PLS-SEM is virtually without competition when path models with latent variables are complex in their structural relationships (Chapter 3). Exhibit 1.9 summarizes rules of thumb for PLS-SEM model characteristics.

ORGANIZATION OF REMAINING CHAPTERS

The remaining chapters provide more detailed information on PLS-SEM, including specific examples of how to use software to estimate simple and complex PLS path models. In doing so, the chapters follow a multistage procedure that should be used as a blueprint when conducting PLS-SEM analyses (Exhibit 1.10).

Specifically, the process starts with the specification of structural and measurement models, followed by the examination of data (Chapter 2). Next, we discuss the PLS-SEM algorithm and provide an overview of important considerations when running the analyses (Chapter 3). On the basis of the results of the computation, the researchers then have to evaluate the results. To do so, researchers must know how to assess both reflective and formative measurement models (Chapters 4 and 5). When the data for the measures are

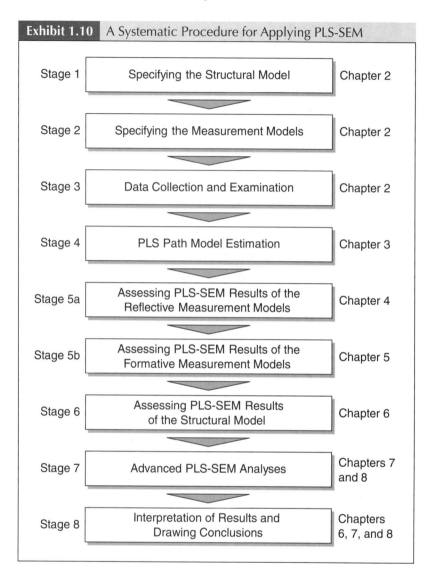

Exhibit 1.10   A Systematic Procedure for Applying PLS-SEM

Stage 1	Specifying the Structural Model	Chapter 2
Stage 2	Specifying the Measurement Models	Chapter 2
Stage 3	Data Collection and Examination	Chapter 2
Stage 4	PLS Path Model Estimation	Chapter 3
Stage 5a	Assessing PLS-SEM Results of the Reflective Measurement Models	Chapter 4
Stage 5b	Assessing PLS-SEM Results of the Formative Measurement Models	Chapter 5
Stage 6	Assessing PLS-SEM Results of the Structural Model	Chapter 6
Stage 7	Advanced PLS-SEM Analyses	Chapters 7 and 8
Stage 8	Interpretation of Results and Drawing Conclusions	Chapters 6, 7, and 8

considered reliable and valid (based on established criteria), researchers can then evaluate the structural model (Chapter 6). Finally, Chapter 7 covers the handling of mediating and moderating effects whose analysis has become standard in PLS-SEM research. On the basis of the results of Chapters 6 and 7, researchers interpret their findings and draw their final conclusions.

SUMMARY

SEM is a powerful statistical method that can identify relationships in social science research that likely would not otherwise be found. This chapter introduced you to the topic, explained why researchers are increasingly using the method, and helped you do the following:

- **Understand the meaning of structural equation modeling (SEM) and its relationship to multivariate data analysis.** SEM is a second-generation multivariate data analysis method. Multivariate data analysis involves the application of statistical methods that simultaneously analyze multiple variables representing measurements associated with individuals, companies, events, activities, situations, and so forth. SEM is used to either explore or confirm theory. Exploratory modeling involves developing theory while confirmatory modeling tests theory. There are two types of SEM—one is covariance-based, and the other is variance-based. CB-SEM is used to confirm (or reject) theories. Variance-based structural equation modeling (i.e., PLS-SEM) is primarily used for exploratory research and the development of theories.

- **Describe the basic considerations in applying multivariate data analysis.** Several considerations are necessary when applying multivariate analysis, including the following five elements: (1) composite variables, (2) measurement, (3) measurement scales, (4) coding, and (5) data distributions. A composite variable (also called variate) is a linear combination of several variables that are chosen based on the research problem at hand. Measurement is the process of assigning numbers to a variable based on a set of rules. Multivariate measurement involves using several variables to indirectly measure a concept to improve measurement accuracy. The anticipated improved accuracy is based on the assumption that using several variables (indicators) to measure a single concept is more likely to represent all the different aspects of the concept and thereby result in a more valid measurement of the concept. The ability to identify measurement error using multivariate measurement also helps researchers obtain more accurate measurements. Measurement error is the difference between the true value of a variable and the value obtained by a measurement. A measurement scale is a tool with a predetermined number of closed-ended responses that can be used to obtain an answer to a question. There are four types of measurement scales: nominal, ordinal, interval, and ratio. When researchers collect quantitative data using scales, the answers to the questions can be shown as a distribution across the available (pre-defined) response categories. The type of distribution must always be considered when working with SEM.

- **Comprehend the basic concepts of partial least squares structural equation modeling (PLS-SEM).** Path models are diagrams used to visually display the hypotheses and variable relationships that are examined when structural equation modeling is applied. Four basic elements must be understood when developing path models: (1) constructs, (2) measured variables, (3) relationships, and (4) error terms. Constructs are latent variables that are not directly measured and are sometimes called unobserved variables. They are represented in path models as circles or ovals. Measured variables are directly measured observations (raw data), generally referred to as either indicators or manifest variables, and are represented in path models as rectangles. Relationships represent hypotheses in path models and are shown as arrows that are single-headed, indicating a predictive/causal relationship. Error terms represent the unexplained variance when path models are estimated and are present for endogenous constructs and reflectively measured indicators. Exogenous constructs and formative indicators do not have error terms. Path models also distinguish between the structural (inner) model and the measurement (outer) models. The role of theory is important when developing structural models. Theory is a set of systematically related hypotheses developed following the scientific method that can be used to explain and predict outcomes. Measurement theory specifies how the latent unobservable variables (constructs) are modeled. Latent variables can be modeled as either reflective or formative. Structural theory shows how the latent unobservable variables are related to each other. Latent variables are classified as either endogenous or exogenous.

- **Explain the differences between covariance-based structural equation modeling (CB-SEM) and PLS-SEM and when to use each.** Compared to CB-SEM, PLS-SEM emphasizes prediction while simultaneously relaxing the demands regarding the data and specification of relationships. PLS-SEM maximizes the endogenous latent variables' explained variance by estimating partial model relationships in an iterative sequence of OLS regressions. In contrast,

CB-SEM estimates model parameters so that the discrepancy between the estimated and sample covariance matrices is minimized. Instead of following a common factor model logic as CB-SEM does, PLS-SEM calculates composites of indicators that serve as proxies for the concpets under research. The method is not constrained by identification issues, even if the model becomes complex—a situation that typically restricts CB-SEM use—and does not require accounting for most distributional assumptions. Moreover, PLS-SEM can better handle formative measurement models and has advantages when sample sizes are relatively small. Researchers should consider the two SEM approaches as complementary and apply the SEM technique that best suits their research objective, data characteristics, and model setup.

REVIEW QUESTIONS

1. What is multivariate analysis?

2. Describe the difference between first- and second-generation multivariate methods.

3. What is structural equation modeling?

4. What is the value of structural equation modeling in understanding relationships between variables?

CRITICAL THINKING QUESTIONS

1. When would SEM methods be more advantageous in understanding relationships between variables?

2. What are the most important considerations in deciding whether to use CB-SEM or PLS-SEM?

3. Under what circumstances is PLS-SEM the preferred method over CB-SEM?

4. Why is an understanding of theory important when deciding whether to use PLS-SEM or CB-SEM?

5. Why should social science researchers consider using SEM instead of multiple regression?

KEY TERMS

CB-SEM

Coding

Composite variable

Confirmatory applications

Constructs

Covariance-based structural equation modeling

Endogenous latent variables

Equidistance

Error terms

Exogenous latent variables

Exploratory

Factor (score) indeterminacy

First-generation techniques

Formative measurement model

Indicators

Inner model

Interval scale

Items

Latent variable

Manifest variables

Measurement

Measurement error

Measurement model

Measurement scale

Measurement theory

Metric data

Minimum sample size

Missing value treatment

Multivariate analyses

Nominal scale

Ordinal scale

Outer models

Partial least squares structural equation modeling

Path models

PLS path modeling

PLS regression

PLS-SEM

Ratio scales

Reflective measurement model

Sample

Second-generation techniques

SEM

Single-item constructs

Statistical power

Structural equation modeling

Structural model

Structural theory

Sum scores

Theory

Variance-based SEM

Variate

SUGGESTED READINGS

Dijkstra, T. K. (2014). PLS' Janus face—response to Professor Rigdon's "Rethinking partial least squares modeling: In praise of simple methods." *Long Range Planning, 47,* 146–153.

Esposito Vinzi, V., Trinchera, L., & Amato, S. (2010). PLS path modeling: From foundations to recent developments and open issues for model assessment and improvement. In V. Esposito Vinzi, W. W. Chin, J. Henseler, & H. Wang (Eds.), *Handbook of partial least squares: Concepts, methods and applications* (Springer Handbooks of Computational Statistics Series, Vol. II, pp. 47–82). New York: Springer.

Gefen, D., Straub, D. W., & Boudreau, M. C. (2000). Structural equation modeling techniques and regression: Guidelines for research practice. *Communications of the AIS, 1,* 1–78.

Hair, J. F., Ringle, C. M., & Sarstedt, M. (2011). PLS-SEM: Indeed a silver bullet. *Journal of Marketing Theory and Practice, 19,* 139–151.

Henseler, J., Dijkstra, T. K., Sarstedt, M., Ringle, C. M., Diamantopoulos, A., Straub, D. W., et al. (2014). Common beliefs and reality about partial least squares: Comments on Rönkkö & Evermann (2013). *Organizational Research Methods, 17,* 182–209.

Henseler, J., Ringle, C. M., & Sarstedt, M. (2012). Using partial least squares path modeling in international advertising research: Basic concepts and recent issues. In S. Okazaki (Ed.), *Handbook of research in international advertising* (pp. 252–276). Cheltenham, UK: Edward Elgar.

Jöreskog, K. G., & Wold, H. (1982). The ML and PLS techniques for modeling with latent variables: Historical and comparative aspects. In H. Wold & K. G. Jöreskog (Eds.), *Systems under indirect observation, Part I* (pp. 263–270). Amsterdam: North-Holland.

Lohmöller, J. B. (1989). *Latent variable path modeling with partial least squares.* Heidelberg, Germany: Physica.

Marcoulides, G. A., & Chin, W. W. (2013). You write but others read: Common methodological misunderstandings in PLS and related methods. In H. Abdi, W. W. Chin, V. Esposito Vinzi, G. Russolillo, & L. Trinchera (Eds.), *New perspectives in partial least squares and related methods* (pp. 31–64). New York: Springer.

Mateos-Aparicio, G. (2011). Partial least squares (PLS) methods: Origins, evolution, and application to social sciences. *Communications in Statistics: Theory and Methods, 40,* 2305–2317.

Rigdon, E. E. (2012). Rethinking partial least squares path modeling: In praise of simple methods. *Long Range Planning, 45,* 341–358.

Specifying the Path Model and Examining Data

1. Understand the basic concepts of structural model specification, including mediation and moderation.

2. Explain the differences between reflective and formative measures and specify the appropriate measurement model.

3. Comprehend that the selection of the mode of measurement model and the indicators must be based on theoretical/conceptual reasoning before data collection.

4. Explain the difference between multi-item and single-item measures and assess when to use each measurement type.

5. Describe the data collection and examination considerations necessary to apply PLS-SEM.

6. Learn how to develop a PLS path model using the SmartPLS 3 software.

CHAPTER PREVIEW

Chapter 2 introduces the basic concepts of structural and measurement model specification when PLS-SEM is used. The concepts are associated with completing the first three stages in the application of

PLS-SEM, as described in Chapter 1. Stage 1 is specifying the structural model. Stage 2 is selecting and specifying the **measurement models.** Stage 3 summarizes the major guidelines for data collection when the application of PLS-SEM is anticipated, as well as the need to examine your data after they have been collected to ensure the results from applying PLS-SEM are valid and reliable. An understanding of these three topics will prepare you for Stage 4, estimating the model, which is the focus of Chapter 3.

STAGE 1: SPECIFYING THE STRUCTURAL MODEL

In the initial stages of a research project that involves the application of SEM, an important first step is to prepare a diagram that illustrates the research hypotheses and displays the variable relationships that will be examined. This diagram is often referred to as a path model. Recall that a path model is a diagram that connects variables/ constructs based on theory and logic to visually display the hypotheses that will be tested (Chapter 1). Preparing a path model early in the research process enables researchers to organize their thoughts and visually consider the relationships between the variables of interest. Path models also are an efficient means of sharing ideas between researchers working on or reviewing a research project.

Path models are made up of two elements: (1) the **structural model** (also called the **inner model** in PLS-SEM), which describes the relationships between the latent variables, and (2) the **measurement models,** which describe the relationships between the latent variables and their measures (i.e., their indicators). We discuss structural models first, which are developed in Stage 1. The next section covers Stage 2, measurement models.

When a structural model is being developed, two primary issues need to be considered: the sequence of the constructs and the relationships between them. Both issues are critical to the concept of modeling because they represent the hypotheses and their relationship to the theory being tested.

The sequence of the constructs in a structural model is based on theory, logic, or practical experiences observed by the researcher. The sequence is displayed from left to right, with independent (predictor) constructs on the left and dependent (outcome) variables on the right-hand side. That is, constructs on the left are assumed to precede and predict constructs on the right. Constructs that act only as independent variables are generally referred to as exogenous latent variables and are on the very left side of the structural model. Exogenous latent variables only have arrows that point out of them and never have arrows pointing into them. Constructs considered dependent in a structural model (i.e., those that have an arrow pointing into them) often are called endogenous latent variables and are on the right side of the structural model. Constructs that operate as both independent and dependent variables in a model also are considered endogenous and, if they are part of a model, appear in the middle of the diagram.

The structural model in Exhibit 2.1 illustrates the three types of constructs and the relationships. The reputation construct on the far left is an exogenous (i.e., independent) latent variable. It is modeled as predicting the satisfaction construct. The satisfaction construct is an endogenous latent variable that has a dual relationship as both independent and dependent. It is a dependent construct because it is predicted by reputation. But it is also an independent construct because it predicts loyalty. The loyalty construct on the right end is an endogenous (i.e., dependent) latent variable predicted by satisfaction.

Determining the sequence of the constructs is seldom an easy task because contradictory theoretical perspectives can lead to different sequencing of latent variables. For example, some researchers assume that customer satisfaction precedes and predicts corporate reputation (e.g., Walsh, Mitchell, Jackson, & Beatty, 2009), while others argue that corporate reputation predicts customer satisfaction (Eberl, 2010; Sarstedt, Wilczynski, & Melewar, 2013). Theory and logic should always determine the sequence of constructs in a conceptual model, but when the literature is inconsistent or unclear, researchers must use their best judgment to determine the sequence. In large, complex models, researchers may adjust the sequence of constructs several times

Exhibit 2.1 Example of Path Model and Types of Constructs

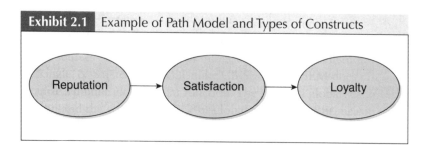

while trying to accurately portray the theoretical concepts. Likewise, it is possible to have alternative competing models that test a different sequence (Sattler, Völckner, Riediger, & Ringle, 2010; Wilson, Callaghan, Ringle, & Henseler, 2007). However, selecting the best sequence among several competing alternatives can be challenging.

Once the sequence of the constructs has been decided, the relationships between them must be established by drawing arrows. The arrows are inserted with the arrow pointed to the right. This approach indicates the sequence and that the constructs on the left predict the constructs on the right side. The predictive relationships are sometimes referred to as **causal links,** if the structural theory supports a causal relationship. In drawing arrows between the constructs, researchers face a trade-off between theoretical soundness (i.e., including those relationships that are strongly supported by theory) and model parsimony (i.e., using fewer relationships). The latter should be of crucial concern as the most nonrestrictive statement "everything is predictive of everything else" is also the most uninformative. As pointed out by Falk and Miller (1992), "A parsimonious approach to theoretical specification is far more powerful than the broad application of a shotgun" (p. 24).

In most instances, researchers examine linear independent-dependent relationships between two or more constructs in the path model. Theory may suggest, however, that model relationships are more complex and involve mediation or **moderation** relationships. In the following section, we briefly introduce these different relationship types. In Chapter 7, we explain how they can be estimated and interpreted using PLS-SEM.

Mediation

A **mediating effect** is created when a third variable or construct intervenes between two other related constructs, as shown in Exhibit 2.2. To understand how mediating effects work, let's consider a path model in terms of direct and indirect effects. **Direct effects** are the relationships linking two constructs with a single arrow; **indirect effects** are those relationships that involve a sequence of relationships with at least one intervening construct involved. Thus, an **indirect effect** is a sequence of two or more direct effects (compound path) that are represented visually by multiple arrows. This indirect effect is characterized as the mediating effect. In Exhibit 2.2, satisfaction is modeled as a possible mediator between reputation and loyalty.

From a theoretical perspective, the most common application of mediation is to "explain" why a relationship between an exogenous and endogenous construct exists. For example, a researcher may observe a relationship between two constructs but not be sure "why" the relationship exists or if the observed relationship is the only relationship between the two constructs. In such a situation, a researcher might posit an explanation of the relationship in terms of an intervening variable that operates by receiving the "inputs" from an exogenous construct and translating them into an "output," which is an endogenous construct. The role of the mediator variable then is to reveal the true relationship between an independent and a dependent construct.

Consider the example in Exhibit 2.2, in which we want to examine the effect of corporate reputation on customer loyalty. On the basis of theory and logic, we know that a relationship exists between reputation and loyalty, but we are unsure how the relationship actually works. As researchers, we might want to explain how companies translate their reputation into higher loyalty among their customers. We may observe that sometimes a customer perceives a company as being highly reputable, but this perception does not translate into high levels of loyalty. In other situations, we observe that some customers with lower reputation assessments are highly loyal. These observations are confusing and lead to the question as to whether there is some other process going on that translates corporate reputation into customer loyalty.

In the diagram, the intervening process (mediating effect) is modeled as satisfaction. If a respondent perceives a company to be highly

Exhibit 2.2 Example of a Mediating Effect

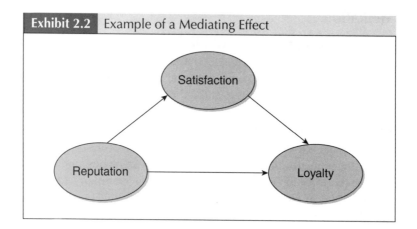

reputable, this assessment may lead to higher satisfaction levels and ultimately to increased loyalty. In such a case, the relationship between reputation and loyalty may be explained by the reputation → loyalty sequence, or the reputation → satisfaction → loyalty sequence, or perhaps even by both sets of relationships (Exhibit 2.2). The reputation → loyalty sequence is an example of a direct relationship. In contrast, the reputation → satisfaction → loyalty sequence is an example of an indirect relationship. After empirically testing these relationships, the researcher would be able to explain how reputation is related to loyalty, as well as the role that satisfaction might play in mediating that relationship. Chapter 7 offers additional details on mediation and explains how to test mediating effects in PLS-SEM.

Moderation

Related to the concept of mediation is moderation. With **moderation,** a third variable could directly affect the relationship between the exogenous and endogenous latent variables but in a different way. Referred to as a **moderator effect,** this situation occurs when the moderator (an independent variable or construct) changes the strength or even the direction of a relationship between two constructs in the model.

For example, income has been shown to significantly affect the strength of the relationship between customer satisfaction and customer loyalty (Homburg & Giering, 2001). In that context, income serves as a moderator variable on the satisfaction → loyalty relationship, as shown in Exhibit 2.3. Specifically, the relationship between satisfaction and loyalty has been shown to be weaker for people with high income than for people with low income. That is, for higher-income individuals, there may be little or no relationship between satisfaction and loyalty. But for lower-income individuals, there often is a strong relationship between the two variables. As can be seen, both the mediator and the moderator concept affect the strength of a relationship between two latent variables. The crucial distinction between both concepts is that the moderator variable (income in our moderator example) does not depend on the exogenous (predictor) latent variable (satisfaction in our moderator example).

There are two types of moderating relationships. One is referred to as *continuous* and the other as *categorical.* The difference in the two types of relationships is that a continuous moderating effect

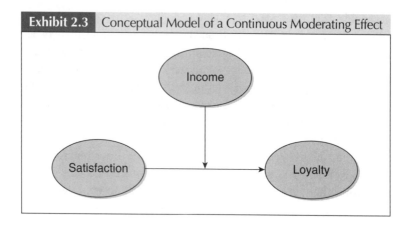

Exhibit 2.3 Conceptual Model of a Continuous Moderating Effect

exists when the moderating variable is metrically measured (e.g., income in Exhibit 2.3), whereas a categorical moderating effect is when the moderating variable is categorical, such as gender.

When a moderator effect is categorical, the variable may serve as a grouping variable that divides the data into subsamples. The same theoretical model is then estimated for each of the distinct subsamples. Since researchers are usually interested in comparing the models and learning about significant differences between the subsamples, the model estimates for the subsamples are usually compared by means of **multigroup analysis** (Sarstedt, Henseler, & Ringle, 2011). Specifically, multigroup analysis enables the researcher to test for differences between identical models estimated for different groups of respondents. The general objective is to see if there are statistically significant differences between individual group models. This procedure is different from testing different theoretical models for the same sample of respondents. With multigroup analysis, we are comparing the same model across different samples of respondents. For example, we might be interested in evaluating whether the effect of satisfaction on loyalty is significantly different for males compared with females (Exhibit 2.4). Specifically, a researcher might want to determine whether the relationship is statistically significant for both males and females and if the strength of the relationship is similar or quite different.

Another situation researchers often encounter is where they have a continuous moderator variable, but instead of modeling its original effect on the relationship as continuous, they transform the continuous

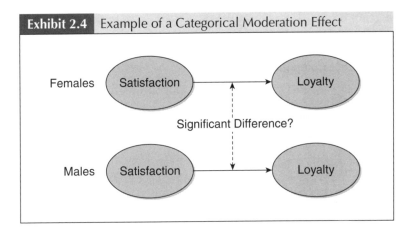

Exhibit 2.4 Example of a Categorical Moderation Effect

variable into a categorical variable and then conduct a multigroup analysis. Different approaches transform the continuous variable into a categorical one, such as mean and median splits. In Chapter 7, we discuss in greater detail how to use categorical and continuous variables for the moderator analysis.

Higher-Order and Hierarchical Component Models

Thus far, we have dealt with first-order components in which we consider a single layer of constructs. However, in some instances, the constructs that researchers wish to examine are quite complex in that they can also be operationalized at higher levels of abstraction. **Higher-order models** or **hierarchical component models (HCMs)** most often involve testing second-order structures that contain two layers of components (e.g., Ringle et al., 2012; Wetzels, Odekerken-Schroder, & van Oppen, 2009). For example, satisfaction can be defined at different levels of abstraction. Specifically, satisfaction can be represented by numerous first-order components that capture separate attributes of satisfaction. In the context of services, these might include satisfaction with the quality of the service, the service personnel, the price, or the servicescape. These first-order components might form the more abstract second-order component satisfaction, as shown in Exhibit 2.5.

Instead of modeling the attributes of satisfaction as drivers of the respondent's overall satisfaction on a single construct layer, higher-order modeling involves summarizing the lower-order components

Exhibit 2.5 Example of a Hierarchical Component Model

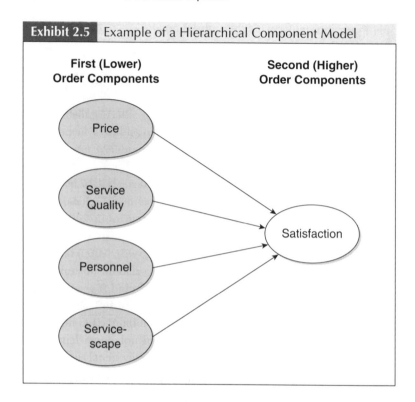

into a single multidimensional higher-order construct. This modeling approach leads to more parsimony and reduces model complexity. Theoretically, this process can be extended to any number of multiple layers, but researchers usually restrict their modeling approach to two layers. More details on hierarchical component models in PLS-SEM are provided in Chapter 8.

STAGE 2: SPECIFYING THE MEASUREMENT MODELS

The structural model describes the relationships between latent variables (constructs). In contrast, the measurement models represent the relationships between constructs and their corresponding indicator variables (generally called the **outer models** in PLS-SEM). The basis for determining these relationships is measurement theory. A sound measurement theory is a necessary condition to obtain useful results from PLS-SEM. Hypothesis tests involving the structural relationships among constructs will be only as reliable or valid as the measurement models are explaining how these constructs are measured.

Researchers typically have several established measurement approaches to choose from, each a slight variant from the others. In fact, almost all social science researchers today use established measurement approaches published in prior research studies or scale handbooks (e.g., Bearden, Netemeyer, & Haws, 2011; Bruner, James, & Hensel, 2001) that performed well (Ramirez, David, & Brusco, 2013). In some situations, however, the researcher is faced with the lack of an established measurement approach and must develop a new set of measures (or substantially modify an existing approach). A description of the general process for developing indicators to measure a construct can be long and detailed. Hair et al. (2010) describe the essentials of this process. Likewise, Diamantopoulos and Winklhofer (2001), DeVellis (2011), and MacKenzie, Podsakoff, and Podsakoff (2011) offer thorough explications of different approaches to measurement development. In each case, decisions regarding how the researcher selects the indicators to measure a particular construct provide a foundation for the remaining analysis.

The path model shown in Exhibit 2.6 shows an excerpt of the path model we use as an example throughout the book. The model has two exogenous constructs—*corporate social responsibility* (*CSOR*) and *attractiveness* (*ATTR*)—and one endogenous construct, which is *competence* (*COMP*). Each of these constructs is measured by means of multiple indicators. For instance, the endogenous construct *COMP* has three measured indicator variables, *comp_1* to *comp_3*. Using a scale from 1 to 7 (*totally disagree* to *completely agree*), respondents had to evaluate the following statements: "[The company] is a top competitor in its market," "As far as I know, [the company] is recognized worldwide," and "I believe that [the company] performs at a premium level." The answers to these three inquiries represent the measures for this construct. The construct itself is measured indirectly by these three indicator variables and for that reason is referred to as a latent variable.

The other two constructs in the model, *CSOR* and *ATTR*, can be described in a similar manner. That is, the two exogenous constructs are measured by indicators that are each directly measured by responses to specific questions. Note that the relationship between the indicators and the corresponding construct is different for *COMP* compared with *CSOR* and *ATTR*. When you examine the *COMP*

Exhibit 2.6 Example of a Path Model With Three Constructs

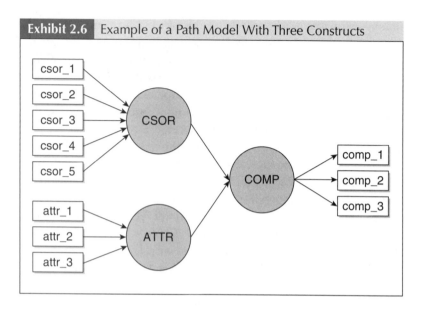

construct, the direction of the arrows goes from the construct to the indicators. This type of measurement model is referred to as *reflective*. When you examine the *CSOR* and *ATTR* constructs, the direction of the arrows is from the measured indicator variables to the constructs. This type of measurement model is called *formative*. As discussed in Chapter 1, an important characteristic of PLS-SEM is that the technique readily incorporates both reflective and formative measures. Likewise, PLS-SEM can easily be used when constructs are measured with only a single item (rather than multiple items). Both of these measurement issues are discussed in the following sections.

Reflective and Formative Measurement Models

When developing constructs, researchers must consider two broad types of measurement specification: reflective and **formative measurement** models. The **reflective measurement** model (also referred to as **Mode A** measurement in PLS-SEM) has a long tradition in the social sciences and is directly based on classical test theory. According to this theory, measures represent the effects (or manifestations) of an underlying construct. Therefore, causality is from the construct to its measures (*COMP* in Exhibit 2.6). Reflective indicators (sometimes referred to as **effect indicators** in the psychometric literature) can be viewed as a representative sample of all the possible items available within the conceptual domain of the construct (Nunnally & Bernstein, 1994). Therefore, since a reflective measure dictates that all indicator items are caused by the same construct (i.e., they stem from the same domain), indicators associated with a particular construct should be highly correlated with each other. In addition, individual items should be interchangeable, and any single item can generally be left out without changing the meaning of the construct, as long as the construct has sufficient reliability. The fact that the relationship goes from the construct to its measures implies that if the evaluation of the latent trait changes (e.g., because of a change in the standard of comparison), all indicators will change simultaneously. A set of reflective measures is commonly called a **scale.**

In contrast, **formative measurement** models (also referred to as **Mode B** measurement in PLS-SEM) are based on the assumption that **causal indicators** form the construct by means of linear combinations. Therefore, researchers typically refer to this type of measurement model as being a formative **index.** An important characteristic of formative indicators is that they are not interchangeable, as is true with reflective indicators. Thus, each indicator for a formative construct captures a specific aspect of the construct's domain. Taken jointly, the items ultimately determine the meaning of the construct, which implies that omitting an indicator potentially alters the nature of the construct. As a consequence, breadth of coverage of the construct domain is extremely important to ensure that the content of the focal construct is adequately captured (Diamantopoulos & Winklhofer, 2001).

Recently, researchers have started distinguishing two types of indicators in the context of formative measurement: composite and causal indicators. **Composite indicators** largely correspond to the above definition of formative measurement models in that they are combined in a linear way to form a variate (Chapter 1), which is also referred to as composite variable in the context of SEM (Bollen, 2011; Bollen & Bauldry, 2011). More precisely, the indicators fully form the composite variable (i.e., the composite variable's R^2 value is 1.0). The resulting composite variable is considered a proxy for a latent concept (Rigdon, 2012), and the indicators do not necessarily need to be conceptually united. In contrast, **causal indicators** do not form the latent variable but, as the name implies, "cause" it. Consequently, causal indicators must correspond to a theoretical definition of the concept under investigation. This subtle distinction from composite indicators has important implications for the modeling of the latent variable, as it is highly unlikely that any set of causal indicators can fully capture every aspect of a latent phenomenon (Diamantopoulos & Winklhofer, 2001). Therefore, latent variables measured with causal indicators have an error term, which captures all the other causes of the latent variable not included in the model (Diamantopoulos, 2006). The use of causal indicators is prevalent in CB-SEM, which allows for explicitly defining the error term of a formatively measured latent variable. But the situation is different with PLS-SEM. The PLS-SEM algorithm relies solely on the concept of composite indicators because of the way the algorithm estimates formative measurement models (e.g., Diamantopoulos, 2011).

In a nutshell, the distinction between composite and causal indicators relates to a difference in measurement philosophy. Causal indicators assume that a certain concept can—at least in principle—be fully measured using a set of indicators and an error term. Composite indicators make no such assumption but view measurement as an approximation of a certain theoretical concept. In social sciences research, viewing measurement as an approximation seems more realistic (e.g., Rigdon, 2014b), which, from a conceptual standpoint, favors the use of composite indicators over causal indicators. For the sake of simplicity and in line with seminal research in the field (e.g., Fornell & Bookstein, 1982), we therefore refer to formative indicators when referring to composite indicators (as used in PLS-SEM) in the remainder of this book. Similarly, we refer to formative measurement models to describe measurement models comprising composite indicators. Henseler et al. (2014) and Henseler, Ringle, and Sarstedt (in press) provide further information on composite models as well as common factor models and their distinction.

Exhibit 2.7 illustrates the key difference between the reflective and formative measurement perspectives. The black circle illustrates the construct domain, which is the domain of content the construct is intended to measure. The gray circles represent the scope each indicator captures. Whereas the reflective measurement approach aims at maximizing the overlap between interchangeable indicators, the formative measurement approach tries to fully cover the domain of the latent concept under investigation (black circle) by the different formative indicators (gray circles), which should have small overlap.

Exhibit 2.7	Difference Between Reflective and Formative Measures

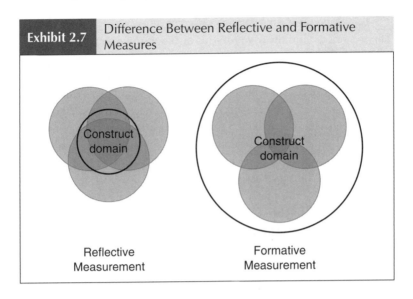

Reflective
Measurement

Formative
Measurement

Unlike the reflective measurement approach whose objective is to maximize the overlap between interchangeable indicators, there are no specific expectations about patterns or the magnitude of intercorrelations between formative indicators (Diamantopoulos, Riefler, & Roth, 2008). Since there is no "common cause" for the items in the construct, there is not any requirement for the items to be correlated, and they may be completely independent. In fact, collinearity among formative indicators can present significant problems because the weights linking the formative indicators with the construct can become unstable and nonsignificant. Furthermore, formative indicators (in the sense of composite indicators) have no individual measurement error terms. That is, they are assumed to be error free in a conventional sense. These characteristics have broad implications for the evaluation of formatively measured constructs, which rely on a totally different set of criteria compared with the evaluation of reflective measures (Chapter 5). For example, a reliability analysis based on item correlations (internal consistency) could remove important items and decrease the validity of the index (Diamantopoulos & Siguaw, 2006). Broadly speaking, researchers need to pay closer attention to the content validity of the measures by determining how well the indicators represent the domain, (or at least its major aspects) of the latent concept under research (e.g., Bollen & Lennox, 1991).

But when do we measure a construct reflectively or formatively? There is not a definite answer to this question since constructs are not inherently reflective or formative. Instead, the specification depends on the construct conceptualization and the objective of the study. Consider Exhibit 2.8, which shows how the construct "satisfaction with hotels" can be operationalized in both ways (Albers, 2010).

The left side of Exhibit 2.8 shows a reflective measurement model setup. This type of model setup is likely to be more appropriate when a researcher wants to test theories with respect to satisfaction. In many managerially oriented business studies, however, the aim is to identify the most important drivers of satisfaction that ultimately lead to customer loyalty. In this case, researchers should consider the different facets of satisfaction, such as satisfaction with the service or the personnel, as shown on the right side of Exhibit 2.8. In the latter case, a formative measurement model specification is more promising as it allows identifying distinct drivers of satisfaction and thus deriving more nuanced recommendations. This especially applies to situations where the corresponding constructs are exogenous. However, formative measurement models may also be used on endogenous constructs when measurement theory supports such a specification.

Exhibit 2.8	Satisfaction as a Formatively and Reflectively Measured Construct

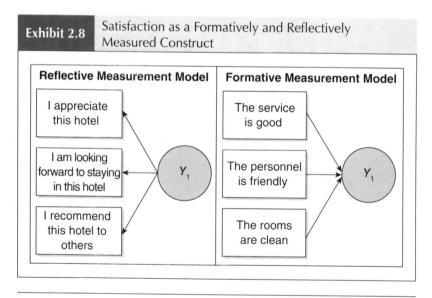

Adapted from source: Albers, S. (2010). PLS and success factor studies in marketing. In V. Esposito Vinzi, W. W. Chin, J. Henseler, & H. Wang (Eds.), *Handbook of partial least squares: Concepts, methods and applications in marketing and related fields* (pp. 409–425). Berlin: Springer.

Apart from the role a construct plays in the model and the recommendations the researcher wants to give based on the results, the specification of the content of the construct (i.e., the domain content the construct is intended to capture) primarily guides the measurement perspective. Still, the decision as to which measurement model is appropriate has been the subject of considerable debate in a variety of disciplines and is not fully resolved. In Exhibit 2.9, we present a set of guidelines that researchers can use in their decision of whether to measure a construct reflectively or formatively. Note that there are also empirical means to determine the measurement perspective. Gudergan, Ringle, Wende, and Will (2008) propose the so-called **confirmatory tetrad analysis for PLS-SEM (CTA-PLS)**, which allows testing the null hypothesis that the construct measures are reflective in nature. Rejecting the null hypothesis in a tetrad test implies, therefore, that formative measures should be used for construct operationalization. We discuss the CTA-PLS technique in greater detail in Chapter 8. Clearly, a purely data-driven perspective needs to be supplemented with theoretical considerations based on the guidelines summarized in Exhibit 2.9.

Single-Item Measures and Sum Scores

Rather than using multiple items to measure a construct, researchers sometimes choose to use a single item. Single items have practical advantages such as ease of application, brevity, and lower costs associated with their use. Unlike long and complicated scales, which often result in a lack of understanding and mental fatigue for respondents, single items promote higher response rates as the questions can be easily and quickly answered (Fuchs & Diamantopoulos, 2009; Sarstedt & Wilczynski, 2009). However, single-item measures do not offer more for less. For instance, when partitioning the data into groups, fewer degrees of freedom are available to calculate a solution when single-item measures are used since scores from only a single variable are available to assign observations into groups. Similarly, information is available from only a single measure instead of several measures when using imputation methods to deal with missing values. Finally, from a psychometric perspective, single-item measures do not allow for removal of measurement error (as is the case with multiple items), and this generally decreases their reliability. Note that, contrary to commonly held beliefs, single-item reliability can be estimated (e.g., Loo, 2002; Wanous, Reichers, & Hudy, 1997).

Exhibit 2.9	Guidelines for Choosing the Measurement Model Mode	
Criterion	**Decision**	**Reference**
Causal priority between the indicator and the construct	• From the construct to the indicators: reflective • From the indicators to the construct: formative	Diamantopoulos and Winklhofer (2001)
Is the construct a trait explaining the indicators or rather a combination of the indicators?	• If trait: reflective • If combination: formative	Fornell and Bookstein (1982)
Do the indicators represent consequences or causes of the construct?	• If consequences: reflective • If causes: formative	Rossiter (2002)
Is it necessarily true that if the assessment of the trait changes, all items will change in a similar manner (assuming they are equally coded)?	• If yes: reflective • If no: formative	Chin (1998)
Are the items mutually interchangeable?	• If yes: reflective • If no: formative	Jarvis, MacKenzie, and Podsakoff (2003)

Most important, from a validity perspective, opting for single-item measures in most empirical settings is a risky decision when it comes to predictive validity considerations. Specifically, the set of circumstances that would favor the use of single-item measures rather than multiple items is very unlikely to be encountered in practice. This conclusion is generally even more relevant for PLS-SEM since the utilization of a small number of items for construct measurement (in the extreme, the use of a single item) increases the differences to CB-SEM results (Chapter 1). Recall that with PLS-SEM, this difference between PLS-SEM and CB-SEM results is reduced when the number of indicators and/or the number of observations increases (i.e., consistency at large). According to guidelines by Diamantopoulos, Sarstedt,

Fuchs, Kaiser, and Wilczynski (2012), single-item measures should be considered only in situations when (1) small sample sizes are present (i.e., $N < 50$), (2) path coefficients (i.e., the coefficients linking constructs in the structural model) of 0.30 and lower are expected, (3) items of the originating multi-item scale are highly homogeneous (i.e., Cronbach's alpha > 0.90), and (4) the items are semantically redundant (Exhibit 2.10). See also Kamakura (2015).

Nevertheless, when setting up measurement models, this purely empirical perspective should be complemented with practical considerations. Some research situations call for or even necessitate the use of single items. Respondents frequently feel they are oversurveyed, which contributes to lower response rates. The difficulty of obtaining large sample sizes in surveys, often due to a lack of willingness to take the time to complete questionnaires, leads to the necessity of considering reducing the length of construct measures where possible. Therefore, if the population being surveyed is small or only a limited sample size is available (e.g., due to budget constraints, difficulties in recruiting respondents, or dyadic data), the use of single-item measures may be a pragmatic solution. Even if researchers accept the consequences of lower predictive validity and use single-item measures anyway, one fundamental question remains: What should this item be? Unfortunately, recent research clearly points to severe difficulties when choosing a single item from a set of candidate items, regardless of whether this selection is based on statistical measures or expert judgment (Sarstedt, Diamantopoulos, Salzberger, & Baumgartner, in press). Against this background, we clearly advise against the use of single items for construct measurement, unless indicated otherwise by Diamantopoulos et al.'s (2012) guidelines. Finally, it is important to note that the above issues must be considered for the measurement of unobservable phenomena, such as perceptions or attitudes. But single-item measures are clearly appropriate when used to measure observable characteristics such as sales, quotas, profits, and so on.

In a similar manner, and as indicated in Chapter 1, we recommend avoiding using regressions based on **sum scores**, which some scholars have recently propagated. Similarly to reflective and formative measurement models, sum scores assume that several indicators represent a latent variable. However, instead of explicitly estimating the outer relationships in the context of the specified model, the sum scores approach uses the average value of the indicators to determine

Exhibit 2.10	Guidelines for Single-Item Use (Diamantopoulos et al., 2012)

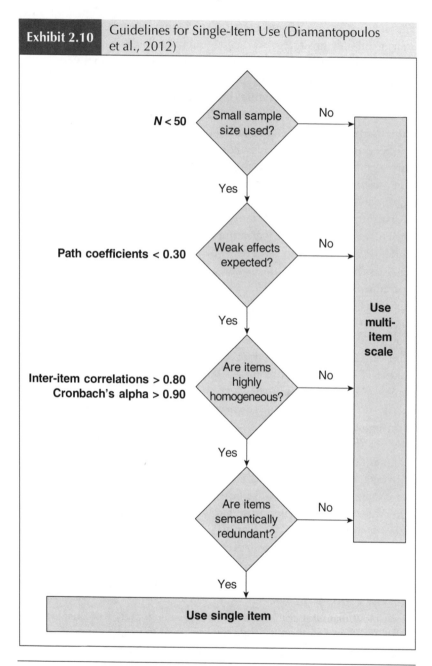

Source: Diamantopoulos, A., Sarstedt, M., Fuchs, C., Kaiser, S., & Wilczynski, P. (2012). Guidelines for choosing between multi-item and single-item scales for construct measurement: A predictive validity perspective. *Journal of the Academy of Marketing Science, 40,* 434–449.

the latent variable scores. Therefore, one can consider sum scores as a special case where all indicator weights in the measurement model are equal. As such, sum scores represent a simplification of PLS-SEM. However, this simplification (i.e., equal relevance of indicators) is not realistic in empirical applications, underlining PLS-SEM's superiority in this regard. In fact, research has shown that sum scores can produce substantial parameter biases and often lag behind PLS-SEM in terms of statistical power (e.g., Thiele et al., 2015). Apart from these construct validity concerns of the sum scores approach, the researcher does not learn which indicator has a higher or lower relative importance. Since PLS-SEM provides this additional information, its use is clearly superior compared with sum scores.

At this point, you should be prepared to create a path model. Exhibit 2.11 summarizes some key guidelines you should consider when preparing your path model. The next section continues with collecting the data needed to empirically test your PLS path model.

Exhibit 2.11 Guidelines for Preparing Your PLS Path Model

- The variables/constructs considered relevant to the study must be clearly identified and defined.
- The measurement discussion states how the constructs are related to each other, that is, which constructs are dependent (endogenous) or independent (exogenous). If applicable, this also includes more complex relationships such as mediators or moderators.
- If possible, the nature (positive or negative) of the relationships as well as the direction is hypothesized on the basis of theory, logic, previous research, or researcher judgment.
- There is a clear explanation of why you expect these relationships to exist. The explanation cites theory, qualitative research, business practice, or some other credible source.
- A conceptual model or framework is prepared to clearly illustrate the hypothesized relationships.
- The measurement discussion states whether constructs are conceptualized as first- or second-order constructs.
- The measurement perspective (i.e., reflective vs. formative) has to be clearly stated and motivated. A construct's conceptualization and the aim of the study guide this decision.
- Single-item measures should be used only if indicated by Diamantopoulos et al.'s (2012) guidelines.
- Do not use regressions based on sum scores.

STAGE 3: DATA COLLECTION AND EXAMINATION

The data collection and examination stage is very important in the application of SEM. This stage is important in all types of research but is particularly important when a researcher anticipates using SEM. With first-generation statistical methods, the general assumption is that the data are error free. With second-generation statistical methods, the measurement model stage attempts to identify the error component of the data and remove it from the analysis. As a result, the research design phase of any project must be carefully planned and executed so the answers to questions are as valid and reliable as possible for social science research.

Application of SEM methods requires that quantitative data are available. Many research applications in scholarly research involve primary data, but it is also possible to use secondary data, particularly the increasingly available archival data from databases such as S&P Capital IQ, WRDS (Wharton Research Data Services), and Compustat. Social science researchers in general have relied on primary data obtained from structured questionnaires for their SEM analyses. This is true for both CB-SEM and PLS-SEM and particularly for academic research. But archival data will be used with SEM, particularly PLS-SEM, much more in the future (Rigdon, 2013).

When empirical data are collected using questionnaires, typically data collection issues must be addressed after the data are collected. The primary issues that need to be examined include missing data, suspicious response patterns (straight lining or inconsistent answers), outliers, and data distribution. We briefly address each of these on the following pages. The reader is referred to more comprehensive discussions of these issues in Hair et al. (2010).

Missing Data

Missing data are often a problem in social science research because many projects obtain data using survey research. Missing data occur when a respondent either purposely or inadvertently fails to answer one or more question(s). When the amount of missing data on a questionnaire exceeds 15%, the observation is typically removed from the data file. Indeed, an observation may be removed from the data file even if the overall missing data on the questionnaire do not exceed 15%. For example, if a high proportion of responses are missing for a single construct, then the entire observation may have to be removed. A high proportion of missing data on a single construct is more likely to occur if the construct is measuring a sensitive topic, such as racism, sexual orientation, or even firm performance.

The proportion of survey data collected in the United States using online data collection methods now exceeds 60% and is above 50% in many developed countries. The increased use of online data collection approaches has reduced missing data, because it is possible to prevent respondents from going to the next question if they do not answer a particular question. This forced-answer approach does motivate some individuals to stop answering the survey. But more often than not, it means respondents answer the question and move on because the reason for skipping questions was inadvertence.

The software used in the book, *SmartPLS 3* (Ringle, Wende, & Becker, 2015), offers three ways of handling missing data. In **mean value replacement,** the missing values of an indicator variable are replaced with the mean of valid values of that indicator. While easy to implement, mean value replacement decreases the variability in the data and likely reduces the possibility of finding meaningful relationships. It should therefore be used only when the data exhibit extremely low levels of missing data. As a rule of thumb, we recommend using mean value replacement when there are less than 5% values missing per indicator.

Alternatively, SmartPLS offers an option to remove all cases from the analysis that include missing values in any of the indicators used in the model (referred to as **casewise deletion** or **listwise deletion**). When casewise deletion is being used, two issues warrant further attention. First, we need to ensure that we do not systematically delete a certain group of respondents. For example, market researchers frequently observe that wealthy respondents are more likely to refuse answering questions related to their income. Running casewise deletion would systematically omit this group of respondents and therefore likely yield biased results. Second, using casewise deletion can dramatically diminish the number of observations in the data set. It is therefore crucial to carefully check the number of observations used in the final model estimation when this type of missing value treatment is used.

Instead of discarding all observations with missing values, **pairwise deletion** uses all observations with complete responses in the calculation of the model parameters. For example, assume we have a measurement model with three indicators $(x_1, x_2, \text{and } x_3)$. To estimate the model parameters, all valid values in $x_1, x_2,$ and x_3 are used in the computation. That is, if a respondent has a missing value in x_3, the valid values in x_1 and x_2 are still used to calculate the model. Consequently, different calculations in the analysis may be based on different sample sizes, which can bias the results. Some researchers therefore call this approach "unwise deletion," and we also generally advise against its use. Exceptions are situations in which many observations have missing values—thus hindering the use of mean replacement and especially casewise deletion—and the aim of the analysis is to gain first insights into the model structure. In addition, more complex procedures for handling missing values can be conducted before analyzing the data with SmartPLS.

Among the best approaches to overcome missing data is to first determine the demographic profile of the respondent with missing data and then calculate the mean for the sample subgroup representing the identified demographic profile. For example, if the respondent with missing data is male, aged 25 to 34, with 14 years of education, then calculate the mean for that group on the questions with missing data. Next determine if the question with missing data is associated with a construct with multiple items. If yes, then calculate an average of the responses to all the items associated with the construct. The final step is to use the subgroup mean and the average of the construct indicator responses to decide what value to insert for the missing response. This approach minimizes the decrease in variability of responses and also enables the researcher to know specifically what is being done to overcome missing data problems. Last, numerous complex statistical procedures rely on regression approaches or the expectation maximization algorithm to impute missing data (Little & Rubin, 2002; Schafer & Graham, 2002). Sarstedt and Mooi (2014) provide an overview and guidelines for their use in multivariate data analysis. However, since knowledge on their suitability specifically in a PLS-SEM context is scarce, we recommend drawing on the methods described above when treating missing values in PLS-SEM analyses.

Suspicious Response Patterns

Before analyzing their data, researchers should also examine response patterns. In doing so, they are looking for a pattern often described as straight lining. **Straight lining** is when a respondent marks the same response for a high proportion of the questions. For example, if a 7-point scale is used to obtain answers and the response pattern is all 4s (the middle response), then that respondent in most cases should be deleted from the data set. Similarly, if a respondent selects only 1s or only 7s, then that respondent should in most cases be removed. Other suspicious response patterns are **diagonal lining** and **alternating extreme pole responses**. A visual inspection of the responses or the analysis of descriptive statistics (e.g., mean, variance, and distribution of the responses per respondent) allows identifying suspicious response patterns.

Inconsistency in answers may also need to be addressed before analyzing the data. Many surveys start with one or more screening questions. The purpose of a screening question is to ensure that only individuals who meet the prescribed criteria complete the survey. For example, a survey of mobile phone users may screen for individuals who own an Apple iPhone. But a question later in the survey is posed and the individual indicates he or she uses an Android device. This respondent would therefore need to be removed from the data set. Surveys often ask the same question with slight variations, especially when reflective measures are used. If a respondent gives a very different answer to the same question asked in a slightly different way, this too raises a red flag and suggests the respondent was not reading the questions closely or simply was marking answers to complete and exit the survey as quickly as possible. Finally, researchers sometimes include specific questions to assess the attention of respondents. For example, in the middle of a series of questions, the researcher may instruct the respondent to check only a 1 on a 7-point scale for the next question. If any answer other than a 1 is given for the question, it is an indication the respondent is not closely reading the question.

Outliers

An **outlier** is an extreme response to a particular question, or extreme responses to all questions. Outliers must be interpreted in the context of the study, and this interpretation should be based on the type of information they provide. Outliers can result from data collection of entry errors (e.g., manual coding of "77" instead of "7" on a 1 to 9 Likert scale). However, exceptionally high or low values can also be part of reality (e.g., an exceptionally high income). Finally, outliers can occur when combinations of variable values are particularly rare (e.g., spending 80% of annual income on holiday trips).

The first step in dealing with outliers is to identify them. Standard statistical software packages offer a multitude of univariate, bivariate, or multivariate graphs and statistics, which allow identifying outliers. For example, when analyzing box plots, one may characterize responses as extreme outliers, which are three times the interquartile range below the first quartile or above the third quartile. Moreover, IBM SPSS Statistics has an option called Explore that develops box plots and stem-and-leaf plots to facilitate the identification of outliers by respondent number (Sarstedt & Mooi, 2014).

Once the outliers are identified, the researcher must decide what to do. If there is an explanation for exceptionally high or low values, outliers are typically retained, because they represent an element of the population. However, their impact on the analysis results should be carefully evaluated. That is, one should run the analyses with and without the outliers to ensure that a very few (extreme) observations do not influence the results substantially. If the outliers are a result of data collection or entry errors, they are always deleted or corrected (e.g., the value of 77 on a 9-point scale). If there is no clear explanation for the exceptional values, outliers should be retained. See Sarstedt and Mooi (2014) for more details about outliers.

Outliers can also represent a unique subgroup of the sample. There are two approaches to use in deciding if a unique subgroup exists. First, a subgroup can be identified based on prior knowledge, for example, based on observable characteristics such as gender, age, or income. Using this information, the researcher partitions the data set into two or more groups and runs a multigroup analysis to disclose significant differences in the model parameters. The second approach to identifying unique subgroups is the application of latent class techniques. Latent class techniques allow researchers to identify and treat unobserved heterogeneity, which cannot be attributed to a specific observable characteristic or a combination of characteristics. Several latent class techniques have recently been proposed that generalize statistical concepts such as finite mixture modeling, typological regression, or genetic algorithms to PLS-SEM (see Sarstedt, 2008, for an early review). In Chapter 8, we discuss several of these techniques in greater detail.

Data Distribution

PLS-SEM is a nonparametric statistical method. Different from maximum likelihood (ML)–based CB-SEM, it does not require the data to be normally distributed. Nevertheless, it is important to verify that the data are not too far from normal as extremely nonnormal data prove problematic in the assessment of the parameters' significances. Specifically, extremely nonnormal data inflate standard errors obtained from bootstrapping (see Chapter 5 for more details) and thus decrease the likelihood that some relationships will be assessed as significant (Hair et al., 2011; Henseler et al., 2009).

The Kolmogorov-Smirnov test and Shapiro-Wilks test are designed to test normality by comparing the data to a normal distribution with the same mean and standard deviation as in the sample (Sarstedt & Mooi, 2014). However, both tests only indicate whether the null hypothesis of normally distributed data should be rejected or not. As the bootstrapping procedure performs fairly robustly when data are nonnormal, these tests provide only limited guidance when deciding whether the data are too far from being normally distributed. Instead, researchers should examine two measures of distributions—skewness and **kurtosis**.

Skewness assesses the extent to which a variable's distribution is symmetrical. If the distribution of responses for a variable stretches toward the right or left tail of the distribution, then the distribution is characterized as skewed. **Kurtosis** is a measure of whether the distribution is too peaked (a very narrow distribution with most of the responses in the center). When both skewness and kurtosis are close to zero (a situation that researchers are very unlikely ever to encounter), the pattern of responses is considered a normal distribution. A general guideline for skewness is that if the number is greater than +1 or lower than −1, this is an indication of a skewed distribution. For kurtosis, the general guideline is that if the number is greater than +1, the distribution is too peaked. Likewise, a kurtosis of less than −1 indicates a distribution that is too flat. Distributions exhibiting skewness and/or kurtosis that exceed these guidelines are considered nonnormal.

Serious effort, considerable amounts of time, and a high level of caution are required when collecting and analyzing the data that you need for carrying out multivariate techniques. Always remember the garbage in, garbage out rule. All your analyses are meaningless if your data are inappropriate. Exhibit 2.12 summarizes some key guidelines you should consider when examining your data and preparing them for PLS-SEM. For more detail on examining your data, see Chapter 2 of Hair et al. (2010).

Exhibit 2.12	Guidelines for Examining Data Used With PLS-SEM

- Missing data must be identified. When missing data for an observation exceed 15%, it should be removed from the data set. Other missing data should be dealt with before running a PLS-SEM analysis. When less than 5% of values *per indicator* are missing, use mean replacement. Otherwise, use casewise deletion, but make sure that the deletion of observations did not occur systematically and that enough observations remain for the analysis. Generally avoid using pairwise deletion. Also consider using more complex imputation procedures before importing the data into the PLS-SEM software.

- Suspicious and inconsistent response patterns typically justify removing a response from the data set.

- Outliers should be identified before running PLS-SEM. Subgroups that are substantial in size should be identified based on prior knowledge or by statistical means (e.g., FIMIX-PLS, PLS-GAS, PLS-POS).

- Lack of normality in variable distributions can distort the results of multivariate analysis. This problem is much less severe with PLS-SEM, but researchers should still examine PLS-SEM results carefully when distributions deviate substantially from normal. *Absolute* skewness and/or kurtosis values of greater than 1 are indicative of nonnormal data.

CASE STUDY ILLUSTRATION—SPECIFYING THE PLS-SEM MODEL

The most effective way to learn how to use a statistical method is to apply it to a set of data. Throughout this book, we use a single example that enables you to do that. We start the example with a simple model, and in Chapter 5, we expand that same model to a much broader, more complex model. For our initial model, we hypothesize a path model to estimate the relationships between corporate reputation, customer satisfaction, and customer loyalty. The example will provide insights on (1) how to develop the structural model representing the underlying concepts/theory, (2) the setup of measurement models for the latent variables, and (3) the structure of the empirical data used. Then, our focus shifts to setting up the SmartPLS 3 software (Ringle et al., 2015) for PLS-SEM.

Application of Stage 1: Structural Model Specification

To specify the structural model, we must begin with some fundamental explications about conceptual/theoretical models. The corporate reputation model by Eberl (2010) is the basis of our theory. The goal of the model is to explain the effects of corporate reputation on customer satisfaction (*CUSA*) and, ultimately, customer loyalty (*CUSL*). Corporate reputation represents a company's overall evaluation by its stakeholders (Helm, Eggert, & Garnefeld, 2010). It is measured using two dimensions. One dimension represents cognitive evaluations of the company, and the construct is the company's competence (*COMP*). The second dimension captures affective judgments, which determine the company's likeability (*LIKE*). This two-dimensional approach to measure reputation was developed by Schwaiger (2004). It has been validated in different countries (e.g., Eberl, 2010; Zhang & Schwaiger, 2009) and applied in various research studies (e.g., Eberl & Schwaiger, 2005; Raithel & Schwaiger, 2015; Raithel, Wilczynski, Schloderer, & Schwaiger, 2010; Sarstedt & Ringle, 2010; Sarstedt & Schloderer, 2010; Schloderer, Sarstedt, & Ringle, 2014; Schwaiger, Raithel, & Schloderer, 2009). Research also shows that the approach performs favorably (in terms of convergent validity and predictive validity) compared with alternative reputation measures (Sarstedt et al., 2013).

Building on a definition of corporate reputation as an attitude-related construct, Schwaiger (2004) further identified four antecedent dimensions of reputation—quality, performance, attractiveness, and corporate social responsibility—measured by a total of 21 formative indicators. These driver constructs of corporate reputation are components of the more complex example we will use in the book and will be added in Chapter 5. Likewise, we do not consider more complex model setups such as mediation or moderation effects yet. These aspects will be covered in the case studies in Chapter 7.

In summary, the simple corporate reputation model has two main conceptual/theoretical components: (1) the target constructs of interest—namely, *CUSA* and *CUSL* (dependent variables)—and (2) the two corporate reputation dimensions *COMP* and *LIKE* (independent variables), which represent key determinants of the target constructs. Exhibit 2.13 shows the constructs and their relationships, which represent the structural model for the PLS-SEM case study.

To propose a theory/concept, researchers usually build on existing research knowledge. When PLS-SEM is applied, the structural model displays the concept/theory with its key elements (i.e., constructs) and cause-effect relationships (i.e., paths). Researchers typically develop hypotheses for the constructs and their path relationships in the structural model. For example, consider Hypothesis 1 (H_1): Customer satisfaction has a positive effect on customer loyalty. PLS-SEM enables statistically testing the significance of the hypothesized relationship (Chapter 6). When conceptualizing the theoretical constructs and their hypothesized structural relationships for PLS-SEM, it is important to make sure the model has no circular relationships (i.e., causal loops). A circular relationship would occur if, for example, we reversed the relationship between COMP and CUSL as this would yield the causal loop COMP → CUSA → CUSL → COMP.

Application of Stage 2: Measurement Model Specification

Since the constructs are not directly observed, we need to specify a measurement model for each construct. The specification of the measurement models (i.e., multi-item vs. single-item measures and reflective vs. formative measures) draws on prior research studies by Schwaiger (2004) and Eberl (2010).

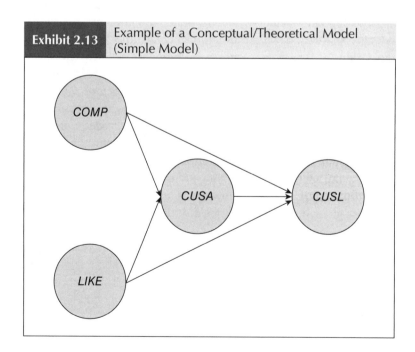

| Exhibit 2.13 | Example of a Conceptual/Theoretical Model (Simple Model) |

In our simple example of a PLS-SEM application, we have three constructs (*COMP, CUSL,* and *LIKE*) measured by multiple items (Exhibit 2.14). All three constructs have reflective measurement models as indicated by the arrows pointing from the construct to the indicators. For example, *COMP* is measured by means of the three reflective items *comp_1, comp_2,* and *comp_3,* which relate to the following survey questions (Exhibit 2.15): "[The company] is a top competitor in its market," "As far as I know, [the company] is recognized worldwide," and "I believe that [the company] performs at a premium level." Respondents had to indicate the degree to which they (dis)agree with each of the statements on a 7-point scale from 1 = *fully disagree* to 7 = *fully agree.*

Different from *COMP, CUSL,* and *LIKE,* the customer satisfaction construct (*CUSA*) is operationalized by a single item (*cusa*) that is related to the following question in the survey: "If you consider your experiences with [company], how satisfied are you with [company]?" The single indicator is measured with a 7-point scale indicating the respondent's degree of satisfaction (1 = *very dissatisfied;* 7 = *very satisfied*). The single item has been used due to practical considerations in an effort to decrease the overall number of items in the questionnaire. As customer satisfaction items are usually highly homogeneous, the loss in predictive validity compared with a

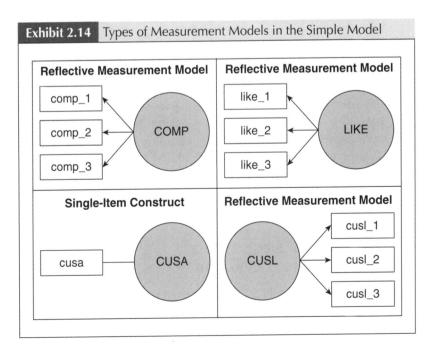

Exhibit 2.14 Types of Measurement Models in the Simple Model

Reflective Measurement Model

comp_1
comp_2   COMP
comp_3

Reflective Measurement Model

like_1
like_2   LIKE
like_3

Single-Item Construct

cusa   CUSA

Reflective Measurement Model

CUSL   cusl_1
cusl_2
cusl_3

Exhibit 2.15	Indicators for Reflective Measurement Model Constructs
Competence (COMP)	
comp_1	[The company] is a top competitor in its market.
comp_2	As far as I know, [the company] is recognized worldwide.
comp_3	I believe that [the company] performs at a premium level.
Likeability (LIKE)	
like_1	[The company] is a company that I can better identify with than other companies.
like_2	[The company] is a company that I would regret more not having if it no longer existed than I would other companies.
like_3	I regard [the company] as a likeable company.
Customer Loyalty (CUSL)	
cusl_1	I would recommend [company] to friends and relatives.
cusl_2	If I had to choose again, I would choose [company] as my mobile phone services provider.
cusl_3	I will remain a customer of [company] in the future.

Note: For data collection, the actual name of the company was inserted in the bracketed space that indicates company.

multi-item measure is not considered severe. As *cusa* is the only item measuring customer satisfaction, construct and item are equivalent (as indicated by the fact that the relationship between construct and single-item measure is always one in PLS-SEM). Therefore, the choice of the measurement perspective (i.e., reflective vs. formative) is of no concern and the relationship between construct and indicator is undirected.

Application of Stage 3: Data Collection and Examination

To estimate the PLS-SEM, data were collected using computer-assisted telephone interviews (Sarstedt & Mooi, 2014) that asked about the respondents' perception of and their satisfaction with four major mobile network providers in Germany's mobile communications market. Respondents rated the questions on 7-point Likert scales, with higher scores denoting higher levels of agreement with a particular statement. In the case of *cusa*, higher scores denote higher levels of satisfaction. Satisfaction and loyalty were measured with respect to the respondents' own service providers. The data set used in this book is a subset of the original set and has a sample size of 344 observations.

Exhibit 2.16 shows the data matrix for the model. The 10 columns represent a subset of all variables (i.e., specific questions in the survey as described in the previous section) that have been surveyed, and the 344 rows (i.e., cases) contain the answers of every respondent to these questions. For example, the first row contains the answers of Respondent 1 while the last row contains the answers of Respondent 344. The columns show the answers to the survey questions. Data in the first nine columns are for the indicators associated with the three constructs, and the tenth column includes the data for the single indicator for *CUSA*. The data set contains further variables that relate to, for example, the driver constructs of *LIKE* and *COMP*. We will cover these aspects in Chapter 5.

If you are using a data set in which a respondent did not answer a specific question, you need to insert a number that does not appear otherwise in the responses to indicate the missing values. Researchers commonly use –99 to indicate missing values, but you can use any other value that does not normally occur in the data set. In the following, we will also use –99 to indicate missing values. If, for example, the first data point of *comp_1* were a missing value, the –99 value would be inserted into the space as a missing value space holder instead of the value of 6 that you see in Exhibit 2.16. Missing value

Exhibit 2.16	Data Matrix for the Indicator Variables									
Case Number	**Variable Name**									
	comp_1	comp_2	comp_3	like_1	like_2	like_3	cusl_1	cusl_2	cusl_3	cusa	...
1	6	7	6	6	6	6	7	7	7	7	...
2	4	5	6	5	5	5	7	7	5	6	...
...	...	...	...	...	...	...	...	...	...	...	...
344	6	5	6	6	7	5	7	7	7	7	7...

treatment procedures (e.g., mean replacement) could then be applied to these data (e.g., Hair et al., 2010). Again, if the number of missing values in your data set per indicator is relatively small (i.e., less than 5% missing per indicator), we recommend mean value replacement instead of casewise deletion to treat the missing values when running PLS-SEM. Furthermore, we need to ascertain that the number of missing values per observation does not exceed 15%. If this was the case, the corresponding observation should be eliminated from the data set.

The data example shown in Exhibit 2.16 (and in the book's example) has only very few missing values. More precisely, *cusa* has one missing value (0.29%), *cusl_1* and *cusl_3* have three missing values (0.87%), and *cusl_2* has four missing values (1.16%). Thus, mean value replacement can be used. Furthermore, none of the observations has more than 15% missing values, so we can proceed analyzing all 344 respondents.

To run outlier diagnostics, we run a series of box plots using IBM SPSS Statistics—see Chapter 5 in Sarstedt and Mooi (2014) for details on how to run these analyses in IBM SPSS Statistics. The results indicate some influential observations but no outliers. Moreover, non-normality of data regarding skewness and kurtosis is not an issue. The kurtosis and skewness values of the indicators are within the −1 and +1 acceptable range. The only exception is the *cusl_2* indicator, which has a skewness of −1.30 and thus exhibits a slight degree of nonnormality. However, as the degree of skewness is not severe and because *cusl_2* is one of three indicators measuring the (reflective) *CUSL* construct, this deviation from normality is not considered an issue and the indicator is retained.

PATH MODEL CREATION USING THE SMARTPLS SOFTWARE

The SmartPLS 3 software (Ringle et al., 2015) is used to execute all the PLS-SEM analyses in this book. The discussion includes an overview of the software's functionalities. The student version of the software is available free of charge at http://www.smartpls.com. The student version offers practically all functionalities of the full version but is restricted to data sets with a maximum of 100 observations. However, as the data set used in this book has more than 100 observations (344 to be precise), you should use the professional version of

SmartPLS, which is available as a 30-day trial version at http://www
.smartpls.com. After the trial period, a license fee applies. Licenses are
available for different periods of time (e.g., 1 month or 2 years) and
can be purchased through the SmartPLS website. The SmartPLS website includes a download area for the software, including the old
SmartPLS 2 (Ringle, Wende, & Will, 2005) software, and many additional resources such as short explanations of PLS-SEM and software
related topics, a list of recommended literature, answers to frequently
asked questions, tutorial videos for getting started using the software,
and the SmartPLS forum, which allows you to discuss PLS-SEM topics with other users.

SmartPLS has a graphical user interface that enables the user to
estimate the PLS path model. Exhibit 2.19 shows the graphical interface for the SmartPLS 3 software, with the simple model already
drawn. In the following paragraphs, we describe how to set up this
model using the SmartPLS 3 software. Before you draw your model,
you need to have data that serve as the basis for running the model.
The data we will use with the reputation model can be downloaded
either as comma-separated value (.csv) or text (.txt) data sets in the
download section at the following URL: http://www.pls-sem.com.
SmartPLS can use both data file formats (i.e., .csv or .txt). Follow the
onscreen instructions to save one of these two files on your hard
drive. Click on **Save Target As . . .** to save the data to a folder on your
hard drive and then **Close**. Now run the SmartPLS 3 software by
clicking on the desktop icon that is available after the software instal-
lation on your computer device. Alternatively, go to the folder where
you installed the SmartPLS software on your computer. Click on the
file that runs SmartPLS and then on the **Run** tab to start the
software.

To create a new project after running SmartPLS 3, click on **File** →
Create New Project. First type a name for the project into the **Name**
box (e.g., **Corporate Reputation**). After clicking **OK**, the new project
is created and appears in the **Project Explorer** window that is in the
upper left below the menu bar. All previously created SmartPLS projects also appear in this window. Next, you need to assign a data set to
the project, in our case, **corporate reputation data.csv** (or whatever
name you gave to the data you downloaded). To do so, click on the
information button labeled **Doubleclick to import data!** below the
project you just created, find and highlight your data folder, and click
Open. It is important to note that if you use your own data set for a
project using the SmartPLS software, the data must not include any

string elements (e.g., respondents' comments to open-ended questions). For example, SmartPLS interprets single dots (such as those produced by IBM SPSS Statistics in case an observation has a system-missing value) as string elements. In our example, the data set does not include any string elements, so this is not an issue. In the screen that follows, you can adjust the name of the data set. In this example, we use the original name (i.e., **Corporate reputation data**) and proceed by clicking **OK**. SmartPLS will open a new tab (Exhibit 2.17), which provides information on the data set and its format (data view).

At the bottom of the screen appears a list with all variables and basic descriptive statistics (i.e., mean, minimum, and maximum values as well as the number of missing values). At the top right of the screen you can see the **Sample Size** as well as the number of indicators and missing values. As we haven't specified any missing values yet, Smart-PLS indicates that there are no missing values in the data set. At the top left of the screen, you can specify the **Delimiter** to determine the separation of the data values in your data set (i.e., comma, semicolon, tabulator, space), the **Value Quote Character** (i.e., none, single quote, double quote) in case the values use quotations (e.g., "7"), and the **Number Format** (i.e., United States with a dot as decimal separator or Europe with a comma as decimal separator). Furthermore, you can specify the coding of missing values. Click on **None** next to **Missing values**. In the screen that follows, you need to specify missing values. Enter **–99** in the field and click on **OK**. SmartPLS dynamically updates the descriptive statistics of the indicators that contain missing values and indicates the number of missing values next to **Total Missing Values**. Note that unlike in other statistical programs such as IBM SPSS Statistics, you can specify only one value for all missing data in SmartPLS. Thus, you have to make sure that all missing values have the same coding (e.g., –99) in your original data set. That is, you need to code all missing values uniformly, regardless of their type (user-defined missing or system missing) and the reason for being missing (e.g., respondent refused to answer, respondent did not know the answer, not applicable). The additional tabs in the data view show the **Indicator Correlations** and the **Raw File** with the imported data. At this point, you can close the data view. Note that you can always reopen the data view by double-clicking on the data set (i.e., **Corporate reputation data**) in the **Project Explorer**.

Each project can have one or more path models and one or more data sets (i.e., .csv or .txt files). When setting up a new project, Smart-PLS will automatically add a model with the same name as the project

Exhibit 2.17 Data View in SmartPLS

Corporate reputation data.txt ⊠

Delimiter:	Semicolon	Encoding: UTF-8
Value Quote Character:	None	Sample size: 344
Number Format:	US (e.g. 1,000.23)	Indicators: 41
Missing Value Marker:	-99	Missing Values: 11

Open External

Re-Analyze

Indicators: **Indicator Correlations** | Raw File | Data Groups

Copy to clipboard

	No.	Missing	Mean	Median	Min	Max	Standard Deviation	Excess Kurtosis	Skewness
serviceprov...	1	0	2.000	2.000	1.000	4.000	1.003	-0.513	0.747
servicetype	2	0	1.637	2.000	1.000	2.000	0.481	-1.684	-0.571
comp_1	3	0	4.648	5.000	1.000	7.000	1.433	-0.324	-0.264
comp_2	4	0	5.424	6.000	1.000	7.000	1.375	-0.616	-0.566
comp_3	5	0	5.221	6.000	1.000	7.000	1.458	-0.188	-0.677
like_1	6	0	4.584	5.000	1.000	7.000	1.547	-0.399	-0.405
like_2	7	0	4.250	4.000	1.000	7.000	1.848	-0.901	-0.312
like_3	8	0	4.480	5.000	1.000	7.000	1.871	-0.941	-0.325
cusl_1	9	3	5.129	5.000	1.000	7.000	1.513	0.268	-0.792
cusl_2	10	4	5.276	6.000	1.000	7.000	1.744	0.040	-0.951
cusl_3	11	3	5.651	6.000	1.000	7.000	1.655	0.930	-1.301

(i.e., **Corporate Reputation**). You can also rename the model by right-clicking on it. In the menu that opens, click on **Rename** and type in the new name for the model. To distinguish our introductory model from the later ones, rename it to **Simple Model** and click on **OK**.

Next, double-click on **Simple Model** in the Project Explorer window and SmartPLS will open the graphical modeling window on the right, where you can create a path model. We start with a new project (as opposed to working with a saved project), so the modeling window is empty and you can start creating the path model shown in Exhibit 2.18. By clicking on **Latent Variable** in the menu bar ( ), you can place one new construct into the modeling window. When you left-click in the modeling window, a new construct represented by a red circle will appear. To add multiple constructs, press the **SHIFT** key and left-click on the icon in the menu. The "1" in the icon changes into an "N" to indicate the changed mode. Alternatively, go to the **Edit** menu and click **Add Latent Variable(s)**. Now a new construct will appear each time you left-click in the modeling window. To leave this mode, click on **Select** in the menu bar ( ). Once you have created all your constructs, you can left-click on any of the constructs to select, resize, or move it in the modeling window. To connect the latent variables with each other (i.e., to draw path arrows), left-click on **Connect** in the menu bar ( ). Next, left-click on an exogenous (independent) construct and move the cursor over the target endogenous (dependent) construct. Now left-click on the endogenous construct, and a path relationship (directional arrow) will be inserted between the two constructs. Repeat the same process and connect all the constructs based on your theory. Analogous to the insertion of latent variables, you can add multiple paths by pressing the **SHIFT** key and left-clicking on the icon in the menu. The "1" in the icon changes into an "N" to indicate the changed mode. Alternatively, go to the Edit menu and click **Add Connection(s)**. When you finish, it will look like Exhibit 2.18.

The next step is to name the constructs. To do so, right-click on the construct to open a menu with different options and left-click on **Rename**. Type the name of your construct in the window of the **Rename** box (i.e., *COMP*) and then click **OK**. The name *COMP* will appear under the construct. Follow these steps to name all constructs. Next, you need to assign indicators to each of the constructs. On the left side of the screen, there is an **Indicators** window that shows all the indicators that are in your data set along with some basic descriptive

Exhibit 2.18 Initial Model

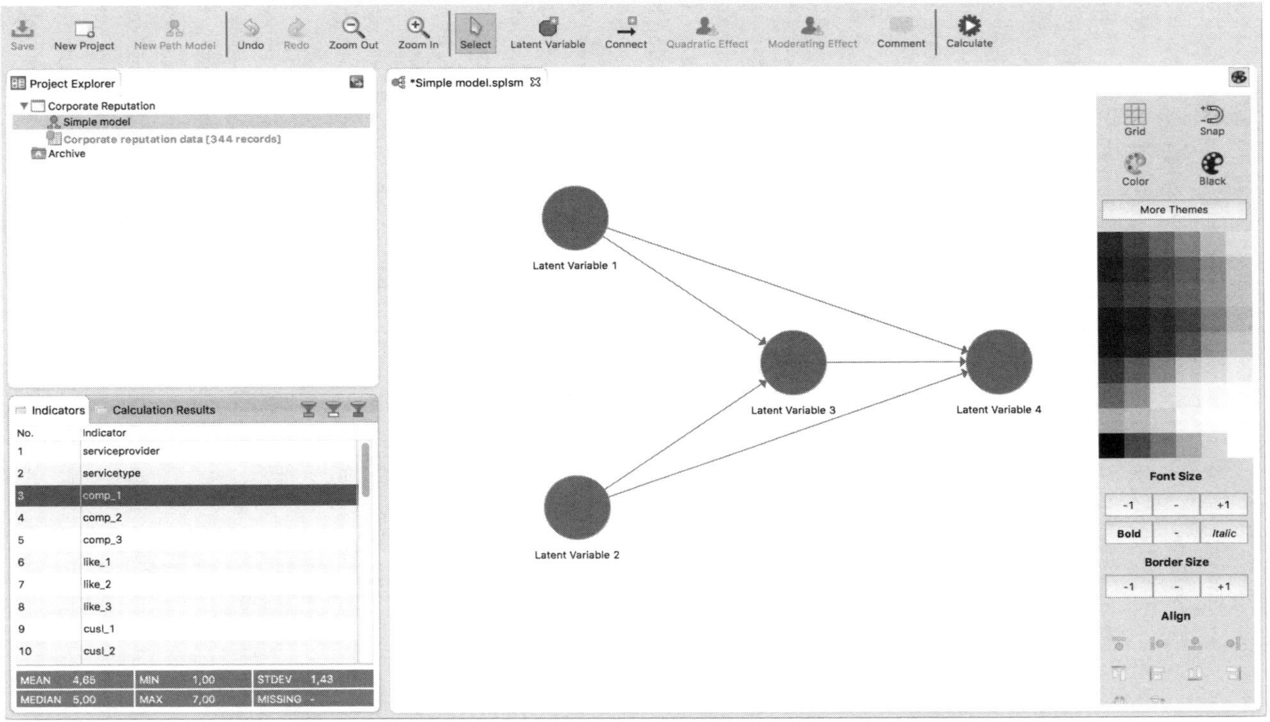

statistics. Start with the *COMP* construct by dragging the first competence indicator *comp_1* from the **Indicators** window and dropping it on the construct (i.e., left-click the mouse and hold the button down, then move it until over a construct, then release). After assigning an indicator to a construct, it appears in the graphical modeling window as a yellow rectangle attached to the construct (as reflective). Assigning an indicator to a construct will also turn the color of the construct from red to blue. You can move the indicator around, but it will remain attached to the construct (unless you delete it). By right-clicking on the construct and choosing one of the options under **Align** (e.g., **Indicators Top**), you can align the indicator(s). You can also hide the indicators of a construct by selecting the corresponding option in the menu that appears when right-clicking on it. You can also access the align indicators option via the **Modeling toolbox** on the right-hand side of the modeling window.

By clicking on the center of the button, you can hide the indicators of the selected construct; by clicking on the boxes next to the construct, you can align the indicators correspondingly. Continue until you have assigned all the indicators to the constructs as shown in Exhibit 2.19. Make sure to save the model by going to **File → Save**.

Clicking on the right mouse button while it is placed on a construct in the graphical modeling window opens a menu with several options. Apart from renaming the constructs, you can invert the measurement model from reflective to formative measurement, and vice versa (**Switch between formative/reflective**), and access more advanced options such as adding interaction and quadratic effects or choosing a different weighting scheme per construct such as sum scores. To add a note to your modeling window, left-click on the **Comment** button ( ) in the menu bar.

Clicking on the right mouse button while the cursor is placed over other elements also opens a menu with additional functions. As a further example, if you place the cursor in the **Project Explorer** window and right-click on the project name, you can create a new model (**Create New Path Model**), create a new project (**Create New Project**), or import a new data set (**Import Data File**). Moreover, you can select the **Copy, Paste,** and **Delete** options for projects and models that appear in the **Project Explorer** window. For example, the **Copy** option is useful when you would like to modify a PLS path model but want to keep your initial model setup. Save your model before using the copy option. The **Import Data File** option allows you to add more

Exhibit 2.19 Simple Model With Names and Data Assigned

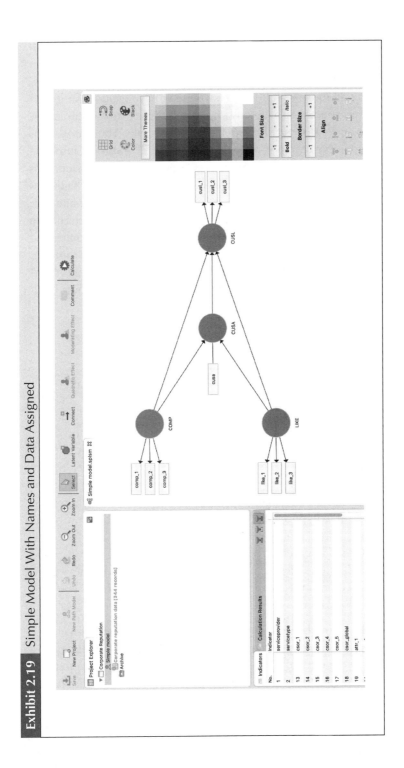

data sets to an existing project (e.g., data from different years if available). You can also export a project by selecting the **Export Project** option. Using this option, SmartPLS will export the entire project, including all models and data sets you may have included in it, in a .zip folder. You can also directly import this "ready-to-use" project by going to **File → Import Project from Backup File.** You can use this option to import the project that includes the PLS-SEM example on corporate reputation. The file name is **Corporate Reputation.zip.** This project is ready to download on your computer system in the download section at http://www.pls-sem.com. Download this file and save it on your computer system. Then, go to **File → Import Project from Backup File.** SmartPLS allows you to browse your computer and select the downloaded project **Corporate_Reputation.zip** for import. After successful import, double-click on the model in this project, and the path model as shown in Exhibit 2.19 will appear in a new modeling window.

SUMMARY

- **Understand the basic concepts of structural model specification, including mediation and moderation.** This chapter includes the first three stages in the application of PLS-SEM. Building in an a priori established theory/concept, the model specification starts with the structural model (Stage 1). Each element of the theory/concept represents a construct in the **structural model** of the PLS path model. Moreover, assumptions for the causal relationships between the elements must be considered. Researchers usually determine hypotheses for the relationships between constructs in the structural model in accordance with their theory/concept. These are the key elements of the structural model (i.e., constructs and their hypothesized relationships), which can also be more complex and contain mediating or moderating relationships. The goal of the PLS-SEM analysis is to empirically test the theory/concept.

- **Explain the differences between reflective and formative measures and specify the appropriate measurement model.** Stage 2 focuses on selecting a measurement model for each theoretical/conceptual construct in the structural model to obtain reliable and valid measurements. Generally, there are two types of measurement models: reflective and formative. The reflective mode has arrows (relationships) pointing from the construct to the observed indicators in the measurement model. If the construct changes, it leads to a simultaneous change of all items in the measurement model. Thus, all indicators are highly correlated. In contrast, the formative mode has arrows pointing from the indicators in the measurement model to the constructs. Hence, all indicators together form the construct, and all major elements of the domain must be represented by the selected formative indicators. Since formative indicators represent independent sources of the construct's content, they do not necessarily need to be correlated (in fact, they shouldn't be highly correlated).

- **Comprehend that the selection of the mode of measurement model and the indicators must be based on theoretical/conceptual reasoning before data collection.** A reflective specification would use different indicators than a formative specification of the same construct. One usually uses reflective constructs as target constructs of the theoretically/conceptually established PLS path model, while formative constructs may be particularly valuable as explanatory sources (independent variables) or drivers of these target constructs. During the data analysis phase, the theoretical/conceptual mode of the measurement models can be empirically tested by using CTA-PLS, which is the confirmatory tetrad analysis for PLS-SEM.

- **Explain the difference between multi-item and single-item measures and assess when to use each measurement type.** Rather than using multiple items to measure a construct, researchers sometimes choose to use a single item. Single items have practical advantages such as ease of application, brevity, and lower costs associated with their use. However, single-item measures do not offer more for less. From a psychometric perspective, single-item measures are less reliable and risky from a predictive validity perspective. The latter aspect is particularly problematic in the context of PLS-SEM, which focuses on prediction. Furthermore, identifying an appropriate single item from a set of candidate items, regardless of whether this selection is based on statistical measures or expert judgment, proves very difficult. For these reasons, the use of single items should generally be avoided. The above issues are important considerations when measuring unobservable phenomena, such as perceptions or attitudes. But single-item measures are clearly appropriate when used to measure observable characteristics such as gender, sales, profits, and so on.

- **Describe the data collection and examination considerations necessary to apply PLS-SEM.** Stage 3 underlines the need to examine your data after they have been collected to ensure that the results from the methods application are valid and reliable. This stage is important in all types of research but is particularly important when a researcher anticipates using SEM. When empirical data are collected using questionnaires, typically data collection issues must be addressed after the data are collected. The primary issues that need to be examined include missing data, suspicious response patterns (straight lining or inconsistent answers), and outliers. Distributional assumptions are of less concern because of PLS-SEM's nonparametric nature. However, as highly skewed data can cause issues in the estimation of significance levels, researchers should ensure that the data are not too far from normal. As a general rule of thumb, always remember the garbage in, garbage out rule. All your analyses are meaningless if your data are inappropriate.

• **Learn how to develop a PLS path model using the SmartPLS 3 software.** The first three stages of conducting a PLS-SEM analysis are explained by conducting a practical exercise. We discuss how to draw a theoretical/conceptual PLS path model focusing on corporate reputation and its relationship with customer satisfaction and loyalty. We also explain several options that are available in the SmartPLS software. The outcome of the exercise is a PLS path model drawn using the SmartPLS software that is ready to be estimated.

REVIEW QUESTIONS

1. What is a structural model?

2. What is a reflective measurement model?

3. What is a formative measurement model?

4. What is a single-item measure?

5. When do you consider data to be "too nonnormal" for a PLS-SEM analysis?

CRITICAL THINKING QUESTIONS

1. How can you decide whether to measure a construct reflectively or formatively?

2. Which research situations favor the use of reflective/formative measures?

3. Discuss the pros and cons of single-item measures.

4. Create your own example of a PLS path model (including the structural model with latent variables and the measurement models).

5. Why is it important to carefully analyze your data prior to analysis? What particular problems do you encounter when the data set has relatively large amounts of missing data per indicator (e.g., more than 5% of the data are missing per indicator)?

KEY TERMS

Alternating extreme pole responses

Casewise deletion

Causal indicators

Causal links

Composite indicators

Confirmatory tetrad analysis for PLS-SEM (CTA-PLS)

CTA-PLS

Diagonal lining

Direct effect

Effect indicators

Formative measurement

HCM

Hierarchical component model (HCM)

Higher-order model

Index

Indirect effect

Inner model

Kurtosis

Listwise deletion

Mean value replacement

Measurement models

Mediating effect

Mode A

Mode B

Moderation

Moderator effect

Multigroup analysis

Outer model

Outlier

Pairwise deletion

Reflective measurement

Scale

Skewness

Straight lining

Structural model

Sum scores

SUGGESTED READINGS

Bollen, K. A. (2011). Evaluating effect, composite, and causal indicators in structural equation models. *MIS Quarterly, 35,* 359–372.

Chin, W. W. (2010). How to write up and report PLS analyses. In V. Esposito Vinzi, W. W. Chin, J. Henseler, & H. Wang (Eds.), *Handbook of partial least squares: Concepts, methods and applications in marketing and related fields* (Springer Handbooks of Computational Statistics Series, Vol. II, pp. 655–690). Berlin: Springer.

Esposito Vinzi, V., Chin, W. W., Henseler, J., & Wang, H. (Eds.). (2010). *Handbook of partial least squares: Concepts, methods and applications* (Springer Handbooks of Computational Statistics Series, Vol. II). Berlin: Springer.

Falk, R. F., & Miller, N. B. (1992). *A primer for soft modeling.* Akron, OH: University of Akron Press.

Garson, G. D. (2014). *Partial least squares: Regression and structural equation models.* Asheboro, NC: Statistical Associates Publishers.

Haenlein, M., & Kaplan, A. M. (2004). A beginner's guide to partial least squares analysis. *Understanding Statistics, 3,* 283–297.

Hair, J. F., Black, W. C., Babin, B. J., & Anderson, R. E. (2010). *Multivariate data analysis.* Englewood Cliffs, NJ: Prentice Hall.

Hair, J. F., Ringle, C. M., & Sarstedt, M. (2011). PLS-SEM: Indeed a silver bullet. *Journal of Marketing Theory and Practice, 19,* 139–151.

Hair, J. F., Celsi, M., Money, A. H., Samouel, P., & Page, M. J. (2016). *Essentials of business research methods* (3rd ed.). Armonk, NY: Sharpe.

Henseler, J., Ringle, C. M., & Sarstedt, M. (2012). Using partial least squares path modeling in international advertising research: Basic concepts and recent issues. In S. Okazaki (Ed.), *Handbook of research in international advertising* (pp. 252–276). Cheltenham, UK: Edward Elgar.

Lohmöller, J.-B. (1989). *Latent variable path modeling with partial least squares.* Heidelberg, Germany: Physica.

Roldán, J. L., & Sánchez-Franco, M. J. (2012). Variance-based structural equation modeling: Guidelines for using partial least squares in information systems research. In M. Mora, O. Gelman, A. L. Steenkamp, & M. Raisinghani (Eds.), *Research methodologies, innovations and philosophies in software systems engineering and information systems* (pp. 193–221). Hershey, PA: IGI Global.

Sarstedt, M., & Mooi, E. A. (2014). *A concise guide to market research: The process, data, and methods using IBM SPSS statistics* (2nd ed.). Berlin: Springer.

Temme, D., Kreis, H., & Hildebrandt, L. (2010). A comparison of current PLS path modeling software: Features, ease-of-use, and performance. In V. Esposito Vinzi, W. W. Chin, J. Henseler, & H. Wang (Eds.), *Handbook of partial least squares: Concepts, methods and applications* (Springer Handbooks of Computational Statistics Series, Vol. II, pp. 737–756). Berlin: Springer.

Tenenhaus, M., Esposito Vinzi, V., Chatelin, Y.-M., & Lauro, C. (2005). PLS path modeling. *Computational Statistics & Data Analysis, 48,* 159–205.

CHAPTER 3

Path Model Estimation

CHAPTER PREVIEW

This chapter covers Stage 4 of the process on how to apply PLS-SEM. Specifically, we focus on the PLS-SEM algorithm and its statistical properties. A basic understanding of the "mechanics" that underlie PLS-SEM, as well as its strengths and weaknesses, is needed to correctly apply the method (e.g., to make decisions regarding software options). Building on these foundations, you will be able to choose the options and **parameter settings** required to run the PLS-SEM algorithm. After explaining how the PLS path model is estimated, we summarize how to interpret the initial results. These will be discussed in much greater detail in Chapters 4 to 6. This chapter closes with an application of the PLS-SEM algorithm to estimate results for the corporate reputation example using the SmartPLS 3 software.

STAGE 4: MODEL ESTIMATION AND THE PLS-SEM ALGORITHM

How the Algorithm Works

The variance-based PLS-SEM algorithm was originally developed by Wold (1975, 1982) and later extended by Lohmöller (1989), Bentler and Huang (2014), Dijkstra (2014), and Dijkstra and Henseler (2015a, 2015b). The algorithm estimates the path coefficients and other model parameters in a way that maximizes the explained variance of the dependent **construct(s)** (i.e., it minimizes the unexplained variance). This section illustrates how the **PLS-SEM algorithm** works.

To start with, you need to understand the data that are used to run the algorithm. Exhibit 3.1 is a matrix showing the data set for the indicator variables (columns) and observations (rows) in the PLS path model shown in Exhibit 3.2. The measured indicator (x) variables (rectangles in the top portion of Exhibit 3.2) are shown in the row at the top of the matrix. The (Y) **constructs** (circles in Exhibit 3.2) are shown at the right side of the matrix. For example, there are seven measured indicator variables in this PLS-SEM example, and the variables are identified as x_1 to x_7. Three constructs identified as Y_1, Y_2, and Y_3 are also shown. Note that the Y constructs are not measured variables. The measured x variables are used as **raw data** input to estimate the Y_1, Y_2, and Y_3 **construct scores** in this example (e.g., for construct Y_1, the scores are data points $Y_{1,1}$ to $Y_{89,1}$) as part of solving the PLS-SEM algorithm.

A **data matrix** like the one in Exhibit 3.1 serves as input for indicators in our hypothetical PLS path model (Exhibit 3.2). The data for the measurement model might be obtained from a company database (e.g., the advertising budget, number of employees, profit, etc.), or it could be responses to survey questions. An ID for the observations is

Exhibit 3.1	Data Matrix for a PLS-SEM Example								
Case	x_1	x_2	x_3	x_4	x_5	x_6	x_7	Y_1	Y_2	Y_3
1	$x_{1,1}$	$x_{2,1}$	$x_{3,1}$	$x_{4,1}$	$x_{5,1}$	$x_{6,1}$	$x_{7,1}$	$Y_{1,1}$	$Y_{2,1}$	$Y_{3,1}$
...	...	...	...	...	...	...	...	...	...	...
89	$x_{89,1}$	$x_{89,2}$	$x_{89,3}$	$x_{89,4}$	$x_{89,5}$	$x_{89,6}$	$x_{89,7}$	$Y_{89,1}$	$Y_{89,2}$	$Y_{89,3}$

listed in the first column to the left under the case label. For example, if your sample includes 89 responses (sample size), then the numbers in this column would be 1 to 89 (assuming you use a number as the ID for each respondent/object).

The minimum sample size for PLS path model estimation should at least meet the **10 times rule** (Chapter 1). Researchers should, however, follow more elaborate guidelines, for example, by following the recommendations made by Cohen (1992) in the context of multiple OLS regression analysis (Chapter 1). In this example, the two (formatively measured) exogenous constructs each have two indicators x_1 and x_2 for Y_1 and x_3 and x_4 for Y_2. Moreover, the structural model has two exogenous (independent) constructs Y_1 and Y_2 to explain the single dependent construct Y_3. The maximum number of arrows pointing at a particular latent variable is two. Thus, according to the 10 times rule, $2 \cdot 10 = 20$ represents the minimum number of observations needed to estimate the PLS path model in Exhibit 3.2. Alternatively, following Cohen's (1992) recommendations for multiple OLS regression analysis or running a power analysis using the G*Power program, one would need 33 observations to detect R^2 values of around 0.25, assuming a significance level of 5% and a statistical power of 80% (see Exhibit 1.7 in Chapter 1).

The PLS-SEM algorithm estimates all unknown elements in the PLS path model. The upper portion of Exhibit 3.2 shows the PLS path model with three **latent variables** and seven measured indicator variables. The four indicator variables (x_1, x_2, x_3, and x_4) for the two **exogenous constructs** (Y_1 and Y_2) are modeled as **formative measures** (i.e., relationships from the indicators to the latent variables). In contrast, the three indicator variables (x_5, x_6, and x_7) for the **endogenous construct** (Y_3) are modeled as **reflective measures** (i.e., relationships from the latent variable to the indicators). This kind of setup for the measurement models is just an example. Researchers can select between a reflective and formative measurement model for every construct. For example, alternatively, Y_1 could be modeled as formative while both Y_2 and Y_3 could be modeled as reflective (assuming theory supported this change and it was considered in designing the questionnaire). In Exhibit 3.2, the relationships between the measured indicator variables of the formative constructs Y_1 and Y_2 (i.e., **outer weights**) are labeled as w_{11}, w_{12}, w_{23}, and w_{24} (the first number is for the construct and the second number is for the arrow; the w stands for weight). Similarly, the relationships between the measured indicator variables of the reflective construct Y_3 (i.e., **outer loadings**) are labeled as l_{35}, l_{36}, and l_{37} (the l stands for loading). Note that the relationships between constructs and indicator variables are considered outer weights for formative constructs, whereas the relationships for reflective constructs are called outer loadings. Outer weights and loadings are initially unknown and are estimated by the PLS-SEM algorithm. Similarly, the relationships between the latent variables (i.e., the path coefficients) in the structural model that are labeled as p (Exhibit 3.2) are also initially unknown and estimated as part of solving the PLS-SEM algorithm. The coefficient p_{13} represents the relationship from Y_1 to Y_3, and p_{23} represents the relationship from Y_2 to Y_3.

The PLS-SEM algorithm uses the known elements to estimate the unknown elements of the model. For this task, the algorithm needs to determine the scores of the constructs Y that are used as input for (single and multiple) partial regression models within the path model. Recall that the construct scores were the Y columns on the right side of the matrix in Exhibit 3.1.

After the algorithm has calculated the construct scores, the scores are used to estimate each partial regression model in the path model. As a result, we obtain the estimates for all relationships in the measurement models (i.e., the loadings and weights) and the structural model (i.e., the path coefficients). The setup of the partial regression model depends on whether the construct under consideration is modeled as reflective or formative. More specifically, when a formative measurement model is assumed for a construct (e.g., latent variables Y_1 and Y_2 in Exhibit 3.2), the w coefficients (i.e., **outer weights**) are estimated by a partial multiple regression where the latent Y construct (e.g., Y_1) represents a dependent variable and its associated indicator variables x (e.g., x_1 and x_2) are the independent variables. In contrast, when a reflective measurement model is assumed for a construct (e.g., latent variable Y_3 in Exhibit 3.2), the l coefficients (i.e., **outer loadings**) are estimated through single regressions (one for each indicator variable) of each indicator variable on its corresponding construct.

Structural model calculations are handled as follows. The partial regressions for the structural model specify a construct as the dependent latent variable (e.g., Y_3 in Exhibit 3.2). This dependent latent variable's direct predecessors (i.e., latent variables with a direct relationship leading to the target construct; here, Y_1 and Y_2) are the independent constructs in a regression used to estimate the path

| Exhibit 3.2 | Path Model and Data for Hypothetical PLS-SEM Example |

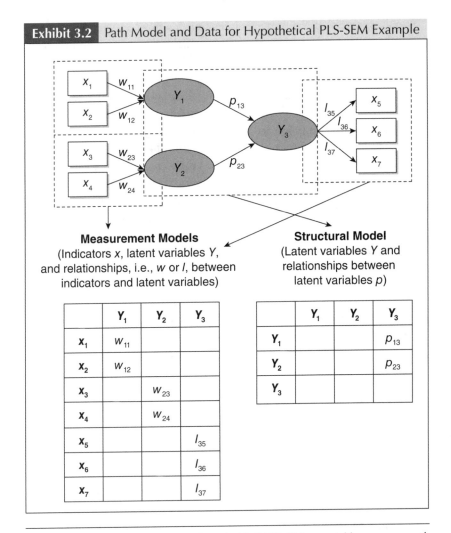

Measurement Models
(Indicators *x*, latent variables *Y*,
and relationships, i.e., *w* or *l*, between
indicators and latent variables)

Structural Model
(Latent variables *Y* and
relationships between
latent variables *p*)

	Y_1	Y_2	Y_3
x_1	w_{11}		
x_2	w_{12}		
x_3		w_{23}	
x_4		w_{24}	
x_5			l_{35}
x_6			l_{36}
x_7			l_{37}

	Y_1	Y_2	Y_3
Y_1			p_{13}
Y_2			p_{23}
Y_3			

Source: Henseler, J., Ringle, C. M., & Sarstedt, M. (2012). Using partial least squares path modeling in international advertising research: Basic concepts and recent issues. In S. Okazaki (Ed.), *Handbook of research in international advertising* (pp. 252–276). Cheltenham, UK: Edward Elgar Publishing. http://www.elgaronline.com/

coefficients. Hence, there is a partial regression model for every endogenous latent variable to estimate all the path coefficients in the structural model.

All partial regression models are estimated by the PLS-SEM algorithm's iterative procedures, which include two stages. In the first stage, the construct scores are estimated. Then, in the second stage, the final estimates of the outer weights and loadings are calculated, as well as the structural model's **path coefficients** and the resulting R^2 **values** of the endogenous latent variables. Henseler et al. (2012) provide a detailed description of the PLS-SEM algorithm's stages.

To run the PLS-SEM algorithm, users can choose from a range of software programs. A popular early example of a PLS-SEM software program is PLS-Graph (Chin, 2003), which is a graphical interface to Lohmöller's (1987) LVPLS, the first program in the field. Compared with LVPLS, which required the user to enter commands via a text editor, PLS-Graph represents a significant improvement, especially in terms of user-friendliness. However, PLS-Graph has not been further developed in recent years. The same holds for several other early software programs such as VisualPLS (Fu, 2006) and SPAD-PLS (Test & Go, 2006)—see Temme, Kreis, and Hildebrandt (2010) for an early software review. With the increasing dissemination of PLS-SEM in a variety of disciplines, several other programs with user-friendly graphical interfaces were introduced to the market such as XLSTAT's PLSPM package, Adanco (Henseler & Dijkstra, 2015); PLS-GUI (Hubona, 2015) WarpPLS (Kock, 2015), and particularly SmartPLS (Ringle et al., 2015; Ringle et al., 2005), which has recently been released in Version 3. To date, SmartPLS 3 is the most comprehensive and advanced program in the field and serves as the basis for all case study examples in this book. Finally, users with experience in the statistical software environment R can also draw on packages such as semPLS (Monecke & Leisch, 2012) and plspm (Sánchez, Trinchera, & Russolillo, 2015), which facilitate flexible analysis of PLS path models.

Statistical Properties

PLS-SEM is an OLS regression-based estimation technique that determines its statistical properties. The method focuses on the **prediction** of a specific set of hypothesized relationships that maximizes the explained variance in the dependent variables, similar to OLS regressions. Therefore, the focus of PLS-SEM is more on prediction than on explanation, which makes PLS-SEM particularly useful for studies on the sources of competitive advantage and success driver studies (Hair, Ringle, & Sarstedt, 2011). Unlike CB-SEM, PLS-SEM does not optimize a unique global scalar function. The lack of a global scalar function and the consequent lack of global goodness-of-fit measures are traditionally considered major drawbacks of PLS-SEM. When using

PLS-SEM, it is important to recognize that the term *fit* has different meanings in the contexts of CB-SEM and PLS-SEM. Fit statistics for CB-SEM are derived from the discrepancy between the empirical and the model-implied (theoretical) covariance matrix, whereas PLS-SEM focuses on the discrepancy between the observed (in the case of manifest variables) or approximated (in the case of latent variables) values of the dependent variables and the values predicted by the model in question (Hair, Sarstedt, Ringle, et al., 2012). While a global goodness-of-fit measure for PLS-SEM has been proposed (Tenenhaus, Amato, & Esposito Vinzi, 2004), research shows that the measure is unsuitable for identifying misspecified models (Henseler & Sarstedt, 2013; see Chapter 6 for a discussion of the measure and its limitations). As a consequence, researchers using PLS-SEM rely on measures indicating the model's predictive capabilities to judge the model's quality. These are going to be introduced in Chapters 4 to 6 on the evaluation of measurement models and the structural model.

While being a regression-based approach, PLS-SEM is nonparametric in nature. This means that it does not make any assumptions regarding the distribution of the data or, more precisely, the residuals, as is the case in regression analysis (Sarstedt & Mooi, 2014). This property has important implications for testing the significances of the model coefficients (e.g., path coefficients) as the technique does not assume any specific distribution. Instead, the research has to derive a distribution from the data using bootstrapping, which is then used as basis for significance testing (Chapter 5).

One of the most important features of PLS-SEM relates to the nature of the construct scores. CB-SEM initially estimates the model parameters without using any case values of the latent variable scores. In contrast, the PLS-SEM algorithm directly and initially computes the construct scores (the scores for Y_1, Y_2, and Y_3 in Exhibit 3.2). The PLS-SEM algorithm treats these scores as perfect substitutes for the indicator variables and therefore uses all the variance from the indicators that can help explain the **endogenous constructs**. This is because the PLS-SEM approach is based on the assumption that all the measured variance in the model's indicator variables is useful and should be included in estimating the construct scores. As a result, PLS-SEM avoids the **factor indeterminacy** problem (difficulty with estimating stable factor scores) and develops more accurate estimates of construct scores compared with CB-SEM (Rigdon, 2012, 2014b; Sarstedt, Ringle, Henseler, & Hair, 2014). In short, the algorithm calculates the construct scores as exact linear combinations of the associated observed indicator variables—for example, the construct score of Y_3 in Exhibit 3.2 as a linear combination of the indicator variables x_5, x_6, and x_7.

The fact that, in PLS-SEM, latent variables are aggregates of observed indicator variables leads to a fundamental problem. Indicator variables always involve some degree of measurement error. This error is present in the latent variable scores and is ultimately reflected in the path coefficients that are estimated using these scores. The error in the latent variable scores, while small, does produce a bias in the model estimates. The result is that the path model relationships are frequently underestimated, while the parameters for the measurement models (i.e., the loadings and weights) typically are overestimated compared with CB-SEM results. This property (structural model relationships underestimated and measurement model relationships overestimated) is referred to as the **PLS-SEM bias.** It should be noted that in this context, inconsistency does not imply the results of the PLS-SEM algorithm are actually biased. Instead, it means that the structural and measurement model relationships in PLS-SEM are not the same as those of CB-SEM as a result of PLS-SEM's different handling of latent variables compared with its covariance-based counterpart (see Chapter 1). Only when the number of observations *and* the number of indicators per latent variable increase to infinity will the latent variable case values approach values similar to CB-SEM and the PLS-SEM inconsistency disappear. This characteristic is commonly described as **consistency at large** (Hui & Wold, 1982; Lohmöller, 1989).

Infinity is a really large number and implies that this difference never fully disappears. However, simulation studies show that the difference between PLS-SEM and CB-SEM is usually very small (Henseler et al., 2014; Reinartz et al., 2009; Ringle et al., 2009) and plays virtually no role in most empirical settings. Simulation studies also show that CB-SEM results can become extremely inaccurate while PLS-SEM produces accurate estimates, even when assuming a common factor model (see Chapter 1). This especially holds when the number of constructs and structural model relationships (i.e., the **model complexity**) is high and sample size is low, a situation in which the bias produced by CB-SEM is oftentimes substantial, particularly when distributional assumptions are violated. In other situations (e.g., when sample sizes are high and model complexity is limited),

CB-SEM estimates are clearly more accurate compared with PLS-SEM estimates, assuming a common factor model holds. Recent research has brought forward the consistent PLS (PLSc) method (Bentler & Huang, 2014; Dijkstra, 2014), a variation of the original PLS-SEM approach. Simulations studies (e.g., Dijkstra & Henseler, 2015a, 2015b) show that PLSc and CB-SEM produce highly similar results in a variety of model constellations. Hence, PLSc is capable of perfectly mimicking CB-SEM. However, while maintaining some of the general PLS-SEM advantages, PLSc is subject to similar problems that have been noted for CB-SEM, such as inferior robustness and highly inaccurate results in certain configurations. Research on PLSc is ongoing, and we expect further improvements of the method in the future. We discuss PLSc in greater detail in the final section of Chapter 8.

Finally, model estimates produced by PLS-SEM generally exhibit higher levels of statistical power than CB-SEM does (Hair, Ringle, & Sarstedt, 2011; Henseler et al., 2014; Reinartz et al., 2009), even when the data originate from a factor model. Consequently, PLS-SEM is better at identifying population relationships and more suitable for exploratory research purposes—a feature that is further supported by the less restrictive requirements of PLS-SEM in terms of model setups, model complexity, and data characteristics (Chapter 1).

Algorithmic Options and Parameter Settings to Run the Algorithm

To estimate a PLS path model, **algorithmic options** and **parameter settings** must be selected. The algorithmic options and parameter settings include selecting the structural model path weighting method, the data metric, **initial values** to start the PLS-SEM algorithm, the stop criterion, and the maximum number of iterations. PLS-SEM allows the user to apply three structural model **weighting schemes:** (1) the centroid weighting scheme, (2) the factor weighting scheme, and (3) the path weighting scheme. While the results differ little across the alternative weighting schemes, path weighting is the recommended approach. This weighting scheme provides the highest R^2 value for endogenous latent variables and is generally applicable for all kinds of PLS path model specifications and estimations. Moreover, when the path model includes higher-order constructs (i.e., constructs measured at different levels of abstraction; Chapter 8), researchers should never use the centroid weighting scheme. Henseler et al. (2009)

provide further details on the three different weighting schemes available in PLS-SEM software.

The PLS-SEM algorithm draws on standardized latent variable scores. Thus, PLS-SEM applications must use **standardized data** for the indicators (more specifically, z-standardization, where each indicator has a mean of 0 and the variance is 1) as input for running the algorithm. This **raw data** transformation is the recommended option (and automatically supported by available software packages such as SmartPLS) when starting the PLS-SEM algorithm. When running the PLS-SEM method, the software package standardizes both the raw data of the indicators and the latent variable scores. As a result, the algorithm calculates standardized coefficients approximately between −1 and +1 for every relationship in the structural model and the measurement models. For example, path coefficients close to +1 indicate a strong positive relationship (and vice versa for negative values). The closer the estimated coefficients are to 0, the weaker the relationships. Very low values close to 0 generally are not statistically significant. Checking for significance of relationships is part of evaluating and interpreting the results discussed in Chapters 4 to 6.

The relationships in the measurement model require **initial values** to start the PLS-SEM algorithm. For the first iteration, any nontrivial linear combination of indicators can serve as values for the latent variable scores. In practice, equal weights are a good choice for the initialization of the PLS-SEM algorithm. Therefore, initialization values of +1 are specified for all relationships in the measurement model during the first iteration. In subsequent iterations of the algorithm, these initial values are replaced by path coefficients for the relationships in the measurement model. If all the indicators have the same direction (e.g., are coded so that a low value is less favorable while a high value is more favorable) and all the relationships in the PLS path model have hypothesized positive relationships, the result should be positive coefficients.

A different initialization setup used in the LVPLS (Lohmöller, 1987) and PLS-Graph (Chin, 2003) software and also offered as an option in SmartPLS 3 assigns the value of +1 to all measurement model relationships except the last one, which obtains the value of −1. Thereby, the PLS-SEM algorithm converges faster, which was primarily an issue when computer capacities were limited. However, this initialization scheme can lead to counterintuitive signs of parameter estimates in the measurement models and structural model. Therefore, using initialization values of +1 for all relationships in the measurement model during the first iteration is generally recommended. Alternatively, programs such as SmartPLS 3 also allow the user to determine specific positive and negative starting values for every single indicator.

The final parameter setting to select is the stopping criterion of the algorithm. The PLS-SEM algorithm is designed to run until the results stabilize. Stabilization is reached when the sum of changes in the outer weights between two iterations is sufficiently low, which means it drops below a predefined limit. A threshold value of $1 \cdot 10^{-7}$ (i.e., **stop criterion**) is recommended to ensure that the PLS-SEM algorithm converges at reasonably low levels of iterative changes in the latent variable scores. One must ensure, however, that the algorithm stops at the predefined stop criterion. Thus, a sufficiently high **maximum number of iterations** must be selected. Since the algorithm is very efficient (i.e., it converges after a relatively low number of iterations even with complex models), the selection of a maximum number of 300 iterations should ensure that **convergence** is obtained at the stop criterion of $1 \cdot 10^{-7}$ (i.e., 0.0000001). Prior research has shown that the PLS-SEM algorithm almost always converges (Henseler, 2010). Only under very extreme and artificial conditions, which very seldom occur in practice, is it possible that the algorithm does not converge, which has, however, practically no implications for the results. Exhibit 3.3 summarizes guidelines for initializing the PLS-SEM algorithm.

Results

When the PLS-SEM algorithm converges, the final outer weights are used to compute the final latent variable scores. Then, these scores serve as input to run OLS regressions to determine final estimates for the path relationships in the structural model. PLS-SEM always provides the outer loadings and outer weights, regardless of the measurement model setup. With reflectively measured constructs, the outer

Exhibit 3.3	Rules of Thumb for Initializing the PLS-SEM Algorithm

- Select the path weighting scheme as the weighting method.
- Use +1 as the initial value for all outer weights.
- Choose a stop criterion of $1 \cdot 10^{-7}$ (i.e., 0.0000001).
- Select a value of at least 300 for the maximum number of iterations.

loadings are single regression results with a particular indicator in the measurement model as a dependent variable (e.g., x_5 in Exhibit 3.2) and the construct as an independent variable (e.g., Y_3 in Exhibit 3.2). In contrast, with formatively measured constructs, the outer weights are resulting coefficients of a multiple regression with the construct as a dependent variable (e.g., Y_1 in Exhibit 3.2) and the indicators as independent variables (e.g., x_1 and x_2 in Exhibit 3.2). The outer loadings or outer weights are computed for all measurement model constructs in the PLS path model. However, outer loadings are primarily associated with the results for the relationships in reflective measurement models, and outer weights are associated with the results for the relationships in formative measurement models.

The estimations for the paths between the latent variables in the structural model are reported as standardized coefficients. In the partial regression models of the structural model, an endogenous latent variable (e.g., Y_3 in Exhibit 3.2) serves as the dependent variable while its direct predecessors serve as independent variables (e.g., Y_1 and Y_2 in Exhibit 3.2). In addition to the coefficients from the estimation of the partial regression models in the structural model (one for each endogenous latent variable), the output includes the R^2 values of each endogenous latent variable in the structural model. The R^2 values are usually between 0 and +1 and represent the amount of explained variance in the construct. For example, an R^2 value of 0.70 for the construct Y_3 in Exhibit 3.2 means that 70% of this construct's variance is explained by the exogenous latent variables Y_1 and Y_2. The goal of the PLS-SEM algorithm is to maximize the R^2 values of the endogenous latent variables and thereby their prediction. Additional criteria must be evaluated to fully understand the results of the PLS-SEM algorithm. These additional criteria are explained in detail in Chapters 4 to 6.

CASE STUDY ILLUSTRATION—PLS PATH MODEL ESTIMATION (STAGE 4)

To illustrate and explain PLS-SEM, we will use a single data set throughout the book and the SmartPLS 3 software (Ringle et al., 2015). The data set is from research that attempts to predict corporate reputation and, ultimately, customer loyalty, as introduced in Chapter 2. The data set (i.e., the **Corporate Reputation data.csv** file) and the ready-to-use SmartPLS project (i.e., the Corporate Reputation.zip file) for this case study are available at http://www.pls-sem.com.

Model Estimation

To estimate the corporate reputation model in SmartPLS, you need to create a new project, import the indicator data (i.e., **Corporate reputation data.csv**), and draw the model as explained in the case study of Chapter 2. Alternatively, you can import the SmartPLS project from a backup file (i.e., **Corporate Reputation.zip**). The procedures to import projects into the SmartPLS software and to open a model are explained in Chapter 2. Once this is done (i.e., you see the PLS path model in the software), you need to navigate to **Calculate → PLS Algorithm,** which you can find at the top of the SmartPLS screen. The menu that shows up provides several algorithms to select from. For estimating the PLS path model, the **PLS Algorithm** is the one to choose. Alternatively, you can left-click on the wheel symbol in the tool bar labeled **Calculate.** After selecting the **PLS Algorithm** function, the dialog box in Exhibit 3.4 appears.

The PLS-SEM algorithm needs three basic parameter settings to run it. The **Path Weighting Scheme** is selected for the inner weights estimation. The PLS-SEM algorithm stops when the maximum number of 300 iterations or the stop criterion of **1.0E-7** (i.e., 0.0000001) has been reached. Finally, one may change the **Initial Weights** in the **Advanced Settings** section of the dialog box. Per default, SmartPLS uses a value of 1.0 for all measurement model relationships to initialize the PLS-SEM algorithm. Alternatively, one can check the box **Use Lohmöller Settings** (i.e., all initial weights are set to +1 except the last one, which is set to −1), configure a specific weight for all indicators in the model (option **Individual Initial Weights**), or use **sum scores** for all constructs by selecting equal initial weights and 0 instead of the default value of 300 for **Maximum Iterations.** In this example, we use the default settings as shown in Exhibit 3.4.

Next, click on the **Missing Values** tab at the top of the dialog box (Exhibit 3.5). Please note that this tab appears only when you have specified the coding of missing values (e.g., −99) in the **Data View** of the data set that you selected for the model estimation (Chapter 2). The **Missing Values** tab shows the number of missing values in the selected data set and alternative missing value treatment options. None of the indicator variables in the simple model has more than 5% missing values (specifically, the maximum number of missing values [four missing values; 1.16%] is in *cusl_2;* see Chapter 2). Thus, use the mean value replacement option by checking the corresponding box.

Exhibit 3.4 PLS-SEM Algorithm Settings

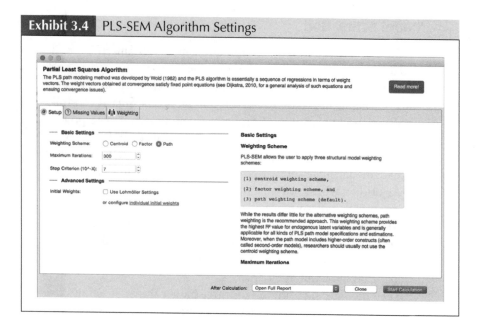

Finally, in the **Weighting** tab, you can specify a weighting variable (labeled **weighting vector** in SmartPLS 3), which assigns each observation a different importance in the PLS-SEM estimation based on some criterion. Weighting variables may serve two purposes. First, a weighting variable may adjust a sample's composition so that it reflects the population's composition. For example, if a certain sample comprises 60% males and 40% females, whereas in the population, gender is evenly distributed (i.e., 50% males and 50% females), the weighting variable would assign a higher importance to female sample respondents. Second, a weighting variable may adjust for the impact of certain sampling methods on the composition of the sample. For example, in simple random sampling, every member of a population has an equal probability of being selected in the sample (Sarstedt & Mooi, 2014). Therefore, every observation in the sample would carry the same weight in the PLS-SEM analysis. However, when using other sampling methods such as quota sampling, members of the population don't have an equal probability of being selected in the sample. Using a weight variable, which adjusts for the differing probabilities, permits making generalizations to the population from which the sample was drawn. In the corporate reputation example, we don't specify a weighting variable, so proceed by clicking on **Start Calculation** at the bottom of the dialog box.

Exhibit 3.5	Missing Values Dialog Box

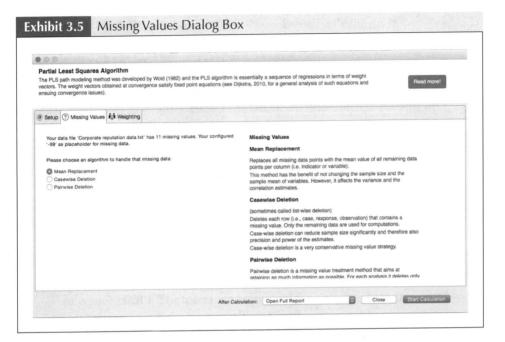

Occasionally, the algorithm does not start and a message appears indicating a **Singular Data Matrix**. There are two potential reasons for this issue. First, one indicator is a constant and thus has zero variance. Second, an indicator is entered twice or is a linear combination of another indicator (e.g., one indicator is a multiple of another such as sales in units and sales in thousands of units). Under these circumstances, PLS-SEM cannot estimate the model, and the researcher has to modify the model by excluding the problematic indicator(s).

Estimation Results

After the estimation of the model, SmartPLS opens the results report per default (note that you can turn this option off by choosing an alternative option for **After Calculation** at the bottom of the **PLS Algorithm** dialog box). At the bottom of the results report, you can select several results tables divided into four categories (**Final Results, Quality Criteria, Interim Results,** and **Base Data**). For example, under **Final Results,** you can find the **Outer Loadings** and **Outer Weights** tables. It is important to note that the results for outer loadings and outer weights are provided by the software for all measurement models, regardless of whether they are reflective or formative. If you have reflective measurement models, you interpret the outer loadings results. In contrast, if you have formative measurement models, then you primarily interpret the outer weights results (the outer loadings also provide a means to evaluate formative measurement models; see Chapter 5). Note the options **Hide Zero Values** (which is switched on as default in SmartPLS 3), **Increase Decimals,** and **Decrease Decimals** in the menu bar on top. Navigate to **Edit Preferences** in the SmartPLS menu if you like to permanently change the number of decimals displayed in the results report (e.g., to 2 decimals). The default report provides various other results menus of which the **Stop Criterion Changes** under **Interim Results** is of initial interest. Here we can see the number of iterations the PLS-SEM algorithm ran. We will discuss these and further menus of the results report in later chapters.

Exhibit 3.6 shows the results report for the path coefficients in matrix format. The table reads from the row to the column. For example, the value 0.504 in the *CUSA* row and the *CUSL* column is the standardized path coefficient of the relationship from *CUSA* to *CUSL*. Clicking on the **Path Coefficients** tab right above the table opens a bar chart (Exhibit 3.7), which visualizes the path coefficients for each model relationship. Each bar's height represents the strength of the relationship, which is displayed at the bottom of each bar.

To get an initial overview of the results, you can switch from the results report view to the modeling window view by left-clicking the tab labeled **Simple Model.** Initially, SmartPLS 3 provides three key results in the modeling window. These are (1) the outer loadings and/ or outer weights for the measurement models, (2) the path coefficients for the structural model relationships, and (3) the R^2 values of the endogenous constructs *CUSA* and *CUSL* (Exhibit 3.8).

Exhibit 3.6	Path Coefficients Report (Matrix Format)

Path Coefficients

⊞ **Matrix** ⋮⋮ **Path Coefficients**

	COMP	CUSA	CUSL	LIKE
COMP		0.162	0.009	
CUSA			0.504	
CUSL				
LIKE		0.424	0.342	

Exhibit 3.7	Path Coefficients Report (Bar Chart)

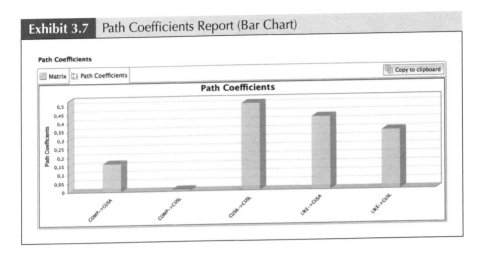

The structural model results enable us to determine, for example, that *CUSA* has the strongest effect on *CUSL* (0.504), followed by *LIKE* (0.342) and *COMP* (0.009). Moreover, the three constructs explain 56.2% of the variance of the endogenous construct *CUSL* (R^2 = 0.562), as indicated by the value in the circle. *COMP* and *LIKE* also jointly explain 29.5% of the variance of *CUSA*. In addition to examining the sizes of the path coefficients, we must also determine if they are statistically significant. Based on their sizes, it would appear that the relationships *CUSA* → *CUSL* and *LIKE* → *CUSL* are significant. But it seems very unlikely that the hypothesized path relationship *COMP* → *CUSL* (0.009) is significant. As a rule of thumb, for sample sizes of up to about 1,000 observations, path coefficients with standardized values above 0.20 are usually significant, and those with values below 0.10 are usually not significant. Nevertheless, making definite statements about a path coefficient's significance requires determining the coefficient estimates' standard error, which is part of more detailed structural model results evaluations presented in Chapter 6.

SmartPLS 3 offers you further options to display estimation results in the modeling window using the **Calculation Results** box at the bottom left of the screen (Exhibit 3.9). Here, you can switch between different types of parameter estimates for the constructs, the inner (i.e., structural) model and the outer (i.e., measurement) models. For example, by clicking on the menu next to **Constructs,** you can switch between the statistics **Average Variance Extracted (AVE), Composite Reliability, Cronbach's Alpha, R Square,** and **R Square Adjusted,**which we will discuss in the following chapters. Depending on the selected setting, SmartPLS 3 will show the corresponding statistic in the center of the

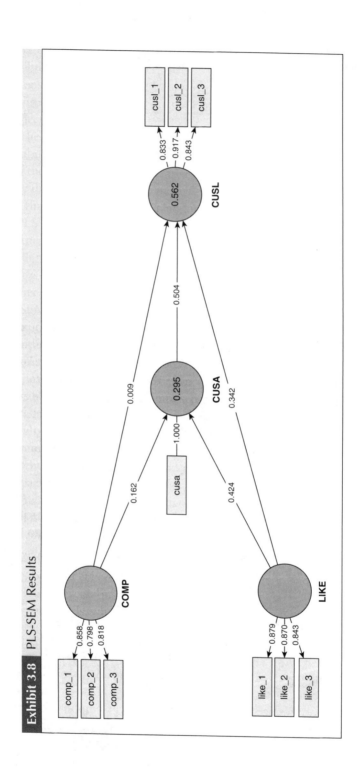

Exhibit 3.8 PLS-SEM Results

Exhibit 3.9	Calculation Results Box

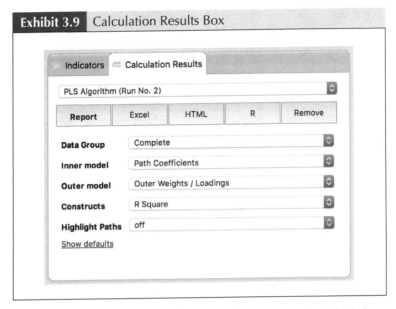

constructs in the modeling window. Note that you can also left-click on the menu to select it and then use the upwards and downwards arrow keys on your keyboard to quickly switch between the alternative results options displayed for **Constructs**. Similarly, you can switch between different types of parameter estimates in the inner model or the outer models. Finally, by clicking on the menu next to **Highlight Paths,** you can highlight the estimated relationships in the inner and outer models. Based on the size of their estimated coefficients, the paths appear as thicker or thinner lines in the SmartPLS **Modeling** window.

On the basis of the path coefficient estimates and their significance, you can determine whether the conceptual model/theoretical hypotheses are substantiated empirically. Moreover, by examining the relative sizes of the significant path relationships, it is possible to make statements about the relative importance of the exogenous latent variables in predicting an endogenous latent variable. In our simple example, *CUSA* and *LIKE* are both moderately strong predictors of *CUSL*, whereas *COMP* does not predict *CUSL* at all.

SUMMARY

- **Learn how the PLS-SEM algorithm functions.** The PLS-SEM algorithm uses the empirical data for the indicators and iteratively determines the construct scores, the path coefficients, indicator loadings and weights, and further statistics such as R^2 values. Specifically, after determining the scores for every construct, the algorithm estimates all remaining unknown relationships in the PLS path model. The algorithm first obtains the measurement model results, which are the relationships between the constructs and their indicator variables. Then, the algorithm calculates the path coefficients, which are the relationships between the constructs in the structural model, along with the R^2 values of endogenous constructs. All results are standardized, meaning that, for example, path coefficients can be compared with each other.

- **Comprehend the options and parameter settings to run the algorithm.** To apply the PLS-SEM algorithm, researchers need to specify several parameter settings. The decisions include selecting the structural model weighting scheme, initial values to start the PLS-SEM algorithm, the **stop criterion,** and the **maximum number of iterations.** The path weighting scheme maximizes the R^2 values of the endogenous constructs, so that option should be selected. Finally, the initial values (e.g., +1) for the relationships in the measurement model, the stop criterion (a small number such as $1 \cdot 10^{-7}$), and a sufficiently large maximum number of iterations (e.g., 300) should be selected. The PLS-SEM algorithm runs until convergence is achieved or the maximum number of iterations has been reached. The resulting construct scores are then used to estimate all partial regression models in the structural model and the measurement models to obtain the final model estimates.

- **Understand the statistical properties of the PLS-SEM method.** PLS-SEM is an OLS regression-based method, which implies that those statistical properties known from OLS also apply to PLS-SEM. PLS-SEM focuses on the prediction of a specific set of hypothesized relationships that maximizes the explained variance of the dependent variable. The initial key results of the PLS path model estimation are the construct scores. These scores are treated as perfect substitutes for the indicator variables in the measurement models and therefore use all the variance that can help explain the endogenous constructs. Moreover, they facilitate estimating all relationships in the PLS path model. The estimation of these relationships is, however, subject to what has been mistakenly referred to as the PLS-SEM bias, which means that measurement model results are usually overestimated while structural model results are usually underestimated compared with CB-SEM results. However, under conditions commonly encountered in research situations, this inconsistency is quite small. Moreover, the parameter estimation efficiency of PLS-SEM delivers high levels of statistical power compared with CB-SEM. Consequently, PLS-SEM better identifies population relationships and is better suited for exploratory research purposes—a feature that is further supported by the method's less restrictive requirements in terms of model setups, model complexity, and data characteristics.

- **Explain how to interpret the results.** The PLS-SEM method estimates the standardized outer loadings, outer weights, and structural model path coefficients. The indicator loadings and indicator weights are computed for any measurement model in the PLS path model. When reflective measurement models are used, the researcher interprets the outer loadings, whereas outer weights are the primary criterion when formative measurement models are interpreted (note, however, that the loadings also play a role in formative measurement model assessment). For the structural model, the standardized coefficients of the relationships between the constructs are provided as well as the R^2 values for the endogenous constructs. Other more advanced PLS-SEM evaluation criteria used in assessing the results are introduced in Chapters 4 to 6.

- **Apply the PLS-SEM algorithm using the SmartPLS 3 software.** The corporate reputation example and the empirical data available with this book enable you to apply the PLS-SEM algorithm using the SmartPLS 3 software. Selected menu options guide the user in choosing the algorithmic options and parameter settings required for running the PLS-SEM algorithm. The SmartPLS 3 results reports enable the user to check if the algorithm converged (i.e., the stop criterion was reached and not the maximum number of iterations) and to evaluate the initial results for the outer weights, outer loadings, structural model path coefficients, and R^2 values. Additional diagnostic measures for more advanced analyses are discussed in later chapters.

REVIEW QUESTIONS

1. Describe how the PLS-SEM algorithm functions.

2. Explain the parameter settings and algorithmic options that you would use (e.g., stopping rules, weighting scheme).

3. What are the key results provided after convergence of the PLS-SEM algorithm?

CRITICAL THINKING QUESTIONS

1. Does the PLS-SEM inconsistency represent a crucial problem in PLS-SEM applications? Explain why or why not.

2. What does consistency at large mean?

3. Explain what factor determinacy means and why this feature makes the PLS-SEM method particularly useful for exploratory research?

KEY TERMS

10 times rule

Algorithmic options

Consistency at large

Construct scores

Constructs

Convergence

Data matrix

Endogenous constructs

Exogenous constructs

Factor indeterminacy

Formative measures

Initial values

Latent variables (endogenous, exogenous)

Maximum number of iterations

Model complexity

Outer loadings

Outer weights

Parameter settings

Path coefficients

PLS-SEM algorithm

PLS-SEM bias

Prediction

R^2 values

Raw data

Reflective measure

Singular data matrix

Standardized data

Stop criterion

Weighting scheme

SUGGESTED READINGS

Dijkstra, T. K. (2010). Latent variables and indices: Herman Wold's basic design and partial least squares. In V. Esposito Vinzi, W. W. Chin, J. Henseler, & H. Wang (Eds.), *Handbook of partial least squares: Concepts, methods and applications* (Springer Handbooks of Computational Statistics Series, Vol. II, pp. 23–46). Berlin: Springer.

Dijkstra, T. K., & Henseler, J. (2015). Consistent partial least squares path modeling. *MIS Quarterly, 39,* 297–316.

Haenlein, M., & Kaplan, A. M. (2004). A beginner's guide to partial least squares analysis. *Understanding Statistics, 3,* 283–297.

Hair, J. F., Ringle, C. M., & Sarstedt, M. (2011). PLS-SEM: Indeed a silver bullet. *Journal of Marketing Theory and Practice, 19,* 139–151.

Henseler, J., Ringle, C. M., & Sarstedt, M. (2012). Using partial least squares path modeling in international advertising research: Basic concepts and recent issues. In S. Okazaki (Ed.), *Handbook of research in international advertising* (pp. 252–276). Cheltenham, UK: Edward Elgar.

Henseler, J., Ringle, C. M., & Sinkovics, R. R. (2009). The use of partial least squares path modeling in international marketing. *Advances in International Marketing, 20,* 277–320.

Jöreskog, K. G., & Wold, H. (1982). The ML and PLS techniques for modeling with latent variables: Historical and comparative aspects. In H. Wold & K. G. Jöreskog (Eds.), *Systems under indirect observation, Part I* (pp. 263–270). Amsterdam: North-Holland.

Lohmöller, J. B. (1989). *Latent variable path modeling with partial least squares.* Heidelberg, Germany: Physica.

Marcoulides, G. A., & Chin, W. W. (2013). You write but others read: Common methodological misunderstandings in PLS and related methods. In H. Abdi, W. W. Chin, V. Esposito Vinzi, G. Russolillo, & L. Trinchera (Eds.), *New perspectives in partial least squares and related methods* (pp. 31–64). New York: Springer.

Reinartz, W., Haenlein, M., & Henseler, J. (2009). An empirical comparison of the efficacy of covariance-based and variance-based SEM. *International Journal of Research in Marketing, 26,* 332–344.

Rigdon, E. E. (2005). Structural equation modeling: Nontraditional alternatives. In B. Everitt & D. Howell (Eds.), *Encyclopedia of statistics in behavioral science* (Vol. 4, pp. 1934–1941). New York: John Wiley.

Rigdon, E. E. (2012). Rethinking partial least squares path modeling: In praise of simple methods. *Long Range Planning, 45,* 341–358.

Tenenhaus, M., Esposito Vinzi, V., Chatelin, Y.-M., & Lauro, C. (2005). PLS path modeling. *Computational Statistics & Data Analysis, 48,* 159–205.

Vilares, M. J., Almeida, M. H., & Coelho, P. S. (2010). Comparison of likelihood and PLS estimators for structural equation modeling: A simulation with customer satisfaction data. In V. Esposito Vinzi, W. W. Chin, J. Henseler, & H. Wang (Eds.), *Handbook of partial least squares: Concepts, methods and applications* (Springer Handbooks of Computational Statistics Series, Vol. II, pp. 289–305). Berlin: Springer.

Wold, H. O. A. (1982). Soft modeling: The basic design and some extensions. In H. Wold & K. G. Jöreskog (Eds.), *Systems under indirect observation, Part II* (pp. 1–54). Amsterdam: North-Holland.

CHAPTER 4

Assessing PLS-SEM Results Part I

Evaluation of Reflective Measurement Models

LEARNING OUTCOMES

1. Gain an overview of Stage 5 of the process for using PLS-SEM, which deals with the evaluation of measurement models.

2. Describe Stage 5a: evaluating reflectively measured constructs.

3. Use the SmartPLS 3 software to assess reflectively measured constructs in the corporate reputation example.

CHAPTER PREVIEW

Having learned how to create and estimate a PLS path model, we now focus on understanding how to assess the quality of the results. Initially, we summarize the primary criteria that are used for PLS path model evaluation and their systematic application. Then, we focus on the evaluation of reflective measurement models. The PLS path model of corporate reputation is a practical application enabling you to review the relevant measurement model **evaluation criteria** and the appropriate reporting of results. This provides a foundation for the overview of formative measurement models in Chapter 5 and how to evaluate structural model results, which is covered in Chapter 6.

OVERVIEW OF STAGE 5: EVALUATION OF MEASUREMENT MODELS

Model estimation delivers empirical measures of the relationships between the indicators and the constructs (measurement models), as well as between the constructs (structural model). The empirical measures enable us to compare the theoretically established measurement and structural models with reality, as represented by the sample data. In other words, we can determine how well the theory fits the data.

PLS-SEM results are reviewed and evaluated using a systematic process. The goal of PLS-SEM is maximizing the **explained variance** (i.e., the R^2 **value**) of the endogenous latent variables in the PLS path model. For this reason, the evaluation of the quality of the PLS-SEM measurement and structural models focuses on metrics indicating the model's predictive capabilities. As with CB-SEM, the most important measurement model metrics for PLS-SEM are reliability, convergent validity, and discriminant validity. For the structural model, the most important evaluation metrics are R^2 (explained variance), f^2 (**effect size**), Q^2 (predictive relevance), and the size and statistical significance of the structural path coefficients. CB-SEM also relies on several of these metrics but in addition provides goodness-of-fit measures based on the discrepancy between the empirical and the model-implied (theoretical) covariance matrix. Since PLS-SEM relies on variances instead of covariances to determine an optimum solution, covariance-based goodness-of-fit measures are not fully transferrable to the PLS-SEM context. Fit measures in PLS-SEM are generally variance based and focus on the discrepancy between the observed (in the case of manifest variables) or approximated (in the case of latent variables) values of the dependent variables and the values predicted by the model in question. Nevertheless, research has proposed several PLS-SEM–based model fit measures, which are, however, in their early stages of development (see Chapter 6 for more details).

The systematic evaluation of these criteria follows a two-step process, as shown in Exhibit 4.1. The process involves separate assessments of the measurement models (Stage 5 of the procedure for using PLS-SEM) and the structural model (Stage 6).

PLS-SEM model assessment initially focuses on the measurement models. Examination of PLS-SEM estimates enables the researcher to

Exhibit 4.1	Systematic Evaluation of PLS-SEM Results

Stage 5: Evaluation of the Measurement Models	
Stage 5a: Reflective Measurement Models	**Stage 5b: Formative Measurement Models**
• Internal consistency (Cronbach's alpha, composite reliability) • Convergent validity (indicator reliability, average variance extracted) • Discriminant validity	• Convergent validity • Collinearity between indicators • Significance and relevance of outer weights
Stage 6: Evaluation of the Structural Model	
• Coefficients of determination (R^2) • Predictive relevance (Q^2) • Size and significance of path coefficients • f^2 effect sizes • q^2 effect sizes	

evaluate the **reliability** and **validity** of the construct measures. Specifically, multivariate measurement involves using several variables (i.e., multi-items) to measure a construct. An example is the customer loyalty (*CUSL*) construct described in the PLS-SEM corporate reputation model, which we discussed earlier.

The logic of using multiple items as opposed to single items for construct measurement is that the measure will be more accurate. The anticipated improved accuracy is based on the assumption that using several indicators to measure a single concept is more likely to represent all the different aspects of the concept. However, even when using multiple items, the measurement is very likely to contain some degree of measurement error. There are many sources of measurement error in social sciences research, including poorly worded questions in a survey, misunderstanding of the scaling approach, and incorrect application of a statistical method, all of which lead to random and/ or systematic errors. The objective is to reduce the measurement error as much as possible. Multivariate measurement enables researchers to more precisely identify measurement error and therefore account for it in research findings.

Measurement error is the difference between the true value of a variable and the value obtained by a measurement. Specifically, the measured value x_m equals the true value x_t plus a measurement error. The measurement error ($e = \varepsilon_r + \varepsilon_s$) can have a random source (random error ε_r), which threatens reliability, or a systematic source (systematic error ε_s), which threatens validity. This relationship can be expressed as follows:

$$x_m = x_t + \varepsilon_r + \varepsilon_s.$$

In Exhibit 4.2, we explain the difference between reliability and validity by comparing a set of three targets. In this analogy, repeated measurements (e.g., of a customer's satisfaction with a specific service) are compared to arrows shot at a target. To measure each true score, we have five measurements (indicated by the black dots). The average value of the dots is indicated by a cross. Validity is indicated when the cross is close to the bull's-eye at the target center. The closer the average value (black cross in Exhibit 4.2) to the true score, the higher the validity. If several arrows are fired, reliability is the distances between the dots showing where the arrows hit the target. If all the dots are close together, the measure is reliable, even though the dots are not necessarily near the bull's-eye. This corresponds to the upper left box, where we have a scenario in which the measure is reliable but not valid. In the upper right box, both reliability and validity are shown. In the lower left box, though, we have a situation in which the measure is neither reliable nor valid. That is, the repeated measurements (dots) are scattered quite widely and the average value (cross) is not close to the bull's-eye. Even if the average value would match the true score (i.e., if the cross were in the bull's-eye), we would still not consider the measure valid. The reason is that an unreliable measure can never be valid, because there is no way we can distinguish the systematic error from the random error (Sarstedt & Mooi, 2014). If we repeat the measurement, say, five more times, the random error would likely shift the cross to a different position. Thus, reliability is a necessary condition for validity. This is also why the not reliable/valid scenario in the lower right box is not possible.

When evaluating the measurement models, we must distinguish between reflectively and formatively measured constructs (Chapter 2). The two approaches are based on different concepts and therefore require consideration of different evaluative measures. Reflective

Exhibit 4.2	Comparing Reliability and Validity (Sarstedt & Mooi, 2014)

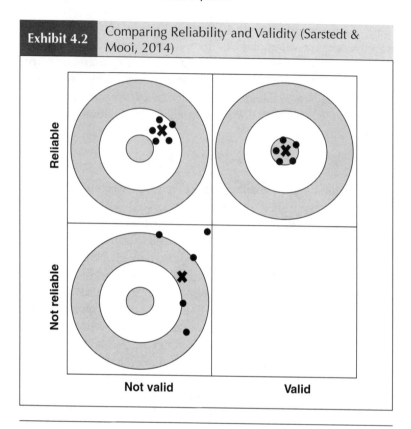

Source: Sarstedt, M., & Mooi, E. A. (2014). *A concise guide to market research* (2nd ed., p. 35). New York: Springer. With kind permission of Springer Science + Business Media.

measurement models are assessed on their **internal consistency reliability** and validity. The specific measures include the composite reliability (as a means to assess the internal consistency reliability), convergent validity, and discriminant validity. The criteria for reflective measurement models cannot be universally applied to formative measurement models. With formative measures, the first step is to ensure **content validity** before collecting the data and estimating the PLS path model. After model estimation, different metrics are used to assess formative measures for **convergent validity,** the significance and relevance of indicator weights, and the presence of **collinearity** among indicators (Exhibit 4.1).

As implied by its name, a single-item construct (Chapter 2) is not represented by a multi-item measurement model. The relationship (i.e., the correlation) between the single indicator and the latent variable is always 1. Put differently, the single indicator and the latent variable have identical values. Thus, the criteria for the assessment of measurement models are not applicable to single-item constructs. To evaluate the reliability and validity of single-item measures, researchers must rely on proxies or different forms of validity assessment. For example, researchers can assess a single-item variable by means of criterion validity. This is done by correlating the single-item measure with an established criterion variable and comparing the resulting correlation with the correlation that results if the predictor construct is measured by a multi-item scale (e.g., Diamantopoulos et al., 2012). In terms of reliability, researchers often assume that one cannot estimate the reliability of single-item measures based on such techniques as common factor analysis and the correction for attenuation formula (e.g., Sarstedt & Wilczynski, 2009). These procedures require that both the multi-item measure and the single-item measure are included in the same survey. Thus, these analyses are of primary interest when researchers want to assess in a pretest or pilot study whether in the main study, a multi-item scale can be replaced with a single-item measure of the same construct. Still, recent research suggests that the reliability and validity of single items are highly context specific, which renders their assessment in pretests or pilot studies problematic (Sarstedt et al., in press).

The structural model estimates are not examined until the reliability and validity of the constructs have been established. If assessment of reflective (i.e., Stage 5a) and formative (i.e., Stage 5b) measurement models provides evidence of the measures' quality, the structural model estimates are evaluated in Stage 6 (Chapter 6). PLS-SEM assessment of the structural model involves the model's ability to predict the variance in the dependent variables. Hence, after reliability and validity are established, the primary evaluation criteria for PLS-SEM results are the **coefficients of determination** (R^2 values) as well as the size and significance of the path coefficients. The f^2 **effect sizes, predictive relevance** (Q^2), and the q^2 **effect sizes** give additional insights about quality of the PLS path model estimations (Exhibit 4.1).

Assessment of PLS-SEM outcomes can be extended to more advanced analyses such as examining mediating or moderating effects, which we discuss in Chapter 7. Similarly, advanced analyses may involve estimating nonlinear effects (e.g., Rigdon, Ringle, & Sarstedt, 2010), conducting an importance-performance matrix analysis (PLS-IPMA; e.g., Rigdon, Ringle, Sarstedt, & Gudergan, 2011;

Schloderer et al., 2014), assessing the mode of measurement model by using the confirmatory tetrad analysis (CTA-PLS; Gudergan et al., 2008), analyzing hierarchical component models (e.g., Becker, Klein, & Wetzels, 2012; Ringle et al., 2012), considering heterogeneity (e.g., Becker, Rai, Ringle, & Völckner, 2013; Sarstedt & Ringle, 2010), executing multigroup analyses (Sarstedt, Henseler, & Ringle, 2011), and assessing measurement model invariance (Henseler, Ringle, & Sarstedt, in press). In Chapter 8, we discuss several of these aspects in greater detail. The objective of these additional analyses is to extend and further differentiate the findings from the basic PLS path model estimation. Some of these advanced analyses are necessary to obtain a complete understanding of PLS-SEM results (e.g., checking for the presence of unobserved heterogeneity and significantly different subgroups), while others are optional.

The primary rules of thumb on how to evaluate PLS-SEM results are shown in Exhibit 4.3. In the following sections, we provide an overview of the process for assessing reflective measurement models (Stage 5a). Chapter 5 addresses the evaluation of formative measurement models (Stage 5b), while Chapter 6 deals with structural model evaluation.

Exhibit 4.3 Rules of Thumb for Evaluating PLS-SEM Results

- Model assessment in PLS-SEM primarily builds on nonparametric evaluation criteria based on bootstrapping and blindfolding. Goodness-of-fit measures used in CB-SEM are not universally transferrable to PLS-SEM, but recent research has brought forward various model fit criteria.

- Begin the evaluation process by assessing the quality of the reflective and formative measurement models (specific rules of thumb for reflective measurement models follow later in this chapter and in Chapter 5 for formative measurement models).

- If the measurement characteristics of constructs are acceptable, continue with the assessment of the structural model results. Path estimates should be statistically significant and meaningful. Moreover, endogenous constructs in the structural model should have high levels of explained variance as expressed in high R^2 values (Chapter 6 presents specific guidelines).

- Advanced analyses that extend and differentiate initial PLS-SEM findings may be necessary to obtain a correct picture of the results (Chapters 7 and 8).

STAGE 5A: ASSESSING RESULTS OF REFLECTIVE MEASUREMENT MODELS

Assessment of reflective measurement models includes composite reliability to evaluate internal consistency, individual **indicator reliability,** and **average variance extracted (AVE)** to evaluate convergent validity. Assessment of reflective measurement models also includes discriminant validity. The **Fornell-Larcker criterion, cross-loadings,** and especially the heterotrait-monotrait (HTMT) ratio of correlations can be used to examine **discriminant validity.** In the following sections, we address each criterion for the evaluation of reflective measurement models.

Internal Consistency Reliability

The first criterion to be evaluated is typically **internal consistency reliability.** The traditional criterion for internal consistency is **Cronbach's alpha,** which provides an estimate of the reliability based on the intercorrelations of the observed indicator variables. This statistic is defined as follows:

$$Cronbach's\,\alpha = \left(\frac{M}{M-1}\right) \cdot \left(1 - \frac{\sum_{i=1}^{M} s_i^2}{s_t^2}\right).$$

In this formula, s_i^2 represents the variance of the indicator variable i of a specific construct, measured with M indicators ($i = 1, \ldots, M$), and s_t^2 is the variance of the sum of all M indicators of that construct. Cronbach's alpha assumes that all indicators are equally reliable (i.e., all the indicators have equal outer loadings on the construct). But PLS-SEM prioritizes the indicators according to their individual reliability. Moreover, Cronbach's alpha is sensitive to the number of items in the scale and generally tends to underestimate the internal consistency reliability. As such, it may be used as a more conservative measure of internal consistency reliability. Due to Cronbach's alpha's limitations, it is technically more appropriate to apply a different measure of internal consistency reliability, which is referred to as **composite reliability.** This measure of reliability takes into account the different outer loadings of the indicator variables and is calculated using the following formula:

$$\rho_c = \frac{\left(\sum_{i=1}^{M} l_i\right)^2}{\left(\sum_{i=1}^{M} l_i\right)^2 + \sum_{i=1}^{M} var(e_i)},$$

where l_i symbolizes the standardized outer loading of the indicator variable i of a specific construct measured with M indicators, e_i is the measurement error of indicator variable i, and $var(e_i)$ denotes the variance of the measurement error, which is defined as $1 - l_i^2$.

The composite reliability varies between 0 and 1, with higher values indicating higher levels of reliability. It is generally interpreted in the same way as Cronbach's alpha. Specifically, composite reliability values of 0.60 to 0.70 are acceptable in exploratory research, while in more advanced stages of research, values between 0.70 and 0.90 can be regarded as satisfactory. Values above 0.90 (and definitely above 0.95) are not desirable because they indicate that all the indicator variables are measuring the same phenomenon and are therefore not likely to be a valid measure of the construct. Specifically, such composite reliability values occur if one uses semantically redundant items by slightly rephrasing the very same question. As the use of redundant items has adverse consequences for the measures' content validity (e.g., Rossiter, 2002) and may boost error term correlations (Drolet & Morrison, 2001; Hayduk & Littvay, 2012), researchers are advised to minimize the number of redundant indicators. Finally, composite reliability values below 0.60 indicate a lack of internal consistency reliability.

Cronbach's alpha is a conservative measure of reliability (i.e., it results in relatively low reliability values). In contrast, composite reliability tends to overestimate the internal consistency reliability, thereby resulting in comparatively higher reliability estimates. Therefore, it is reasonable to consider and report both criteria. When analyzing and assessing the measures' internal consistency reliability, the true reliability usually lies between Cronbach's alpha (representing the lower bound) and the composite reliability (representing the upper bound).

Convergent Validity

Convergent validity is the extent to which a measure correlates positively with alternative measures of the same construct. Using the domain sampling model, indicators of a reflective construct are treated as different (alternative) approaches to measure the same construct. Therefore, the items that are indicators (measures) of a specific reflective construct should converge or share a high proportion of variance. To evaluate convergent validity of reflective constructs, researchers consider the outer loadings of the indicators and the average variance extracted (AVE).

High outer loadings on a construct indicate the associated indicators have much in common, which is captured by the construct. The size of the outer loading is also commonly called **indicator reliability**. At a minimum, the outer loadings of all indicators should be statistically significant. Because a significant outer loading could still be fairly weak, a common rule of thumb is that the standardized outer loadings should be 0.708 or higher. The rationale behind this rule can be understood in the context of the square of a standardized indicator's outer loading, referred to as the **communality** of an item. The square of a standardized indicator's outer loading represents how much of the variation in an item is explained by the construct and is described as the variance extracted from the item. An established rule of thumb is that a latent variable should explain a substantial part of each indicator's variance, usually at least 50%. This also implies that the variance shared between the construct and its indicator is larger than the measurement error variance. This means that an indicator's outer loading should be above 0.708 since that number squared (0.708^2) equals 0.50. Note that in most instances, 0.70 is considered close enough to 0.708 to be acceptable.

Researchers frequently obtain weaker outer loadings (<0.70) in social science studies, especially when newly developed scales are used (Hulland, 1999). Rather than automatically eliminating indicators when their outer loading is below 0.70, researchers should carefully examine the effects of item removal on the composite reliability, as well as on the content validity of the construct. Generally, indicators with outer loadings between 0.40 and 0.70 should be considered for removal from the scale only when deleting the indicator leads to an increase in the composite reliability (or the average variance extracted; see next section) above the suggested threshold value. Another consideration in the decision of whether to delete an indicator is the extent to which its removal affects content validity. Indicators with weaker outer loadings are sometimes retained on the basis of their contribution to content validity. Indicators with very low outer loadings (below 0.40) should, however, always be eliminated from the construct (Bagozzi, Yi, & Philipps, 1991; Hair et al., 2011). Exhibit 4.4 illustrates the recommendations regarding indicator deletion based on outer loadings.

A common measure to establish convergent validity on the construct level is the **average variance extracted (AVE)**. This criterion is defined as the grand mean value of the squared loadings of the indicators associated with the construct (i.e., the sum of the squared loadings divided by the number of indicators). Therefore, the AVE is

Exhibit 4.4 Outer Loading Relevance Testing

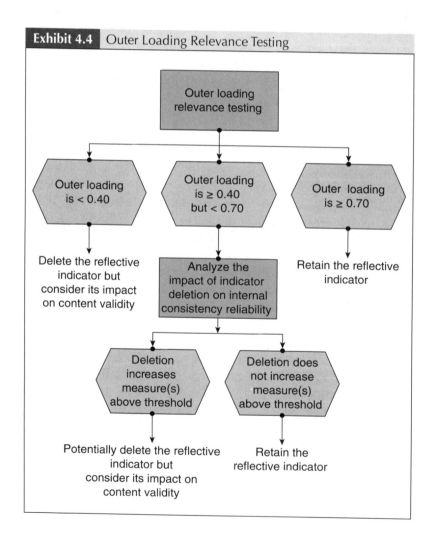

equivalent to the **communality** of a construct. The AVE is calculated using the following formula:

$$AVE = \left(\frac{\sum_{i=1}^{M} l_i^2}{M} \right).$$

Using the same logic as that used with the individual indicators, an AVE value of 0.50 or higher indicates that, on average, the construct explains more than half of the variance of its indicators. Conversely, an AVE of less than 0.50 indicates that, on average, more variance remains in the error of the items than in the variance explained by the construct.

The AVE of each reflectively measured construct should be evaluated. In the example introduced in Chapter 2, an AVE estimate is needed only for constructs COMP, CUSL, and LIKE. For the single-item construct CUSA, the AVE is not an appropriate measure since the indicator's outer loading is fixed at 1.00.

Discriminant Validity

Discriminant validity is the extent to which a construct is truly distinct from other constructs by empirical standards. Thus, establishing discriminant validity implies that a construct is unique and captures phenomena not represented by other constructs in the model. Traditionally, researchers have relied on two measures of discriminant validity. The **cross-loadings** are typically the first approach to assess the discriminant validity of the indicators. Specifically, an indicator's outer loading on the associated construct should be greater than any of its cross-loadings (i.e., its correlation) on other constructs. The best way to assess and report cross-loadings is in a table with rows for the indicators and columns for the latent variable. Exhibit 4.5 illustrates this analysis in an example with three latent variables (Y_1, Y_2, and Y_3), each measured with two indicators. As can be seen, the loadings always exceed the cross-loadings. For example, x_{11} loads high on its corresponding construct Y_1 (0.75) but much lower on constructs Y_2 (0.49) and Y_3 (0.41). In this example, the analysis of cross-loadings suggests that discriminant validity has been established. On the contrary, the presence of cross-loadings that exceed the indicators' outer loadings would represent a discriminant validity problem.

The **Fornell-Larcker criterion** is the second approach to assessing discriminant validity. It compares the square root of the AVE values

Exhibit 4.5 Cross-Loadings Analysis			
	Y_1	Y_2	Y_3
x_{11}	**0.75**	0.49	0.41
x_{12}	**0.83**	0.27	0.35
x_{21}	0.55	**0.82**	0.60
x_{22}	0.45	**0.82**	0.42
x_{31}	0.43	0.53	**0.87**
x_{32}	0.42	0.55	**0.84**

Note: One expects that an indicator has the highest loading value (in bold) with the construct to which it has been assigned to.

with the latent variable correlations. Specifically, the square root of each construct's AVE should be greater than its highest correlation with any other construct. An alternative approach to evaluating the results of the Fornell-Larcker criterion is to determine whether the AVE is larger than the squared correlation with any other construct. The logic of the Fornell-Larcker method is based on the idea that a construct shares more variance with its associated indicators than with any other construct.

Exhibit 4.6 illustrates this concept. In the example, the AVE values of the constructs Y_1 and Y_2 are 0.55 and 0.65, respectively. The AVE values are obtained by squaring each outer loading, obtaining the sum of the three squared outer loadings, and then calculating the average value. For example, with respect to construct Y_1, 0.60, 0.70, and 0.90 squared are 0.36, 0.49, and 0.81, respectively. The sum of these three numbers is 1.66, and the average value is therefore 0.55 (i.e., 1.66/3). The correlation between constructs Y_1 and Y_2 (as indicated by the double-headed arrow linking the two constructs) is 0.80. Squaring the correlation of 0.80 indicates that 64% (i.e., the squared correlation; $0.80^2 = 0.64$) of each construct's variation is explained by the other construct. Therefore, Y_1 explains less variance in its indicator measures x_1 to x_3 than it shares with Y_2, which implies that the two constructs (Y_1 and Y_2), which are conceptually different, are not sufficiently different in terms of their empirical standards. Thus, in this example, discriminant validity is not established.

The analysis and presentation of the results of the Fornell-Larcker criterion are illustrated in Exhibit 4.7—for a PLS path model with

Exhibit 4.6	Visual Representation of the Fornell-Larcker Criterion

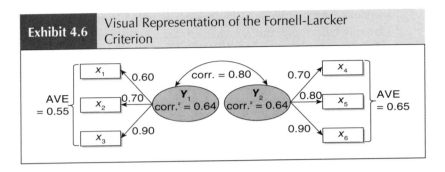

two reflective constructs (i.e., Y_1 and Y_2), one formative construct (i.e., Y_3), and a single-item construct (i.e., Y_4). The first consideration is that only reflective multi-item constructs are evaluated using the Fornell-Larcker criterion. Therefore, constructs Y_3 and Y_4 are exceptions to this type of evaluation since the AVE value is not a meaningful criterion for formative and single-item measures. Looking only at constructs Y_1 and Y_2, note that the square root of each construct's AVE is on the diagonal. The nondiagonal elements represent the correlations between the latent variables. To establish discriminant validity, the square root of each construct's AVE must be larger than its correlation with other constructs. To evaluate the reflective construct Y_2 in Exhibit 4.7, one would compare all correlations in the row of Y_2 and the column of Y_2 with its square root of the AVE. In the case study illustration of the corporate reputation path model later in this chapter, the actual estimated values for this type of analysis are provided.

Recent research that critically examined the performance of cross-loadings and the Fornell-Larcker criterion for discriminant validity assessment has found that neither approach reliably detects

Exhibit 4.7	Example of Fornell-Larcker Criterion Analysis		
	Y_1	**Y_2**	**Y_3**	**Y_4**
---	---	---	---	---
Y_1	$\sqrt{AVE_{Y_1}}$			
Y_2	$CORR_{Y_1 Y_2}$	$\sqrt{AVE_{Y_2}}$		
Y_3	$CORR_{Y_1 Y_3}$	$CORR_{Y_2 Y_3}$	*Formative measurement model*	
Y_4	$CORR_{Y_1 Y_4}$	$CORR_{Y_2 Y_4}$	$CORR_{Y_3 Y_4}$	*Single-item construct*

discriminant validity issues (Henseler et al., 2015). Specifically, cross-loadings fail to indicate a lack of discriminant validity when two constructs are perfectly correlated, which renders this criterion ineffective for empirical research. Similarly, the Fornell-Larcker criterion performs very poorly, especially when indicator loadings of the constructs under consideration differ only slightly (e.g., all indicator loadings vary between 0.60 and 0.80). When indicator loadings vary more strongly, the Fornell-Larcker criterion's performance in detecting discriminant validity issues improves but is still rather poor overall. (also see Voorhees, Brady, Calantone, & Ramirez, 2016).

As a remedy, Henseler et al. (2015) propose assessing the **heterotrait-monotrait ratio (HTMT)** of the correlations. In short, **HTMT** is the ratio of the between-trait correlations to the within-trait correlations. HTMT is the mean of all correlations of indicators across constructs measuring different constructs (i.e., the **heterotrait-heteromethod correlations**) relative to the (geometric) mean of the average correlations of indicators measuring the same construct (i.e., the monotrait-heteromethod correlations; for a formal definition of the HTMT statistic, see Henseler et al., 2015). Technically, the HTMT approach is an estimate of what the true correlation between two constructs would be, if they were perfectly measured (i.e., if they were perfectly reliable). This true correlation is also referred to as **disattenuated correlation.** A disattenuated correlation between two constructs close to 1 indicates a lack of discriminant validity.

Exhibit 4.8 illustrates the HTMT approach. The average **heterotrait-heteromethod correlations** equal all pairwise correlations between variables x_1, x_2, and x_3 and x_4, x_5, and x_6 (gray-shaded area in the correlation matrix in Exhibit 4.8). In the example, the average heterotrait-heteromethod correlation is 0.341. The average **monotrait-heteromethod correlations** of Y_1 equal the mean of all pairwise correlations between x_1, x_2, and x_3 (i.e., 0.712). Similarly, the mean of all pairwise correlations between x_4, x_5, and x_6 (i.e., 0.409) defines the average monotrait-heteromethod correlations of Y_2. The HTMT statistic for the relationship between Y_1 and Y_2 therefore equals

$$HTMT(Y_1, Y_2) = \frac{0.341}{\sqrt{0.712 \cdot 0.409}} = 0.632.$$

The exact threshold level of the HTMT is debatable; after all, "when is a correlation close to 1?" Based on prior research and their study results, Henseler et al. (2015) suggest a threshold value of 0.90

| Exhibit 4.8 | Visual Representation of the HTMT Approach |

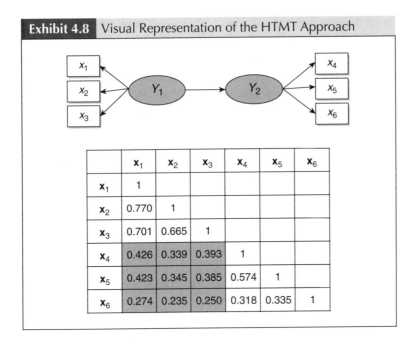

	x₁	**x₂**	**x₃**	**x₄**	**x₅**	**x₆**
x₁	1					
x₂	0.770	1				
x₃	0.701	0.665	1			
x₄	0.426	0.339	0.393	1		
x₅	0.423	0.345	0.385	0.574	1	
x₆	0.274	0.235	0.250	0.318	0.335	1

if the path model includes constructs that are conceptually very similar (e.g., affective satisfaction, cognitive satisfaction, and loyalty). In other words, an HTMT value above 0.90 suggests a lack of discriminant validity. When the constructs in the path model are conceptually more distinct, a lower and thus more conservative threshold value of 0.85 seems warranted (Henseler et al., 2015). Furthermore, the HTMT can serve as the basis of a statistical discriminant validity test. However, as PLS-SEM does not rely on any distributional assumptions, standard parametric significance tests cannot be applied to test whether the HTMT statistic is significantly different from 1. Instead, researchers have to rely on a procedure called **bootstrapping** to derive a distribution of the HTMT statistic (see Chapter 5 for more details on the bootstrapping procedure).

In bootstrapping, subsamples are randomly drawn (with replacement) from the original set of data. Each subsample is then used to estimate the model. This process is repeated until a large number of random subsamples have been created, typically about 5,000. The estimated parameters from the subsamples (in this case, the HTMT statistic) are used to derive standard errors for the estimates. With this information, it is possible to derive a **bootstrap confidence interval.** The confidence interval is the range into which the true HTMT population value will fall, assuming a certain level of confidence (e.g., 95%).

A confidence interval containing the value 1 indicates a lack of discriminant validity. Conversely, if the value 1 falls outside the interval's range, this suggests that the two constructs are empirically distinct. Since the HTMT-based assessment using a confidence interval relies on inferential statistics, one should primarily rely on this criterion, especially in light of the limitations of cross-loadings and the Fornell-Larcker criterion. However, the latter two measures still constitute standard means for discriminant validity assessment.

What should researchers do if any of the criteria signal a lack of discriminant validity? There are different ways to handle discriminant validity problems (Exhibit 4.9). The first approach retains the constructs that cause discriminant validity problems in the model and aims at increasing the average monotrait-heteromethod correlations and/or decreasing the average heteromethod-heterotrait correlations of the constructs measures.

To decrease the HTMT by increasing a construct's average monotrait-heteromethod correlations, one can eliminate items that have low correlations with other items measuring the same construct. Likewise, heterogeneous subdimensions in the construct's set of items could also deflate the average monotrait-heteromethod correlations. In this case, the construct (e.g., quality) can be split into homogeneous subconstructs (e.g., product quality and service quality), perhaps using a higher-order construct, if the measurement theory supports this step (e.g., Kocyigit & Ringle, 2011). These subconstructs then replace the more general construct in the model. When following this approach, however, the discriminant validity of the newly generated constructs with all the other constructs in the model needs to be reevaluated.

To decrease the average heteromethod-heterotrait correlations, one can (1) eliminate items that are strongly correlated with items in the opposing construct, or (2) reassign these indicators to the other construct, if theoretically plausible. It is important to note that the elimination of items purely on statistical grounds can have adverse consequences for the content validity of the constructs. Therefore, this step entails carefully examining the scales (based on prior research results or on a pretest when newly developed measures are involved) to determine whether all the construct domain facets have been captured. At least two expert coders should conduct this judgment independently to ensure a high degree of objectivity.

Another approach to treating discriminant validity problems involves merging the constructs that cause the problems into a more general construct. Again, measurement theory must support this step.

Exhibit 4.9   Handling Discriminant Validity Problems

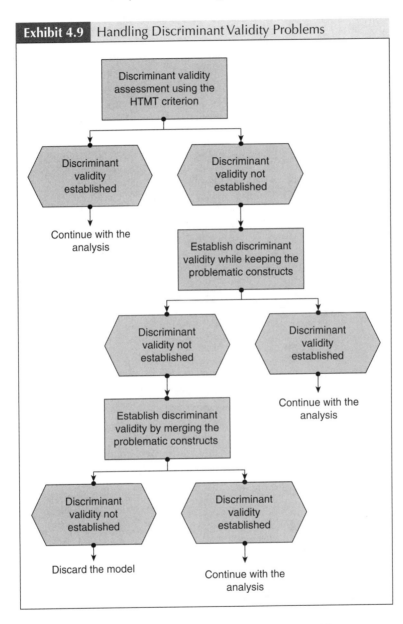

In this case, the more general construct replaces the problematic constructs in the model. This step may entail modifications to increase a construct's average monotrait-heteromethod correlations and/or to decrease the average heteromethod-heterotrait correlations.

In Exhibit 4.10, we summarize the criteria used to assess the reliability and validity of reflective construct measures. If the criteria are

Exhibit 4.10	Rules of Thumb for Evaluating Reflective Measurement Models

- Internal consistency reliability: composite reliability should be higher than 0.70 (in exploratory research, 0.60 to 0.70 is considered acceptable). Consider Cronbach's alpha as the lower bound and composite reliability as the upper bound of internal consistency reliability.

- Indicator reliability: the indicator's outer loadings should be higher than 0.70. Indicators with outer loadings between 0.40 and 0.70 should be considered for removal only if the deletion leads to an increase in composite reliability and AVE above the suggested threshold value.

- Convergent validity: the AVE should be higher than 0.50.

- Discriminant validity:

  o Use the HTMT criterion to assess discriminant validity in PLS-SEM.

  o The confidence interval of the HTMT statistic should not include the value 1 for all combinations of constructs.

  o According to the traditional discriminant validity assessment methods, an indicator's outer loadings on a construct should be higher than all its cross-loadings with other constructs. Furthermore, the square root of the AVE of each construct should be higher than its highest correlation with any other construct (Fornell-Larcker criterion).

not met, the researcher may decide to remove single indicators from a specific construct in an attempt to more closely meet the criteria. However, removing indicators should be carried out with care since the elimination of one or more indicators may improve the reliability or discriminant validity but at the same time may decrease the measurement's content validity.

CASE STUDY ILLUSTRATION—REFLECTIVE MEASUREMENT MODELS

Running the PLS-SEM Algorithm

We continue working with our PLS-SEM example on corporate reputation. In Chapter 3, we explained how to estimate the PLS path model and how to obtain the results by opening the default report in the SmartPLS 3 software. Recall that to do so, you must first load the simple corporate reputation model and then run the model by clicking on the icon at the top right or by using the pull-down menu by going to **Calculate** → **PLS Algorithm.** After running the **PLS Algorithm,** the SmartPLS results report automatically opens; if not, go to the **Calculation Results** tab on the bottom left of the screen and click on **Report.**

Before analyzing the results, you need to quickly check if the algorithm converged (i.e., the stop criterion of the algorithm was reached and not the maximum number of iterations). To do so, go to **Interim Results** → **Stop Criterion Changes** in the results report. You will then see the table shown in Exhibit 4.11, which shows the number of iterations of the PLS-SEM algorithm. This number should be lower than the maximum number of iterations (e.g., 300) that you defined in the PLS-SEM algorithm parameter settings (Chapter 2). At the bottom left side of the table, you will see that the algorithm converged after Iteration 5.

If the PLS-SEM algorithm does not converge in fewer than 300 iterations (the default setting in the software), the algorithm could not find a stable solution. This kind of situation almost never occurs. But if it does occur, there are two possible causes of the problem: (1) the selected stop criterion is at a very small level (e.g., 1.0E-10) so that little changes in the coefficients of the measurement models prevent the PLS-SEM algorithm from stopping, or (2) there are problems with the data and they need to be checked carefully. For example, data problems may occur if the sample size is too small or if an indicator has many identical values (i.e., the same data points, which results in insufficient variability).

When your PLS path model estimation converges, which it practically always does, you need to examine the following PLS-SEM calculation results tables from the results report for reflective measurement model assessment: **Outer Loadings, Composite Reliability, Cronbach's Alpha, Average Variance Extracted** (AVE), and **Discriminant Validity.** We examine other information in the report in Chapters 5 and 6, when we extend the simple path model by including formative measures and examine the structural model results.

Exhibit 4.11	Stop Criterion Table in SmartPLS

Stop Criterion Changes

Matrix

	comp_1	comp_2	comp_3	cusa	cusl_1	cusl_2	cusl_3	like_1	like_2	like_3
Iteration 0	1.000	1.000	1.000	1.000	1.000	1.000	1.000	1.000	1.000	1.000
Iteration 1	0.536	0.341	0.328	1.000	0.368	0.421	0.365	0.419	0.378	0.359
Iteration 2	0.536	0.340	0.328	1.000	0.369	0.420	0.365	0.418	0.378	0.360
Iteration 3	0.536	0.340	0.328	1.000	0.369	0.420	0.365	0.418	0.378	0.360
Iteration 4	0.536	0.340	0.328	1.000	0.369	0.420	0.365	0.418	0.378	0.360
Iteration 5	0.536	0.340	0.328	1.000	0.369	0.420	0.365	0.418	0.378	0.360

Reflective Measurement Model Evaluation

The simple corporate reputation model has three latent variables with reflective measurement models (i.e., *COMP, CUSL,* and *LIKE*) as well as a single-item construct (*CUSA*). For the reflective measurement models, we need the estimates for the relationships between the reflective latent variables and their indicators (i.e., outer loadings). Exhibit 4.12 displays the results table for the outer loadings, which can be found under **Final Results** → **Outer Loadings**. By default, the outer loadings are also displayed in the modeling window after running the PLS-SEM algorithm. All outer loadings of the reflective constructs *COMP, CUSL,* and *LIKE* are well above the threshold value of 0.70, which suggests sufficient levels of indicator reliability. The indicator *comp_2* (outer loading: 0.798) has the smallest indicator reliability with a value of 0.637 (0.798^2), while the indicator *cusl_2* (outer loading: 0.917) has the highest indicator reliability, with a value of 0.841 (0.917^2).

To evaluate the composite reliability of the construct measures, left-click on the **Construct Reliability and Validity** tab under **Quality Criteria** in the results report. Here, you have the option of displaying the composite reliability values using a bar chart or in a matrix format. Exhibit 4.13 shows the bar chart of the constructs' composite reliability values. The horizontal blue line indicates the common minimum threshold level for composite reliability (i.e., 0.70). If a composite reliability value is above this threshold value, the corresponding bar is colored green. If the composite reliability value is lower than 0.70, the bar is colored red. In our example, all composite reliability values exceed the threshold. Clicking on the **Matrix** tab shows the specific composite reliability values. With values of 0.865 (*COMP*), 0.899 (*CUSL*), and 0.899 (*LIKE*), all three reflective constructs have high

Exhibit 4.12	Outer Loadings

Outer Loadings

☐ Matrix

	COMP	CUSA	CUSL	LIKE
comp_1	0.858			
comp_2	0.798			
comp_3	0.818			
cusa		1.000		
cusl_1			0.833	
cusl_2			0.917	
cusl_3			0.843	
like_1				0.879
like_2				0.870
like_3				0.843

Exhibit 4.13 Composite Reliability

Construct Reliability and Validity

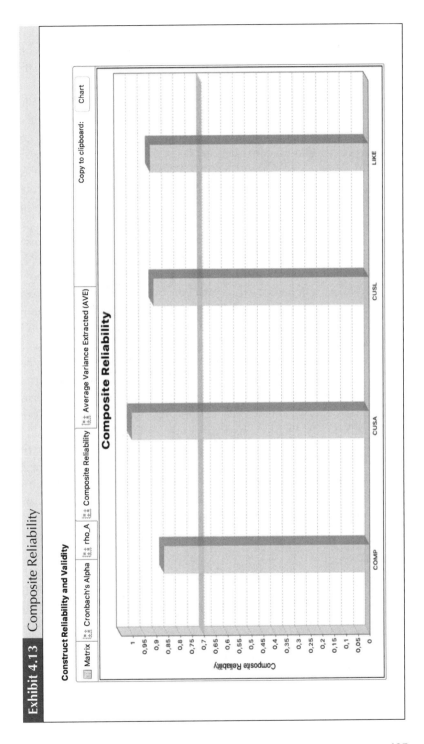

125

levels of internal consistency reliability. Note that the composite reliability value of the single-item variable *CUSA* is 1.00. But this cannot be interpreted as evidence that the construct exhibits perfect reliability and should not be reported with other measures of reliability.

Going to **Quality Criteria** → **Construct Reliability and Validity** gives you the option to show the chart of Cronbach's alpha values for all constructs (Exhibit 4.14). All bars in the chart appear in green, indicating that all construct measures are above the 0.70 threshold. The specific Cronbach's alpha (0.776 for *COMP*, 0.831 for *CUSL*, and 0.831 for *LIKE*) values can be accessed by left-clicking on the **Matrix** tab. Again, as *CUSA* is measured using a single item, interpreting this construct's Cronbach's alpha value is not meaningful.

Convergent validity assessment is based on the AVE values, which can be accessed by going to **Quality Criteria** → **Construct Reliability and Validity** in the results report. As with composite reliability and Cronbach's alpha, SmartPLS offers the option of displaying the results using bar charts (Exhibit 4.15) or in a matrix format. In this example, the AVE values of *COMP* (0.681), *CUSL* (0.748), and *LIKE* (0.747) are well above the required minimum level of 0.50. Thus, the measures of the three reflective constructs have high levels of convergent validity.

Finally, in the **Discriminant Validity** tab under **Quality Criteria,** SmartPLS 3 offers several means to assess whether the construct measures discriminate well empirically. According to the Fornell-Larcker criterion, the square root of the AVE of each construct should be higher than the construct's highest correlation with any other construct in the model (this notion is identical to comparing the AVE with the squared correlations between the constructs). Exhibit 4.16 shows the results of the Fornell-Larcker criterion assessment with the square root of the reflective constructs' AVE on the diagonal and the correlations between the constructs in the off-diagonal position. For example, the reflective construct *COMP* has a value of 0.825 for the square root of its AVE, which needs to be compared with all correlation values in the column of *COMP*. Note that for *CUSL*, you need to consider the correlations in both the row and column. Overall, the square roots of the AVEs for the reflective constructs *COMP* (0.825), *CUSL* (0.865), and *LIKE* (0.864) are all higher than the correlations of these constructs with other latent variables in the path model, thus indicating all constructs are valid measures of unique concepts.

Another alternative to assessing discriminant validity is the cross-loadings. One can check the cross-loadings (click on **Cross Loadings** in the **Discriminant Validity** section of the results report) to make this evaluation. Discriminant validity is established when an indicator's

Exhibit 4.14 Cronbach's Alpha

Construct Reliability and Validity

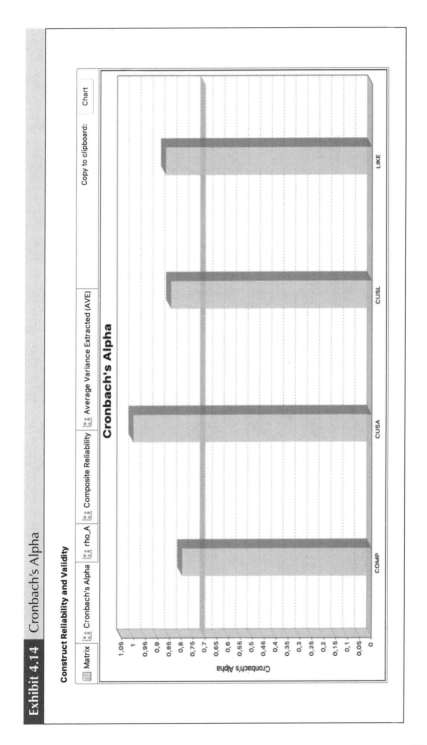

Exhibit 4.15 Average Variance Extracted (AVE)

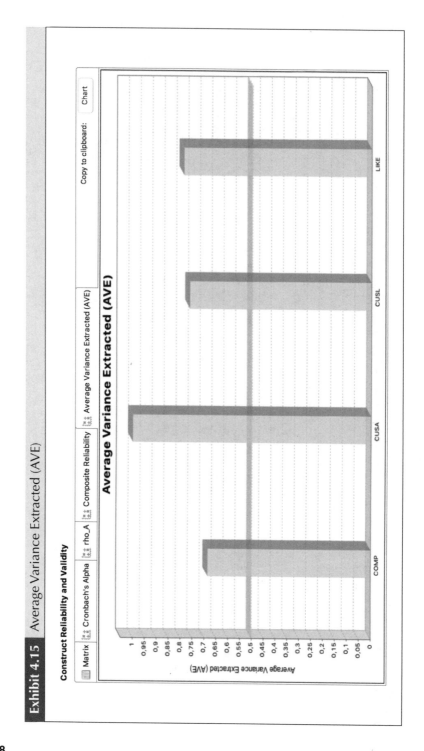

Exhibit 4.16	Fornell-Larcker Criterion

Discriminant Validity

🗒 Fornell–Larcker Criterium	🗒 Cross Loadings	🗒 Heterotrait–Monotrait Ratio (HTMT)

	COMP	CUSA	CUSL	LIKE
COMP	0.825			
CUSA	0.436	1.000		
CUSL	0.450	0.689	0.865	
LIKE	0.645	0.528	0.615	0.864

loading on its assigned construct is higher than all of its cross-loadings with other constructs. Exhibit 4.17 shows the loadings and cross-loadings for every indicator. For example, the indicator *comp_1* has the highest value for the loading with its corresponding construct *COMP* (0.858), while all cross-loadings with other constructs are considerably lower (e.g., *comp_1* on *CUSA*: 0.464). The same finding holds for the other indicators of *COMP* as well as the indicators measuring *CUSL* and *LIKE*. Overall, cross-loadings as well as the Fornell-Larcker criterion provide evidence for the constructs' discriminant validity.

However, note that while frequently used in applied research, neither the Fornell-Larcker criterion nor the cross-loadings allow for reliably detecting discriminant validity issues. Therefore, an alternative, more reliable criterion, HTMT, should be applied. The **Discriminant Validity** section of the results report includes the **Heterotrait-Monotrait Ratio (HTMT)**. Exhibit 4.18 shows the HTMT values for all pairs of constructs in a matrix format. The next tab also shows these HTMT values in bar charts, using 0.85 as the relevant threshold level. As can be seen, all HTMT values are

Exhibit 4.17	Cross-Loadings

Discriminant Validity

🗒 Fornell–Larcker Criterium	🗒 Cross Loadings	🗒 Heterotrait–Monotrait Ratio (HTMT)

	COMP	CUSA	CUSL	LIKE
comp_1	0.858	0.464	0.465	0.607
comp_2	0.798	0.286	0.304	0.460
comp_3	0.818	0.272	0.296	0.497
cusa	0.436	1.000	0.689	0.528
cusl_1	0.430	0.536	0.833	0.557
cusl_2	0.396	0.655	0.917	0.573
cusl_3	0.341	0.593	0.843	0.461
like_1	0.602	0.510	0.561	0.879
like_2	0.523	0.434	0.530	0.870
like_3	0.544	0.420	0.499	0.843

Exhibit 4.18 HTMT

Discriminant Validity

Fornell-Larcker Criterion	Cross Loadings	Heterotrait-Monotrait Ratio (HTMT)	Heterotrait-Monotrait Ratio (HTMT)
	COMP	CUSA	CUSL	LIKE

	COMP	CUSA	CUSL	LIKE
COMP				
CUSA	0.465			
CUSL	0.532	0.755		
LIKE	0.780	0.577	0.737	

clearly lower than the more conservative threshold value of 0.85, even for *CUSA* and *CUSL*, which, from a conceptual viewpoint, are very similar. Recall that the threshold value for conceptually similar constructs is 0.90.

In addition to examining the HTMT ratios, you should test whether the HTMT values are significantly different from 1. This requires computing bootstrap confidence intervals obtained by running the bootstrapping option. To run the bootstrapping procedure, go back to the modeling window and left-click on **Calculate** → **Bootstrapping** in the pull-down menu. In the dialog box that opens, choose the bootstrapping options as displayed in Exhibit 4.19 (Chapter 5 includes a more detailed introduction to the bootstrapping procedure and the parameter settings). Make sure to select the **Complete Bootstrapping** option, which, unlike the **Basic Bootstrapping** option, includes the results for HTMT. Finally, click on **Start Calculation**.

After running bootstrapping, open the results report. Go to **Quality Criteria** → **Heterotrait-Monotrait (HTMT)** and left-click on the tab **Confidence Intervals Bias Corrected**. The menu that opens up (Exhibit 4.20) shows the original HTMT values (column **Original Sample (O)**) for each combination of constructs in the model, along with the average HTMT values computed from the 5,000 bootstrap samples (column **Sample Mean (M)**). Note that the results in Exhibit 4.20 will differ from your results and will change when rerunning the bootstrapping procedure. The reason is that bootstrapping builds on randomly drawn bootstrap samples, which will differ every time the procedure is run. The differences in the overall bootstrapping results are marginal, however, provided that a sufficiently large number of bootstrap samples have been drawn (e.g., 5,000). The columns labeled **2.5%** and **97.5%** show the lower and upper bounds of the 95% (bias-corrected and accelerated) confidence interval. As can be seen, neither of the confidence

Exhibit 4.19 Bootstrapping Options in SmartPLS

Bootstrapping

Bootstrapping is a nonparametric procedure that can be applied to test whether coefficients such as outer weights, outer loadings and path coefficients are significant by estimating standard errors for the estimates.

Read more!

Setup ⚙ Partial Least Squares 👥 Weighting

— **Basic Settings**

Basic Settings

Subsamples

5000 ⟨⟩

Subsamples

In bootstrapping, subsamples are created with observations randomly drawn from the original set of data (with replacement). To ensure stability of results, the number of subsamples should be large.

☑ Do Parallel Processing

Sign Changes

◉ No Sign Changes
○ Construct Level Changes
○ Individual Changes

For an initial assessment, one may wish to choose a smaller number of bootstrap subsamples (e.g., 500) to be randomly drawn and estimated with the PLS-SEM algorithm, since that requires less time. For the final results preparation, however, one should use a large number of bootstrap subsamples (e.g., 5,000).

Amount of Results

○ Basic Bootstrapping
◉ Complete Bootstrapping

Note: Larger numbers of bootstrap subsamples increase the computation time.

Do Parallel Processing

— **Advanced Settings**

Confidence Interval Method

○ Percentile Bootstrap
○ Studentized Bootstrap
◉ Bias-Corrected and Accelerated (BCa) Bootstrap
○ Davision Hinkley's Double Bootstrap
○ Shi's Double Bootstrap

If chosen the bootstrapping algorithm will be performed on multiple processors (if your computer offers more than one core). As each subsample can be calculated individually, subsamples can be computed in parallel mode. Using parallel computing will reduce computation time.

Sign Changes

Test Type

○ One Tailed ◉ Two Tailed

Significance Level

0,05

Sets the method for dealing with sign changes during the bootstrapping iterations. The following options are available:

After Calculation: Open Full Report ⟨⟩

Close

Start Calculation

| Exhibit 4.20 | Confidence Intervals for HTMT |

Heterotrait-Monotrait Ratio (HTMT)

| Mean, STDEV, T-Values, P-Values | Confidence Intervals | Confidence Intervals Bias Corrected | Samples |

	Original Sample (O)	Sample Mean (M)	Bias	2.5%	97.5%
CUSA -> COMP	0.465	0.465	0.000	0.364	0.565
CUSL -> COMP	0.532	0.533	0.000	0.421	0.638
CUSL -> CUSA	0.755	0.754	-0.000	0.684	0.814
LIKE -> COMP	0.780	0.778	-0.001	0.690	0.853
LIKE -> CUSA	0.577	0.577	-0.000	0.489	0.861
LIKE -> CUSL	0.737	0.736	-0.001	0.653	0.816

intervals includes the value 1. For example, the lower and upper bounds of the confidence interval of HTMT for the relationship between *CUSA* and *COMP* are 0.364 and 0.565, respectively (again, your values will likely look slightly different because bootstrapping is a random process). As expected, since the conservative HTMT threshold of 0.85 already supports discriminant validity (Exhibit 4.18), the bootstrap confidence interval results of the HTMT criterion also clearly speak in favor of the discriminant validity of the constructs.

Exhibit 4.21 summarizes the results of the reflective measurement model assessment. As can be seen, all model evaluation criteria have been met, providing support for the measures' reliability and validity.

| Exhibit 4.21 | Results Summary for Reflective Measurement Models | | | | | |

Latent Variable	Indicators	Convergent Validity			Internal Consistency Reliability		Discriminant Validity
		Loadings	Indicator Reliability	AVE	Composite Reliability	Cronbach's Alpha	
		>0.70	>0.50	>0.50	0.60–0.90	0.60–0.90	HTMT confidence interval does not include 1
COMP	comp_1	0.858	0.736	0.681	0.865	0.776	Yes
	comp_2	0.798	0.637				
	comp_3	0.818	0.669				
CUSL	cusl_1	0.833	0.694	0.748	0.899	0.831	Yes
	cusl_2	0.917	0.841				
	cusl_3	0.843	0.711				
LIKE	like_1	0.879	0.773	0.747	0.899	0.831	Yes
	like_2	0.870	0.757				
	like_3	0.843	0.711				

SUMMARY

• **Gain an overview of Stage 5 of the process for using PLS-SEM, which deals with the evaluation of measurement models.** PLS-SEM results are reviewed and evaluated using a systematic process. The goal of PLS-SEM is maximizing the explained variance (i.e., the R^2 value) of the endogenous latent variables in the PLS path model. For this reason, the evaluation of the quality of the PLS-SEM measurement and structural models focuses on metrics indicating the model's predictive capabilities. Evaluation of PLS-SEM results is a two-step approach (Stages 5 and 6) that starts with evaluating the quality of the measurement models (Stage 5). Each type of measurement model (i.e., reflective or formative) has specific evaluation criteria. With reflective measurement models, reliability and validity must be assessed (Stage 5a). In contrast, evaluation of formative measurement models (Stage 5b) involves testing the measures' convergent validity and the significance and relevance of the indicator weights as well as collinearity. Satisfactory outcomes for the measurement model are a prerequisite for evaluating the relationships in the structural model (Stage 6), which includes testing the significance of path coefficients and the **coefficient of determination** (R^2 value). Depending on the specific model and the goal of the study, researchers may want to use additional advanced analyses such as mediation or moderation, which we discuss in Chapters 7 and 8.

• **Describe Stage 5a: Evaluating reflectively measured constructs.** The goal of reflective measurement model assessment is to ensure the reliability and validity of the construct measures and therefore provide support for the suitability of their inclusion in the path model. The key criteria include indicator reliability, composite reliability, convergent validity, and discriminant validity. Convergent validity means the construct includes more than 50% of the indicator's variance. Discriminant validity means that every reflective construct must share more variance with its own indicators than with other constructs in the path model. Reflective constructs are appropriate for PLS-SEM analyses if they meet all these requirements.

• **Use the SmartPLS 3 software to assess reflectively measured constructs in the corporate reputation example.** The case study illustration uses the corporate reputation path model and the data set introduced in Chapter 2. The SmartPLS 3 software provides all relevant results for the evaluation of the measurement models.

Tables and figures for this example demonstrate how to correctly report and interpret the PLS-SEM results. This hands-on example not only summarizes the concepts that have been introduced before but also provides additional insights for their practical application.

REVIEW QUESTIONS

1. What is indicator reliability and what is the minimum threshold value for this criterion?

2. What is composite reliability and what is the minimum threshold value for this criterion?

3. What is average variance extracted and what is the minimum threshold value for this criterion?

4. Explain the idea behind discriminant validity and how it can be established.

CRITICAL THINKING QUESTIONS

1. Why are the criteria for reflective measurement model assessment not applicable to formative measures?

2. How do you evaluate single-item constructs? Why is internal consistency reliability a meaningless criterion when evaluating single-item constructs?

3. Should researchers rely purely on statistical evaluation criteria to select a final set of indicators to include in the path model? Discuss the trade-off between statistical analyses and content validity.

KEY TERMS

AVE	Collinearity
Average variance extracted (AVE)	Communality (construct)
Bootstrap confidence interval	Communality (item)
Bootstrapping	Composite reliability
Coefficient of determination (R^2)	Content validity

Convergent validity

Cronbach's alpha

Cross-loadings

Disattenuated correlation

Discriminant validity

Evaluation criteria

Explained variance

f^2 effect size

Formative measurement
  models

Fornell-Larcker criterion

Heterotrait-heteromethod
  correlations

Heterotrait-monotrait ratio
  (HTMT)

HTMT

Indicator reliability

Internal consistency reliability

Monotrait-heteromethod
  correlations

Predictive relevance (Q^2)

q^2 effect size

Q^2 value

R^2 value

Reliability

Validity

SUGGESTED READINGS

Boudreau, M. C., Gefen, D., & Straub, D. W. (2001). Validation in information systems research: A state-of-the-art assessment. *MIS Quarterly, 25*, 1–16.

Chin, W. W. (1998). The partial least squares approach to structural equation modeling. In G. A. Marcoulides (Ed.), *Modern methods for business research* (pp. 295–358). Mahwah, NJ: Erlbaum.

Chin, W. W. (2010). How to write up and report PLS analyses. In V. Esposito Vinzi, W. W. Chin, J. Henseler, & H. Wang (Eds.), *Handbook of partial least squares: Concepts, methods and applications in marketing and related fields* (Springer Handbooks of Computational Statistics Series, Vol. II, pp. 655–690). Berlin: Springer.

Do Valle, P. O., & Assaker, G. (in press). Using partial least squares structural equation modeling in tourism research: A review of past research and recommendations for future applications. *Journal of Travel Research*.

Gefen, D., Rigdon, E. E., & Straub, D. W. (2011). Editor's comment: An update and extension to SEM guidelines for administrative and social science research. *MIS Quarterly, 35*, iii–xiv.

Götz, O., Liehr-Gobbers, K., & Krafft, M. (2010). Evaluation of structural equation models using the partial least squares (PLS) approach. In V. Esposito Vinzi, W. W. Chin, J. Henseler, & H. Wang (Eds.), *Handbook of partial least squares: Concepts, methods and applications* (Springer Handbooks of Computational Statistics Series, Vol. II, pp. 691–711). Berlin: Springer.

Hair, J. F., Ringle, C. M., & Sarstedt, M. (2011). PLS-SEM: Indeed a silver bullet. *Journal of Marketing Theory and Practice, 19*, 139–151.

Hair, J. F., Ringle, C. M., & Sarstedt, M. (2013). Partial least squares structural equation modeling: Rigorous applications, better results and higher acceptance. *Long Range Planning, 46,* 1–12.

Hair, J. F., Sarstedt, M., Ringle, C. M., & Mena, J. A. (2012). An assessment of the use of partial least squares structural equation modeling in marketing research. *Journal of the Academy of Marketing Science, 40,* 414–433.

Henseler, J., Ringle, C. M., & Sarstedt, M. (2015). A new criterion for assessing discriminant validity in variance-based structural equation modeling. *Journal of the Academy of Marketing Science, 43,* 115–135.

Henseler, J., Ringle, C. M., & Sinkovics, R. R. (2009). The use of partial least squares path modeling in international marketing. *Advances in International Marketing, 20,* 277–320.

Ringle, C. M., Sarstedt, M., & Straub, D. W. (2012). A critical look at the use of PLS-SEM in *MIS Quarterly. MIS Quarterly, 36,* iii–xiv.

Roldán, J. L., & Sánchez-Franco, M. J. (2012). Variance-based structural equation modeling: Guidelines for using partial least squares in information systems research. In M. Mora, O. Gelman, A. L. Steenkamp, & M. Raisinghani (Eds.), *Research methodologies, innovations and philosophies in software systems engineering and information systems* (pp. 193–221). Hershey, PA: IGI Global.

Straub, D., Boudreau, M. C., & Gefen, D. (2004). Validation guidelines for IS positivist research. *Communications of the Association for Information Systems, 13,* 380–427.

Tenenhaus, M., Esposito Vinzi, V., Chatelin, Y. M., & Lauro, C. (2005). PLS path modeling. *Computational Statistics & Data Analysis, 48,* 159–205.

Voorhees, C. M., Brady, M. K., Calantone, R., & Ramirez, E. (2016). Discriminant validity testing in marketing: An analysis, causes for concern, and proposed remedies. *Journal of the Academy of Marketing Science, 44,* 119-134.

C H A P T E R 5

Assessing PLS-SEM Results Part II

Evaluation of the Formative Measurement Models

LEARNING OUTCOMES

1. Explain the criteria used for the assessment of formative measurement models.

2. Understand the basic concepts of bootstrapping for significance testing in PLS-SEM and apply them.

3. Use the SmartPLS 3 software to apply the formative measurement model assessment criteria and learn how to properly report the results of the practical example on corporate reputation.

CHAPTER PREVIEW

Having learned how to evaluate reflective measurement models in the previous chapter (Stage 5a of applying PLS-SEM), our attention now turns to the assessment of formative measurement models (Stage 5b of applying PLS-SEM). The internal consistency perspective that underlies reflective measurement model evaluation cannot be applied to formative models since formative measures do not necessarily covary. Thus, any attempt to purify formative indicators based on correlation patterns can have negative consequences for a construct measure's content validity. This notion especially holds for PLS-SEM, which assumes that the formative indicators (more precisely, composite indicators) fully capture the content domain of the construct under consideration. Therefore, instead of employing measures such as composite reliability or AVE, researchers should rely on other criteria to assess the quality of formative measurement models.

The chapter begins with an introduction to the criteria needed to evaluate formative measures. This includes a discussion of the bootstrapping routine that facilitates significance testing of PLS-SEM estimates, including formative indicator weights. These criteria are then applied to the corporate reputation model that is extended for this purpose. While the simple model contains only three reflectively measured constructs as well as one single-item construct, the extended model also includes four antecedent constructs of corporate reputation that are measured using formative indicators. This chapter concludes with the evaluation of measurement models. In Chapter 6, we move to the evaluation of the structural model (Stage 6 of applying PLS-SEM).

STAGE 5B: ASSESSING RESULTS OF FORMATIVE MEASUREMENT MODELS

Many researchers incorrectly use reflective measurement model evaluation criteria to assess the quality of formative measures in PLS-SEM, as revealed by the review of PLS-SEM studies in the strategic management and marketing disciplines (Hair, Sarstedt, Pieper, et al., 2012b; Hair, Sarstedt, Ringle, & Mena, 2012). However, the statistical evaluation criteria for reflective measurement scales cannot be directly transferred to formative measurement models where indicators are likely to represent the construct's independent causes and thus do not necessarily correlate highly. Furthermore, formative indicators are assumed to be error free (Diamantopoulos, 2006; Edwards & Bagozzi, 2000), which means that the internal consistency reliability concept is not appropriate.

Assessing convergent validity and discriminant validity of formatively measured constructs using criteria similar to those associated with reflective measurement models is not meaningful (Chin, 1998). Instead, researchers should focus on establishing content validity before empirically evaluating formatively measured constructs. This step requires ensuring that the formative indicators capture all (or at least major) facets of the construct. In creating formative constructs, content validity issues are addressed by the **content specification** in which the researcher clearly specifies the domain of content the indicators are intended to measure. Researchers must include a comprehensive set of indicators that exhausts the formative construct's domain as defined by the researcher. The set of comprehensive indicators for formatively measured constructs should be identified using a rigorous qualitative approach. Failure to consider all major aspects of the construct (i.e., relevant indicators) entails an exclusion of important parts of the construct itself. In this context, experts' assessment helps safeguard that proper sets of indicators have been used. In addition to specific reasons for operationalizing the construct as formative (Chapter 2), researchers should conduct a thorough literature review and ensure a reasonable theoretical grounding when developing measures (Diamantopoulos & Winklhofer, 2001; Jarvis, MacKenzie, & Podsakoff, 2003). The evaluation of PLS-SEM results for formative measurement models may include reviewing these aspects.

In this chapter, we examine the PLS-SEM results of formative measurement models following the procedure outlined in Exhibit 5.1. The first step involves assessing the formative measurement model's convergent validity by correlating the formatively measured construct with a reflective measure of the same construct (Step 1). At the indicator level, the question arises as to whether each formative indicator indeed

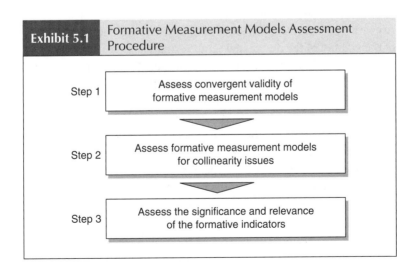

| Exhibit 5.1 | Formative Measurement Models Assessment Procedure |

Step 1	Assess convergent validity of formative measurement models
Step 2	Assess formative measurement models for collinearity issues
Step 3	Assess the significance and relevance of the formative indicators

delivers a contribution to the formative index by representing the intended meaning. There are two situations in which researchers should critically examine whether a particular indicator should be included in the index: First, an indicator's information could be redundant if it exhibits high correlations with other indicators of the same construct. This requires examining collinearity among the indicators (Step 2). Second, a formative indicator may not significantly contribute to the construct both relatively and absolutely. The latter aspects can be assessed by examining the (statistical) significance and relevance of the formative indicators (Step 3). Depending on the outcomes of Steps 2 and 3, you may need to revisit the previous steps, starting with establishing convergent validity of the revised set of formative indicators.

Step 1: Assess Convergent Validity

Convergent validity is the extent to which a measure correlates positively with other (e.g., reflective) measures of the same construct using different indicators. Hence, when evaluating formative measurement models, we have to test whether the formatively measured construct is highly correlated with a reflective measure of the same construct. This type of analysis is also known as **redundancy analysis** (Chin, 1998). The term redundancy analysis stems from the information in the model being redundant in the sense that it is included in the formative construct and again in the reflective one. Specifically, one has to use the formatively measured construct as an exogenous latent variable predicting an endogenous latent variable operationalized through one or more reflective indicators (Exhibit 5.2). The strength of the path coefficient linking the two constructs is indicative of the validity of the designated set of formative indicators in tapping the construct of interest. Ideally, a magnitude of 0.80, but at a minimum 0.70 and above, is desired for the path between $Y_1^{formative}$ and $Y_1^{reflective}$, which translates into an R^2 value of 0.64—or at least 0.50. If the analysis exhibits lack of convergent validity (i.e., the R^2 value of $Y_1^{reflective} < 0.50$), then the formative indicators of the construct $Y_1^{formative}$ do not contribute at a sufficient degree to its intended content. The formative construct needs to be theoretically/conceptually refined by exchanging and/or adding indicators. Note that to execute this approach, the reflective latent variable must be specified in the research design phase and included in data collection for the research.

To identify suitable reflective measures of the construct, researchers can draw on scales from prior research, many of which are

Exhibit 5.2	Redundancy Analysis for Convergent Validity Assessment

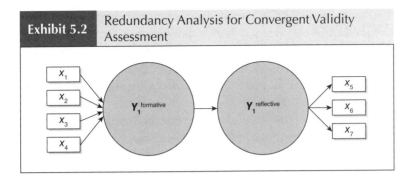

reviewed in scale handbooks (e.g., Bearden et al., 2011; Bruner et al., 2001). Including sets of reflective multi-item measures is not always desirable, however, since they increase the survey length. Long surveys are likely to result in respondent fatigue, decreased response rates, and an increased number of missing values. Furthermore, established reflective measurement instruments may not be available, and constructing a new scale is difficult and time-consuming.

An alternative is to use a global item that summarizes the essence of the construct the formative indicators purport to measure (Sarstedt et al., 2013). For the PLS-SEM example on corporate reputation in Chapter 3, an additional statement, "Please assess the extent to which [the company] acts in socially conscious ways," was developed and measured on a scale of 0 (*not at all*) to 10 (*definitely*). This question can be used as an endogenous single-item construct to validate the formative measurement of corporate social responsibility (*CSOR*). Later in this chapter, we explain how to access the full data set for this PLS-SEM example on corporate reputation and how to conduct this procedure. Note that while the use of single items is generally not recommended, especially in the context of PLS-SEM (Chapter 2), their role in redundancy analyses is different because single items only serve as a proxy for the constructs under consideration. In other words, the aim is not to fully capture the content domain of the construct but only to consider its salient elements, which serves as standard of comparison for the formative measurement approach of the construct.

Step 2: Assess Formative Measurement Models for Collinearity Issues

Unlike reflective indicators, which are essentially interchangeable, high correlations are not expected between items in formative measurement models. In fact, high correlations between two formative indicators, also referred to as collinearity, can prove problematic from a methodological and interpretational standpoint. Note that when more than two indicators are involved, this situation is called **multicollinearity**. To simplify our comments, we only refer to collinearity in the following discussion.

The most severe form of collinearity occurs if two (or more) formative indicators are entered in the same block of indicators with exactly the same information in them (i.e., they are perfectly correlated). This situation may occur because the same indicator is entered twice or because one indicator is a linear combination of another indicator (e.g., one indicator is a multiple of another indicator such as *sales in units* and *sales in thousand units*). Under these circumstances, PLS-SEM cannot estimate one of the two coefficients (technically, a singular matrix occurs during the model estimation; Chapter 3). Collinearity problems may also appear in the structural model (Chapter 6) if, for example, redundant indicators are used as single items to measure two (or more) constructs. If this occurs, researchers need to eliminate the redundant indicators. While perfect collinearity occurs rather seldom, high levels of collinearity are much more common.

High levels of collinearity between formative indicators are a crucial issue because they have an impact on the estimation of weights and their statistical significance. More specifically, in practice, high levels of collinearity often affect the results of analyses in two respects. First, collinearity boosts the standard errors and thus reduces the ability to demonstrate that the estimated weights are significantly different from zero. This issue is especially problematic in PLS-SEM analyses based on smaller sample sizes where standard errors are generally larger due to sampling error. Second, high collinearity can result in the weights being incorrectly estimated, as well as in their signs being reversed. The following example (Exhibit 5.3) illustrates sign reversal due to high correlations between two formative indicators.

On examining the correlation matrix in Exhibit 5.3 (right side), note that indicators x_1 and x_2 are both positively correlated with construct Y_1 (0.38 and 0.14, respectively) but have a higher intercorrelation (0.68). Although both bivariate correlations of the indicators are positive with the construct Y_1 in this situation, and the two indicators are positively intercorrelated, when the final parameter estimates are computed in the last stage of the algorithm (Chapter 3), the outer weight of x_1 is positive (0.53), whereas the outer weight of x_2 is negative (−0.17) as in Exhibit 5.3 (left side). This demonstrates a situation where high collinearity unexpectedly reverses the signs of the weaker

Exhibit 5.3	Correlation Matrix Demonstrating Collinearity

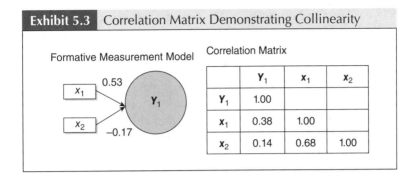

Formative Measurement Model   Correlation Matrix

	Y_1	x_1	x_2
Y_1	1.00		
x_1	0.38	1.00	
x_2	0.14	0.68	1.00

indicator (i.e., the indicator less correlated with the construct) which can entail a false interpretation of results and misleading conclusions.

How to Assess Collinearity and Deal With Critical Levels

To assess the level of collinearity, researchers should compute the **tolerance (TOL)**. The tolerance represents the amount of variance of one formative indicator not explained by the other indicators in the same block. For example, in a block of formative indicators, the tolerance for the first indicator x_1 can be obtained in two steps:

1. Take the first formative indicator x_1 and regress it on all remaining indicators in the same block. Calculate the proportion of variance of x_1 associated with the other indicators ($R_{x_1}^2$).
2. Compute the tolerance for indicator x_1 (TOL_{xs}) using $1 - R_{x_1}^2$. For example, if the other indicators explain 75% of the first indicator's variance (i.e., $R_{x_1}^2 = 0.75$), the tolerance for x_1 is 0.25 ($TOL_{xs} = 1.00 - 0.75 = 0.25$).

A related measure of collinearity is the **variance inflation factor (VIF)**, defined as the reciprocal of the tolerance (i.e., $VIF_{xs} = 1/TOL_{xs}$). Therefore, a tolerance value of 0.25 for x_1 (TOL_{xs}) translates into a VIF value of $1/0.25 = 4.00$ for x_1 (VIF_{xs}). The term VIF is derived from its square root ($\sqrt{VIF}$) being the degree to which the standard error has been increased due to the presence of collinearity. In the example above, a VIF value of 4.00 therefore implies that the standard error has been doubled ($\sqrt{4} = 2.00$) due to collinearity. Similarly, the TOL and VIF values are computed for every indicator per formative measurement model. Both collinearity statistics carry the same information, but the reporting of VIF values has become standard practice.

In the context of PLS-SEM, a tolerance value of 0.20 or lower and a VIF value of 5 and higher respectively indicate a potential collinearity problem (Hair et al., 2011). More specifically, an indicator's

VIF level of 5 indicates that 80% of its variance is accounted for by the remaining formative indicators associated with the same construct. Besides the VIF, researchers may also consider using the condition index (CI) to assess the presence of critical collinearity levels in formative measurement models (Götz, Liehr-Gobbers, & Krafft, 2010). However, the CI is more difficult to interpret and not yet included in any PLS-SEM software. Another alternative approach to evaluating collinearity is a bivariate correlation. While not common, in practice, bivariate correlations higher than 0.60 have resulted in collinearity issues with formative indicators in PLS path models.

If the level of collinearity is very high, as indicated by a VIF value of 5 or higher, one should consider removing one of the corresponding indicators. However, this requires that the remaining indicators still sufficiently capture the construct's content from a theoretical perspective. Combining the collinear indicators into a single (new) composite indicator (i.e., an index)—for example, by using their average values, their weighted average value, or their factor scores—is another option for treating collinearity problems. However, the latter step is not without problems because the individual effects of the indicators become confounded, which can have adverse consequences for the content validity of the index. Alternatively, setting up formative-formative higher-order constructs (Becker et al., 2012; Kuppelwieser & Sarstedt, 2014; Ringle et al., 2012) is a solution to address the collinearity problem, if measurement theory supports such a step (Chapter 8).

Exhibit 5.4 displays the process to assess collinearity in formative measurement models based on the VIF. Outer weights in formative measurement models should be analyzed for their significance and relevance only if collinearity is not at a critical level. When this is not the case and collinearity issues cannot be treated, one cannot use and interpret the results of the outer weights in formative measurement models. As a consequence, the results of the formative measurement must not be interpreted. Even though it is still possible to analyze the relationships of such a constructs with other constructs in the structural model (Chapter 6). However, in such a situation, the researcher may want to reconsider or dismiss the operationalization of the formative measurement model.

Step 3: Assess the Significance and Relevance of the Formative Indicators

Another important criterion for evaluating the contribution of a formative indicator, and thereby its relevance, is its outer weight. The

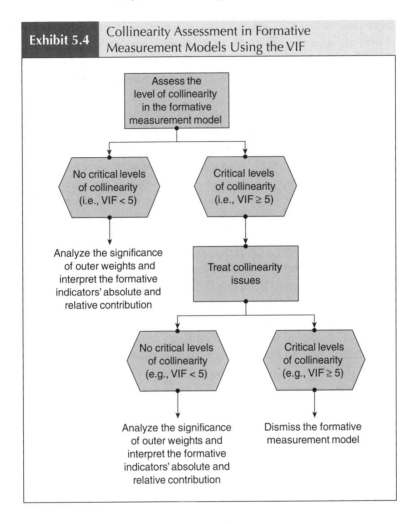

| Exhibit 5.4 | Collinearity Assessment in Formative Measurement Models Using the VIF |

outer weight is the result of a multiple regression (Hair et al., 2010) with the latent variable scores as the dependent variable and the formative indicators as the independent variables (see the PLS-SEM algorithm in Chapter 3). Since the construct itself is formed by its underlying formative indicators as a linear combination of the indicator scores and the outer weights, running such a multiple regression analysis yields an R^2 value of 1.0. That is, 100% of the construct is explained by the indicators. This characteristic distinguishes formative (i.e., composite) indicators from causal indicators commonly used in CB-SEM. In the latter case, the construct measured is not automatically explained in full by its (causal) indicators (Chapter 2). The values of the outer weights are standardized and can therefore be compared with each other. They express each indicator's **relative contribution** to the construct, or its relative importance to forming the construct. The estimated values of outer weights in formative measurement models are frequently smaller than the outer loadings of reflective indicators.

The key question that arises is whether formative indicators truly contribute to forming the construct. To answer this question, we must test if the outer weights in formative measurement models are significantly different from zero by means of the bootstrapping procedure. Note that bootstrapping also plays a crucial role in other elements of the PLS path model analysis, particularly in the evaluation of the structural model path coefficients (Chapter 6). We explain bootstrapping in more detail later in this chapter.

It is important to note that the values of the formative indicator weights are influenced by other relationships in the model (see the PLS-SEM algorithm in Chapter 3). Hence, the exogenous formative construct(s) can have different contents and meanings depending on the endogenous constructs used as outcomes. This is also known as **interpretational confounding** and represents a situation in which the empirically observed meaning between the construct and its measures differs from the theoretically imposed meaning (Kim, Shin, & Grover, 2010). Such outcomes are not desirable since they limit the generalizability of the results (Bagozzi, 2007). Therefore, comparing formatively measured constructs across several PLS path models with different setups (e.g., different endogenous latent variables) should be approached with caution.

Implications of the Numbers of Indicators Used on the Indicator Weights

With larger numbers of formative indicators used to measure a single construct, it becomes more likely that one or more indicators will have low or even nonsignificant outer weights. Unlike reflective measurement models, where the number of indicators has little bearing on the measurement results, formative measurement has an inherent limit to the number of indicators that can retain a statistically significant weight (Cenfetelli & Bassellier, 2009). Specifically, when indicators are assumed to be uncorrelated, the maximum possible outer weight is $1/\sqrt{n}$, where n is the number of indicators. For example, with 2 (or 5 or 10) uncorrelated indicators, the maximum possible outer weight is $1/\sqrt{2} = 0.707$ (or $1/\sqrt{5} = 0.447$ or $1\sqrt{10} = 0.316$). Similarly, just as the maximum possible outer weight declines with the number of indicators, the average value of outer weights significantly declines with larger numbers of items. Thus, it becomes more likely that additional formative indicators will become nonsignificant.

To deal with the potential impact of a large number of indicators, Cenfetelli and Bassellier (2009) propose grouping indicators into two or more distinct constructs. This approach, of course, requires the indicator groups to be conceptually aligned and that the grouping makes sense from theoretical and conceptual perspectives. For example, the indicators of the *performance* construct, which we introduce as a driver construct of corporate reputation later in this chapter (see Exhibit 5.13), could be grouped into two sets, as shown in Exhibit 5.5. The indicator items "[the company] is a very well-managed company" (*perf_1*) and "[the company] has a clear vision about the future" (*perf_5*) could be used as formative indicators of a separate construct called *management competence*. Similarly, the indicators "[the company] is an economically stable company" (*perf_2*), "I assess the business risk for [the company] as modest compared to its competitors" (*perf_3*), and "I think that [the company] has growth potential" (*perf_4*) could be used as formative indicators of a second construct labeled *economic performance*. An alternative is to create a formative-formative hierarchical component model (Becker et al., 2012; Kuppelwieser & Sarstedt, 2014; Ringle et al., 2012). The higher-order component itself (*performance*) is then formed by the formatively measured lower-order components *management competence* and *economic performance* (Exhibit 5.5).

Dealing With Nonsignificant Indicator Weights

Nonsignificant indicator weights should not automatically be interpreted as indicative of poor measurement model quality. Rather, researchers should also consider a formative indicator's **absolute contribution** to (or **absolute importance** for) its construct—that is, the information an indicator provides without considering any other indicators. The absolute contribution is given by the formative indicator's outer loading, which is always provided along with the indicator weights. Different from the outer weights, the outer loadings stem from simple regressions of each indicator on its corresponding construct (which in PLS-SEM is equivalent to the bivariate correlation between each indicator and the construct).

Exhibit 5.5   Example of a Higher-Order Construct

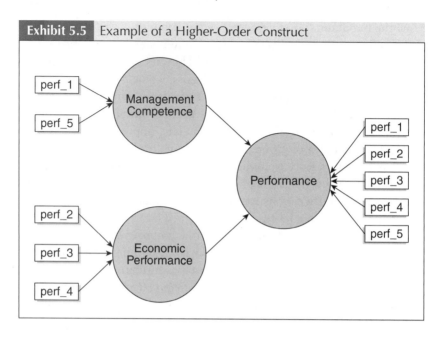

When an indicator's outer weight is nonsignificant but its outer loading is high (i.e., above 0.50), the indicator should be interpreted as absolutely important but not as relatively important. In this situation, the indicator would generally be retained. But when an indicator has a nonsignificant weight and the outer loading is below 0.50, researchers should decide whether to retain or delete the indicator by examining its theoretical relevance and potential content overlap with other indicators of the same construct.

If the theory-driven conceptualization of the construct strongly supports retaining the indicator (e.g., by means of expert assessment), it should be kept in the formative measurement model. But if the conceptualization does not strongly support an indicator's inclusion, the nonsignificant indicator should most likely be removed from further analysis. In contrast, if the outer loading is low (e.g., say below 0.10) and nonsignificant, there is no empirical support for the indicator's relevance in providing content to the formative index (Cenfetelli & Bassellier, 2009). Therefore, such an indicator should be removed from the formative measurement model.

Eliminating formative indicators that do not meet threshold levels in terms of their contribution has, from an empirical perspective, almost no effect on the parameter estimates when reestimating the model. Nevertheless, formative indicators should never be discarded simply on the basis of statistical outcomes. Before removing an indicator from the formative measurement model, researchers need to check its relevance from a content validity point of view. Again, omitting a formative indicator results in the omission of some of the construct's content. Exhibit 5.6 summarizes the decision-making process for keeping or deleting formative indicators.

In summary, the evaluation of formative measurement models requires establishing the measures' convergent validity, assessing the indicators' collinearity, and analyzing the indicators' relative and absolute contributions, including their significance. Exhibit 5.7 summarizes the rules of thumb for evaluating formative measurement models.

Bootstrapping Procedure

Concept

PLS-SEM does not assume the data are normally distributed. Lack of normality means that parametric significance tests used in regression analyses cannot be applied to test whether coefficients such as outer weights, outer loadings, and path coefficients are significant. Instead, PLS-SEM relies on a nonparametric bootstrap procedure (Davison & Hinkley, 1997; Efron & Tibshirani, 1986) to test coefficients for their significance.

In bootstrapping, a large number of samples (i.e., **bootstrap samples**) are drawn from the original sample with replacement. Replacement means that each time an observation is drawn at random from the sampling population, it is returned to the sampling population before the next observation is drawn (i.e., the population from which the observations are drawn always contains all the same elements). Therefore, an observation for any bootstrap sample can be selected more than once or may not be selected at all for the sample. Each bootstrap sample has the same number of observations (often termed **bootstrap cases**) as the original sample. For example, if the original sample has 130 valid (!) observations (e.g., after applying casewise deletion to treat missing values; see Chapter 2), then each bootstrap sample contains 130 observations. The number of bootstrap samples should be high but must be at least equal to the number of valid observations in the data set. As a rule, 5,000 bootstrap samples are recommended. Exhibit 5.8 illustrates how the bootstrap technique works.

Exhibit 5.6	Decision-Making Process for Keeping or Deleting Formative Indicators

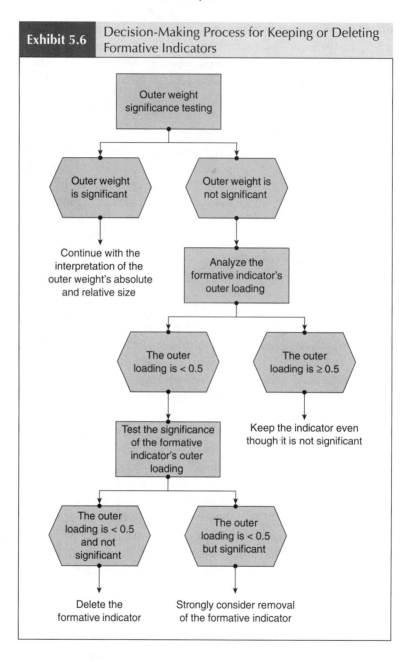

The bootstrap samples are used to estimate the PLS path model. That is, when using 5,000 bootstrap samples, 5,000 PLS path models are estimated. The estimates of the coefficients form a bootstrap distribution, which can be viewed as an approximation of the sampling

Exhibit 5.7	Rules of Thumb for the Evaluation of Formative Measurement Indicators

- Assess the formative construct's convergent validity by examining its correlation with an alternative measure of the construct, using reflective measures or a global single item (redundancy analysis). The correlation between the constructs should be 0.70 or higher.
- Collinearity of indicators: Each indicator's VIF value should be lower than 5. Otherwise, consider eliminating indicators, merging indicators into a single index, or creating higher-order constructs to treat collinearity problems.
- Examine each indicator's outer weight (relative importance) and outer loading (absolute importance) and use bootstrapping to assess their significance.
- When an indicator's weight is significant, there is empirical support to retain the indicator.
- When an indicator's weight is not significant but the corresponding item loading is relatively high (i.e., ≥0.50), or statistically significant, the indicator should generally be retained.
- If the outer weight is non-significant and the outer loading relatively low (i.e., <0.5), you should strongly consider to remove the formative indicator from the model.

distribution. Based on this distribution, it is possible to determine the standard error and the standard deviation of the estimated coefficients. We refer to the estimated bootstrap standard error by using se^*, whereby the asterisk denotes that the estimated standard error has been obtained by using the bootstrap method. The bootstrap distribution can be viewed as a reasonable approximation of an estimated coefficient's distribution in the population, and its standard deviation can be used as a proxy for the parameter's standard error in the population.

For example, the bootstrap method allows for the statistical testing of the hypothesis that a specific outer weight w_1 is in fact zero in the population. Using the standard error derived from the bootstrap distribution, a Student's t test can be calculated to test whether w_1 is significantly different from zero (i.e., $H_0: w_1 = 0$ and $H_1: w_1 \neq 0$) using the following formula:

$$t = \frac{w_1}{se^*_{w_1}},$$

Exhibit 5.8 Bootstrapping

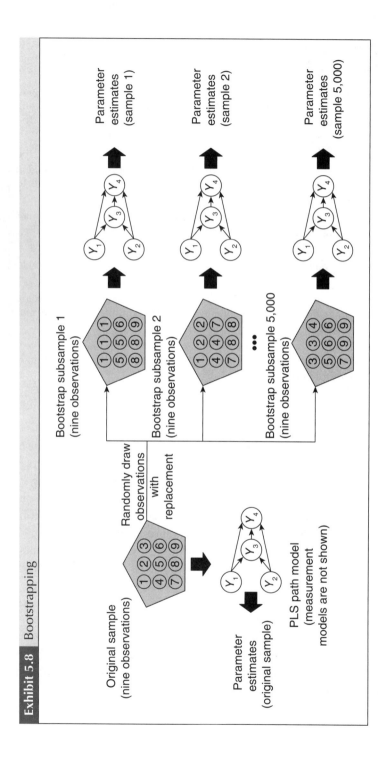

where w_1 is the weight obtained from the original model estimation using the original set of empirical data, and $se_{w_1}^*$ is the bootstrap standard error of w_1.

As indicated by its name, the test statistic follows a t distribution with **degrees of freedom** *(df)* (which is the number of values in the final calculation of the test statistic that are free to vary) equal to the number of observations minus the number of indicators in the formative measurement model minus 1. As a general rule, the t distribution is well approximated by the normal (Gaussian) distribution for more than 30 observations. As the number of observations usually exceeds this threshold, the normal (Gaussian) quantiles can be used to determine **critical t values** (or **theoretical t values**) for significance testing. Therefore, when the size of the resulting **empirical t value** is above 1.96, we can assume that the path coefficient is significantly different from zero at a significance level of 5% ($\alpha = 0.05$; two-tailed test). The critical t values for significance levels of 1% ($\alpha = 0.01$; two-tailed test) and 10% ($\alpha = 0.10$; two-tailed test) probability of error are 2.57 and 1.65, respectively.

PLS-SEM software programs such as SmartPLS 3 also report **p values** (i.e., probability values) that equal the probability of obtaining an empirical t value at least as extreme as the one that is actually observed, conditional on the null hypothesis being supported. With regard to the example above, the p value is the answer to the following question: If w_1 is in fact zero (i.e., in reality H_0 holds), what is the probability that random sampling using bootstrapping would yield a t value of at least 1.96 (in case of a 5% significance level, two-tailed)? In other words, the p value is the probability of erroneously rejecting a true null hypothesis (i.e., assuming a significant effect when there is no significance). In most settings, researchers choose a significance level of 5%, which implies that the p value must be smaller than 0.05 in order to render the relationship under consideration significant. When researchers are very conservative or strict in their testing of relationships (e.g., when conducting experiments), the significance level is set to 1%. In studies that are exploratory, however, a significance level of 10% is commonly used.

An important consideration in the use of bootstrapping in PLS-SEM is that the signs of the latent variable scores are indeterminate (Wold, 1985). This **sign indeterminacy** of latent variable scores may, however, result in arbitrary sign changes in the bootstrap estimates of the coefficients, compared with the estimates obtained from the original sample. Such occurrence of sign changes "pulls" the mean value of bootstrap results (e.g., for an outer weight w_1) toward zero and inflates the corresponding bootstrap standard error ($se^*_{w_1}$) upward, thereby decreasing the t value.

Three options for dealing with sign changes have been proposed: the **no sign change option**, the **individual-level sign change option**, and the **construct-level sign change option**. No sign change simply means to not do anything and to accept the negative impact of sign changes on the results for the empirical t value. The individual-level sign change option reverses sign if an estimate for a bootstrap sample results in a different sign compared with that resulting from the original sample. Thus, the signs in the measurement and structural models of each bootstrap sample are made consistent with the signs in the original sample to avoid sign change–related problems. A third option, the construct-level sign change, considers a group of coefficients (e.g., all outer weights) simultaneously and compares the signs of the original PLS path model estimation with those of a bootstrapping sample. If the majority of signs need to be reversed in a bootstrap run to match the signs of the model estimation using the original sample, all signs are reversed in that bootstrap run. Otherwise, no signs are changed. As such, the construct-level sign change is a compromise between the two extremes of no sign changes and individual-level sign changes: Some signs are changed for improvement, but the results do not 100% match the signs of the original model estimation.

The individual-level and construct-level sign change options have been introduced in connection with the Lohmöller scheme for initializing the outer weights when initializing the PLS-SEM algorithm (i.e., all initial weights are set to +1 except the last one, which is set to –1; see Chapter 3). The Lohmöller initialization leads to faster convergence of the PLS-SEM algoirithm but is well known to entail unexpected sign changes. In practice, the results of the three different options usually do not differ much, provided that the original estimates are not close to zero. However, if the original estimates are close to zero, the sign reversal may systematically reduce the bootstrapping standard error. We strongly recommend using the no sign change option because it results in the most conservative outcome. Conservative means that if coefficients are significant under the no sign change option, they will also be significant when using the alternative options.

Bootstrap Confidence Intervals

Instead of just reporting the significance of a parameter, it is valuable to also report the bootstrap confidence interval that provides additional information on the stability of a coefficient estimate. The confidence interval is the range within which the true population parameter will fall assuming a certain level of confidence (e.g., 95%). In a PLS-SEM context, we also talk about bootstrap confidence intervals because the construction of the interval is based on the standard errors obtained from the bootstrapping procedure (Henseler et al., 2009). A null hypothesis H_0 that a certain parameter such as an outer weight w_1 equals zero (i.e., H_0: $w_1 = 0$) in the population is rejected at a given level α, if the corresponding $(1 - \alpha)\%$ bootstrap confidence interval does *not* include zero. In other words, if a confidence interval for an estimated coefficient such as an outer weight w_1 does not include zero, the hypothesis that w_1 equals zero is rejected, and we assume a significant effect. In addition to the significance testing aspect, the range of the confidence interval provides the researcher with an indication of how stable the estimate is. If the confidence interval of a coefficient is wider, then its stability is lower. The confidence interval offers a range of plausible population values for a certain parameter dependent on the variation in the data and the sample size.

There are several approaches for constructing bootstrap confidence intervals (Davison & Hinkley, 1997; Efron & Tibshirani, 1986). The logical approach is to order all estimates of a certain parameter (e.g., an outer weight w_1) as obtained from the bootstrapping samples and compute an interval that excludes the 2.5% lowest and 2.5% highest values. For example, suppose that we draw 5,000 bootstrap samples and thus obtain 5,000 estimates for the indicator weight w_1. After ordering these values from smallest to largest, let us denote these values as $w^*_{(1)}, w^*_{(2)}, ..., w^*_{(5,000)}$. Here, the asterisk denotes that the estimated weight has been obtained by using the bootstrap method. The number in brackets in subscript indicates the bootstrap sample. The lower bound of the 95% bootstrap confidence interval would be the bootstrap estimate of w_1 that separates the lowest 2.5% from the highest 97.5% of the bootstrap values (i.e., $w^*_{(125)}$). Similarly, the upper bound would be the value separating the 97.5% lowest from the 2.5% highest bootstrap values (i.e., $w^*_{(4,875)}$). Exhibit 5.9 illustrates this approach, known as the **percentile method,** by showing

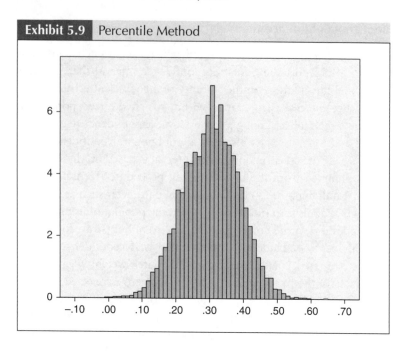

Exhibit 5.9 Percentile Method

a histogram of the distribution of the indicator weight w_1 (more precisely, *csor_1*), resulting from 5,000 bootstrap samples. The resulting confidence interval is [0.138, 0.462], which suggests that the population value of w_1 will be somewhere in between 0.138 and 0.462 with a 95% probability. As this confidence interval does not include the value zero, we would conclude that w_1 is significant.

A shortcoming of the percentile method is its assumption that the expected value of a certain parameter derived by computing its mean value across all bootstrapping samples (e.g., $\hat{w}_1$) is an unbiased estimate of the true value. However, this assumption does not necessarily hold, especially when sample sizes are small or when the distribution of the parameter is asymmetric. In these situations, the percentile method is subject to **coverage error** (e.g., a 95% confidence interval may actually be a 90% confidence interval). As a remedy, researchers have introduced bias corrections, which adjust for resulting deviations in the bootstrap distribution from the empirical distribution of the parameters. The most prominent among this set of approaches is Efron's (1987) **bias-corrected and accelerated (BCa) bootstrap confidence intervals,** which adjust for biases and skewness in the bootstrap distribution. Henseler et al. (2009) provide more details on the use of the BCa bootstrap method in PLS-SEM—see also Gudergan et al. (2008) and Sarstedt, Henseler, and Ringle (2011).

An alternative to the previously described approaches is the **studentized bootstrap method**. The studentized bootstrap confidence interval is computed similar to a confidence interval based on the t distribution, except that the standard error is derived from the bootstrapping results. For example, if an outer weight w_1 has a bootstrap standard error $(se_{w_1}^*)$, then the corresponding approximate $100 \cdot (1 - \alpha)\%$ confidence interval is

$$\left[w_1 - t_{(1-\alpha/2)} \cdot se_{w_1}^* \, ; w_1 + t_{(1-\alpha/2)} \cdot se_{w_1}^* \right],$$

where $t_{(1-\alpha/2)}$ stems from the t distribution table. If the probability of error is 5% (i.e., $\alpha = 0.05$), then $t_{(1-\alpha/2)} = t_{0.975} = 1.96$. Thus, the lower bound of the bootstrap confidence interval is $w_1 - 1.96 \cdot se_{w_1}^*$, and the upper bound is $w_1 + 1.96 \cdot se_{w_1}^*$ (i.e., $[w_1 - 1.96 \cdot se_{w_1}^* \, ; w_1 + 1.96 \cdot se_{w_1}^*]$). For example, assume that an outer weight of an indicator in a formative measurement model has the value 0.306 and a bootstrap standard error of 0.083. The lower bound of the 95% bootstrap confidence interval has a value of $0.306 - 1.96 \cdot 0.083 = 0.143$, while the upper bound has a value of $0.306 + 1.96 \cdot 0.083 = 0.469$. Thus, the 95% bootstrap confidence interval is [0.143, 0.469]. Since zero does not fall in this confidence interval, we conclude that the outer weight of 0.306 is significant at the 5% probability of error level.

Double bootstrapping offers yet another way of establishing confidence intervals. Double bootstrapping follows the same principles as regular bootstrapping in that samples (i.e., bootstrap samples) are drawn from the original sample with replacement. Different from regular bootstrapping, further subsamples are drawn from each bootstrap sample (i.e., bootstrap the bootstrap samples). That way, the method produces a larger number of samples and subsamples, which provide the basis for parameter estimation (Exhibit 5.10; for further details, see Sarstedt, Henseler, & Ringle, 2011). However, this increase in bootstrap (sub)samples comes at the expense of computational demands. For example, following general recommendations of drawing 5,000 (sub)samples would require estimating the PLS path model $5,000 \cdot 5,000 + 5,000 = 25,005,000$ times. Different types of double bootstrapping methods have been proposed, two of which have recently been implemented in SmartPLS 3. **Shi (1992)** extends the percentile method to double bootstrapping, accounting for coverage

Exhibit 5.10 Double Bootstrapping

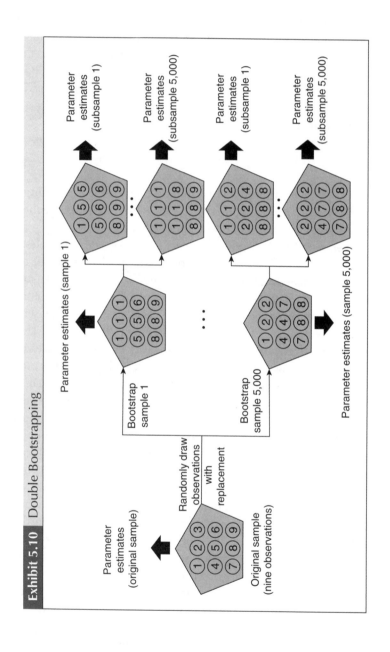

errors. **Davison and Hinkley** (1997) introduced a bias correction based on differences between parameter estimates derived from samples and corresponding subsamples.

A fundamental question remains, however: Which method should we use? Prior research indicates that while the percentile method is intuitive and easy to implement, it does not work very well with small sample sizes, especially when the distribution of the parameter is asymmetric (e.g., Chernick, 2008). Against this background, researchers routinely suggest using the BCa bootstrap method as it has reasonable computation requirements and produces comparably narrow confidence intervals. Initial research in the PLS-SEM context by Henseler et al. (2014) provides support for these results (e.g., in terms of low levels of Type I errors), but future research needs to provide a more detailed assessment of the approach's properties. Finally, confidence intervals derived from double bootstrap methods have been proven to be more accurate than those from regular bootstrapping. However, their performance has not been examined in the context of PLS-SEM. In light of the considerable computational demand, their application should be restricted to models with limited complexity (i.e., four constructs or less) when sample size is small (i.e., fewer than 300; a number of 300 bootstrap samples would result in the computation 300 · 300 = 90,000 samples when applying the double bootstrap method). Instead, you should primarily rely on the BCa method. Exhibit 5.11 summarizes the rules of thumb for significance testing using the bootstrapping routine in PLS-SEM.

CASE STUDY ILLUSTRATION—EVALUATION OF FORMATIVE MEASUREMENT MODELS

Extending the Simple Path Model

The simple path model introduced in Chapter 2 describes the relationships between the two dimensions of corporate reputation (i.e., competence and likeability) as well as the two outcome variables (i.e., customer satisfaction and loyalty). While the simple model is useful to explain how corporate reputation affects customer satisfaction and customer loyalty, it does not indicate how companies can manage (i.e., improve) their corporate reputation effectively.

Exhibit 5.11	Rules of Thumb for Bootstrapping in PLS-SEM

- The number of bootstrap samples must be larger than the number of valid observations in the original data set but should be higher; generally, 5,000 bootstrap samples are recommended.
- The bootstrap routine provides the standard error of an estimated coefficient (e.g., an indicator weight), which serves as the basis for determining the empirical *t* value and its corresponding *p* value.
- Use the no sign change option to obtain the most conservative results when running the bootstrap routine.
- Bootstrap confidence intervals provide additional information on the stability of coefficient estimates. Use the BCa method for constructing confidence intervals. When models are not complex (i.e., fewer than four constructs) and sample size is small (i.e., <300), use double bootstrapping. However, the running time can be extensive.

Schwaiger (2004) identified four driver constructs of corporate reputation that companies can steer by means of corporate-level marketing activities. Specifically, the driver constructs of corporate reputation are (1) the quality of a company's products and services as well as its quality of customer orientation (*QUAL*), (2) its economic and managerial performance (*PERF*), (3) the company's corporate social responsibility (*CSOR*), and (4) its attractiveness (*ATTR*). All four driver constructs are related to the competence and likeability dimensions of corporate reputation. Exhibit 5.12 shows the constructs and their relationships, which represent the extended structural model for our PLS-SEM example in the remaining chapters of the text. To summarize, the extended corporate reputation model has three main conceptual/theoretical components: (1) the target constructs of interest (namely, *CUSA* and *CUSL*); (2) the two corporate reputation dimensions, *COMP* and *LIKE*, that represent key determinants of the target constructs; and (3) the four exogenous driver constructs (i.e., *ATTR*, *CSOR*, *PERF*, and *QUAL*) of the two corporate reputation dimensions.

The endogenous latent variables on the right-hand side in Exhibit 5.12 include a single-item construct (i.e., *CUSA*) and three reflective constructs (i.e., *COMP*, *CUSL*, and *LIKE*). In contrast, the four new driver constructs (i.e., exogenous latent variables) on the left-hand side of the exhibit (i.e., *ATTR*, *CSOR*, *PERF*, and

QUAL) have formative measurement models in accordance with their role in the reputation model (Schwaiger, 2004). Specifically, the four new constructs are measured by a total of 21 formative indicators that have been derived from literature, qualitative studies, and quantitative pretests (for more details, see Schwaiger, 2004). Exhibit 5.13 shows a complete list of the formative indicators and the corresponding survey questions.

Again, we use a data set with 344 observations for our empirical PLS-SEM analyses. Unlike in the simple model that we used in the prior chapters, we now also have to consider the formative measurement models when deciding on the minimum sample size required to estimate the model. The maximum number of arrowheads pointing at a particular construct occurs in the measurement model of *QUAL*. All other formatively measured constructs have fewer indicators. Similarly, there are fewer arrows pointing at each of the endogenous constructs in the structural model. Therefore, when building on the 10 times rule of thumb, we would need 8 · 10 = 80 observations. Alternatively, following Cohen's (1992) recommendations for

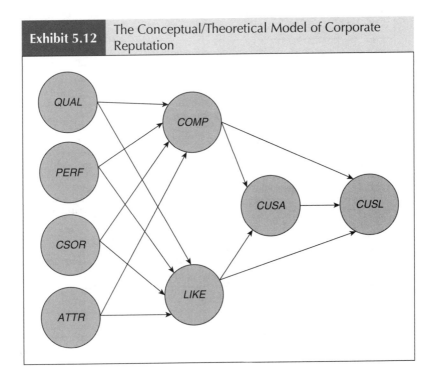

| Exhibit 5.12 | The Conceptual/Theoretical Model of Corporate Reputation |

Exhibit 5.13	Indicators of the Formative Measurement Models

Quality (QUAL)	
qual_1	The products/services offered by [the company] are of high quality.
qual_2	[The company] is an innovator, rather than an imitator with respect to [industry].
qual_3	[The company]'s products/services offer good value for money.
qual_4	The services [the company] offered are good.
qual_5	Customer concerns are held in high regard at [the company].
qual_6	[The company] is a reliable partner for customers.
qual_7	[The company] is a trustworthy company.
qual_8	I have a lot of respect for [the company].
Performance (PERF)	
perf_1	[The company] is a very well-managed company.
perf_2	[The company] is an economically stable company.
perf_3	The business risk for [the company] is modest compared to its competitors.
perf_4	[The company] has growth potential.
perf_5	[The company] has a clear vision about the future of the company.
Corporate Social Responsibility (CSOR)	
csor_1	[The company] behaves in a socially conscious way.
csor_2	[The company] is forthright in giving information to the public.
csor_3	[The company] has a fair attitude toward competitors.
csor_4	[The company] is concerned about the preservation of the environment.
csor_5	[The company] is not only concerned about profits.
Attractiveness (ATTR)	
attr_1	[The company] is successful in attracting high-quality employees.
attr_2	I could see myself working at [the company].
attr_3	I like the physical appearance of [the company] (company, buildings, shops, etc.).

multiple OLS regression analysis or running a power analysis using the G*Power program, one would need only 54 observations to detect R^2 values of around 0.25, assuming a significance level of 5% and a statistical power of 80% (Chapter 1).

The SmartPLS project and data files for the extended corporate reputation model can be downloaded at http://www.pls-sem.com (i.e., Corporate Reputation.zip). Click with the right mouse button on **Corporate Reputation.zip** and save the file on your hard drive. Then, run the SmartPLS software and click on **File → Import project from backup file** in the menu. In the box that appears on the screen, locate and open the **Corporate Reputation.zip** file that you just downloaded. Thereafter, a new project appears with the name **Corporate Reputation** in the SmartPLS **Project Explorer** window on the left-hand side. This project contains several models (.splsm files) labeled **Simple model, Extended model, Redundancy analysis ATTR, Redundancy analysis CSOR,** and so forth, plus the data file **Corporate reputation data.csv.** Note that you do not see the file extensions such as .splsm and .csv in the SmartPLS Project Explorer window. Next, double-click on **Extended model,** and the extended PLS path model for the corporate reputation example opens as displayed in Exhibit 5.14.

Alternatively, if you want to practice using the SmartPLS software, you can create the extended model by yourself. Following the description in Chapter 2, we use the SmartPLS software to extend the simple model. For this purpose, right-click on **Simple model** in the **Project Explorer** window and select the option **Copy** (Exhibit 5.15). Next, right-click on the Corporate Reputation project file and select **Paste** (Exhibit 5.16). A menu opens and gives you the option to select a name for the copy of the existing project; for example, type in the name **Extended Model** or something similar. By clicking on **OK,** SmartPLS will copy the simple model under a new name within the **Corporate Reputation** project. Alternatively, you can use the **Duplicate** option. While copy and paste uses the model when the SmartPLS session was started or from the last time it was saved, the duplicate option creates a copy of the model with all its changes as it is shown in the modeling window. In this case, since we did not change the simple model, both options will lead to the same results.

You can now start extending the simple PLS path model on corporate reputation. Double-click on **Extended Model** in the **Corporate Reputation** project and the existing PLS path model elements will open it in the **Modeling** window. Click on the **Modeling** window and select everything by pressing on the CTRL and A keys on your

Exhibit 5.14 Extended Model in SmartPLS

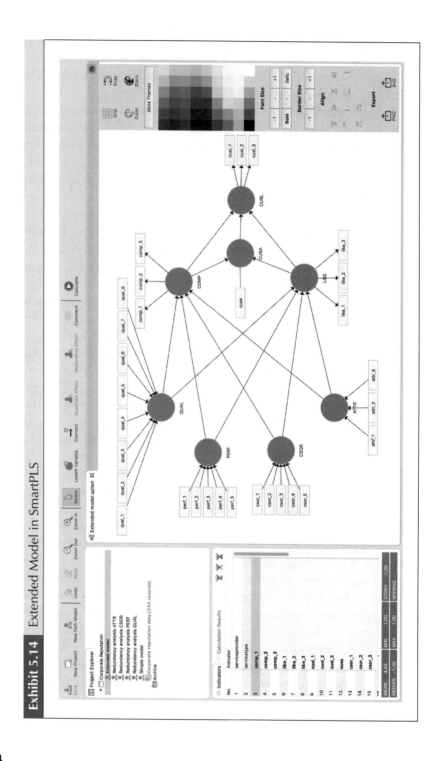

keyboard. Move all existing PLS path model elements further to the right-hand side of the **Modeling** window (simply left-click and hold down anywhere on the model, and move your mouse to the right). Note that if your simple model filled the screen, you may wish to reduce the model size by clicking on the **Zoom Out** button at the top of the **Modeling** window. Next, go to the **Edit** menu, click on **Add Latent Variable(s)**, and place four additional constructs into the **Modeling** window. Refer to Exhibit 5.14 to see where to place the new constructs. Right-click on any of the constructs, and a dialog box opens with several options (Exhibit 5.17). The **Rename** option allows you to rename each construct in accordance with the extended model setup shown in Exhibit 5.14.

Next draw the path relationships between the constructs. Go to the **Edit** menu, click on **Add Connection(s),** and connect the new constructs with the existing ones as shown in Exhibit 5.14. To draw path relationships, you need to first click on the starting constructs and then click on the target construct.

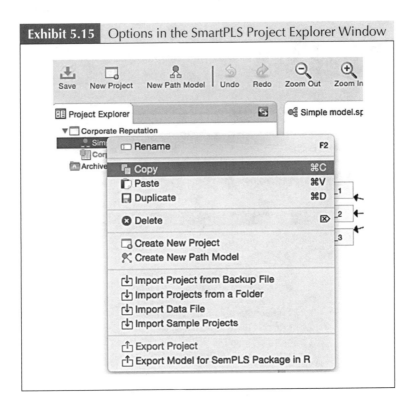

Exhibit 5.15   Options in the SmartPLS Project Explorer Window

Finally, drag and drop the corresponding indicators from the **Indicators** window to each of the constructs. Initially, the indicators will be associated with the constructs as reflective indicators. To change the measurement model setup to formative, right-click on the construct and select **Switch between formative/reflective** (Exhibit 5.17). Doing so will switch the indicators from reflective to formative. The final model in your SmartPLS **Modeling** window should look similar to the one shown in Exhibit 5.14. At this point, be sure to save your newly drawn extended model.

Once the model is set up, we click on **Calculate → PLS Algorithm** and run PLS-SEM using the options presented in Chapter 3 (i.e., path weighting scheme, 300 iterations, stop criterion: 1.0E-7) and as displayed in Exhibit 5.18. Just like the indicator data that we used in the previous chapters, the **Corporate reputation data.csv** data set has almost no missing values. Only the indicators *cusl_1* (three missing values; 0.87% of all responses on this indicator), *cusl_2* (four missing values; 1.16% of all responses on this indicator), *cusl_3* (three missing values; 0.87% of all responses on this indicator), and

Exhibit 5.16	Paste Option in the SmartPLS Project Explorer Window

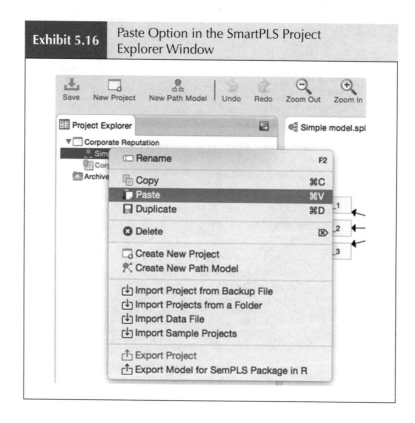

cusa (one missing value; 0.29% of all responses on this indicator) have missing values. Since the number of missing values is relatively small (i.e., less than 5% missing values per indicator; Chapter 2), we use mean value replacement instead of casewise or pairwise deletion to treat the missing values when running the PLS-SEM algorithm. Then, click on **Start Calculation.**

When the PLS-SEM algorithm stops running, check whether the algorithm converged (Chapter 3). For this example, the PLS-SEM algorithm will stop when the maximum number of **300** iterations or the stop criterion of **1.0E-7** (i.e., 0.0000001) has been reached. Go to **Interim Results → Stop Criterion Changes** in the results report to determine how the algorithm stopped. If the algorithm stopped based on the stop criterion, continue with the measurement model evaluation. If the algorithm stopped based on the number of iterations (which is, however, practically never the case; see Henseler, 2010), the calculation results cannot be reliably interpreted and the model setup and/or data need to be reconsidered. In the present example, the algorithm converged after eight iterations, so we can proceed with the analysis.

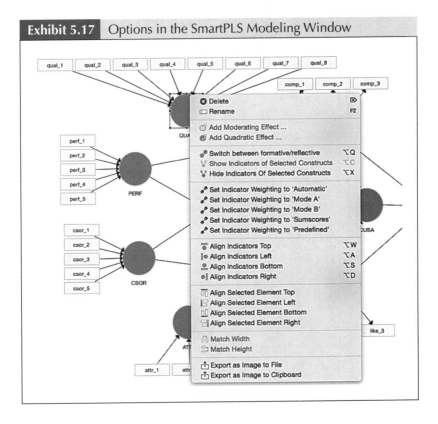

Exhibit 5.17 Options in the SmartPLS Modeling Window

Exhibit 5.18 Settings to Start the PLS-SEM Algorithm

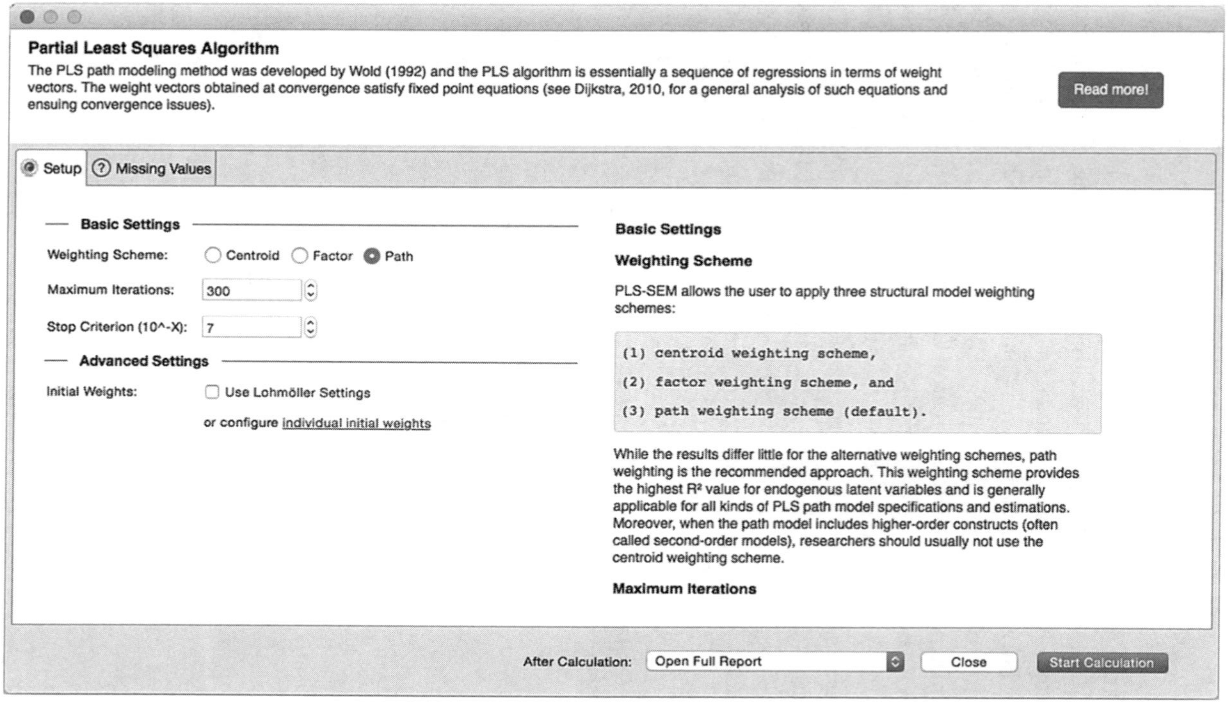

Partial Least Squares Algorithm

The PLS path modeling method was developed by Wold (1992) and the PLS algorithm is essentially a sequence of regressions in terms of weight vectors. The weight vectors obtained at convergence satisfy fixed point equations (see Dijkstra, 2010, for a general analysis of such equations and ensuing convergence issues).

Read more!

Setup ⑦ Missing Values

— **Basic Settings**

Weighting Scheme: ○ Centroid ○ Factor ● Path

Maximum Iterations: 300 ‹›

Stop Criterion (10^−X): 7 ‹›

— **Advanced Settings**

Initial Weights: ☐ Use Lohmöller Settings

or configure individual initial weights

Basic Settings

Weighting Scheme

PLS-SEM allows the user to apply three structural model weighting schemes:

(1) centroid weighting scheme,

(2) factor weighting scheme, and

(3) path weighting scheme (default).

While the results differ little for the alternative weighting schemes, path weighting is the recommended approach. This weighting scheme provides the highest R² value for endogenous latent variables and is generally applicable for all kinds of PLS path model specifications and estimations. Moreover, when the path model includes higher-order constructs (often called second-order models), researchers should usually not use the centroid weighting scheme.

Maximum Iterations

After Calculation: Open Full Report ‹› Close Start Calculation

The results presentation in the **Modeling** window gives you a first overview of the outcomes. As shown in Exhibit 5.19, you see the standardized outer weights for the formative measurement models (e.g., *QUAL*), standardized outer loadings for the reflective measurement models (e.g., *CUSL*), and a 1.000 for the relationship between the *CUSA* construct and its single-item measure. In the latter case, the outer relationship is always 1 regardless of whether the mode of the single-item construct is formative or reflective. The standardized path relationships between the constructs in the structural model are also shown, as well as the R^2 values for the endogenous latent variables (i.e., the values in the circles). Note that the exogenous constructs *ATTR, CSOR, PERF,* and *QUAL,* by definition, have no R^2 value. Clicking on the **Calculation Results** tab on the bottom left of the screen enables you to browse different parameter estimates for the constructs, as well as the inner and the outer models (see Chapter 3).

Reflective Measurement Model Evaluation

An important characteristic of PLS-SEM is that the model estimates always depend on the model under consideration. For instance, eliminating or adding certain indicators or constructs will also have an effect on the model estimates in different parts of the model. Since we extended the initial model by adding four constructs, we need to reassess the reflective measurement models according to the criteria presented in Chapter 4. However, we present the assessment in a much more concise way, which gives the reader some guidance on how to write up his or her own report in a straight-to-the-point manner—see, for example, the assessment of PLS-SEM results in applications such as Klarner, Sarstedt, Höck, and Ringle (2013), Ringle, Sarstedt, and Zimmermann (2011), and Schloderer et al. (2014).

To examine the results, go to the SmartPLS 3 results report. If this report did not open automatically after running the **PLS Algorithm**, go to the **Calculation Results** tab on the bottom left of the screen and click on **Report**. First check for the measures' convergent validity and internal consistency reliability (i.e., Cronbach's alpha and composite reliability) under **Quality Criteria → Construct Reliability and Validity**. The results reveal that all reflectively measured constructs have AVE values of 0.688 (*COMP*) or higher, which is considerably above the critical value of 0.5 (Chapter 4). In addition, all Cronbach's alpha and composite reliability values are well above the critical threshold of 0.70.

Exhibit 5.19 PLS-SEM Results

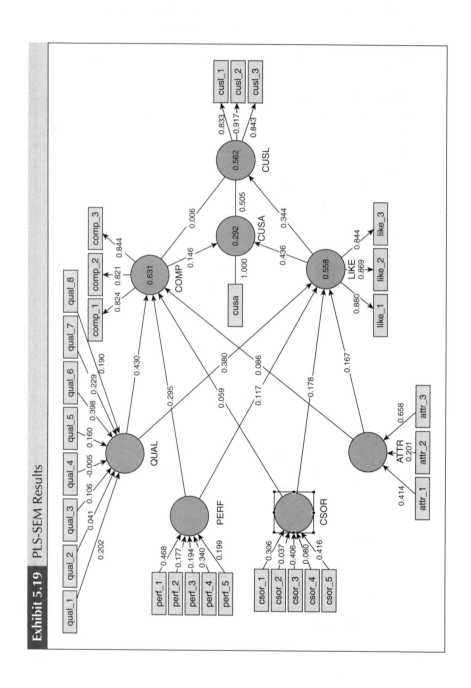

Looking at the indicator loadings (**Final Results → Outer Loadings** in the results report) reveals that all indicators of the reflective constructs *COMP, LIKE* and *CUSL* have loadings of 0.821 and higher, as shown in Exhibit 5.20. It is important to note that PLS software applications such as SmartPLS 3 always provide outer loadings and outer weights for all constructs in the PLS path model, regardless of whether they are measured reflectively or formatively. Thus, the report shown in Exhibit 5.20 displays the outer loadings for both the reflective and formative constructs. For the reflective measurement model evaluation, however, the assessment focuses only on the outer loadings of the reflective constructs (i.e., *COMP, LIKE,* and *CUSL*).

In the next step, we examine the measures' discriminant validity. Examining the cross-loadings (**Quality Criteria → Discriminant Validity → Cross Loadings** in the results report) provides initial support for the reflective constructs' discriminant validity as each reflective indicator loads highest on the construct it is linked to (Chapter 4). Reviewing the Fornell-Larcker criterion (**Quality Criteria → Discriminant Validity → Fornell-Larcker Criterion** in the results report) shown in Exhibit 5.21 also suggests that the constructs discriminate well because the square root of the AVE of each reflective construct (shown on the diagonal) is larger than the correlations with the remaining constructs in the model (Chapter 4). Note that when assessing the Fornell-Larcker criterion in a model that includes formative constructs, one needs to compare the reflective construct's AVE values (more precisely their square root) with *all* latent variable correlations (i.e., also those of formative constructs). However, the AVEs of formatively measured constructs should not be compared with the correlations. In fact, the AVEs are not even reported for formative constructs in SmartPLS (see the empty cells on the diagonal in Exhibit 5.21).

Several shortcomings of these traditional approaches to discriminant validity assessment have been identified. As a result, you should primarily consider the HTMT statistics, which you can also find under **Quality Criteria → Discriminant Validity → Heterotrait-Monotrait Ratio (HTMT)**. The assessment of cross-loadings and the Fornell-Larcker criterion can be different when additional constructs are added to a model, as when our example moved from a simple model to the extended model by adding the four formative exogenous constructs. In contrast, the HTMT results of the extended model do not change compared with those produced in the simple model. The reason is that the HTMT statistic is purely based on correlations among items of the reflectively measured constructs. Adding formative constructs

Exhibit 5.20	PLS-SEM Results for Outer Loadings

Outer Loadings

▦ Matrix

	ATTR	COMP	CSOR	CUSA	CUSL	LIKE	PERF	QUAL
attr_1	0.754							
attr_2	0.506							
attr_3	0.891							
comp_1		0.824						
comp_2		0.821						
comp_3		0.844						
csor_1			0.771					
csor_2			0.571					
csor_3			0.838					
csor_4			0.617					
csor_5			0.846					
cusa				1.000				
cusl_1					0.833			
cusl_2					0.917			
cusl_3					0.843			
like_1						0.880		
like_2						0.869		
like_3						0.844		
perf_1							0.846	
perf_2							0.690	
perf_3							0.573	
perf_4							0.717	
perf_5							0.638	
qual_1								0.741
qual_2								0.570
qual_3								0.749
qual_4								0.664
qual_5								0.787
qual_6								0.856
qual_7								0.722
qual_8								0.627

has no bearing on the computation of heterotrait-heteromethod and monotrait-heteromethod correlations. The results therefore parallel those presented in Chapter 4, which clearly showed that all reflectively measured constructs exhibit discriminant validity. Recall that an HTMT value above 0.90—or above 0.85 when the constructs in the path model are conceptually more distinct—suggests a lack of discriminant validity. Thus, all constructs in the extended model exhibit discriminant validity based on the HTMT method.

Formative Measurement Model Evaluation

To evaluate the formative measurement models of the extended corporate reputation model, we follow the formative measurement models assessment procedure (Exhibit 5.1). First, we need to examine whether the formative constructs exhibit convergent validity. To do so, we carry out separate redundancy analyses for each construct.

Exhibit 5.21	Fornell-Larcker Criterion

Discriminant Validity

▦ Fornell-Larcker Criterium	▦ Cross Loadings	▦ Heterotrait-Monotrait Ratio (HTMT)

	ATTR	COMP	CSOR	CUSA	CUSL	LIKE	PERF	QUAL
ATTR								
COMP	0.613	0.829						
CSOR	0.592	0.596						
CUSA	0.416	0.423	0.422	1.000				
CUSL	0.439	0.439	0.417	0.689	0.865			
LIKE	0.612	0.638	0.617	0.529	0.615	0.864		
PERF	0.665	0.728	0.626	0.425	0.479	0.639		
QUAL	0.689	0.763	0.700	0.489	0.532	0.712	0.788	

The original questionnaire contained global single-item measures with generic assessments of the four phenomena—*attractiveness, corporate social responsibility, performance,* and *quality*—that we can use as measures of the dependent construct in the redundancy analyses. Note that when you are designing your own research study that includes formatively measured constructs, you need to include this type of global measure in the survey to be able to conduct this type of test for your formative constructs.

To assess convergent validity, we need to create the new models, as shown in Exhibit 5.22. Each model is included in the SmartPLS project file **Corporate Reputation** that you can download and import into the SmartPLS software. Each model opens after double-clicking on it. Alternatively, you can create these four models for the convergent validity assessment in the **Corporate Reputation** project in SmartPLS 3. To do so, select **Corporate Reputation** in the **Project** window (click with the left mouse button) and then click the right mouse button. A box with several options appears (Exhibit 5.15). Select the option **Create New Path Model.** Thereafter, you can select a name for the new model (e.g., **Redundancy analysis ATTR**). After pressing on the **OK** button, the new model (e.g., **Redundancy analysis ATTR**) appears in the **Corporate Reputation** project, and an empty modeling window shows up. Now, we follow the steps explained in the earlier chapters to create one of the models displayed in Exhibit 5.22 (e.g., the first one, **Redundancy analysis ATTR**).

The first box in Exhibit 5.22 shows the results for the redundancy analysis for the *ATTR* construct. The original formative construct is labeled with *ATTR_F,* whereas the global assessment of the

Exhibit 5.22	Redundancy Analysis Assessment of Formative Measurement Models

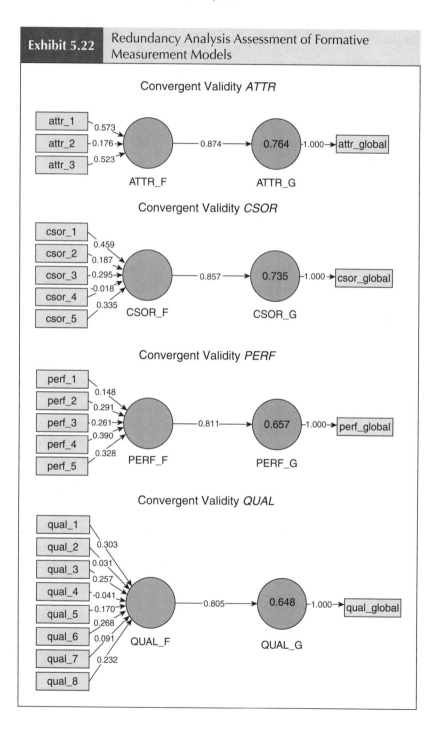

company's attractiveness using a single-item construct is labeled with *ATTR_G*. As can be seen, this analysis yields a path coefficient of 0.874, which is above the recommended threshold of 0.70, thus providing support for the formative construct's convergent validity. The redundancy analyses of *CSOR*, *PERF*, and *QUAL* yield estimates of 0.857, 0.811, and 0.805, respectively. Thus, all formatively measured constructs exhibit convergent validity.

In the next step, we check the formative measurement models for collinearity of indicators by looking at the formative indicators' VIF values. To do so, go to **Quality Criteria → Collinearity Statistics (VIF) → Outer VIF Values** in the results report. Note that SmartPLS 3 also provides VIF values for reflective indicators. However, since we would expect high correlations among reflective indicators, we do not interpret these results but focus on the formative indicators' VIF values.

According to the results in Exhibit 5.23, *qual_3* has the highest VIF value (2.269). Hence, VIF values are uniformly below the threshold value of 5. We conclude, therefore, that collinearity does not reach critical levels in any of the formative constructs and is not an issue for the estimation of the PLS path model in the extended example on corporate reputation.

Next we need to analyze the outer weights for their significance and relevance. We first consider the significance of the outer weights by means of bootstrapping. To run the bootstrapping procedure, go to **Calculate → Bootstrapping** in the SmartPLS menu or left-click on the wheel symbol in the tool bar labeled **Calculate** and select **Bootstrapping**. Then, the menu opens as displayed in Exhibit 5.24.

We retain all previous settings for the PLS-SEM algorithm (**Partial Least Squares** tab) and the missing value treatment (**Missing Values** tab) as in the initial model estimation. Instead, we focus on the **Setup** tab where we can make the additional selections required to run the bootstrapping procedure (shown in Exhibit 5.24). In terms of bootstrap samples, we recommend using **5,000** bootstrap samples. Since using such a great number of samples requires much computational time, you may choose a smaller number of samples (e.g., 500) for the initial model estimation. For the final results preparation, however, you should use the suggested number of 5,000 bootstrap samples. The selection **Do Parallel Processing** allows you to use all processors of your computer device. We recommend using this option since it makes bootstrapping much faster. Next, select the **No Sign Changes** option as it is the most conservative among the three sign change options. The choice between **Basic Bootstrapping** and **Complete Bootstrapping** returns a reduced (basic) and a complete basic results report. While the first option is faster, the latter option provides more details that are relevant for the model evaluation. Hence, for the

Exhibit 5.23	VIF Values

Collinearity Statistic (VIF)

Inner VIF Values | Outer VIF Values

	VIF
attr_1	1.275
attr_2	1.129
attr_3	1.264
comp_1	1.397
comp_2	1.787
comp_3	1.888
csor_1	1.560
csor_2	1.487
csor_3	1.735
csor_4	1.556
csor_5	1.712
cusa	1.000
cusl_1	1.802
cusl_2	2.564
cusl_3	1.933
like_1	1.945
like_2	2.000
like_3	1.811
perf_1	1.560
perf_2	1.506
perf_3	1.229
perf_4	1.316
perf_5	1.331
qual_1	1.806
qual_2	1.632
qual_3	2.269
qual_4	1.957
qual_5	2.201
qual_6	2.008
qual_7	1.623
qual_8	1.362

initial model estimation, you may use **Basic Bootstrapping,** but we select **Complete Bootstrapping.**

Next you need to select an approach to compute the bootstrap confidence intervals. Since our data set has more than 300 observations (i.e., it has 344 observations), we do not use the computationally intensive double bootstrap routines. Instead, we use the default option **Bias Corrected and Accelerated (BCa) Bootstrap.** Finally, we select the **0.05** significance level and follow general convention by using **two-tailed** testing. Finally, click on **Start Calculation.**

After running the bootstrapping procedure, SmartPLS 3 shows the bootstrapping results for the measurement models and structural model in the **Modeling** window. At this point in the analysis, we are primarily interested in the significance of the weights and therefore consider only the measurement models for now. Using the **Calculation Results** box at the bottom left of the screen, you can choose whether SmartPLS should display t values or p values in the **Modeling** window, individually or jointly with the path coefficients. Exhibit 5.25 shows t values for the measurement and structural model relationships that the bootstrapping procedure produces. Note that the results will differ from your results and will change again when rerunning the bootstrapping routine. This is because bootstrapping builds on randomly drawn samples, and each time you run the bootstrapping routine, different samples will be drawn. The differences become very small, however, if the number of bootstrapping samples is sufficiently large (e.g., 5,000). In terms of the measurement models, we can compare the t values shown in Exhibit 5.26 with the critical values from the standard normal distribution to decide whether the coefficients are significantly different from zero. For example, the critical values for significance levels of 1% ($\alpha = 0.01$) and 5% ($\alpha = 0.05$) probability of error are 2.57 and 1.96 (two-tailed), respectively. Alternatively, you can choose to display p values, as shown in Exhibit 5.26, by clicking on the menu next to **Inner model** in the **Calculation Results** box at the bottom left of the screen. These correspond to the t values; for example, a t value of 1.96 translates into a p value of 0.05. The p values in the formative measurement models displayed in Exhibit 5.26 must be lower than 0.05 to establish significant outer weights at a significance level of 5% (i.e., $\alpha = 0.05$). Finally, you can also let SmartPLS display t or p values in conjunction with the path coefficients.

(Text continues on page 180)

Exhibit 5.24 Bootstrapping Options in SmartPLS

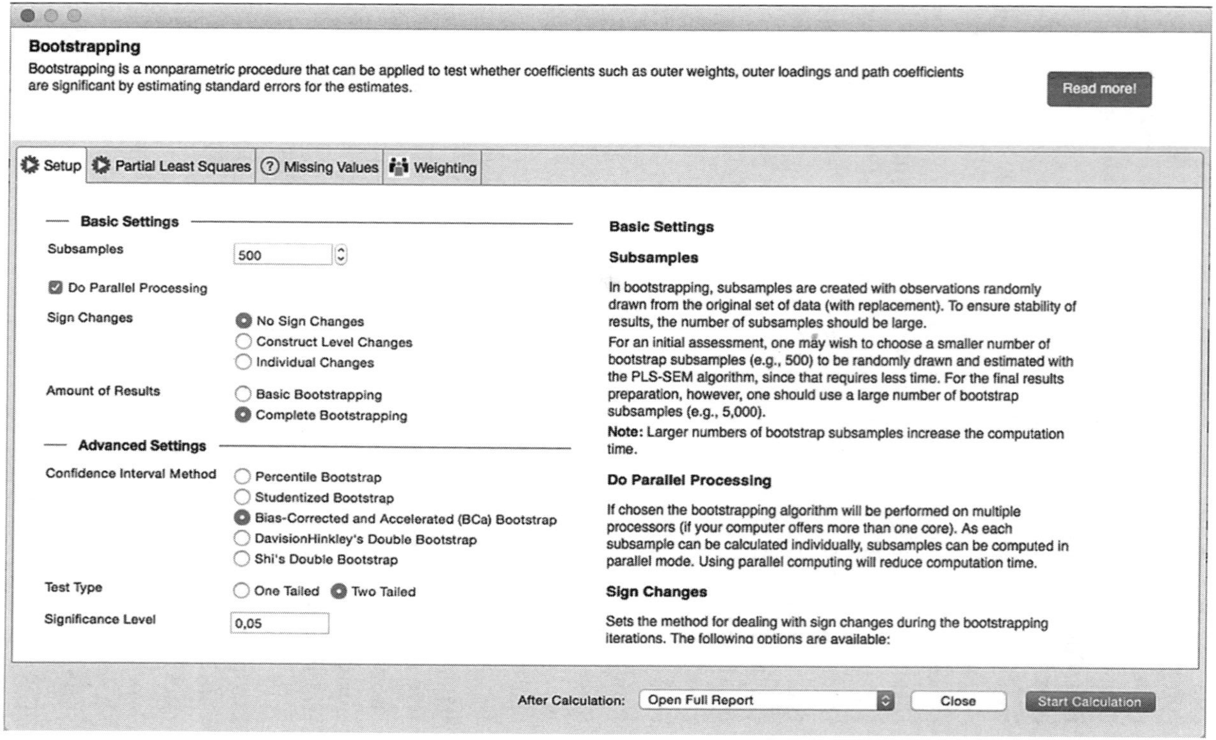

Bootstrapping

Bootstrapping is a nonparametric procedure that can be applied to test whether coefficients such as outer weights, outer loadings and path coefficients are significant by estimating standard errors for the estimates.

Read more!

✿ Setup ✿ Partial Least Squares ⑦ Missing Values ᐧᐧ Weighting

— Basic Settings —

Basic Settings

Subsamples
500 〈 〉

☑ Do Parallel Processing

Sign Changes
◉ No Sign Changes
○ Construct Level Changes
○ Individual Changes

Amount of Results
○ Basic Bootstrapping
◉ Complete Bootstrapping

— Advanced Settings —

Confidence Interval Method
○ Percentile Bootstrap
○ Studentized Bootstrap
◉ Bias-Corrected and Accelerated (BCa) Bootstrap
○ DavisionHinkley's Double Bootstrap
○ Shi's Double Bootstrap

Test Type
○ One Tailed ◉ Two Tailed

Significance Level
0,05

Subsamples

In bootstrapping, subsamples are created with observations randomly drawn from the original set of data (with replacement). To ensure stability of results, the number of subsamples should be large.

For an initial assessment, one may wish to choose a smaller number of bootstrap subsamples (e.g., 500) to be randomly drawn and estimated with the PLS-SEM algorithm, since that requires less time. For the final results preparation, however, one should use a large number of bootstrap subsamples (e.g., 5,000).

Note: Larger numbers of bootstrap subsamples increase the computation time.

Do Parallel Processing

If chosen the bootstrapping algorithm will be performed on multiple processors (if your computer offers more than one core). As each subsample can be calculated individually, subsamples can be computed in parallel mode. Using parallel computing will reduce computation time.

Sign Changes

Sets the method for dealing with sign changes during the bootstrapping iterations. The following options are available:

After Calculation: Open Full Report 〈 〉   Close   Start Calculation

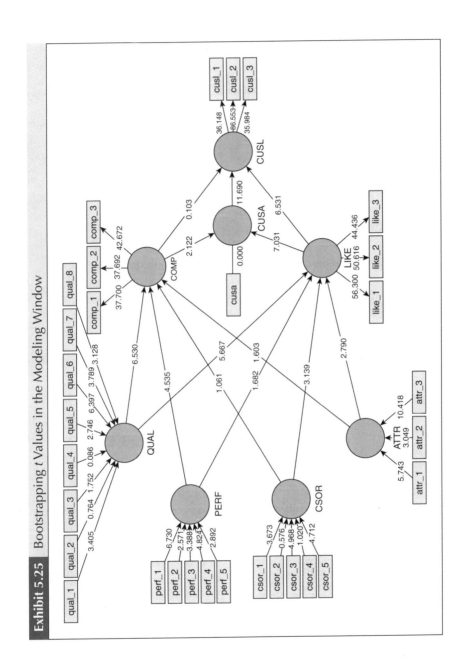

Exhibit 5.25 Bootstrapping *t* Values in the Modeling Window

179

By going to the bootstrapping results report, we get a more detailed overview of the results. The table under **Final Results →
Outer Weights** provides us with an overview of results, including standard errors, bootstrap mean values, *t* values, and *p* values (Exhibit 5.27; again, your results will look slightly different because bootstrapping is a random process). The original estimate of an outer weight (shown in the second column, Original Sample (O); Exhibit 5.27) divided by the bootstrap standard error (column: **Standard Error (STERR)**) for that outer weight results in its empirical *t* value as displayed in the second to last column in Exhibit 5.27. The *t* values translate into *p* values as shown in the last column.

The bootstrapping results report also provides bootstrap confidence intervals. Clicking on the **Confidence Intervals Bias Corrected** tab in the bootstrapping results report shows the confidence intervals as derived from the BCa method (Exhibit 5.28). In addition, you can access the confidence interval without bias correction by clicking the corresponding tab in the results report. Finally, you can access all bootstrap sample–specific estimates by clicking the **Samples** tab.

Exhibit 5.29 summarizes the results for the formatively measured constructs *ATTR, CSOR, PERF,* and *QUAL* by showing the original outer weights estimates, *t* values, *p* values, and the confidence intervals derived from the percentile method.

Looking at the significance levels, we find that all formative indicators are significant at a 5% level, except *csor_2, csor_4, qual_2, qual_3,* and *qual_4*. The results report of the SmartPLS 3 software also provides their outer loadings, *t* values, and *p* values in the results table for the outer loadings. Using this information, we note that the lowest outer loading of these five formative indicators occurs for *qual_2* (0.570). Furthermore, the *p* values of the five indicator loadings (i.e., *csor_2, csor_4, qual_2, qual_3,* and *qual_4*) are clearly below 0.01, suggesting that all loadings are significant at a level of 1%. Moreover, prior research and theory also provide support for the relevance of these indicators for capturing the corporate social responsibility and quality dimensions of corporate reputation (Eberl, 2010; Sarstedt et al., 2013; Schwaiger, 2004; Schwaiger, Sarstedt, & Taylor, 2010). Thus, we retain the indicators in the formative constructs, even though their outer weights are not significant.

The analysis of outer weights concludes the evaluation of the formative measurement models. Considering the results from Chapters 4 and 5 jointly, all reflective and formative constructs exhibit satisfactory levels of quality. Thus, we can proceed with the evaluation of the structural model (Chapter 6).

(Text continues on page 185)

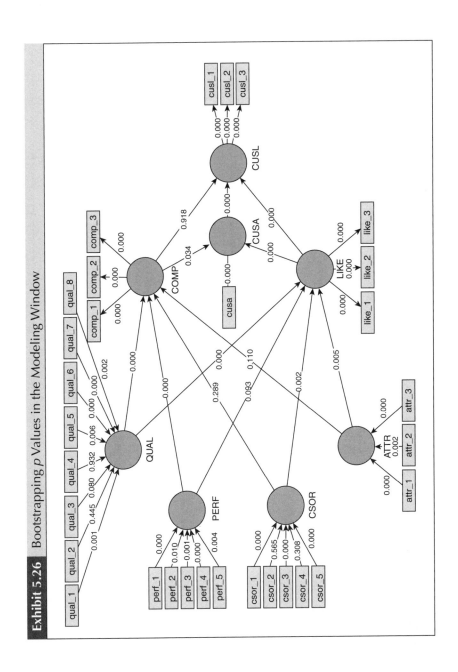

Exhibit 5.26 Bootstrapping *p* Values in the Modeling Window

Outer Weights

Exhibit 5.27 | Bootstrapping Results for Outer Weights

	Original Sample (O)	Sample Mean (M)	Standard Error (STERR)	T Statistics (|O/STERR|)	P Values
attr_1 -> ATTR	0.414	0.411	0.072	5.743	0.000
attr_2 -> ATTR	0.201	0.203	0.066	3.049	0.002
attr_3 -> ATTR	0.658	0.653	0.063	10.418	0.000
comp_1 <- COMP	0.469	0.469	0.021	21.990	0.000
comp_2 <- COMP	0.365	0.365	0.018	19.944	0.000
comp_3 <- COMP	0.372	0.372	0.015	25.344	0.000
csor_1 -> CSOR	0.306	0.306	0.083	3.673	0.000
csor_2 -> CSOR	0.037	0.037	0.065	0.576	0.565
csor_3 -> CSOR	0.406	0.398	0.082	4.968	0.000
csor_4 -> CSOR	0.080	0.077	0.078	1.020	0.308
csor_5 -> CSOR	0.416	0.417	0.088	4.712	0.000
cusa <- CUSA	1.000	1.000	0.000		
cusl_1 <- CUSL	0.369	0.369	0.016	22.402	0.000
cusl_2 <- CUSL	0.420	0.421	0.015	28.531	0.000
cusl_3 <- CUSL	0.365	0.365	0.016	23.062	0.000
like_1 <- LIKE	0.419	0.419	0.015	28.081	0.000
like_2 <- LIKE	0.374	0.374	0.013	28.235	0.000
like_3 <- LIKE	0.363	0.363	0.014	25.597	0.000
perf_1 -> PERF	0.468	0.461	0.070	6.730	0.000
perf_2 -> PERF	0.177	0.177	0.069	2.571	0.010
perf_3 -> PERF	0.194	0.191	0.057	3.388	0.001
perf_4 -> PERF	0.340	0.340	0.071	4.824	0.000
perf_5 -> PERF	0.199	0.202	0.069	2.892	0.004
qual_1 -> QUAL	0.202	0.207	0.059	3.405	0.001
qual_2 -> QUAL	0.041	0.040	0.054	0.764	0.445
qual_3 -> QUAL	0.106	0.106	0.060	1.752	0.080
qual_4 -> QUAL	-0.005	-0.009	0.053	0.086	0.932
qual_5 -> QUAL	0.160	0.159	0.058	2.746	0.006
qual_6 -> QUAL	0.398	0.396	0.062	6.397	0.000
qual_7 -> QUAL	0.229	0.224	0.060	3.789	0.000
qual_8 -> QUAL	0.190	0.189	0.061	3.128	0.002

Mean, STDEV, T-Values, P-Values   Confidence Intervals   Confidence Intervals   Confidence Intervals Bias Corrected   Samples

Exhibit 5.28 BCa Confidence Intervals for Outer Weights

Outer Weights

Mean, STDEV, T-Values, P-Values | Confidence Intervals | Confidence Intervals Bias Corrected | Samples

	Original Sample (O)	Sample Mean (M)	Bias	2.5 %	97.5 %
attr_1 -> ATTR	0.414	0.411	-0.003	0.273	0.554
attr_2 -> ATTR	0.201	0.203	0.002	0.073	0.332
attr_3 -> ATTR	0.658	0.653	-0.004	0.516	0.761
comp_1 <- COMP	0.469	0.469	0.000	0.427	0.508
comp_2 <- COMP	0.365	0.365	0.000	0.327	0.402
comp_3 <- COMP	0.372	0.372	0.001	0.344	0.402
csor_1 -> CSOR	0.306	0.306	-0.000	0.145	0.458
csor_2 -> CSOR	0.037	0.037	0.000	-0.082	0.167
csor_3 -> CSOR	0.406	0.398	-0.008	0.229	0.550
csor_4 -> CSOR	0.080	0.077	-0.003	-0.063	0.219
csor_5 -> CSOR	0.416	0.417	0.001	0.260	0.611
cusa <- CUSA	1.000	1.000	0.000	1.000	1.000
cusl_1 <- CUSL	0.369	0.369	0.000	0.336	0.398
cusl_2 <- CUSL	0.420	0.421	0.001	0.394	0.452
cusl_3 <- CUSL	0.365	0.365	-0.000	0.334	0.392
like_1 <- LIKE	0.419	0.419	-0.000	0.393	0.452
like_2 <- LIKE	0.374	0.374	-0.000	0.348	0.400
like_3 <- LIKE	0.363	0.363	0.000	0.334	0.392
perf_1 -> PERF	0.468	0.461	-0.007	0.310	0.582
perf_2 -> PERF	0.177	0.177	0.001	0.044	0.311
perf_3 -> PERF	0.194	0.191	-0.004	0.069	0.298
perf_4 -> PERF	0.340	0.340	-0.001	0.205	0.479
perf_5 -> PERF	0.199	0.202	0.004	0.070	0.350
qual_1 -> QUAL	0.202	0.207	0.005	0.103	0.332
qual_2 -> QUAL	0.041	0.040	-0.001	-0.074	0.148
qual_3 -> QUAL	0.106	0.106	0.001	-0.004	0.227
qual_4 -> QUAL	-0.005	-0.009	-0.005	-0.119	0.081
qual_5 -> QUAL	0.160	0.159	-0.001	0.045	0.267
qual_6 -> QUAL	0.398	0.396	-0.002	0.275	0.501
qual_7 -> QUAL	0.229	0.224	-0.005	0.094	0.328
qual_8 -> QUAL	0.190	0.189	-0.001	0.060	0.303

Exhibit 5.29	Formative Constructs Outer Weights Significance Testing Results					
Formative Constructs	Formative Indicators	Outer Weights (Outer Loadings)	t Value	p Value	95% BCa Confidence Interval	Significance[a] (p < 0.05)?
ATTR	attr_1	0.414 (0.755)	5.743	0.000	[0.273, 0.554]	Yes
	attr_2	0.201 (0.506)	3.049	0.002	[0.073, 0.332]	Yes
	attr_3	0.658 (0.891)	10.418	0.000	[0.516, 0.761]	Yes
CSOR	csor_1	0.306 (0.771)	3.673	0.000	[0.145, 0.458]	Yes
	csor_2	0.037 (0.571)	0.576	0.565	[−0.082, 0.167]	No
	csor_3	0.406 (0.838)	4.968	0.000	[0.229, 0.550]	Yes
	csor_4	0.080 (0.617)	1.020	0.308	[−0.063, 0.219]	No
	csor_5	0.416 (0.848)	4.712	0.000	[0.260, 0.611]	Yes
PERF	perf_1	0.468 (0.846)	6.730	0.000	[0.310, 0.582]	Yes
	perf_2	0.177 (0.690)	2.571	0.010	[0.044, 0.311]	Yes
	perf_3	0.194 (0.573)	3.388	0.001	[0.069, 0.298]	Yes
	perf_4	0.340 (0.717)	4.824	0.000	[0.205, 0.479]	Yes
	perf_5	0.199 (0.638)	2.892	0.004	[0.070, 0.350]	Yes
QUAL	qual_1	0.202 (0.741)	3.405	0.001	[0.103, 0.332]	Yes
	qual_2	0.041 (0.570)	0.764	0.445	[−0.074, 0.148]	No
	qual_3	0.106 (0.749)	1.752	0.080	[−0.004, 0.227]	No
	qual_4	−0.005 (0.664)	0.086	0.932	[−0.119, 0.081]	No
	qual_5	0.160 (0.787)	2.746	0.006	[0.045, 0.267]	Yes
	qual_6	0.398 (0.856)	6.397	0.000	[0.275, 0.501]	Yes
	qual_7	0.229 (0.722)	3.789	0.000	[0.094, 0.328]	Yes
	qual_8	0.190 (0.627)	3.128	0.002	[0.060, 0.303]	Yes

[a]We refer to the bootstrap confidence intervals for significance testing, as recommended in this chapter.

SUMMARY

- **Explain the criteria used for the assessment of formative measurement models.** The statistical evaluation criteria for reflective measurement scales cannot be directly transferred to formative measurement models where indicators are likely to represent the construct's independent causes and thus do not necessarily correlate highly. Researchers must include a comprehensive set of indicators that fully exhausts the formative construct's domain. Failure to consider all major facets of the construct—as defined by the researcher—entails an exclusion of important parts of the construct itself. The evaluation of formative measurement models starts with convergent validity to ensure that the entire domain of the construct and all of its relevant facets have been covered by the formative indicators. The next step involves examining whether each indicator contributes to forming the index. Hence, the significance and relevance of the indicator weights must be assessed, and it is valuable also to report the bootstrap confidence interval that provides additional information on the stability of the coefficient estimates. Nonsignificant indicator weights should not automatically be interpreted as indicating poor measurement model quality. Rather, researchers should also consider a formative indicator's absolute contribution to its construct (i.e., its loading). Only if both weights and loadings are low or even nonsignificant should a formative indicator be deleted. In addition, potential collinearity issues among sets of formative indicators need to be addressed in the measurement model assessment. By accounting for these issues, one makes sure that the formative construct can be used for the PLS-SEM analysis and that the estimations of outer weights are correctly interpreted.

- **Understand the basic concepts of bootstrapping for significance testing in PLS-SEM and apply them.** PLS-SEM is a distribution-free multivariate data analysis technique and, as such, does not rely on distributional assumptions. As a consequence and different from, for example, OLS regression, PLS-SEM does not initially provide t or p values to evaluate the estimates' significance. Instead, researchers have to rely on the bootstrapping procedure that provides bootstrap standard errors. These standard errors can be used to approximate t values and, in turn, p values. Bootstrapping is a resampling approach that draws random samples (with replacement) from the data and uses these samples to estimate the path model multiple times under slightly changed data constellations. When running the bootstrapping procedure, researchers should draw 5,000 bootstrap samples, each of which includes the same number of cases as there are observations in the original data set. The random nature of the bootstrapping procedure might cause arbitrary sign changes in the model estimates that researchers can correct for by using the construct-level or individual-level sign change options. However, choosing the no sign change option is strongly recommended because it is the most conservative option. Bootstrap confidence intervals provide further information on the stability of the model estimates. Researchers should draw on the BCa method to construct bootstrap confidence intervals.

- **Use the SmartPLS software to apply the formative measurement model assessment criteria and learn how to properly report the results of the practical example on corporate reputation.** Expanding the corporate reputation model example by four formatively measured constructs allows us to continue the SmartPLS application of the previous chapters. The SmartPLS 3 software generates results for the evaluation of the formative measurement models. Besides the outcomes of the PLS-SEM algorithm, running the bootstrapping routine delivers the results required for testing the significance of formative indicators' outer weights. Tables and figures for the PLS path model example on corporate reputation demonstrate how to correctly report and interpret the PLS-SEM results. This hands-on example not only reinforces the concepts that have been introduced before but also provides additional insights for their practical application.

REVIEW QUESTIONS

1. How do you assess the content validity of formative constructs?

2. Why do you need to consider the significance and relevance of formative indicators?

3. What VIF level indicates critical levels of indicator collinearity?

4. What is the basic idea underlying bootstrapping?

5. Which sign changes procedure and number of samples should you choose when running the bootstrap procedure?

CRITICAL THINKING QUESTIONS

1. What is the difference between reflectively and formatively measured constructs? Explain the difference between outer loadings and outer weights.

2. Why are formative constructs particularly useful as exogenous latent variables in a PLS path model?

3. Why is indicator collinearity an issue in formative measurement models?

4. Critically discuss the following statement: "Nonsignificant indicators should be eliminated from a formative measurement model as they do not contribute to forming the index."

5. What value added do bootstrap confidence intervals offer over p values?

KEY TERMS

Absolute contribution

Absolute importance

Bias-corrected and accelerated (BCa) bootstrap confidence intervals

Bootstrap cases

Bootstrap samples

Confidence interval

Construct-level sign change option

Content specification

Coverage error

Critical t value

Davison and Hinkley's double bootstrap

Degrees of freedom (df)

Double bootstrapping

Empirical t value

Individual-level sign change option

Interpretational confounding

Multicollinearity

No sign change option

p value	Studentized bootstrap method
Percentile method	Theoretical t value
Redundancy analysis	TOL
Relative contribution	Tolerance
Shi's double bootstrap	Variance inflation factor (VIF)
Sign indeterminacy	VIF

SUGGESTED READINGS

Albers, S. (2010). PLS and success factor studies in marketing. In V. Esposito Vinzi, W. W. Chin, J. Henseler, & H. Wang (Eds.), *Handbook of partial least squares: Concepts, methods and applications* (Springer Handbooks of Computational Statistics Series, Vol. II, pp. 409–425). Berlin: Springer.

Cenfetelli, R. T., & Bassellier, G. (2009). Interpretation of formative measurement in information systems research. *MIS Quarterly, 33*, 689–708.

Chin, W. W. (2010). How to write up and report PLS analyses. In V. Esposito Vinzi, W. W. Chin, J. Henseler, & H. Wang (Eds.), *Handbook of partial least squares: Concepts, methods and applications in marketing and related fields* (Springer Handbooks of Computational Statistics Series, Vol. II, pp. 655–690). Berlin: Springer.

Diamantopoulos, A. (2008). Formative indicators: Introduction to the special issue. *Journal of Business Research, 61*, 1201–1202.

Diamantopoulos, A., & Winklhofer, H. M. (2001). Index construction with formative indicators: An alternative to scale development. *Journal of Marketing Research, 38*, 269–277.

Gudergan, S. P., Ringle, C. M., Wende, S., & Will, A. (2008). Confirmatory tetrad analysis in PLS path modeling. *Journal of Business Research, 61*, 1238–1249.

Hair, J. F., Ringle, C. M., & Sarstedt, M. (2011). PLS-SEM: Indeed a silver bullet. *Journal of Marketing Theory and Practice, 19*, 139–151.

Hair, J. F., Sarstedt, M., Pieper, T., & Ringle, C. M. (2012). The use of partial least squares structural equation modeling in strategic management research: A review of past practices and recommendations for future applications. *Long Range Planning, 45*, 320–340.

Hair, J. F., Sarstedt, M., Ringle, C. M., & Mena, J. A. (2012). An assessment of the use of partial least squares structural equation modeling in marketing research. *Journal of the Academy of Marketing Science, 40*, 414–433.

Henseler, J., Ringle, C. M., & Sinkovics, R. R. (2009). The use of partial least squares path modeling in international marketing. *Advances in International Marketing, 20*, 277–320.

Petter, S., Straub, D., & Rai, A. (2007). Specifying formative constructs in information systems research. *MIS Quarterly, 31*(4), 623–656.

Ringle, C. M., Sarstedt, M., & Straub, D. W. (2012). A critical look at the use of PLS-SEM in *MIS Quarterly. MIS Quarterly, 36*, iii–xiv.

C H A P T E R 6

Assessing PLS-SEM Results Part III

Evaluation of the Structural Model

LEARNING OUTCOMES

1. Understand the concept of model fit in a PLS-SEM context.

2. Assess the path coefficients in the structural model.

3. Evaluate the coefficients of determination (R^2 values).

4. Understand and evaluate the f^2 effect size.

5. Use the blindfolding procedure to assess the predictive relevance (Q^2 value) of the path model.

6. Understand how to report and interpret the structural model results.

CHAPTER PREVIEW

Chapters 4 and 5 provided insights into the evaluation of reflective and formative measurement models. This chapter continues the analysis and focuses on the structural model that represents the underlying structural theories/concepts of the path model. Assessment of the structural model results enables you to determine the model's capability to predict one or more target constructs. We first discuss the concept of model fit in a PLS-SEM context and then introduce a range of measures that should be used to assess the structural model. The chapter concludes with a practical application and assessment of the PLS-SEM results of the structural model by means of our corporate reputation example and using the SmartPLS 3 software.

STAGE 6: ASSESSING PLS-SEM STRUCTURAL MODEL RESULTS

Once we have confirmed that the construct measures are reliable and valid, the next step addresses the assessment of the structural model results. This involves examining the model's predictive capabilities and the relationships between the constructs. Exhibit 6.1 shows a systematic approach to the assessment of structural model results.

Before we describe these analyses, however, we need to examine the structural model for collinearity (Step 1). The reason is that the estimation of path coefficients in the structural models is based on OLS regressions of each endogenous latent variable on

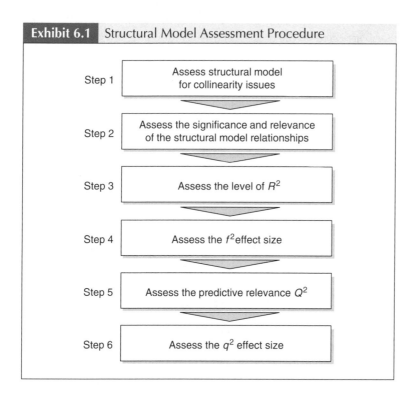

Exhibit 6.1 Structural Model Assessment Procedure

Step 1 Assess structural model for collinearity issues

Step 2 Assess the significance and relevance of the structural model relationships

Step 3 Assess the level of R^2

Step 4 Assess the f^2 effect size

Step 5 Assess the predictive relevance Q^2

Step 6 Assess the q^2 effect size

its corresponding predecessor constructs. Just as in a regular multiple regression, the path coefficients might be biased if the estimation involves critical levels of collinearity among the predictor constructs.

When examining the structural model, it is important to understand that PLS-SEM estimates the parameters so that the explained variance of the endogenous latent variable(s) is maximized. This aspect of PLS-SEM is different from CB-SEM, which estimates parameters so that the differences between the sample covariances and those predicted by the theoretical/conceptual model are minimized. As a result, with CB-SEM, the covariance matrix estimated by the theoretical/ conceptual model is as close as possible to the sample covariance matrix. Goodness-of-fit measures such as the chi-square (χ^2) statistic or the various fit indices associated with CB-SEM are based on the difference between the two covariance matrices. The notion of fit is therefore not fully transferrable to PLS-SEM as the method seeks a solution based on a different statistical objective when estimating model parameters (i.e., maximizing the explained variance instead of minimizing the differences between covariance matrices).

Instead of assessing goodness-of-fit, the structural model is primarily assessed on the basis of heuristic criteria that are determined by the model's predictive capabilities. These criteria, by definition, do not allow for testing the overall goodness of the model fit in a CB-SEM sense. Rather, the model is assessed in terms of how well it predicts the endogenous variables/constructs (see Sarstedt, Ringle, Henseler, & Hair, 2014, for a discussion of model fit in CB-SEM vis-à-vis PLS-SEM's prediction orientation). The key criteria for assessing the structural model in PLS-SEM are the significance of the path coefficients (Step 2), the level of the R^2 values (Step 3), the f^2 effect size (Step 4), the predictive relevance Q^2 (Step 5), and the q^2 effect size (Step 6).

Nevertheless, research has proposed several PLS-SEM–based model fit measures, which are, however, in their early stages of development. We therefore provide an outlook on these developments in Exhibit 6.2.

Step 1: Collinearity Assessment

To assess collinearity, we apply the same measures as in the evaluation of formative measurement models (i.e., tolerance and VIF values) in Chapter 5. In doing so, we need to examine each set of predictor constructs separately for each subpart of the structural model.

Exhibit 6.2   Model Fit Measures in PLS-SEM

While PLS-SEM was originally designed for prediction purposes, research has sought to extend its capabilities for theory testing by developing model fit measures. Model fit indices enable judging how well a hypothesized model structure fits the empirical data and, thus, help to identify model misspecifications.

One of the earliest proposed indices was by Tenenhaus et al. (2004) and Tenenhaus, Esposito Vinzi, Chatelin, and Lauro (2005), who proposed the **goodness-of-fit index (GoF)** as "an operational solution to this problem as it may be meant as an index for validating the PLS model globally" (Tenenhaus et al., 2005, p. 173). Henseler and Sarstedt (2013) challenged the usefulness of the GoF both conceptually and empirically. Their research shows that the GoF does not represent a goodness-of-fit criterion for PLS-SEM. In particular, the GoF is, unlike fit measures in CB-SEM, not able to separate valid models from invalid ones. Since the GoF is also not applicable to formatively measured models and does not penalize overparametrization efforts, researchers are advised not to use this measure.

More recently, Henseler et al. (2014) assessed the efficacy of the **standardized root mean square residual (SRMR)**, a model fit measure well known from CB-SEM, which has previously not been applied in a PLS-SEM context. The SRMR is defined as the root mean square discrepancy between the observed correlations and the model-implied correlations. Because the SRMR is an absolute measure of fit, a value of zero indicates perfect fit. When applying CB-SEM, a value less than 0.08 is generally considered a good fit (Hu & Bentler, 1998). But this threshold is likely too low for PLS-SEM. The reason is that the discrepancy between the observed correlations and the model-implied correlations plays different roles in CB-SEM and PLS-SEM. Whereas the CB-SEM algorithm aims at minimizing the discrepancy, in PLS-SEM, the discrepancy results from the model estimation, whose aim is to maximize the explained variance of the endogenous construct(s). That is, minimizing the discrepancy is the target criterion of CB-SEM, whereas this is not the case in PLS-SEM.

As an alternative model fit measure, researchers may use the **root mean square residual covariance (RMS$_{theta}$)**, which follows the same logic as SRMR but relies on covariances. The criterion was introduced by Lohmöller (1989) but has not been explored by PLS-SEM researchers until recently. Initial simulation results suggest a (conservative) threshold value for RMS$_{theta}$ of 0.12. That is, RMS$_{theta}$ values below 0.12 indicate a well-fitting model, whereas higher values indicate a lack of fit (Henseler et al., 2014).

(Continued)

Exhibit 6.2	(Continued)

Finally, Dijkstra and Henseler (2015a) recently introduced the **exact fit test**. Their chi-square–based test applies bootstrapping to derive p values of the discrepancy between the observed correlations and the model-implied correlations. Different from SRMR, the discrepancy is not expressed in the form of residuals but in terms of distances, which are calculated in two forms (Euclidean and geodesic distance).

Initial simulation results suggest that the SRMR, RMS$_{theta}$, and exact fit test are capable of identifying a range of model misspecifications (Dijkstra & Henseler, 2015a; Henseler et al., 2014). At this time, too little is known about these measures' behavior across a range of data and model constellations, so more research is needed. Furthermore, these criteria are not readily implemented in standard PLS-SEM software. However, SmartPLS 3 offers the SRMR measure thus far and future releases will include the exact fit measures and other extensions of PLS-SEM.

Apart from these developments, it is an open question whether fit measured as described above adds any value to PLS-SEM analyses in general. PLS-SEM focuses on prediction rather than on explanatory modeling and therefore requires a different type of validation. More precisely, validation of PLS-SEM results is concerned with generalization, which is the ability to predict sample data, or, preferably, out-of-sample data—see Shmueli (2010) for details. Against this background researchers increasingly call for the development of evaluation criteria that better support the prediction-oriented nature of PLS-SEM (e.g., Rigdon, 2012, 2014b) and for an emancipation of PLS-SEM from its CB-SEM sibling (Sarstedt, Ringle, Henseler, & Hair, 2014). In this context, fit (as put into effect by SRMR), RMS$_{theta}$, and the exact fit test offer little value. In fact, their use can even be harmful as researchers may be tempted to sacrifice predictive power to achieve better "fit." Therefore, we advise against the routine use of such statistics in the context of PLS-SEM.

For instance, in the model shown in Exhibit 6.3, Y_1 and Y_2 jointly explain Y_3. Likewise, Y_2 and Y_3 act as predictors of Y_4. Therefore, one needs to check whether there are critical levels of collinearity between each set of predictor variables, that is, Y_1 and Y_2 as well as Y_2 and Y_3.

Analogous to the assessment of formative measurement models, we consider tolerance values below 0.20 (VIF value above 5) in the predictor constructs as critical levels of collinearity. If a critical level of collinearity is indicated by the tolerance or VIF guidelines, one should consider eliminating constructs, merging predictors into a single construct, or creating higher-order constructs (Chapter 8) to treat collinearity problems.

Exhibit 6.3	Collinearity in the Structural Model

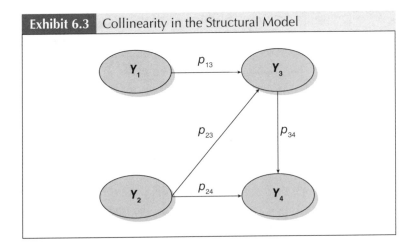

Step 2: Structural Model Path Coefficients

After running the PLS-SEM algorithm, estimates are obtained for the structural model relationships (i.e., the path coefficients), which represent the **hypothesized relationships** among the constructs. The path coefficients have **standardized values** approximately between –1 and +1 (values can be smaller/larger but usually fall in between these bounds). Estimated path coefficients close to +1 represent strong positive relationships (and vice versa for negative values) that are usually statistically significant (i.e., different from zero in the population). The closer the estimated coefficients are to 0, the weaker are the relationships. Very low values close to 0 are usually not significantly different from zero.

Whether a coefficient is significant ultimately depends on its **standard error** that is obtained by means of bootstrapping. The bootstrapping routine is applied as described in Chapter 5, where we used the procedure to assess whether a formative indicator significantly contributes to its corresponding construct. The bootstrap standard error enables computing the empirical t values and p values for all structural path coefficients. When an empirical t value is larger than the **critical value,** we conclude that the coefficient is statistically significant at a certain error probability (i.e., significance level). Commonly used critical values for **two-tailed tests** are 1.65 (significance level = 10%), 1.96 (significance level = 5%), and 2.57 (significance level = 1%). Critical values for **one-tailed tests** are 1.28 (significance level = 10%), 1.65 (significance level = 5%), and

2.33 (significance level = 1%). In marketing, researchers usually assume a significance level of 5%. This does not always apply, however, since consumer research studies sometimes assume a significance level of 1%, especially when experiments are involved. In general, when a study is exploratory in nature, researchers often assume a significance level of 10%. Ultimately, the choice of the significance level and type of test (one or two tails) depends on the field of study and the study's objective.

Most researchers use p values to assess significance levels. A p value is equal to the probability of obtaining a t value at least as extreme as the one that is actually observed, conditional on the null hypothesis being supported. In other words, the p value is the probability of erroneously rejecting a true null hypothesis (i.e., assuming a significant path coefficient when in fact it is not significant). When assuming a significance level of 5%, the p value must be smaller than 0.05 to conclude that the relationship under consideration is significant at a 5% level. For example, when we assume a significance level of 5% and the analysis yields a p value of 0.03 for a certain coefficient, we would conclude that the coefficient is significant at a 5% level. Correspondingly, when researchers want to be stricter in their testing of relationships and therefore assume a 1% significance level, the corresponding p value must be smaller than 0.01 to indicate a relationship is significant.

The bootstrap confidence interval also allows testing whether a path coefficient is significantly different from zero. The confidence interval provides information on the stability of the estimated coefficient by offering a range of plausible population values for the parameter dependent on the variation in the data and the sample size. As discussed in Chapter 5, the bootstrap confidence interval is based on standard errors derived from bootstrapping and specifies the range into which the true population parameter will fall assuming a certain level of confidence (e.g., 95%). If a confidence interval for an estimated path coefficient does not include zero, the hypothesis that the path equals zero is rejected, and we assume a significant effect. While research has brought forward a range of different bootstrap confidence intervals, we recommend using the BCa approach in line with prior research (see Chapter 5 for a discussion). Alternatively, when models are not complex (i.e., fewer than four constructs) and sample size is relatively small (e.g., <300), using the double bootstrap routine is beneficial.

When interpreting the results of a path model, we need to test the significance of all structural model relationships using t values, p values, and the bootstrap confidence intervals. When reporting results, researchers usually provide t values or p values. Reporting of the bootstrapping confidence interval is less common despite their value added but is likely to increase in the future.

After examining the significance of relationships, it is important to assess the **relevance of significant relationships.** Many studies do not undertake this important step in their analyses but simply focus on the significance of effects. However, the path coefficients in the structural model may be significant, but their size may be very small. Such situations often occur with large sample sizes. An analysis of the relative importance of relationships is crucial for interpreting the results and drawing conclusions since such small coefficients, even though significant, may not warrant managerial attention.

The structural model path coefficients can be interpreted relative to one another. If one path coefficient is larger than another, its effect on the endogenous latent variable is greater. More specifically, the individual path coefficients of the path model can be interpreted just as the standardized beta coefficients in an OLS regression: A one-unit change of the exogenous construct changes the endogenous construct by the size of the path coefficient when everything else (i.e., all other constructs and their path coefficients) remains constant (ceteris paribus; Hair et al., 2010). If the path coefficient is statistically significant (i.e., the coefficient is significantly different from zero in the population), its value indicates the extent to which the exogenous construct is associated with the endogenous construct. Researchers have also proposed formal tests for assessing whether two path coefficients differ significantly in one model (Chin, Kim, & Lee, 2013). Such a test should be used when hypotheses relate to differences in path coefficients in the model, which, however, is rather rarely the case.

Researchers are often interested in evaluating not only one construct's direct effect on another but also its indirect effects via one or more mediating constructs. The sum of direct and indirect effects is referred to as the **total effect.** The interpretation of total effects is particularly useful in studies aimed at exploring the differential impact of several driver constructs on a criterion construct via one or more mediating variables. In Exhibit 6.4, for example, constructs Y_1 and Y_3 are linked by a direct effect ($p_{13} = 0.20$). In addition, there is an indirect effect between the two constructs via the mediating construct Y_2.

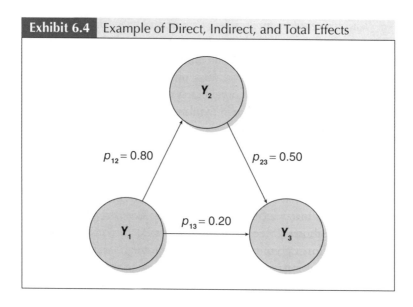

Exhibit 6.4   Example of Direct, Indirect, and Total Effects

This indirect effect can be calculated as the product of the two effects p_{12} and p_{23} ($p_{12} \cdot p_{23} = 0.80 \cdot 0.50 = 0.40$). The total effect is 0.60, which is calculated as $p_{13} + p_{12} \cdot p_{23} = 0.20 + 0.80 \cdot 0.50 = 0.60$.

Although the direct effect of Y_1 to Y_3 is not very strong (i.e., 0.20), the total effect (both direct and indirect combined) is quite pronounced (i.e., 0.60), indicating the relevance of Y_1 in explaining Y_3. This type of result suggests that the direct relationship from Y_1 to Y_3 is mediated by Y_2. In Chapter 7, we will deal with the question of how to analyze mediating effects.

Step 3: Coefficient of Determination (R^2 Value)

The most commonly used measure to evaluate the structural model is the **coefficient of determination** (R^2 **value**). This coefficient is a measure of the model's predictive power and is calculated as the squared correlation between a specific endogenous construct's actual and predicted values. The coefficient represents the exogenous latent variables' combined effects on the endogenous latent variable. That is, the coefficient represents the amount of variance in the endogenous constructs explained by all of the exogenous constructs linked to it. Because the R^2 is the squared correlation of actual and predicted values and, as such, includes all the data that have been used for model estimation to judge the model's predictive power, it represents a measure of **in-sample predictive power** (Rigdon, 2012; Sarstedt, Ringle, Henseler, & Hair, 2014).

The R^2 value ranges from 0 to 1, with higher levels indicating higher levels of predictive accuracy. It is difficult to provide rules of thumb for acceptable R^2 values as this depends on the model complexity and the research discipline. Whereas R^2 values of 0.20 are considered high in disciplines such as consumer behavior, in success driver studies (e.g., in studies that aim at explaining customer satisfaction or loyalty), researchers expect much higher values, such as 0.75 and above. In scholarly research that focuses on marketing issues, R^2 values of 0.75, 0.50, or 0.25 for endogenous latent variables can, as a rule of thumb, be respectively described as substantial, moderate, or weak (Hair et al., 2011; Henseler et al., 2009).

Problems often arise if we use the R^2 value to compare models that are specified differently (e.g., different exogenous constructs predicting the same endogenous construct). For example, adding nonsignificant constructs to a structural model that are slightly correlated with the endogenous latent variable will increase the R^2 value. This type of impact is most noticeable if the sample size is close to the number of exogenous latent variables predicting the endogenous latent variable under consideration. Thus, if we use the R^2 value as the only basis for understanding the model's predictive power, there is an inherent bias toward selecting models with many exogenous constructs, including ones that may be only slightly related to the endogenous constructs.

Selecting a model solely based on the R^2 value is not a good approach. Adding additional (nonsignificant) constructs to explain an endogenous latent variable in the structural model always increases its R^2 value. The more paths pointing toward a target construct, the higher its R^2 value. However, researchers typically prefer models that are good at explaining the data (thus, with high R^2 values) but also have fewer exogenous constructs. Such models are called **parsimonious.**

As with multiple regression, the **adjusted coefficient of determination** (R^2_{adj}) can be used as the criterion to avoid bias toward complex models. This criterion is modified according to the number of exogenous constructs relative to the sample size. The value is formally defined as

$$R^2_{adj} = 1 - \left(1 - R^2\right) \cdot \frac{n-1}{n-k-1},$$

where n is the sample size and k is the number of exogenous latent variables used to predict the endogenous latent variable under consideration. The R^2_{adj} **value** reduces the R^2 **value** by the number of explaining constructs and the sample size and thus systematically compensates for adding nonsignificant exogenous constructs merely to increase the explained variance R^2. Note that we cannot interpret the R^2_{adj} just like the regular R^2. Rather, the R^2_{adj} is used for comparing PLS-SEM results involving models with different numbers of exogenous latent variables and/or data sets with different sample sizes. See Sarstedt et al. (2013) for an example application.

Consider the sample path model in Exhibit 6.5. We are interested in comparing the R^2_{adj} values of the endogenous construct Y_3 of the original model that includes the two exogenous constructs Y_1 and Y_2 with an extended model that additionally includes the exogenous construct Y_0. As indicated by the path coefficient of 0.06, Y_0 has a very weak (and likely nonsignificant) effect on Y_3. The underlying data set has many missing values in the indicators of Y_0, which requires the use of casewise deletion. Therefore, the estimation of the extended model with three exogenous constructs is based on only 100 observations (i.e., $n = 100$). In contrast, the original model without Y_0 can be estimated with 160 observations (i.e., $n = 160$); 60 observations were eliminated because of missing data in Y_0. Estimating the original and extended model shows that the inclusion of Y_0 slightly increases the R^2 of Y_3 from 0.595 to 0.598. Therefore, from a prediction standpoint, one might consider it beneficial to include Y_0 in the model. But a different picture emerges when comparing the adjusted R^2 values, which also take the model complexity and sample sizes into account, for the original situation ($n = 160$) and the extended situation ($n = 100$):

$$R^2_{adj,Original} = 1 - (1 - 0.595) \cdot \frac{160 - 1}{160 - 2 - 1} = 0.590,$$

$$R^2_{adj,Extended} = 1 - (1 - 0.598) \cdot \frac{100 - 1}{100 - 3 - 1} = 0.585.$$

Based on the R^2_{adj} values, the original model is preferable. While the differences in (adjusted) R^2 values are not very pronounced in this example, they can vary in different setups that involve comparing models with a great number of exogenous latent variables and/or different sample sizes. Note that one can also use the bootstrapping routine to test for significant differences between (adjusted) R^2 values between two models (for an example, see Sarstedt et al., 2013).

Exhibit 6.5	Original and Extended Path Model

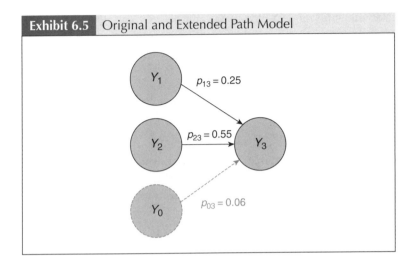

Step 4: Effect Size f^2

In addition to evaluating the R^2 values of all endogenous constructs, the change in the R^2 value when a specified exogenous construct is omitted from the model can be used to evaluate whether the omitted construct has a substantive impact on the endogenous constructs. This measure is referred to as the f^2 **effect size** and is increasingly encouraged by journal editors and reviewers. The effect size can be calculated as

$$f^2 = \frac{R^2_{included} - R^2_{excluded}}{1 - R^2_{included}},$$

where $R^2_{included}$ and $R^2_{excluded}$ are the R^2 values of the endogenous latent variable when a selected exogenous latent variable is included in or excluded from the model. Technically, the change in the R^2 values is calculated by estimating the PLS path model twice. It is estimated the first time with the exogenous latent variable included (yielding $R^2_{included}$) and the second time with the exogenous latent variable excluded (yielding $R^2_{excluded}$). Guidelines for assessing f^2 are that values of 0.02, 0.15, and 0.35, respectively, represent small, medium, and large effects (Cohen, 1988) of the exogenous latent variable. Effect size values of less than 0.02 indicate that there is no effect.

For example, consider the extended path model with the three exogenous constructs Y_0, Y_1, and Y_2 as shown in Exhibit 6.5.

Estimating this model yields an R^2 value of 0.598 (i.e., $R^2_{included} = 0.598$). However, when, for example, excluding Y_1 from the path model, the R^2 value drops to 0.501 (i.e., $R^2_{excluded} = 0.501$), yielding the following f^2 effect size for Y_1:

$$f^2 = \frac{0.598 - 0.501}{1 - 0.598} = 0.241.$$

Hence, we would consider the effect size of construct Y_1 on the endogenous latent variable Y_3 as medium. Another application of f^2 effect size computations follows later in this chapter when we work with the example on corporate reputation.

Step 5: Blindfolding and Predictive Relevance Q^2

In addition to evaluating the magnitude of the R^2 values as a criterion of predictive accuracy, researchers should also examine Stone-Geisser's **Q^2 value** (Geisser, 1974; Stone, 1974). This measure is an indicator of the model's **out-of-sample predictive power** or predictive relevance. When a PLS path model exhibits predictive relevance, it accurately predicts data not used in the model estimation. In the structural model, Q^2 values larger than zero for a specific reflective endogenous latent variable indicate the path model's predictive relevance for a particular dependent construct.

The Q^2 value is obtained by using the **blindfolding** procedure for a specified omission distance D. Blindfolding is a sample reuse technique that omits every dth data point in the endogenous construct's indicators and estimates the parameters with the remaining data points (Chin, 1998; Henseler et al., 2009; Tenenhaus et al., 2005). The omitted data points are considered missing values and treated accordingly when running the PLS-SEM algorithm (e.g., by using pairwise deletion or mean value replacement; Chapter 2). The resulting estimates are then used to predict the omitted data points. The difference between the true (i.e., omitted) data points and the predicted ones is then used as input for the Q^2 measure. Blindfolding is an iterative process that repeats until each data point has been omitted and the model reestimated. The blindfolding procedure is usually applied to endogenous constructs that have a reflective measurement model specification as well as to endogenous single-item constructs.

When applying the blindfolding procedure to the path model shown in Exhibit 6.6, the data points in the measurement model of the reflective endogenous construct are estimated by means of a two-step approach. First, the information from the structural model is used to predict the scores of latent variable Y_3. More precisely, after running the PLS-SEM algorithm, the scores of the latent variables Y_1, Y_2, and Y_3 are available. Instead of directly using the Y_3 scores, the blindfolding procedure predicts these scores by using the available information for the structural model (i.e., the latent variable scores of Y_1 and Y_2, as well as the structural model coefficients p_{13} and p_{23}). Specifically, the prediction of Y_3 equals the standardized scores of the following equation: $\hat{Y}_3 = p_{13} \cdot Y_1 + p_{23} \cdot Y_2$, whereby $\hat{Y}_3$ represents the structural model's prediction. These scores differ from the scores of Y_3, which were obtained by applying the PLS-SEM algorithm because they result from the structural model estimates rather than those from the measurement model (Chapter 3).

In the second step, the predicted scores ($\hat{Y}_3$) of the reflective endogenous latent variable are used to predict systematically omitted (or eliminated) data points of the indicators x_5, x_6, and x_7 in the measurement model. The systematic pattern of data point elimination and prediction depends on the **omission distance (D)**, which must be determined to run the blindfolding procedure. An omission distance of 3, for example, implies that every third data point of the indicators x_5, x_6, and x_7 is eliminated in a single blindfolding round. Since the blindfolding procedure has to omit and predict every data point of the indicators used in the measurement model of a reflective endogenous latent variable, it has to include three rounds. Hence, the number of blindfolding rounds always equals the omission distance D.

Exhibit 6.6 Path Model Example of the Blindfolding Procedure

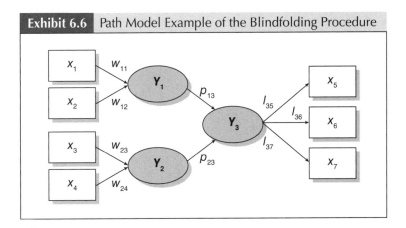

Exhibit 6.7 shows the application of the blindfolding procedure with respect to the reflective endogenous latent variable Y_3 shown in Exhibit 6.6. For illustrative purposes, the number of observations for the standardized data of indicators x_5, x_6, and x_7 is reduced to seven. We select an omission distance of 3 in this example. We use this number for illustrative reasons. In applications, a higher omission distance D between 5 and 10 should be used (Apel and Wold, 1982; Hair, Sarstedt, Ringle, et al., 2012), which represents an omission between approximately 20% (i.e., $D = 5$) and 10% (i.e., $D = 10$) of the data points per blindfolding round. Note that [$d1$], [$d2$], and [$d3$] in Exhibit 6.7 are not entries in the data matrix but are used to show how the data elimination pattern is applied to the data points of x_5, x_6, and x_7. For example, the first data point of indicator x_5 has a value of -0.452 and is connected to [$d1$], which indicates that this data point is eliminated in the first blindfolding round. The assignment of the omission distance (e.g., [$d1$], [$d2$], and [$d3$] in Exhibit 6.7) occurs per column. When the assignment of the pattern ends with [$d1$] in the last observation (i.e., Observation 7) in the first column of indicator x_5 (Exhibit 6.7), the procedure continues assigning [$d2$] to the first observation in the second column of indicator x_6.

Exhibit 6.7 displays the assignment of the data omission pattern for the omission distance D of 3. It is important to note that the omission distance D has to be chosen so that the number of observations used in the model estimation divided by D is not an integer. If the number of observations divided by D results in an integer, you would always delete the same set of observations in each round from the data matrix. For example, if you have 90 observations, the omission distance must not be 9 or 10 as $90/9 = 10$ and $90/10 = 9$ are integers. Rather, you should use omission distances of 7 or 8.

As shown in Exhibit 6.7, the data points [$d1$] are eliminated in the first blindfolding round. The remaining data points are now used to estimate the path model in Exhibit 6.6. A missing value treatment function (e.g., the mean value replacement) is used for the deleted data points when running the PLS-SEM algorithm. These PLS-SEM estimates differ from the original model estimation and from the results of the two following blindfolding rounds. The outcomes of the first blindfolding round are used to first predict the $\hat{Y}_3$ scores of the selected reflective endogenous latent variable. Thereafter, the predicted values of $\hat{Y}_3$ and the estimations of the outer loadings (i.e., l_{35}, l_{36}, and l_{37}; Exhibit 6.7) in the first blindfolding round allow every single eliminated data point to be predicted in this first round. The second and the third blindfolding rounds follow a similar process.

Exhibit 6.7 Blindfolding Procedure

| | Standardized Indicator Data | | | | | | First Blindfolding Round: Omission of Data Points [d1] | | | | | |
| | Indicators of the Reflective Construct Y_3 | | | | | | Indicators of the Reflective Construct Y_3 | | | | | |
Observations	x_5		x_6		x_7		x_5		x_6		x_7	
1	−0.452	[d1]	−0.309	[d2]	−0.152	[d3]			−0.309	[d2]	−0.152	[d3]
2	0.943	[d2]	1.146	[d3]	0.534	[d1]	0.943	[d2]	1.146	[d3]		
3	−0.452	[d3]	−0.309	[d1]	−2.209	[d2]	−0.452	[d3]			−2.209	[d2]
4	0.943	[d1]	−1.036	[d2]	−0.837	[d3]			−1.036	[d2]	−0.837	[d3]
5	0.943	[d2]	−1.036	[d3]	0.534	[d1]	0.943	[d2]	−1.036	[d3]		
6	−1.150	[d3]	−1.036	[d1]	−0.837	[d2]	−1.150	[d3]			−0.837	[d2]
7	1.641	[d1]	−0.309	[d2]	1.220	[d3]			−0.309	[d2]	1.220	[d3]

(Continued)

Exhibit 6.7 (Continued)

Observations	Second Blindfolding Round: Omission of Data Points [d2]						Third Blindfolding Round: Omission of Data Points [d3]					
	Indicators of the Reflective Construct Y_3						Indicators of the Reflective Construct Y_3					
	x_5		x_6		x_7		x_5		x_6		x_7	
1	−0.452	[d1]			−0.152	[d3]	−0.452	[d1]	−0.309	[d2]		
2			1.146	[d3]	0.534	[d1]	0.943	[d2]			0.534	[d1]
3	−0.452	[d3]	−0.309	[d1]					−0.309	[d1]	−2.209	[d2]
4	0.943	[d1]			−0.837	[d3]	0.943	[d1]	−1.036	[d2]		
5			−1.036	[d3]	0.534	[d1]	0.943	[d2]			0.534	[d1]
6	−1.150	[d3]	−1.036	[d1]					−1.036	[d1]	−0.837	[d2]
7	1.641	[d1]			1.220	[d3]	1.641	[d1]	−0.309	[d2]		

After the last blindfolding round, each data point of the indicators of a selected reflective endogenous latent variable has been removed and then predicted. Thus, the blindfolding procedure can compare the original values with the predicted values. If the prediction is close to the original value (i.e., there is a small prediction error), the path model has a high predictive accuracy. The **prediction errors** (calculated as the difference between the true values [i.e., the omitted values] and the predicted values), along with a trivial prediction error (defined as the mean of the remaining data), are then used to estimate the Q^2 value (Chin, 1998). Q^2 values larger than 0 suggest that the model has predictive relevance for a certain endogenous construct. In contrast, values of 0 and below indicate a lack of predictive relevance.

It is important to note that the Q^2 value can be calculated by using two different approaches. The **cross-validated redundancy** approach—as described in this section—builds on the path model estimates of both the structural model (scores of the antecedent constructs) and the measurement model (target endogenous construct) of data prediction. Therefore, prediction by means of cross-validated redundancy fits the PLS-SEM approach perfectly. An alternative method, the **cross-validated communality** approach, uses only the construct scores estimated for the target endogenous construct (without including the structural model information) to predict the omitted data points. We recommend using the cross-validated redundancy as a measure of Q^2 since it includes the structural model, the key element of the path model, to predict eliminated data points.

Step 6: Effect Size q^2

The Q^2 values estimated by the blindfolding procedure represent a measure of how well the path model can predict the originally observed values. Similar to the f^2 effect size approach for assessing R^2 values, the relative impact of predictive relevance can be compared by means of the measure to the q^2 **effect size**, formally defined as follows:

$$q^2 = \frac{Q^2_{\text{included}} - Q^2_{\text{excluded}}}{1 - Q^2_{\text{included}}}.$$

For example, to determine the q^2 effect size of construct Y_1 on the reflective endogenous latent variable Y_3 in Exhibit 6.6, one would compute the PLS-SEM results of the model with construct Y_1 (Q^2_{included}) and, thereafter, of the path model without construct Y_1 (Q^2_{excluded}). In doing so, one has to use identical values for the omission distance D when computing the results of $Q^2_{included}$ and $Q^2_{excluded}$. As a relative measure of predictive relevance, values of 0.02, 0.15, and 0.35 indicate that an exogenous construct has a small, medium, or large predictive relevance, respectively, for a certain endogenous construct. An application of q^2 effect size to the reputation model follows later in this chapter. Exhibit 6.8 summarizes the key criteria for evaluating structural model results.

Exhibit 6.8   Rules of Thumb for Structural Model Evaluation

- Examine each set of predictors in the structural model for collinearity. Each predictor construct's tolerance (VIF) value should be higher than 0.20 (lower than 5). Otherwise, consider eliminating constructs, merging predictors into a single construct, or creating higher-order constructs to treat collinearity problems.

- Use bootstrapping to assess the significance of path coefficients. The minimum number of bootstrap samples must be at least as large as the number of valid observations but should be 5,000. Critical t values for a two-tailed test are 1.65 (significance level = 10%), 1.96 (significance level = 5%), and 2.57 (significance level = 1%). Alternatively, examine the p value, which should be lower than 0.10 (significance level = 10%), 0.05 (significance level = 5%), or 0.01 (significance level = 1%). In applications, you should usually assume a 5% significance level.

- Bootstrap confidence intervals provide additional information on the stability of path coefficient estimates. Use the percentile method for constructing confidence intervals. When models are not complex (i.e., fewer than four constructs) and sample size is small, use double bootstrapping. However, the running time can be extensive.

- PLS-SEM aims at maximizing the R^2 values of the endogenous latent variable(s) in the path model. While the exact interpretation of the R^2 value depends on the particular model and research discipline, in general R^2 values of 0.75, 0.50, or 0.25 for the endogenous construct can be described as respectively substantial, moderate, and weak.

- Use the R^2_{adj} when comparing models with different exogenous constructs and/or different numbers of observations.

- The effect size f^2 allows assessing an exogenous construct's contribution to an endogenous latent variable's R^2 value. f^2 values of 0.02, 0.15, and 0.35 indicate an exogenous construct's small, medium, or large effect, respectively, on an endogenous construct.

- Predictive relevance: Use blindfolding to obtain cross-validated redundancy measures for each endogenous construct. Make sure the number of observations used in the model estimation divided by the omission distance D is not an integer. Choose D values between 5 and 10. The resulting Q^2 values larger than 0 indicate that the exogenous constructs have predictive relevance for the endogenous construct under consideration.

- The effect size q^2 allows assessing an exogenous construct's contribution to an endogenous latent variable's Q^2 value. As a relative measure of predictive relevance, q^2 values of 0.02, 0.15, and 0.35, respectively, indicate that an exogenous construct has a small, medium, or large predictive relevance for a certain endogenous construct.

- For theory testing, consider using SRMR, RMS_{theta}, or the exact fit test. Apart from conceptual concerns, these measures' behaviors have not been researched in a PLS-SEM context in depth, and threshold values have not been derived yet. Following a conservative approach, an SRMR (RMS_{theta}) value of less than 0.08 (0.12) indicates good fit. Do not use the GoF to determine model fit.

CASE STUDY ILLUSTRATION—HOW ARE PLS-SEM STRUCTURAL MODEL RESULTS REPORTED?

We continue with the extended corporate reputation model as introduced in Chapter 5. If you do not have the PLS path model readily available in SmartPLS, download the file **Corporate Reputation.zip** from the http://www.pls-sem.com website and save it on your hard drive. Then, run the SmartPLS software and click on **File → Import project from backup file** in the menu. In the box that appears on the screen, locate and open the **Corporate Reputation.zip** file that you just downloaded. Thereafter, a new project appears with the name **Corporate Reputation** in the SmartPLS **Project Explorer** window on the left-hand side. This project contains several models (.splsm files) labeled **Simple model, Extended model, Redundancy analysis ATTR, Redundancy analysis CSOR,** and so forth, plus the data file **Corporate reputation data.csv.** Next, double-click on **Extended model,** and the extended PLS path model for the corporate reputation example opens.

The assessment of the structural model builds on the results from the standard model estimation, the bootstrapping routine, and the blindfolding procedure. After running the PLS-SEM algorithm using the same algorithm and missing values settings as in the previous chapters, SmartPLS shows the key results of the model estimation in the **Modeling** window (Exhibit 6.9). Per default, we see the path coefficients as well as the R^2 values of the endogenous constructs (shown in the circles).

For a more detailed assessment, we need to examine the Smart-PLS results report. Following the structural model assessment procedure (Exhibit 6.1), we first need to check the structural model for collinearity issues by examining the VIF values of all sets of predictor constructs in the structural model. To do so, go to **Quality Criteria → Collinearity Statistic (VIF)** and click on the **Inner VIF Values** tab. The results table that opens (Exhibit 6.10) shows the VIF values of all combinations of endogenous constructs (represented by the columns) and corresponding exogenous (i.e., predictor) constructs (represented by the rows). Specifically, we assess the following sets of (predictor) constructs for collinearity: (1) *ATTR, CSOR, PERF,* and *QUAL* as predictors of *COMP* (and *LIKE*); (2) *COMP* and *LIKE* as predictors of *CUSA;* and (3) *COMP, LIKE,* and *CUSA* as predictors of *CUSL.* As can be seen in Exhibit 6.10 all VIF values are clearly below the threshold of 5. Therefore, collinearity among the predictor constructs is not a critical issue in the structural model, and we can continue examining the results report.

To start with, we examine the R^2 values of the endogenous latent variables, which are available under **Quality Criteria → R Square** (select the **Matrix** view). Following our rules of thumb, the R^2 values of *COMP* (0.631), *CUSL* (0.562), and *LIKE* (0.558) can be considered moderate, whereas the R^2 value of *CUSA* (0.292) is rather weak.

To obtain the effect sizes f^2 for all structural model relationships, go to **Quality Criteria → f Square** (select the **Matrix** view). Exhibit 6.11 shows the f^2 values for all combinations of endogenous constructs (represented by the columns) and corresponding exogenous (i.e., predictor) constructs (represented by the rows). For example, *LIKE* has a medium effect size of 0.159 on *CUSA* and of 0.138 on *CUSL.* On the contrary, *COMP* has no effect on *CUSA* (0.018) or *CUSL* (0.000). Please note that these results differ from a manual computation of the f^2 values by using the aforementioned equation with values for $R^2_{included}$ and $R^2_{excluded}$. This difference results because SmartPLS 3 uses the latent variable scores of the model that includes all latent variables and then internally excludes latent variables to obtain the $R^2_{excluded}$. On the contrary, when manually computing the f^2 values by estimating the model with and without a latent variable, the model changes and, thus, the latent variable scores. Hence, the difference of the manually computed

Exhibit 6.9 Results in Modeling Window

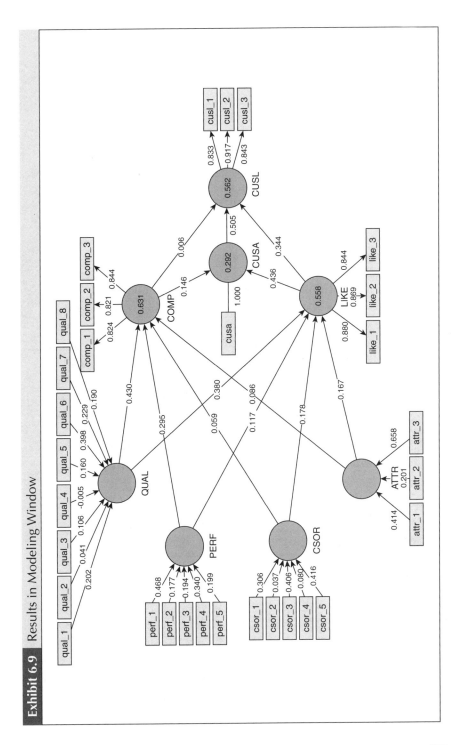

Exhibit 6.10	VIF Values in the Structural Model

Collinearity Statistic (VIF)

| | Inner VIF Values | | Outer VIF Values | | | | | | |

	ATTR	COMP	CSOR	CUSA	CUSL	LIKE	PERF	QUAL
ATTR		2.122				2.122		
COMP				1.686	1.716			
CSOR		2.083				2.083		
CUSA					1.412			
CUSL								
LIKE				1.686	1.954			
PERF		2.889				2.889		
QUAL		3.487				3.487		

f^2 values results from the changes in the latent variable scores due to a model modification, which is, however, incorrect.

Under **Final Results → Path Coefficients,** we find the path coefficients as shown in the modeling window. Looking at the relative importance of the exogenous driver constructs for the perceived competence (*COMP*), one finds that the customers' perception of the company's quality of products and services (*QUAL*) is most important, followed by its performance (*PERF*). In contrast, the perceived attractiveness (*ATTR*) and degree to which the company acts in socially conscious ways (*CSOR*) have very little bearing on the perceived competence. These two drivers are, however, of increased importance for establishing a company's likeability. Moving on in the model, we also find that likeability is the primary driver for the customers' satisfaction and loyalty, as illustrated by the increased path coefficients compared with those of competence.

More interesting, though, is the examination of total effects. Specifically, we can evaluate how strongly each of the four formative

Exhibit 6.11	f^2 Effect Sizes

f Square

| | f Square | | Matrix | | | | | | |

	ATTR	COMP	CSOR	CUSA	CUSL	LIKE	PERF	QUAL
ATTR		0.009				0.030		
COMP				0.018	0.000			
CSOR		0.005				0.035		
CUSA					0.412			
CUSL								
LIKE				0.159	0.138			
PERF		0.082				0.011		
QUAL		0.143				0.094		

driver constructs (*ATTR, CSOR, PERF,* and *QUAL*) ultimately influences the key target variable *CUSL* via the mediating constructs *COMP, LIKE,* and *CUSA*. Total effects are shown under **Final Results → Total Effects** in the results report. We read the table shown in Exhibit 6.12 column to row. That is, each column represents a target construct, whereas the rows represent predecessor constructs. For example, with regard to loyalty, we can see that among the four exogenous driver constructs, quality has the strongest total effect on loyalty (0.248), followed by corporate social responsibility (0.105), attractiveness (0.101), and performance (0.089). Therefore, it is advisable for companies to focus on marketing activities that positively influence the customers' perception of the quality of their products and services. By also taking the construct's indicator weights into consideration, we can even identify which specific element of quality needs to be addressed. Looking at the outer weights (**Final Results → Outer Weights**) reveals that *qual_6* has the highest outer weight (0.398). This item relates to the survey question "[the company] is a reliable partner for customers." Thus, marketing managers should try to enhance the customers' perception of the reliability of their products and services by means of marketing activities.

The analysis of structural model relationships showed that several path coefficients (e.g., *COMP → CUSL*) had rather low values. To assess whether these relationships are significant, we run the bootstrapping procedure. The extraction of bootstrapping results for the structural model estimates is analogous to the descriptions in the context of formative measurement model assessment (Chapter 5). To run the bootstrapping procedure, go to **Calculate → Bootstrapping** in

---

Exhibit 6.12   Total Effects

Total Effects

▦ Matrix

	ATTR	COMP	CSOR	CUSA	CUSL	LIKE	PERF	QUAL
ATTR	1.000	0.086		0.085	0.101	0.167		
COMP		1.000		0.146	0.079			
CSOR		0.059	1.000	0.086	0.105	0.178		
CUSA				1.000	0.505			
CUSL					1.000			
LIKE				0.436	0.564	1.000		
PERF		0.295		0.094	0.089	0.117	1.000	
QUAL		0.430		0.228	0.248	0.380		1.000

the SmartPLS menu or go to the **Modeling** window and click on the **Calculate** icon, followed by **Bootstrapping** (note that you first may need to go back to the **Modeling** window before the **Calculate** icon appears). We retain all settings for missing value treatment and the PLS-SEM algorithm as in the initial model estimation and select the **No Sign Changes** option, **5,000** bootstrap samples and select the **Complete Bootstrapping** option. In the advanced settings, we choose **Bias-Corrected and Accelerated (BCa) Bootstrap, two-tailed** testing, and a significance level of **0.05**. Next, we click **Start Calculation.**

After running the procedure, SmartPLS shows the bootstrapping results for the measurement models and structural model in the **Modeling** window. Using the **Calculation Results** box at the bottom left of the screen, you can choose whether SmartPLS should display t values or p values in the **Modeling** window. Exhibit 6.13 shows p values for the structural model relationships as resulting from the bootstrapping procedure. Note that the results will differ from your results and will change again when rerunning bootstrapping as the procedure builds on randomly drawn samples.

Assuming a 5% significance level, we find that all relationships in the structural model are significant, except $PERF \rightarrow LIKE$ ($p = 0.084$), $ATTR \rightarrow COMP$ ($p = 0.102$), $CSOR \rightarrow COMP$ ($p = 0.261$), and $COMP \rightarrow CUSL$ ($p = 0.920$). These results suggest that companies should concentrate their marketing efforts on enhancing their likeability (by strengthening customers' quality perceptions) rather than their perceived competence to maximize customer loyalty. This is not surprising, considering that customers rated mobile network operators. As their services (provision of network capabilities) are intangible, affective judgments play a much more important role than cognitive judgments for establishing customer loyalty. Furthermore, we learn that $ATTR$ and $CSOR$ only influence $LIKE$, which is also not surprising since these two driver constructs are also more affective in nature.

By going to the bootstrapping report, we get a more detailed overview of the results. The table under **Final Results** $\rightarrow$ **Path Coefficients** provides us with an overview of results, including standard errors, bootstrap mean values, t values and p values. Clicking on the **Confidence Intervals** tab in the bootstrapping results report shows the confidence interval as derived from the BCa method (Exhibit 6.14; again, your results will look slightly different because bootstrapping is a random process). In addition, you can access the bias-corrected confidence interval by clicking the corresponding tab.

Finally, clicking on the **Samples** tab in the bootstrapping results report shows the results of each bootstrap run as shown in

Exhibit 6.13 Bootstrapping Results in the Modeling Window

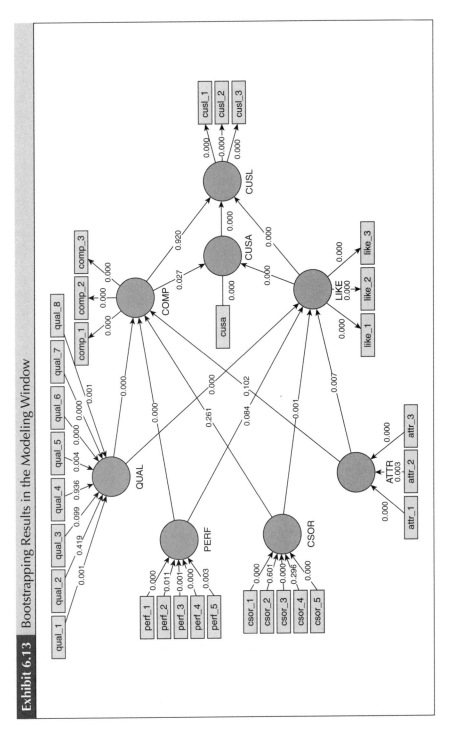

Exhibit 6.14 Bootstrapping Results

Path Coefficients

| Mean, STDEV, T-Values, P-Values | Confidence Intervals | Confidence Intervals Bias Corrected | Samples |

	Original Sample (O)	Sample Mean (M)	Bias	2.5 %	97.5 %
ATTR -> COMP	0.086	0.088	0.002	-0.013	0.187
ATTR -> LIKE	0.167	0.161	-0.007	0.032	0.273
COMP -> CUSA	0.146	0.151	0.005	0.033	0.275
COMP -> CUSL	0.006	0.004	-0.001	-0.111	0.113
CSOR -> COMP	0.059	0.060	0.001	-0.036	0.156
CSOR -> LIKE	0.178	0.183	0.005	0.084	0.288
CUSA -> CUSL	0.505	0.505	0.000	0.428	0.580
LIKE -> CUSA	0.436	0.435	-0.001	0.312	0.544
LIKE -> CUSL	0.344	0.346	0.002	0.241	0.453
PERF -> COMP	0.295	0.298	0.003	0.172	0.417
PERF -> LIKE	0.117	0.119	0.002	-0.012	0.254
QUAL -> COMP	0.430	0.429	-0.001	0.295	0.560
QUAL -> LIKE	0.380	0.387	0.007	0.278	0.514

Exhibit 6.15. Note that the exhibit displays only a fraction of the results table (i.e., the first 20 bootstrap samples). The full table includes the estimates of all the path coefficients for all 5,000 sub-samples. These estimates are used to compute the bootstrapping mean values, standard errors, t values, and p values of all the path coefficients, shown in the **Mean, STDEV, T-Values, P-Values** table of the bootstrapping results report.

Exhibit 6.16 provides a summary of the path coefficient estimates, t values, p values, and confidence intervals. Again, the user usually reports either the t values (and their significance levels) *or the* p values *or* the confidence intervals. We find that all criteria come to the same outcome for the significance of path coefficients. Otherwise, we recommend relying on the bootstrap confidence intervals for **significance testing** (see Chapter 5 for details); Exhibit 6.16 only shows all results for illustrative purposes.

To examine the bootstrapping results for the total effects, go to **Final Results → Total Effects.** Exhibit 6.17 summarizes the results for the total effects of the exogenous constructs *ATTR, CSOR, PERF,* and *QUAL* on the target constructs *CUSA* and *CUSL* taken from the **Mean, STDEV, T-Values, P-Values** table of the bootstrapping results report. As can be seen, all total effects are significant at a 5% level.

Next, we run the blindfolding procedure to assess the predictive relevance of the path model. To run the procedure, go to **Calculate → Blindfolding** in the SmartPLS menu or go to the **Modeling** window and click on the **Calculate** icon, followed by **Blindfolding.** In the dialog box that opens, we keep all the information of the missing value treatment and the PLS-SEM algorithm as in the initial model estimation in the **Partial Least Squares** and **Missing Values** tabs. However, in the **Setup** tab, we need to specify the omission distance D. Remember that dividing the sample size by D must not yield an integer. As we have 344 observations, we can choose an omission distance of $D = 7$. Finally, click on **Start Calculation.**

Exhibit 6.18 shows the blindfolding results report. The only results table we need to focus on is the one for the **Construct Cross-validated Redundancy** estimates. The first tab of the results table (as displayed on the right in Exhibit 6.18) presents the summary with the total outcomes of the blindfolding procedure (the other tabs labeled **Case1** to **Case7** show the outcomes of each of the seven blindfolding rounds). In the table, **SSO** shows the sum of the squared observations, **SSE** the sum of the squared prediction errors, and the last column (i.e., 1 − SSE/SSO) the final value Q^2, which we interpret to judge the

(Text continues on page 220)

Exhibit 6.15 Bootstrap Samples

Path Coefficients

☐ Mean, STDEV, T-Values, P-Values   ☐ Confidence Intervals   ☐ Confidence Intervals Bias Corrected   ☐ Samples

	ATTR -> COMP	ATTR -> LIKE	COMP -> CUSA	COMP -> CUSL	CSOR -> COMP	CSOR -> LIKE	CUSA -> CUSL	LIKE -> CUSA	LIKE -> CUSL	PERF -> C
Sample 1	0.142	0.206	0.115	0.071	0.082	0.145	0.538	0.474	0.236	
Sample 2	0.112	0.132	0.011	-0.034	0.045	0.137	0.520	0.611	0.298	
Sample 3	-0.002	0.135	0.231	-0.015	0.050	0.164	0.483	0.448	0.336	
Sample 4	0.063	0.231	0.242	0.029	0.076	0.186	0.458	0.389	0.386	
Sample 5	0.093	0.140	0.196	0.042	0.087	0.135	0.467	0.459	0.383	
Sample 6	0.163	0.155	0.142	0.047	0.102	0.103	0.536	0.466	0.292	
Sample 7	0.042	0.136	0.186	-0.028	0.173	0.114	0.487	0.450	0.408	
Sample 8	0.047	0.068	0.173	0.190	-0.003	0.161	0.480	0.382	0.187	
Sample 9	0.046	0.176	0.044	0.032	0.056	0.267	0.523	0.477	0.315	
Sample 10	0.025	0.137	0.062	-0.110	0.048	0.222	0.510	0.524	0.464	
Sample 11	0.012	0.172	0.252	0.006	0.102	0.084	0.507	0.365	0.372	
Sample 12	0.120	0.122	0.183	-0.013	0.045	0.187	0.509	0.399	0.339	
Sample 13	0.007	0.040	0.121	0.004	0.088	0.289	0.409	0.439	0.458	
Sample 14	0.119	0.215	0.279	-0.028	0.077	0.226	0.563	0.334	0.348	
Sample 15	0.041	0.099	0.233	0.052	-0.036	0.190	0.459	0.357	0.381	
Sample 16	0.098	0.170	0.066	0.041	0.070	0.160	0.553	0.491	0.234	
Sample 17	0.133	0.129	0.031	0.053	0.064	0.210	0.500	0.576	0.278	
Sample 18	0.104	0.284	0.232	0.027	0.039	0.164	0.540	0.377	0.305	
Sample 19	0.090	0.224	0.262	-0.019	0.057	0.204	0.519	0.312	0.393	
Sample 20	0.016	0.011	0.093	-0.124	0.063	0.299	0.515	0.528	0.417	

Exhibit 6.16	Significance Testing Results of the Structural Model Path Coefficients				
	Path Coefficients	t Values	p Values	95% Confidence Intervals	Significance[a] (p < 0.05)?
ATTR → COMP	0.086	1.636	0.102	[-0.013, 0.187]	No
ATTR → LIKE	0.167	2.724	0.007	[0.032, 0.273]	Yes
COMP → CUSA	0.146	2.211	0.027	[0.033, 0.275]	Yes
COMP → CUSL	0.006	0.100	0.920	[-0.111, 0.113]	No
CSOR → COMP	0.059	1.126	0.261	[-0.036, 0.156]	No
CSOR → LIKE	0.178	3.472	0.001	[0.084, 0.288]	Yes
CUSA → CUSL	0.505	12.329	0.000	[0.428, 0.580]	Yes
LIKE → CUSA	0.436	7.469	0.000	[0.312, 0.544]	Yes
LIKE → CUSL	0.344	5.989	0.000	[0.241, 0.453]	Yes
PERF → COMP	0.295	4.578	0.000	[0.172, 0.417]	Yes
PERF → LIKE	0.117	1.731	0.084	[-0.012, 0.254]	No
QUAL → COMP	0.430	6.661	0.000	[0.295, 0.560]	Yes
QUAL → LIKE	0.380	6.018	0.000	[0.278, 0.514]	Yes

[a]We refer to the bootstrap confidence intervals for significance testing, as described in Chapter 5.

Exhibit 6.17	Significance Testing Results of the Total Effects				
	Total Effect	t Values	p Values	95% Confidence Intervals	Significance[a] (p < 0.05)?
ATTR → CUSA	0.086	2.856	0.004	[0.024, 0.133]	Yes
ATTR → CUSL	0.101	2.783	0.006	[0.026, 0.166]	Yes
CSOR → CUSA	0.086	3.321	0.001	[0.044, 0.144]	Yes
CSOR → CUSL	0.105	3.369	0.001	[0.053, 0.169]	Yes
PERF → CUSA	0.094	2.492	0.013	[0.027, 0.173]	Yes
PERF → CUSL	0.089	2.026	0.043	[0.011, 0.179]	Yes
QUAL → CUSA	0.228	6.390	0.000	[0.172, 0.310]	Yes
QUAL → CUSL	0.248	5.970	0.000	[0.186, 0.344]	Yes

[a]We refer to the bootstrap confidence intervals for significance testing, as described in Chapter 5.

Exhibit 6.18	Q^2 Values

Construct Crossvalidated Redundancy

▦ Total	▦ Case1	▦ Case2	▦ Case3	▦ Case4	▦ Case5	▦ Case6	▦ Case7

	SSO	SSE	Q^2 (=1-SSE/SSO)
ATTR	1,032.000	1,032.000	
COMP	1,032.000	603.416	0.415
CSOR	1,720.000	1,720.000	
CUSA	344.000	247.704	0.280
CUSL	1,032.000	604.012	0.415
LIKE	1,032.000	612.624	0.406
PERF	1,720.000	1,720.000	
QUAL	2,752.000	2,752.000	

model's predictive relevance with regard to each endogenous construct. As can be seen, the Q^2 values of all four endogenous constructs are considerably above zero. More precisely, *CUSL* and *COMP* have the highest Q^2 values (0.415), followed by *LIKE* (0.406) and, finally, *CUSA* (0.280). These results provide clear support for the model's predictive relevance regarding the endogenous latent variables.

The final assessment addresses the q^2 effect sizes. These must be computed manually because the SmartPLS software does not provide them. To compute the q^2 value of a selected endogenous latent variable, we need the $Q^2_{included}$ and $Q^2_{excluded}$ values. The $Q^2_{included}$ results from the previous blindfolding estimation are available from Exhibit 6.18. The $Q^2_{excluded}$ value is obtained from a model reestimation after deleting a specific predecessor of that endogenous latent variable. For example, the endogenous latent variable *CUSL* has an original Q^2 value of 0.415 ($Q^2_{included}$). When *CUSA* is deleted from the path model and the model is reestimated, the Q^2 of *CUSL* drops to 0.281 ($Q^2_{excluded}$). These two values are the inputs for computing the q^2 effect size of *CUSA* on *CUSL*:

$$q^2_{CUSA \rightarrow CUSL} = \frac{Q^2_{included} - Q^2_{excluded}}{1 - Q^2_{included}} = \frac{0.415 - 0.281}{1 - 0.415} = 0.229.$$

Following the rules of thumb, the q^2 effect size for this relationship can be considered medium. Exhibit 6.19 summarizes the results of the q^2 effect sizes with respect to all the relationships in the model. The endogenous constructs appear in the first row, whereas the predictor constructs are in the first column.

Exhibit 6.19	q^2 Effect Sizes			
	COMP	**CUSA**	**CUSL**	**LIKE**
ATTR	0.000			0.016
COMP		0.006	−0.002	
CSOR	−0.005			0.018
CUSA			0.229	
LIKE		0.151	0.077	
PERF	0.039			0.003
QUAL	0.052			0.050

SUMMARY

• **Understand the concept of model fit in a PLS-SEM context.** The notion of model fit as known from CB-SEM is not fully transferrable to PLS-SEM as the method follows a different aim when estimating model parameters (i.e., maximizing the explained variance instead of minimizing the divergence between covariance matrices). Instead, the structural model is primarily assessed on the basis of heuristic criteria that are determined by the model's predictive capabilities. These criteria, by definition, do not allow for testing the overall goodness of the model fit in a CB-SEM sense. Rather, the model is assessed in terms of how well it predicts the endogenous variables/constructs. Nevertheless, research has brought forward several PLS-SEM–based model fit measures such as SRMR, RMS_{theta}, and the exact fit test. While these measures have been shown to identify model misspecifications in various model settings, they are still in the early stages of development.

• **Assess the path coefficients in the structural model.** When initially assessing the PLS-SEM results for the structural model, the first issues to examine are the significance and the relevance of coefficients. Testing for significance requires application of the bootstrapping routine and examination of t values, p values, or bootstrapping confidence intervals. Next, the relative sizes of path coefficients are compared, as well as the total effects, f^2 effect size, and q^2 effect size. By interpreting these results, you can identify the key constructs with the highest relevance to explain the endogenous latent variable(s) in the structural model.

- **Evaluate the coefficients of determination (R^2 values).** The PLS-SEM method was developed primarily for prediction purposes. The R^2 values (i.e., coefficients of determination) represent the amount of explained variance of the endogenous constructs in the structural model. A well-developed path model to explain certain key target constructs (e.g., customer satisfaction, customer loyalty, or technology acceptance) should deliver sufficiently high R^2 values. The exact interpretation of the R^2 value depends on the particular research discipline. In general, R^2 values of 0.25, 0.50, and 0.75 for target constructs are considered as weak, medium, and substantial, respectively.

- **Understand and evaluate the f^2 effect size.** The f^2 effect size enables you to analyze the relevance of constructs in explaining selected endogenous constructs. More specifically, you analyze how much a predictor construct contributes to the R^2 value of a target construct in the structural model. Initially, you estimate the R^2 value with a particular predecessor construct. Without the predecessor construct, the result is a lower R^2 value. On the basis of the difference of the R^2 values for estimating the model with and without the predecessor construct, you obtain the f^2 effect size. Results of 0.02, 0.15, and 0.35 are interpreted as small, medium, and large f^2 effect sizes, respectively.

- **Use the blindfolding procedure for assessing the predictive relevance (Q^2 value) of the path model.** The blindfolding procedure is a resampling technique that systematically deletes and predicts every data point of the indicators in the reflective measurement model of endogenous constructs. By comparing the original values with the predictions, the prediction error of the path model for this particular reflective target construct is obtained. The computation of the Q^2 value for assessing predictive relevance uses this prediction error. The path model has predictive relevance for a selected reflective endogenous construct if the Q^2 value is above zero. In accordance with the f^2 effect size for the R^2 values, you can also compute the q^2 effect size for the Q^2 values. The q^2 effect size of a selected construct and its relationship to an endogenous construct in the structural model use the same critical values for assessment used for the f^2 effect size evaluation.

• **Learn how to report and interpret structural model results.** By extending the example on corporate reputation to include additional constructs, you can learn to systematically apply the structural model assessment criteria. The SmartPLS 3 software provides all relevant results for the evaluation of the structural model. The tables and figures for this example described in the chapter demonstrate how to correctly interpret and report the PLS-SEM results. The hands-on example not only summarizes the previously introduced concepts but also provides additional insights for practical applications of PLS-SEM.

REVIEW QUESTIONS

1. What are the key criteria for assessing the results of the structural model?

2. Why do you assess the significance of path coefficients?

3. What is an appropriate R^2 value level?

4. Which is the critical Q^2 value to establish predictive relevance?

5. What are the critical values for interpreting the f^2 and q^2 effect sizes?

CRITICAL THINKING QUESTIONS

1. What problems do you encounter in evaluating the structural model results of PLS-SEM? How do you approach this task?

2. Why is the use of the GoF index for PLS-SEM not advisable? Which other means for model fit testing have been proposed?

3. Why use the bootstrapping routine for significance testing? Explain the algorithm options and parameters you need to select.

4. Explain the f^2 effect size.

5. How does the blindfolding procedure function and what are the consequences of increasing and decreasing the omission distance D? Explain the Q^2 value and the q^2 effect size results.

KEY TERMS

Adjusted coefficient of determination R^2_{adj}

Blindfolding

Critical value

Cross-validated communality

Cross-validated redundancy

Exact fit test

f^2 effect size

GoF

GoF f^2

Goodness-of-fit index (GoF)

Hypothesized relationships

In-sample predictive power

Omission distance (D)

One-tailed test

Out-of-sample predictive power

Parsimonious models

Prediction error

q^2 effect size

Q^2 value

R^2 value

R^2_{adj} value

Q^2 value

Relevance of significant relationships

RMS_{theta}

Root mean square residual covariance (RMS_{theta})

SRMR

Significance testing

Standard error

Standardized root mean square residual (SRMR)

Total effect

Two-tailed test

SUGGESTED READINGS

Albers, S. (2010). PLS and success factor studies in marketing. In V. Esposito Vinzi, W. W. Chin, J. Henseler, & H. Wang (Eds.), *Handbook of partial least squares: Concepts, methods and applications* (Springer Handbooks of Computational Statistics Series, Vol. II, pp. 409–425). Berlin: Springer.

Chin, W. W. (2010). How to write up and report PLS analyses. In V. Esposito Vinzi, W. W. Chin, J. Henseler, & H. Wang (Eds.), *Handbook of partial least squares: Concepts, methods and applications in marketing and related fields* (Springer Handbooks of Computational Statistics Series, Vol. II, pp. 655–690). Berlin: Springer.

Dijkstra, T. K., & Henseler, J. (2015). Consistent and asymptotically normal PLS estimators for linear structural equations. *Computational Statistics & Data Analysis, 81,* 10–23.

Gefen, D., Rigdon, E. E., & Straub, D. W. (2011). Editor's comment: An update and extension to SEM guidelines for administrative and social science research. *MIS Quarterly, 35,* iii–xiv.

Hair, J. F., Ringle, C. M., & Sarstedt, M. (2011). PLS-SEM: Indeed a silver bullet. *Journal of Marketing Theory and Practice, 19,* 139–151.

Hair, J. F., Sarstedt, M., Pieper, T., & Ringle, C. M. (2012). The use of partial least squares structural equation modeling in strategic management research: A review of past practices and recommendations for future applications. *Long Range Planning, 45,* 320–340.

Hair, J. F., Sarstedt, M., Ringle, C. M., & Mena, J. A. (2012). An assessment of the use of partial least squares structural equation modeling in marketing research. *Journal of the Academy of Marketing Science, 40,* 414–433.

Henseler, J., Dijkstra, T. K., Sarstedt, M., Ringle, C. M., Diamantopoulos, A., Straub, D. W., et al. (2014). Common beliefs and reality about partial least squares: Comments on Rönkkö & Evermann (2013). *Organizational Research Methods, 17,* 182–209.

Henseler, J., Ringle, C. M., & Sinkovics, R. R. (2009). The use of partial least squares path modeling in international marketing. *Advances in International Marketing, 20,* 277–320.

Hulland, J. (1999). Use of partial least squares (PLS) in strategic management research: A review of four recent studies. *Strategic Management Journal, 20,* 195–204.

Ringle, C. M., Sarstedt, M., & Straub, D. W. (2012). A critical look at the use of PLS-SEM in *MIS Quarterly. MIS Quarterly, 36,* iii–xiv.

Roldán, J. L., & Sánchez-Franco, M. J. (2012). Variance-based structural equation modeling: Guidelines for using partial least squares in information systems research. In M. Mora, O. Gelman, A. L. Steenkamp, & M. Raisinghani (Eds.), *Research methodologies, innovations and philosophies in software systems engineering and information systems* (pp. 193–221). Hershey, PA: IGI Global.

Sarstedt, M., Ringle, C. M., Henseler, J., & Hair, J. F. (2014). On the emancipation of PLS-SEM: A commentary on Rigdon (2012). *Long Range Planning, 47,* 154–160.

Sarstedt, M., Wilczynski, P., & Melewar, T. (2013). Measuring reputation in global markets: A comparison of reputation measures' convergent and criterion validities. *Journal of World Business, 48,* 329–339.

Tenenhaus, M., Esposito Vinzi, V., Chatelin, Y. M., & Lauro, C. (2005). PLS path modeling. *Computational Statistics & Data Analysis, 48,* 159–205.

CHAPTER 7

Mediator and Moderator Analysis

LEARNING OUTCOMES

1. Understand the basic concepts of mediation in a PLS-SEM context.

2. Execute a mediation analysis using SmartPLS.

3. Comprehend the basic concepts of moderation in a PLS-SEM context.

4. Use the SmartPLS software to run a moderation analysis.

CHAPTER PREVIEW

Cause-effect relationships in PLS path models imply that exogenous constructs directly affect endogenous constructs without any systematic influences of other variables. In many instances, however, this assumption does not hold, and including a third variable in the analysis can change our understanding of the nature of the model relationships. The two most prominent examples of such extensions include mediation and moderation.

Mediation occurs when a third variable, referred to as a **mediator variable,** intervenes between two other related constructs. More precisely, a change in the exogenous construct results in a change of the mediator variable, which, in turn, changes the endogenous construct. Analyzing the strength of the mediator variable's relationships with the other constructs allows substantiating the mechanisms that under-lie the cause-effect relationship between an exogenous construct and an endogenous construct. In the simplest form, the analysis considers only one mediator variable, but the path model can include a multitude of mediator variables simultaneously.

When **moderation** is present, the strength or even the direction of a relationship between two constructs depends on a third variable. In other words, the nature of the relationship differs depending on the values of the third variable. As an example, the relationship between two constructs is not the same for all customers but differs depending on their income. As such, moderation can (and should) be seen as a means to account for **heterogeneity** in the data.

Mediation and moderation are similar in that they describe situations in which the relationship between two constructs depends on a third variable. There are fundamental differences, however, in terms of their theoretical foundation, modeling, and interpretation. In this chapter, we explain and differentiate mediation and moderation, as well as illustrate their implementation using the corporate reputation PLS path model.

MEDIATION

Introduction

Mediation occurs when a third mediator variable intervenes between two other related constructs. More precisely, a change in the exogenous construct causes a change in the mediator variable, which, in turn, results in a change in the endogenous construct in the PLS path model. Thereby, a mediator variable governs the nature (i.e., the underlying mechanism or process) of the relationship between two constructs. Strong a priori theoretical/conceptual support is a key requirement to explore meaningful **mediating effects**. When that support is present, mediation can be a useful statistical analysis, if carried out properly.

Consider Exhibit 7.1 for an illustration of mediating effects in terms of direct and indirect effects. Direct effects are the relationships linking two constructs with a single arrow. Indirect effects are those relationships that involve a sequence of relationships with at least one intervening construct involved. Thus, an indirect effect is a sequence of two or more direct effects and is represented visually by multiple

Exhibit 7.1 General Mediation Model

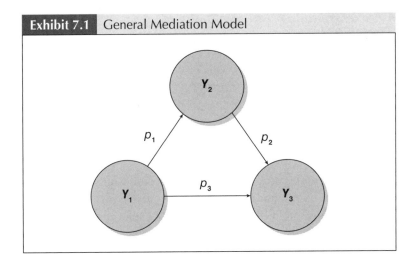

arrows. Exhibit 7.1 shows both a direct effect p_3 between Y_1 and Y_3 and an indirect effect of Y_1 on Y_3 in the form of a $Y_1 \rightarrow Y_2 \rightarrow Y_3$ sequence. The indirect effect of $p_1 \cdot p_2$ represents the mediating effect of the construct Y_2 on the relationship between Y_1 and Y_3.

To understand the conceptual basis of mediation, consider the following example of the relationship between seawater temperature and the number of incidents (e.g., swimmers needing to be rescued). We could, for example, hypothesize the following (H_1): The higher the seawater temperature (Y_1), the lower the number of incidents (e.g., swimmers needing to be rescued) (Y_3). The rationale behind this hypothesis is that the body temperature declines much faster in cold water and, thus, exhausts swimmers more quickly. Therefore, they are more likely to misjudge their chances of swimming out in the sea and returning safely. Hence, in accordance with H_1, we assume that swimming in warmer water is less dangerous. The logic of this simple cause-effect relationship is shown in Exhibit 7.2.

Many coastal cities and lifeguard organizations have daily empirical data readily available on the seawater temperature and the number of swimming incidents over many years. When using these data and estimating the relationship (i.e., the correlation between the seawater temperature and the number of incidents), however, either a nonsignificant or a significantly positive result for the hypothesized relationship is generally obtained. In the latter case, we may conclude that swimming in warmer water is more dangerous. Since we had

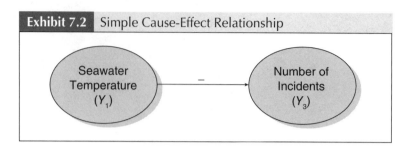

Exhibit 7.2   Simple Cause-Effect Relationship

theoretical reasoning suggesting a negative relationship, there must be something we do not understand about the model.

This finding reminds us that simple data exploration may lead to misleading and false conclusions. A priori theoretical assumptions and logical reasoning are key requirements when applying multivariate analysis techniques. When the results do not match the expectations, researchers may find an explanation based on (1) theoretical/conceptual considerations, (2) certain data-related issues, and/or (3) technical peculiarities of the statistical method used. In this example, theoretical/conceptual considerations enable us to adjust our previous considerations.

To better understand the relationship between the seawater temperature (Y_1) and the number of incidents (Y_3), it makes sense to include the number of swimmers at the selected shoreline (Y_2) in the modeling considerations. More specifically, the higher the seawater temperature, the more swimmers there will be at the specific beach (H_2). Moreover, the more swimmers there are in the water, the higher the likelihood of incidents occurring in terms of swimmers needing to be rescued (H_3). Exhibit 7.3 illustrates this more complex cause-effect relationship.

Empirical data might substantiate the positive effects illustrated in Exhibit 7.3. When the complex cause-effect relationship is examined, however, it is still possible to conclude that swimming in warmer water is more dangerous than swimming in colder water since the two relationships both have a positive sign. We therefore combine the simple and the more complex cause-effect relationship models in the **mediation model** shown in Exhibit 7.4, which includes the **mediator variable** (Y_2). In addition to H_1, H_2, and H_3, we could propose the following hypothesis (H_4): The direct relationship between the seawater temperature and number of incidents is mediated by the number of swimmers.

Exhibit 7.3 Complex Cause-Effect Relationship

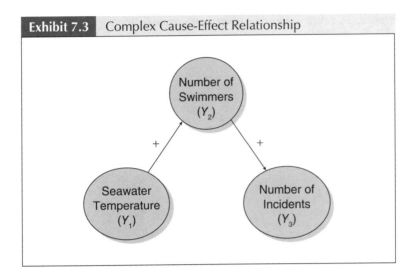

If we use the available data to empirically estimate the model in Exhibit 7.4, we may obtain the estimated relationships with the expected signs. The counterintuitive positive relationship between the seawater temperature and the number of incidents becomes negative, as expected, when extending the model by the mediator variable number of swimmers. In this **mediation model,** the number of swimmers represents an appropriate mechanism to explain the relationship between the seawater temperature and the number of incidents.

Exhibit 7.4 Mediation Model

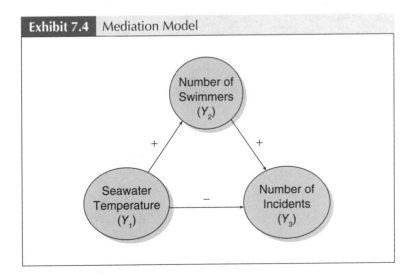

Hence, the positive indirect effect via the mediator variable reveals the "true" relationship between the seawater temperature and the number of incidents.

This example points out that mediation is a challenging field. An estimated cause-effect relationship may not be the "true" effect because a systematic influence—a certain phenomenon (i.e., a mediator)—has not been accounted for in the model. Many PLS path models include mediation effects, but these are usually not explicitly hypothesized and tested (Hair, Sarstedt, Ringle, et al., 2012). Only when the possible mediation is theoretically taken into account and also empirically tested can the nature of the cause-effect relationship be fully and accurately understood. Again, theory is always the foundation of empirical analyses.

Types of Mediation Effects

The question of how to test mediation has attracted considerable attention in methodological research over the past decades. Three decades ago, Baron and Kenny (1986) presented an approach to mediation analysis, which many researchers still routinely draw upon. More recent research, however, points to conceptual and methodological problems with Baron and Kenny's (1986) approach (e.g., Hayes, 2013). Against this background, our description builds on Zhao, Lynch, and Chen (2010), who offer a synthesis of prior research on mediation analysis and corresponding guidelines for future research (see also Nitzl, Roldán, & Cepeda, in press). The authors characterize two types of nonmediation:

- **Direct-only nonmediation:** The direct effect is significant but not the indirect effect.

- **No-effect nonmediation:** Neither the direct nor indirect effect are significant.

In addition, they identify three types of mediation:

- **Complementary mediation:** The indirect effect and the direct effect both are significant and point in the same direction.

- **Competitive mediation:** The indirect effect and the direct effect both are significant and point in opposite directions.

- **Indirect-only mediation:** The indirect effect is significant but not the direct effect.

Hence, mediation may not exist at all (i.e., direct-only nonmediation and no-effect nonmediation) or, in case of a mediation, the mediator construct accounts either for some (i.e., complementary and competitive mediation) or for all of the observed relationship between two latent variables (i.e., indirect-only mediation). In that sense, Zhao et al.'s (2010) procedure closely corresponds to Baron and Kenny's (1986) concept of **partial mediation** and **full mediation.**

Testing for the type of mediation in a model requires running a series of analyses, which Exhibit 7.5 illustrates. The first step addresses the significance of the indirect effect $(p_1 \cdot p_2)$ via the mediator variable (Y_2). If the indirect effect is not significant (right-hand side of Exhibit 7.5), we conclude that Y_2 does not function as a mediator in the tested relationship. While this result may seem disappointing at first sight, as it does not provide empirical support for a hypothesized mediating relationship, further analysis of the direct effect p_3 can point to as yet undiscovered mediators. Specifically, if the direct effect is significant, we can conclude it is possible there is an omitted mediator, which potentially explains the relationship between Y_1 and Y_3 (direct-only nonmediation). If the direct effect is also nonsignificant (no-effect nonmediation), however, we have to conclude that our theoretical framework is flawed. In this case, we should go back to theory and reconsider the path model setup. Note that this situation can occur despite a significant total effect of Y_1 on Y_3.

Exhibit 7.5   Mediation Analysis Procedure

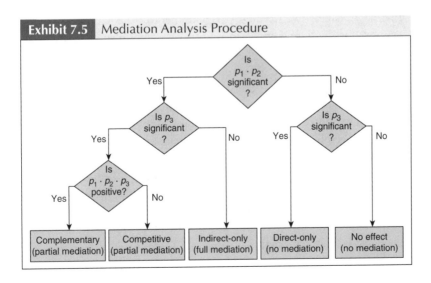

We may, however, find general support for a hypothesized mediating relationship in our initial analysis based on a significant indirect effect (left-hand side of Exhibit 7.5). As before, our next interest is with the significance of the direct effect p_3. If the direct effect is nonsignificant, we face the situation of indirect-only mediation. This situation represents the best-case scenario as it suggests that our mediator fully complies with the hypothesized theoretical framework. If the direct effect p_3 is significant, we still find support for the hypothesized mediating relationship. However, this result may point to a potentially incomplete theoretical framework as there is likely another mediator, which potentially explains a greater share of the relationship between Y_1 and Y_3.

When both the direct and indirect effects are significant, we can distinguish between complementary and competitive mediation. Complementary mediation describes a situation in which the direct effect and the indirect effect $p_1 \cdot p_2$ point in the same direction. In other words, the product of the direct effect and the indirect effect (i.e., $p_1 \cdot p_2 \cdot p_3$) is positive (Exhibit 7.5). While providing support for the hypothesized mediating relationship, complementary mediation also provides a cue that another mediator may have been omitted whose indirect path has the same direction as the direct effect.

On the contrary, in competitive mediation—also referred to as **inconsistent mediation** (MacKinnon, Krull, & Lockwood, 2000)—the direct effect p_3 and either indirect effect p_1 or p_2 have opposite signs. In other words, the product of the direct effect and the indirect effect $p_1 \cdot p_2 \cdot p_3$ is negative (Exhibit 7.5). Competitive mediation provides support for the hypothesized mediating effect but also suggests that another mediator may be present whose indirect effect's sign equals that of the direct effect. It is important to note that in competitive mediation, the mediating construct acts as a **suppressor variable**, which substantially decreases the magnitude of the total effect of Y_1 on Y_3. Therefore, when competitive mediation occurs, researchers need to carefully analyze the theoretical substantiation of all effects involved. Our introductory example on the relationship between seawater temperature and number of incidents as mediated by the number of swimmers constitutes a case of competitive mediation. The opposite signs of the direct and indirect effects can offset each other, so that the total effect of seawater temperature on the number of incidents is relatively small.

Testing Mediating Effects

Prior testing of the significance of mediating effects relied on the Sobel (1982) test. The **Sobel test** compares the direct relationship between the independent variable and the dependent variable with the indirect relationship between the independent variable and dependent variable that includes the mediation construct (Helm et al., 2010). The Sobel test assumes a normal distribution that is not, however, consistent with the nonparametric PLS-SEM method. Moreover, the parametric assumptions of the Sobel test usually do not hold for the indirect effect $p_1 \cdot p_2$, since the multiplication of two normally distributed coefficients results in a nonnormal distribution of their product. Furthermore, the Sobel test requires unstandardized path coefficients as input for the test statistic and lacks statistical power, especially when applied to small sample sizes. For these reasons, research has dismissed the Sobel test for evaluating mediation analysis, especially in PLS-SEM studies (e.g., Klarner et al., 2013; Sattler et al., 2010).

Instead of using the Sobel test, researchers should bootstrap the sampling distribution of the indirect effect. This approach has also been brought forward in a regression context (Preacher & Hayes, 2004, 2008a) and has been implemented in Hayes's SPSS-based PRO-CESS macro (http://www.processmacro.org/). Bootstrapping makes no assumptions about the shape of the variables' distribution or the sampling distribution of the statistics and can be applied to small sample sizes with more confidence. The approach is therefore perfectly suited for the PLS-SEM method and implemented in the SmartPLS 3 software. In addition, bootstrapping the indirect effect yields higher levels of statistical power compared with the Sobel test.

Measurement Model Evaluation in Mediation Analysis

Evaluating mediation models requires that all quality criteria of the measurement models as discussed in Chapters 4 to 6 have been met. For example, a lack of the mediator construct's discriminant validity with the exogenous and/or endogenous latent variable may entail a strong and significant but substantially biased indirect effect, leading to incorrect implications regarding the mediation. Moreover, lack of reliability in the case of reflective mediator constructs has a strong effect on the estimated relationships in the PLS path model (i.e., the indirect paths can become considerably smaller than expected). For this reason, it is important to ensure a high reliability of reflective mediator constructs.

After establishing reliable and valid measurement models for the mediator construct as well as the exogenous and the endogenous latent variables, it is important to consider all structural model evaluation criteria. For instance, it is important to ensure that collinearity is not at a critical level, which, otherwise, may entail substantially biased path coefficients. Thus, as a result of collinearity, the direct effect may become nonsignificant, suggesting nonmediation even though, for example, a complementary mediation may be present. Likewise, high collinearity levels may result in unexpected sign changes, rendering any differentiation between complementary and competitive mediation useless.

Multiple Mediation

In the previous sections, we considered the case of a single mediator variable, which accounts for the relationship between an exogenous and an endogenous construct. Analyzing such a model setup is also referred to as **simple mediation analysis**. More often than not, however, when evaluating structural models, exogenous constructs exert their influence through more than one mediating variable. This situation requires running **multiple mediation analyses**. For an example of multiple mediation with two mediators, consider Exhibit 7.6. In the model, p_3 represents the direct effect between the exogenous construct and the endogenous construct. The **specific indirect effect** of Y_1 on Y_3 via mediator Y_2 is quantified as $p_1 \cdot p_2$, whereas for the second mediator Y_4, the specific indirect effect is given by $p_4 \cdot p_5$. The **total indirect effect** is the sum of the specific indirect effects (i.e., $p_1 \cdot p_2 + p_4 \cdot p_5$). Finally, the total effect of Y_1 on Y_3 is the sum of the direct effect and the total indirect effects (i.e., $p_3 + p_1 \cdot p_2 + p_4 \cdot p_5$).

To test a model such as the one shown in Exhibit 7.6, researchers may be tempted to run a set of simple mediation analyses, one for each proposed mediator. However, as Preacher and Hayes (2008a, 2008b) point out, this approach is problematic for at least two reasons. First, one cannot simply add up the indirect effects calculated in several simple mediation analyses to derive the total indirect effect, as the mediators in a multiple mediation model typically will be correlated. As a result, the specific indirect effects estimated using several simple mediation analyses will be biased and will not sum to the total

Exhibit 7.6	Multiple Mediation Model

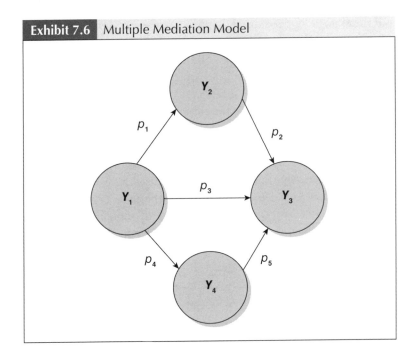

indirect effect through the multiple mediators. Second, hypothesis tests and confidence intervals calculated for specific indirect effects may not be accurate due to the omission of other, potentially important mediators. The latter situation is equivalent to complementary and competitive mediation, as described in Zhao et al. (2010).

By considering all mediators simultaneously in one model, we gain a more complete picture of the mechanisms through which an exogenous construct affects an endogenous construct. In a multiple mediation model, a specific indirect effect can be interpreted as the indirect effect of Y_1 on Y_3 through a given mediator, controlling for all other included mediators. Note that this indirect effect is different from the one we would obtain when examining multiple mediators separately in a simple mediation analysis. In the latter case, the indirect effect may be significantly inflated except in the very unlikely circumstance that all other mediators are uncorrelated with the mediator under consideration.

The analysis of a multiple mediation model follows the same steps as shown in Exhibit 7.5 for simple mediation. That is, researchers should test the significance of each indirect effect (i.e., the specific indirect effects) and the direct effect between the exogenous construct and the endogenous construct. In addition, the researcher should test whether the total indirect effect is significant. Assessing the significance of the total indirect effect and the direct effect can be immediately done using the SmartPLS 3 outputs. In multiple mediation models, however, the total indirect effect may consist of several specific indirect effects. Assessing the significance of the specific indirect effects requires manually calculating each effect's standard error. For this purpose, use the SmartPLS 3 results report from the bootstrapping routine and simply copy and paste the path coefficients of all bootstrap samples into spreadsheet software such as Microsoft Excel. The spreadsheet software's formula tool enables you to manually calculate the specific indirect effects of all bootstrap samples. By using the manually calculated bootstrapping results as input, you can compute the standard error (i.e., which equals the standard deviation in bootstrapping) of each specific indirect effect in the multiple mediation model. Dividing the specific indirect effect—as obtained when multiplying the direct effects from the standard PLS-SEM analysis of the path model—by the standard error yields the t value of the specific indirect effect. Please visit the Download section at http://www.pls-sem.com, where you can download an Excel file, which illustrates the testing of multiple mediation using a modified version of the corporate reputation model. See Nitzl, Roldán, and Cepeda (in press) for more details.

Exhibit 7.7 summarizes the rules of thumb for running a mediation analysis in PLS-SEM.

Case Study Illustration—Mediation

To illustrate the estimation of mediating effects, let's consider the extended corporate model again. If you do not have the model readily available, please go back to the case study in the previous chapter and import the SmartPLS **Project** file **Corporate Reputation.zip** by going to **File → Import Project from Backup File** in the SmartPLS menu. Next, open the model by double-clicking on **Extended Model**. The model shown in Exhibit 7.8 will appear in the **Modeling** window.

In the following discussion, we will further explore the relationship between the two dimensions of corporate reputation (i.e., likeability and competence) and the target construct customer loyalty. According to Festinger's (1957) theory of cognitive dissonance, customers who perceive that a company has a favorable reputation are likely to show higher levels of satisfaction in an effort to avoid cognitive dissonance. At the same time, previous research has demonstrated

Exhibit 7.7	Rules of Thumb for Mediation Analyses in PLS-SEM

- Running mediation requires a series of analyses, which address the significance of the indirect and direct effects. Researchers distinguish between different types of mediation and nonmediation, depending on whether the model relationships are significant and their relationship to each other.
- To test mediating effects, use bootstrapping instead of the Sobel test, which is not applicable in a PLS-SEM context.
- Consider all standard model evaluation criteria in the assessment of mediation models, such as convergent validity, discriminant validity, reliability, multicollinearity, R^2, and so forth.
- To test multiple mediation models, include all mediators simultaneously and distinguish between specific indirect effects and total indirect effects.

that customer satisfaction is the primary driver of customer loyalty. Therefore, we expect that customer satisfaction mediates the relationship between likeability and customer loyalty as well as competence and customer loyalty. To test this notion, we apply the procedure shown in Exhibit 7.5.

To begin the mediation analysis, we test the significance of the indirect effects. The indirect effect from *COMP* via *CUSA* to *CUSL* is the product of the path coefficients from *COMP* to *CUSA* and from *CUSA* to *CUSL* (Mediation Path 1). Similarly, the indirect effect from *LIKE* via *CUSA* to *CUSL* is the product of the path coefficients from *LIKE* to *CUSA* and from *CUSA* to *CUSL* (Mediation Path 2). To test the significance of these path coefficients' products, we run the bootstrap routine. To do so, go to **Calculate** → **Bootstrapping** in the SmartPLS menu or click on the **Calculate** icon, above the **Modeling** window, followed by **Bootstrapping** (note that you first may need to go back to the **Modeling** window before the **Calculate** icon appears). We retain all settings for the PLS-SEM algorithm and the missing value treatment as before and select the **No Sign Changes** option, 5,000 bootstrap samples and select the **Complete Bootstrapping** option. In the advanced settings, we choose **Bias-Corrected and Accelerated (BCa) Bootstrap, two-tailed** testing and a significance level of 0.05. Next, we click **Start Calculation**.

After running the procedure, open the SmartPLS bootstrapping report. The table under **Final Results** → **Indirect Effects** provides us with an overview of results, including standard errors, bootstrap

Exhibit 7.8 Extended Model in SmartPLS

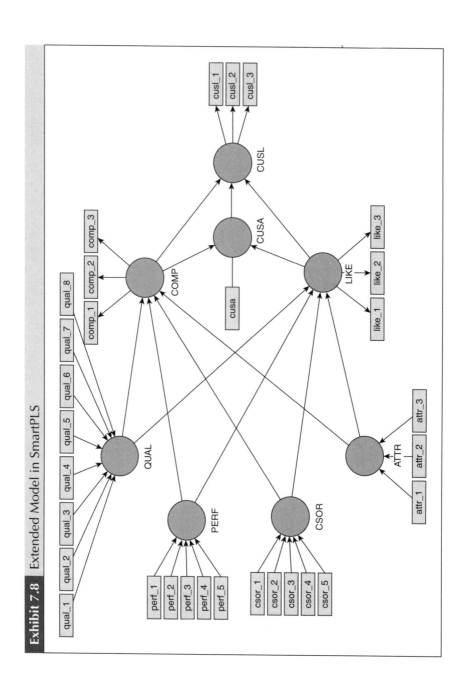

mean values, t values, and p values. Clicking on the **Bias-Corrected Confidence Intervals** tab in the bootstrapping results report shows the confidence interval as derived from the BCa method. Similarly, the table under **Final Results** → **Path Coefficients** offers the corresponding results for the direct effects, which we need in the further analysis. Exhibit 7.9 summarizes the bootstrapping results for the relationships between *COMP* and *CUSL* as well as *LIKE* and *CUSL*.

We find that both indirect effects are significant since neither of the 95% confidence intervals includes zero (see Chapter 5 for how to use confidence intervals for hypothesis testing). Even though it is not necessary to report the t value and p value when drawing on the bootstrap confidence intervals for significance testing, we check them for the completeness of our analysis. The empirical t value of the indirect effect (0.074) for the *COMP* → *CUSL* relationship is 2.162, yielding a p value of 0.031. Please note that your results will slightly differ due to the random nature of the bootstrapping process. Similarly, for the indirect effect (0.220) of the *LIKE* → *CUSL* relationship, we obtain a t value of 6.207, indicating a p value of less than 0.01.

We now continue the mediation analysis procedure as shown in Exhibit 7.5. The next step focuses on the significance of the direct effects from *COMP* to *CUSL* and *LIKE* to *CUSL*. As determined in Chapter 6 and shown in Exhibit 7.8, the relationship from *COMP* to *CUSL* is weak (0.006) and statistically nonsignificant ($t = 0.105$; $p = 0.916$). Following the mediation analysis procedure in Exhibit 7.5, we conclude that *CUSA* fully mediates the *COMP* to *CUSL* relationship. On the contrary, *LIKE* exerts a pronounced (0.344) and significant ($t = 6.207$; $p < 0.001$) effect on *CUSL*. We therefore conclude that *CUSA* partially mediates the relationship since both the direct and the indirect effects are significant (Exhibit 7.5). To further substantiate the type of partial mediation, we next compute the product of the direct effect and the indirect effect. Since the direct and indirect effects are both positive, the sign of their product is also positive (i.e., 0.344 · 0.220 = 0.076). Hence, we conclude that *CUSA* represents complementary mediation of the relationship from *LIKE* to *CUSL*.

Our findings provide empirical support for the mediating role of customer satisfaction in the reputation model. More specifically, customer satisfaction represents a mechanism that underlies the relationship between competence and customer loyalty. Competence leads to customer satisfaction, and customer satisfaction in turn leads to customer loyalty. For the relationship between likeability

Exhibit 7.9 Significance Analysis of the Direct and Indirect Effects

	Direct Effect	95% Confidence Interval of the Direct Effect	t Value	Significance (p < 0.05)?	Indirect Effect	95% Confidence Interval of the Indirect Effect	t Value	Significance (p < 0.05)?
COMP → CUSL	0.006	[−0.101, 0.112]	0.105	No	0.074	[0.007, 0.143]	2.162	Yes
LIKE → CUSL	0.344	[0.235, 0.452]	6.207	Yes	0.220	[0.152, 0.293]	6.207	Yes

and customer loyalty, customer satisfaction serves as a complementary mediator. Higher levels of likeability increase customer loyalty directly but also increase customer satisfaction, which in turn leads to customer loyalty. Hence, some of likeability's effect on loyalty is explained by satisfaction.

MODERATION

Introduction

Moderation describes a situation in which the relationship between two constructs is not constant but depends on the values of a third variable, referred to as a **moderator variable.** The moderator variable (or construct) changes the strength or even the direction of a relationship between two constructs in the model. For example, prior research has shown that the relationship between customer satisfaction and customer loyalty differs as a function of the customers' income. More precisely, income has a pronounced negative effect on the satisfaction-loyalty relationship—the higher the income, the weaker the relationship between satisfaction and loyalty. In other words, income serves as a moderator variable that accounts for heterogeneity in the satisfaction-loyalty link. Thus, this relationship is not the same for all customers but instead differs depending on their income. As such, moderation can (and should) be seen as a means to account for **heterogeneity** in the data.

Moderating relationships are hypothesized a priori by the researcher and specifically tested. The testing of the moderating relationship depends on whether the researcher hypothesizes whether *one* specific model relationship or whether *all* model relationships depend on the scores of the moderator. In the prior example, we hypothesized that only the satisfaction-loyalty link is significantly influenced by income. These considerations also apply for the relationship between *CUSA* and *CUSL* in the corporate reputation model example. In such a setting, we would examine if and how the respondents' income influences the relationship. Exhibit 7.10 shows the conceptual model of such a moderating relationship, which only focuses on the satisfaction-loyalty link in the corporate reputation model.

Alternatively, we could also hypothesize that several relationships in the corporate reputation model depend on some customer characteristic, such as gender (of corporate reputation [i.e., likeability and competence] on satisfaction and loyalty is different Exhibit 7.11).

For example, we could hypothesize that the effect of corporate reputation (i.e., likeability and competence) on satisfaction and loyalty is different for females compared with males. Gender would then serve as a grouping variable that divides the data into two subsamples, as illustrated in Exhibit 7.11. The same model is then estimated for each of the distinct subsamples. Since researchers are usually interested in comparing the models and learning about significant differences between the subsamples, the model estimates for the subsamples are usually compared by means of a multigroup analysis (Sarstedt, Henseler, & Ringle, 2011; Chapter 8). Specifically, multigroup analysis enables the researcher to test for differences between identical models estimated for different groups of respondents (e.g., females vs. males). The general objective is to see if there are statistically significant differences between individual group models. For example, with regard to the models in Exhibit 7.11, the multigroup analysis would enable testing whether the 0.34 relationship between *LIKE* and *CUSL* for female customers is significantly higher than the corresponding relationship for male customers (0.10).

In this section, our focus is on the modeling and interpretation of **interaction effects** that occur when a moderator variable is assumed to influence one specific relationship. In Chapter 8, we provide a brief introduction to the basic concepts of multigroup analysis.

Types of Moderator Variables

Moderators can be present in structural models in different forms. They can represent observable traits such as gender, age, or income. But

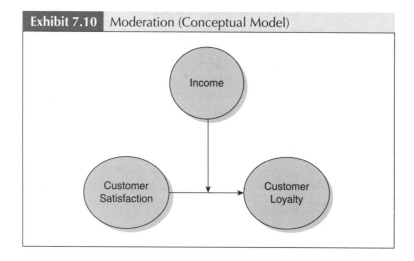

Exhibit 7.10 Moderation (Conceptual Model)

Exhibit 7.11 Multigroup Analysis

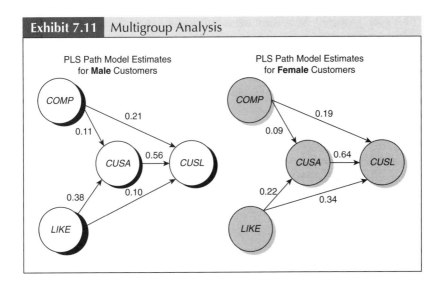

PLS Path Model Estimates
for **Male** Customers

PLS Path Model Estimates
for **Female** Customers

they can also represent unobservable traits such as risk attitude, attitude toward a brand, or ad liking. Moderators can be measured with a single item or multiple items and using reflective or formative indicators. The most important differentiation, however, relates to the moderator's measurement scale, which involves distinguishing between categorical (typically dichotomous) and continuous moderators.

In the case study on corporate reputation in the mobile phone industry, we could, for example, use the service-type variable (contract vs. prepaid) as a **categorical moderator variable.** These categorical variables are usually dummy coded (i.e., 0/1), whereby the zero represents the reference category. Note that a categorical moderator does not necessarily have to represent only two groups. For example, in the case of three groups (e.g., short-term contract, long-term contract, and prepaid), we could split up the moderator into two dummy variables, which are simultaneously included in the model. In the latter case, both dummy variables would take the value zero for the reference category (e.g., prepaid). The other two categories would be indicated by the value 1 in the corresponding dummy variable. Similar to OLS regressions, categorical moderators can be included in a PLS path model to affect a specific relationship. For example, in the case study on corporate reputation, we could evaluate whether the customers' gender has a significant bearing on the satisfaction-loyalty link. In most cases, however, researchers use a categorical moderator variable to split up the data set into two or more groups and estimate the models separately for each group of data. Running a multigroup analysis enables identification of model relationships that differ significantly between the groups (Chapter 8). This approach offers a more complete picture of the moderator's influence on the analysis results as the focus shifts from examining its impact on one specific model relationship to examining its impact on all model relationships. As indicated earlier, however, such an analysis must be grounded in theory.

In many situations, researchers have a **continuous moderator variable** they believe can affect the strength of one specific relationship between two latent variables. Returning to our case study on corporate reputation, we could, for example, hypothesize that the relationship between satisfaction and loyalty is influenced by the customers' income. More precisely, we could hypothesize that the relationship between customer satisfaction and customer loyalty is weaker for high-income customers and stronger for low-income customers. Such a moderator effect would indicate that the satisfaction-loyalty relationship changes, depending on the level of the income. If this moderator effect is not present, we would assume that the strength of the relationship between satisfaction and loyalty is constant.

Continuous moderators are typically measured with multiple items but can, in principle, also be measured using only a single item. When the moderator variable represents some abstract unobservable trait (as opposed to some observable phenomenon such as income), however, we clearly advise against the use of single items for construct measurement. Single items significantly lag behind multi-item scales in terms of predictive validity (Diamantopoulos et al., 2012; Sarstedt et al., in press), which can be particularly problematic in the context of moderation. The reason is that moderation is usually associated with rather limited effect sizes (Aguinis, Beaty, Boik, & Pierce, 2005) so that any lack of predictive power will make it harder to identify significant relationships. Furthermore, when modeling moderating effects, the moderator's measurement model is included twice in the model—in the moderator variable itself as well as in the **interaction term** (see next section). This characteristic amplifies the limitations of single-item measurement in the context of moderation.

Modeling Moderating Effects

To gain an understanding of how **moderating effects** are modeled, consider the path model shown in Exhibit 7.12. This model illustrates our previous example in which income serves as a moderator variable

(M), influencing the relationship between customer satisfaction (Y_1) and customer loyalty (Y_2). The **moderating effect** (p_3) is represented by an arrow pointing at the effect p_1 linking Y_1 and Y_2. Furthermore, when including the moderating effect in a PLS path model, there is also a direct relationship (p_2) from the moderator to the endogenous construct. This additional path is important (and a frequent source of mistake) as it controls for the direct impact of the moderator on the endogenous construct. If the path p_2 were to be omitted, the effect of M on the relationship between Y_1 and Y_2 (i.e., p_3) would be inflated. As can be seen, moderation is similar to mediation in that a third variable (i.e., a mediator or moderator variable) affects the strength of a relationship between two latent variables. The crucial distinction between both concepts is that the moderator variable does not depend on the exogenous construct. In contrast, with mediation there is a direct effect between the exogenous construct and the mediator variable.

The path model in Exhibit 7.12 can also be expressed mathematically using the following formula:

$$Y_2 = (p_1 + p_3 \cdot M) \cdot Y_1 + p_2 \cdot M.$$

As can be seen, the influence of Y_1 on Y_2 depends not only on the strength of the **simple effect** p_1 but also on the product of p_3 and M. To understand how a moderator variable can be integrated in the model, we need to rewrite the equation as follows:

$$Y_2 = p_1 \cdot Y_1 + p_2 \cdot M + p_3 \cdot (Y_1 \cdot M).$$

This equation shows that including a moderator effect requires the specification of the effect of the exogenous latent variable

Exhibit 7.12 Example of a Moderating Effect

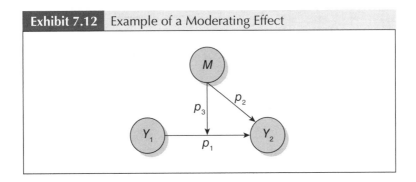

(i.e., $p_1 \cdot Y_1$), the effect of the moderator variable (i.e., $p_2 \cdot M$), and the product term $p_3 \cdot (Y_1 \cdot M)$, which is also called the **interaction term**. As a result, the coefficient p_3 expresses how the effect p_1 changes when the moderator variable M is increased or decreased by one standard deviation. Exhibit 7.13 illustrates the concept of an interaction term. As can be seen, the model includes the interaction term as an additional latent variable covering the product of the exogenous latent variable Y_1 and the moderator M. Because of this interaction term, researchers often refer to **interaction effects** when modeling moderator variables.

So far, we have looked at a **two-way interaction** because the moderator interacts with one other variable, the exogenous latent variable Y_1. However, it is also possible to model higher levels of interaction where the moderating effect is again moderated. Such a setup is also referred to as **cascaded moderator analysis**. The most common form of a cascaded moderator analysis is a **three-way interaction**. For example, we could imagine that the moderating effect of income is not constant but is itself influenced by some other variable such as age, which would serve as a second moderator variable in the model. See Henseler and Fassott (2010) for more details.

Creating the Interaction Term

In the previous section, we introduced the concept of an interaction term to facilitate the inclusion of a moderator variable in the PLS path model. But one fundamental question remains: How should the

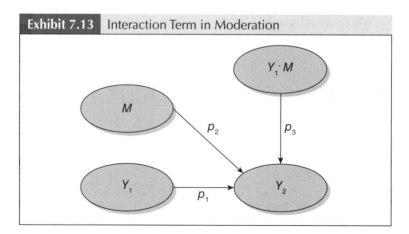

Exhibit 7.13 Interaction Term in Moderation

interaction term be operationalized? Research has proposed several approaches for creating the interaction term (e.g., Henseler & Chin, 2010; Henseler & Fassott, 2010; Rigdon et al., 2010). In the following pages, we discuss three prominent approaches: (1) the product indicator approach, (2) the orthogonalizing approach, and (3) the two-stage approach.

Product Indicator Approach

The **product indicator approach** is the standard approach for creating the interaction term in regression-based analyses and also features prominently in PLS-SEM. As we will describe later, however, its use is not universally recommended in PLS-SEM. The product indicator approach involves multiplying each indicator of the exogenous latent variable with each indicator of the moderator variable (Chin, Marcolin, & Newsted, 2003). These so-called **product indicators** become the indicators of the interaction term. Exhibit 7.14 illustrates the interaction term when both Y_1 and M are measured by means of two indicators. Thus, the interaction term has four product indicators. The indicator multiplication builds on the assumption that the indicators of the exogenous construct and the moderator each stem from a certain construct domain and are in principle interchangeable. Therefore, the product indicator approach is not applicable when the exogenous construct and/or the moderator are measured formatively. Since formative indicators do not have to correspond to a predefined theoretical concept, multiplying them with another set of indicators will confound the conceptual domain of the interaction term.

The product indicator approach requires the indicators of the exogenous construct and the moderator variable to be reused in the measurement model of the interaction term. This procedure, however, inevitably introduces collinearity in the path model. To reduce collinearity problems, researchers typically standardize the indicators of the moderator prior to creating the interaction term. Standardization converts each variable to a mean of 0 and a standard deviation of 1, which reduces the collinearity that is introduced by indicator reuse. Furthermore, standardizing the indicators facilitates the interpretation of the moderating effect, a characteristic that we will discuss later in this chapter in greater detail.

Exhibit 7.14 Product Indicator Approach

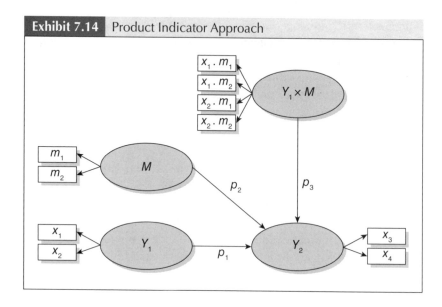

Orthogonalizing Approach

The **orthogonalizing approach** is an extension of the product indicator approach. Little, Bovaird, and Widaman (2006) developed the approach to address two issues that are the result of the standardization of variables as implemented in the product indicator approach. First, while indicator standardization reduces the level of collinearity in the PLS path model, it does not fully eliminate it. So despite the standardization, collinearity in the path model may still be substantial, yielding inflated standard errors or biased path coefficient estimates (Chapter 6). Second, when the variables are standardized, one cannot readily compare the direct effect between Y_1 and Y_2 when no interaction term is included (i.e., the **main effect**), with the effect between Y_1 and Y_2 when the interaction term is included (i.e., the **simple effect**). We will further clarify the distinction between main effect and simple effect when discussing the interpretation of results.

The orthogonalizing approach builds on the product indicator approach and requires creating all product indicators of the interaction term. For the model in Exhibit 7.15, this would mean creating four product indicators: $x_1 \cdot m_1, x_1 \cdot m_2, x_2 \cdot m_1,$ and $x_2 \cdot m_2$. The next step is to regress each product indicator on all indicators of the exogenous construct and the moderator variable. For the example in

Exhibit 7.15, we would need to establish and estimate the following four regression models:

$$x_1 \cdot m_1 = b_{1,11} \cdot x_1 + b_{2,11} \cdot x_2 + b_{3,11} \cdot m_1 + b_{4,11} \cdot m_2 + e_{11}$$
$$x_1 \cdot m_2 = b_{1,12} \cdot x_1 + b_{2,12} \cdot x_2 + b_{3,12} \cdot m_1 + b_{4,12} \cdot m_2 + e_{12}$$
$$x_2 \cdot m_1 = b_{1,21} \cdot x_1 + b_{2,21} \cdot x_2 + b_{3,21} \cdot m_1 + b_{4,21} \cdot m_2 + e_{21}$$
$$x_2 \cdot m_2 = b_{1,22} \cdot x_1 + b_{2,22} \cdot x_2 + b_{3,22} \cdot m_1 + b_{4,22} \cdot m_2 + e_{22}$$

In each regression model, a product indicator (e.g., $x_1 \cdot m_1$) represents the dependent variable, while all indicators of the exogenous construct (here, x_1 and x_2) and the moderator (here, m_1 and m_2) act as independent variables. When looking at the results, we are not interested in the regression coefficients b. Rather, the residual term e is the outcome of interest. The orthogonalizing approach uses the standardized residuals e as indicators for the interaction term, as shown in Exhibit 7.15.

This analysis ensures that the indicators of the interaction term do not share any variance with any of the indicators of the exogenous construct and the moderator. In other words, the interaction term is orthogonal to the other two constructs, precluding any collinearity issues among the constructs involved. Another consequence of the orthogonality is that the path coefficient estimates in the model without the interaction term are identical to those with the interaction term. This characteristic greatly facilitates the interpretation of the moderating effect's strength compared with the product indicator approach. However, because of its reliance on product indicators, the orthogonalizing approach is only applicable when the exogenous construct and the moderator variable are measured reflectively.

Two-Stage Approach

Chin et al. (2003) proposed the **two-stage approach** as a means to run a moderation analysis when the exogenous construct and/or the moderator are measured formatively. The general applicability of the two-stage approach has its roots in its explicit exploitation of PLS-SEM's advantage to estimate latent variable scores (Henseler & Chin, 2010; Rigdon et al., 2010). The two stages are as follows:

Stage 1: The main effects model (i.e., without the interaction term) is estimated to obtain the scores of the latent variables. These are saved for further analysis in the second stage.

Exhibit 7.15 The Orthogonalizing Approach

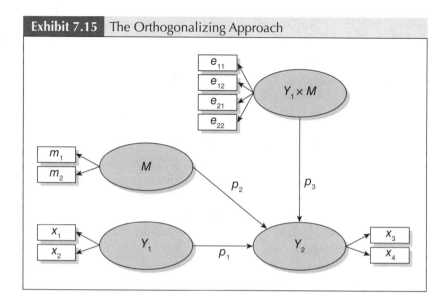

Stage 2: The latent variable scores of the exogenous latent variable and moderator variable from Stage 1 are multiplied to create a single-item measure used to measure the interaction term. All other latent variables are represented by means of single items of their latent variable scores from Stage 1.

Exhibit 7.16 illustrates the two-stage approach for our previous model, but two formative indicators are used in Stage 1 to measure the moderator variable. The main effects model in Stage 1 is run to obtain the latent variable scores for Y_1, Y_2, and M (i.e., $LVS(Y_1)$, $LVS(Y_2)$, and $LVS(M)$). The latent variable scores of Y_2 and M are then multiplied to form the single item used to measure the interaction term $Y_1 \cdot M$ in Stage 2. The latent variables Y_1, Y_2, and M are each measured with a single item of the latent variable scores from Stage 1. It is important to note that the limitations identified when using single items do not apply in this case, since the single item represents the latent variable scores as obtained from a multi-item measurement in Stage 1.

Guidelines for Creating the Interaction Term

Which approach should be preferred to create the interaction term? To answer this question, Henseler and Chin (2010) ran an

Exhibit 7.16   Two-Stage Approach

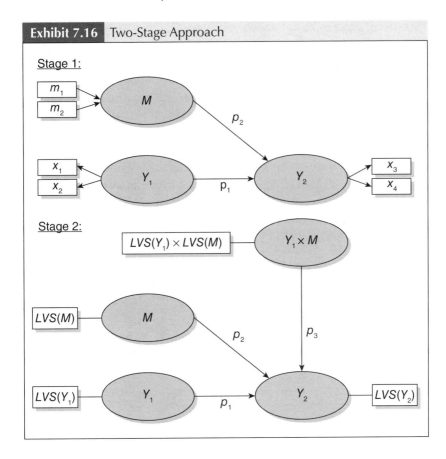

extensive simulation study, comparing the approaches in terms of their statistical power, point estimation accuracy, and prediction accuracy. Exhibit 7.17 summarizes their results, taking into account conceptual differences between the approaches as outlined before.

To begin with, neither the product indicator approach nor the orthogonalizing approach is applicable when the exogenous construct and/or the moderator have a formative measurement model. Therefore, when formative measures are involved, the two-stage approach must be used. If the exogenous construct and the moderator are measured reflectively, the further choice of method depends on the aim of the analysis. When the objective is to determine whether or not the moderator exerts a significant effect on the relationship, the two-stage approach is preferred. This approach yields high levels of statistical power compared with the orthogonalization approach and especially to the product indicator approach. However, when the primary concern is minimizing estimation bias, the orthogonalizing approach should be preferred as it performs best in terms of point accuracy. Similarly, when the aim is to maximize prediction of the endogenous construct, researchers should apply the orthogonalizing approach as this approach yields high prediction accuracy.

Henseler and Chin's (2010) study also points out that when using the product indicator approach, the path coefficient of the interaction term must not be used to quantify the strength of the moderating effect. Because of the PLS-SEM algorithm's characteristic, the coefficient needs to be adjusted. This adjustment is, however, not implemented in standard PLS-SEM software programs, including SmartPLS 3. Against this background and in light of Henseler and Chin's (2010) simulation

Exhibit 7.17 Guidelines for Creating the Interaction Term

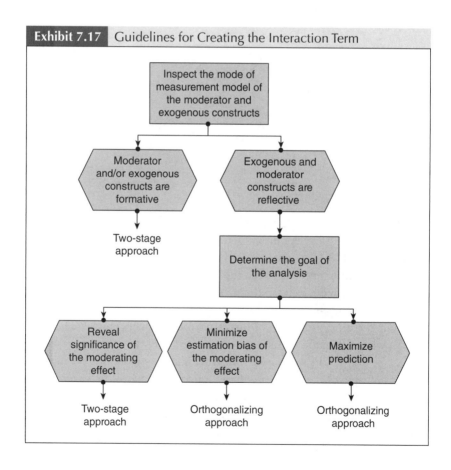

results, we generally advise against the use of the product indicator approach. Instead, the orthogonalizing approach and particularly the two-stage approach are viable alternatives. The latter stands out due to its universal applicability, regardless of whether the moderator variable and/or the exogenous construct are measured formatively. Since the two-stage approach also exhibits a higher level of statistical power compared with the orthogonalizing approach, we generally recommend using it for modeling the interaction term.

Model Evaluation

Measurement and structural model evaluation criteria, as discussed in Chapters 4 to 6, also apply to moderator models. When assessing reflective measurement models, the moderator variable must meet all relevant criteria in terms of internal consistency reliability, convergent validity, and discriminant validity. Similarly, all formative measurement model criteria universally apply to the moderator variable. For the interaction term, however, there is no such requirement. The product indicator approach and the orthogonalizing approach require multiplying the indicators from two conceptual domains (see domain sampling model; Chapter 2) to form the interaction term. This does not imply that the product of the indicators stems from one specific conceptual domain. Rather, the interaction term's measurement model should be viewed as an auxiliary measurement that incorporates the interrelationships between the moderator and the exogenous construct in the path model. This characteristic, however, renders any measurement model assessment of the interaction term meaningless. Furthermore, reusing the indicators of the moderator variable and exogenous construct introduces high construct correlations by design, violating common discriminant validity standards. Similarly, common measurement model evaluation standards do not apply when using the two-stage approach since the interaction term is measured with a single item. Therefore, the interaction term does not have to be assessed in the measurement model evaluation step.

Finally, it is also important to consider the standard criteria for structural model assessment. In the context of moderation, particular attention should be paid to the f^2 effect size of the interaction effect. As explained in Chapter 6, this criterion enables an assessment of the change in the R^2 value when an exogenous construct is omitted from the model. In case of the interactions effect, the f^2 effect size indicates how much the moderation contributes to the explanation of the endogenous latent variable. Recall that the effect size can be calculated as

$$f^2 = \frac{R^2_{\text{included}} - R^2_{\text{excluded}}}{1 - R^2_{\text{included}}},$$

where R^2_{included} and R^2_{excluded} are the R^2 values of the endogenous latent variable when the interaction term of the moderator model is included in or excluded from the PLS path model. General guidelines for assessing f^2 suggest that values of 0.02, 0.15, and 0.35 represent small, medium, and large effect sizes, respectively (Cohen, 1988). However, Aguinis et al. (2005) have shown that the average effect size in tests of moderation is only 0.009. Against this background, Kenny (2016) proposes that 0.005, 0.01, and 0.025 constitute more realistic standards for small, medium, and large effect sizes, respectively, but also points out that even these values are optimistic given Aguinis et al.'s (2005) review.

Results Interpretation

When interpreting the results of a moderation analysis, the primary interest is with the significance of the interaction term. If the interaction term's effect on the endogenous construct is significant, we conclude that the moderator M has a significant moderating effect on the relationship between Y_1 and Y_2. The bootstrapping procedure, as explained in Chapters 5 and 6, facilitates this assessment. In case of a significant moderation, the next step is to determine the strength of the moderating effect. This analysis depends on the way the interaction term was created. Specifically, we need to distinguish between the product indicator approach and the two-stage approach, on one hand, and the orthogonalizing approach, on the other.

In a model without moderation (i.e., without the moderator variable M) where there is only an arrow linking Y_1 and Y_2, the effect p_1 is referred to as a direct effect or **main effect.** In the case of the product indicator and the two-stage approaches, such main effects are, however, different from the corresponding relationship in a moderator model shown in Exhibit 7.14 (product indicator approach) and Exhibit 7.16 (two-stage approach). Here, in contrast, p_1 is referred to as a **simple effect,** expressing the effect of

Y_1 on Y_2 that is moderated by M. More specifically, the estimated value of p_1 represents the strength of the relationship between Y_1 and Y_2 when the moderator variable M has a value of zero. If the level of the moderator variable is increased (or decreased) by one standard deviation unit, the simple effect p_1 is expected to change by the size of p_3. For example, if the simple effect p_1 equals 0.30 and the moderating effect p_3 has a value of −0.10, one would expect the relationship between Y_1 and Y_2 to decrease to a value of 0.30 + (−0.10) = 0.20, if (ceteris paribus) the mean value of the moderator variable M increases by one standard deviation unit (Henseler & Fassott, 2010).

In many model setups, however, zero is not a number on the scale of M or, as in the case in our example, is not a sensible value for the moderator. If this is the case, the interpretation of the simple effect becomes problematic. This is the reason why we need to standardize the indicators of the moderator as described earlier. Standardization is done by subtracting the variable's mean from each observation and dividing the result by the variable's standard error (Sarstedt & Mooi, 2014). The standardization shifts the reference point from an income of zero to the average income and thus facilitates interpretation of the effects. Furthermore, as indicated before, the standardization reduces collinearity among the interaction term, the moderator, and the exogenous constructs, resulting from the reuse of indicators in the case of the product indicator approach.

As the nature of the effect between Y_1 and Y_2 (i.e., p_1) differs for models with and without the moderator when using the product indicator or two-stage approach, we need to include an important note of caution. If one is interested in testing the significance of the main effect p_1 between Y_1 and Y_2, the PLS-SEM analysis should be initially executed without the moderator. The evaluation and interpretation of results should follow the procedures outlined in Chapter 6. Then, the moderator analysis follows as complementary analysis for the specific moderating relationship. This issue is important because the direct effect becomes a simple effect in the moderator model, which differs in its estimated value, meaning, and interpretation. The simple effect represents the relationship between an exogenous and an endogenous latent variable when the moderator variable's value is equal to its mean value (provided standardization has been applied). Hence, interpreting the simple effect results of a moderator model as if it were a direct effect (e.g., for testing the hypothesis of a significant relationship p_1 between Y_1 and Y_2) may involve incorrect and misleading conclusions (Henseler & Fassott, 2010).

The above considerations are relevant only when using the product indicator or two-stage approach for creating the interaction term. The situation is different when using the orthogonalizing approach. As a consequence of the orthogonality of the interaction term, the estimates of the simple effect in a model with an interaction term are (almost) identical to the parameter estimates of the direct effect in a model without interaction. That is, for example, the differentiation between a direct effect or main effect and a simple effect is not relevant when the orthogonalizing approach has been used. Hypotheses relating to the direct and the moderating effect can be assessed in one model.

Beyond understanding these aspects of moderator analysis, interpretation of moderation results is often quite challenging. For this reason, graphical illustrations of results support understanding them and drawing conclusions. A common way to illustrate the results of a moderation analysis is by slope plots. Webpages such as those by Jeremy Dawson (http://www.jeremydawson.co.uk/slopes.htm) or Kristopher Preacher (http://quantpsy.org/interact/mlr2.htm) provide online tools for corresponding computations and simple slope plot extractions. In our example of a two-way interaction (Exhibit 7.13), suppose that the relationship between Y_1 and Y_2 has a value of 0.50, the relationship between M and Y_2 has a value of 0.10, and the interaction term $(Y_1 \cdot M)$ has a 0.25 relationship with Y_2. Exhibit 7.18 shows the slope plot for such a setting, where the x-axis represents the exogenous construct (Y_1) and the y-axis the endogenous construct (Y_2).

The two lines in Exhibit 7.18 represent the relationship between Y_1 and Y_2 for low and high levels of the moderator construct M. Usually, a low level of M is one standard deviation unit below its average (straight line in Exhibit 7.18) while a high level of M is one standard deviation unit above its average (dotted line in Exhibit 7.18). Because of the positive moderating effect as expressed in the 0.25 relationship between the interaction term and the endogenous construct, the high moderator line's slope is steeper. That is, the relationship between Y_1 and Y_2 becomes stronger with high levels of M. For low levels of M, the slope is much flatter, as shown in Exhibit 7.18. Hence, with low levels of the moderator construct M, the relationship between Y_1 and Y_2 becomes weaker.

Exhibit 7.18	Slope Plot

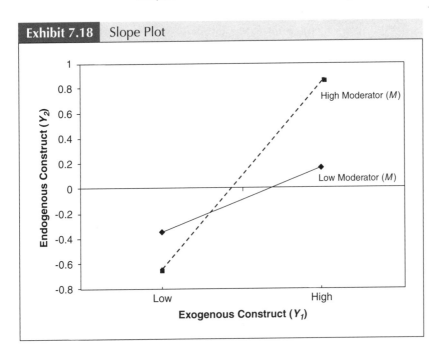

Moderated Mediation and Mediated Moderation

With the advent of mediation and moderation analyses, there have been occasional discussions of how to combine these two analytic strategies in theoretically interesting ways. These analyses are framed in terms of a **moderated mediation** or a mediated moderation, depending on the way the researcher defines the influence of the moderator or mediator variable.

Moderated mediation occurs when a moderator variable interacts with a mediator variable such that the value of the indirect effect changes depending on the value of the moderator variable. Such a situation is also referred to as a **conditional indirect effect** because the value of the indirect effect is conditional on the value of the moderator variable. In other words, if the mechanism linking an exogenous construct to an endogenous construct through a mediator is a function of another variable, then it can be said to be moderated by that variable. Consider Exhibit 7.19 for an example of a moderated mediation. In this model, the relationship between the exogenous construct Y_1 and the mediator variable Y_2 is assumed to be moderated by M. Following the standard approach for testing moderation in a

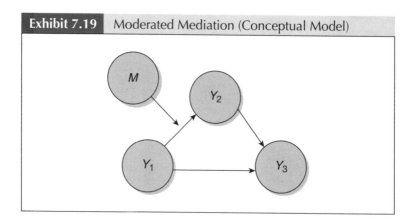

Exhibit 7.19   Moderated Mediation (Conceptual Model)

path model, we would establish an interaction term of the indicators measuring the moderator variable M and the exogenous construct Y_1, as shown in Exhibit 7.20.

To claim that mediation is moderated, researchers traditionally note that there needs to be evidence of a significant moderation of the path linking Y_1 to Y_2 (e.g., Muller, Judd, & Yzerbyt, 2005; Preacher, Rucker, & Hayes, 2007), which is equivalent to observing a significant path p_5 in Exhibit 7.20. More recently, however, Hayes (2015) has stressed that a nonsignificant moderation does not necessarily imply that the indirect effect of Y_1 on Y_3 is not moderated by M. The author points out that researchers have to consider the moderator's impact on the indirect effect as a whole rather than on one element of the mediating effect in isolation (in this case, the path p_2). To formally test such an impact, Hayes (2015) proposes the **index of moderated mediation**, which is defined as follows:

$$w = p_1 \cdot p_2 + p_2 \cdot p_5 \cdot M.$$

In this formula, the path coefficients refer to the relationships between the constructs, as shown in Exhibit 7.20, while M refers to the latent variable scores of the moderator variable. If the index w is significantly different from zero, we can conclude that the indirect effect of Y_1 on Y_3 through Y_2 is not independent of M but, rather, depends on M. To test whether this is the case, we can use the bootstrap sample–specific path coefficients and latent variable scores of M as input to compute w for each bootstrap sample. Using this information, we can easily derive a standard error and t value for w.

Exhibit 7.20	Interaction Term in a Moderated Mediation Model

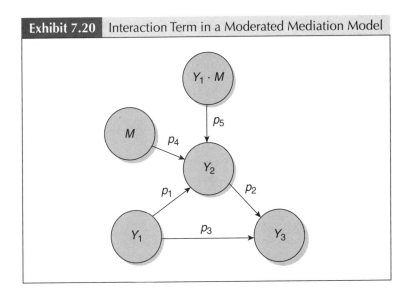

Other types of moderated mediation can occur such as when the relationship between the mediator Y_2 and the endogenous construct Y_3 is moderated or when M additionally influences the simple effect between Y_1 and Y_3. Furthermore, moderation can also occur in multiple mediation models, affecting one or more model relationships. See Hayes (2015) for further details and Coelho and Henseler (2012) for an application of a moderated mediation model in the field of marketing.

The second way of combining mediation and moderation is by means of a **mediated moderation.** Again, consider the moderator model in Exhibit 7.13. In the case of a mediated moderation, the moderating effect p_3 from the interaction term $Y_1 \cdot M$ to the dependent variable Y_2 is mediated by another construct. Hence, the mediator variable intervenes with the moderating effect in that a change in the interaction term results in a change of the mediator variable, which, in turn, translates to a variation of the dependent variable in the moderator model. In other words, the mediator variable governs the nature (i.e., the underlying mechanism or process) of the moderating effect. With respect to these considerations, Hayes (2013) advises against the explicit testing of mediated moderation since the corresponding analysis provides no additional insights into the path model effects. More specifically, the interaction term in a mediated moderation model "has no substantive grounding in the measurement or manipulation process. The product does not quantify anything. And if . . . [the interaction term] has no meaning and no substantive interpretation, then what does the indirect effect of a product mean? The answer, in my opinion, is that it means nothing" (Hayes, 2013, p. 388). Furthermore, it is usually very challenging and oftentimes impossible to establish theoretically/conceptually reasonable underpinnings of mediated moderation models that researchers can test empirically. For these reasons, we follow Hayes's (2013) call to disregard the concept of mediated moderation. Instead, researchers should focus on moderated mediation.

Exhibit 7.21 summarizes the rules of thumb for running a moderation analysis in PLS-SEM.

Case Study Illustration—Moderation

To illustrate the estimation of moderating effects, let's consider the extended corporate model again, as shown in Exhibit 7.8 earlier in this chapter. In the following discussion, we focus on the relationship between customer satisfaction and customer loyalty. Specifically, we introduce switching costs as a moderator variable that can be assumed to negatively influence the relationship between satisfaction and loyalty. The higher the perceived switching costs, the weaker the relationship between these two constructs. We use an extended form of Jones, Mothersbaugh, and Beatty's (2000) scale and measure switching costs reflectively using four indicators (*switch_1* to *switch_4*; Exhibit 7.22), each measured on a 5-point Likert scale (1 = *fully disagree*, 5 = *fully agree*).

We first need to extend the original model by including the moderator variable. To do so, enter a new construct in the model (see Chapter 2 for detailed explanations), rename it as *SC* (i.e., switching costs), and draw a path relationship from the newly added moderator variable to the *CUSL* construct. Next, we need to assign the indicators *switch_1*, *switch_2*, *switch_3*, and *switch_4* to the *SC* construct. Exhibit 7.23 shows the resulting main effects model (i.e., the extended model plus *SC* linked to *CUSL*) in the SmartPLS **Modeling** window.

In the next step, we need to create the interaction term. The SmartPLS 3 software offers an option to automatically include an interaction term based on the product indicator, orthogonalizing, or two-stage approach. In this case study, our primary concern is with disclosing the significance of a moderating effect (which is usually the

Exhibit 7.21	Rules of Thumb for Moderator Analyses in PLS-SEM

- For the creation of the interaction term, use the two-stage approach when the exogenous construct and/or the moderator are measured formatively or when the aim is to disclose a significant moderating effect. Alternatively, use the orthogonalizing approach, especially when the aim is to minimize estimation bias of the moderating effect or to maximize prediction. Independent from these aspects, the two-stage approach is very versatile and should generally be given preference for creating the interaction term.
- The moderator variable must be assessed for reliability and validity following the standard evaluation procedures for reflective and formative measures. However, this does not hold for the interaction term, which relies on an auxiliary measurement model generated by reusing indicators of the exogenous construct and the moderator variable.
- Standardize the data when running a moderator analysis.
- In the results interpretation and testing of hypotheses, differentiate between the direct effect (or main effect), on one hand, and simple effect, on the other. The direct effect expresses the relationship between two constructs when no moderator is included. On the contrary, the simple effect expresses the relationship between two constructs when moderated by a third variable, and this moderator has an average value (provided the data are standardized).
- When testing a moderated mediation model, use Hayes's (2015) index of moderated mediation.
- Do not use mediated moderation models.

case in PLS-SEM applications), making the two-stage approach the method of choice. Furthermore, the two-stage approach is the most versatile approach as it also works when the exogenous construct and/or the moderator are measured formatively. To include an interaction term, right-click in the target construct *CUSL* and choose the option **Add Moderating Effect** (Exhibit 7.24).

In the screen that follows, specify *SC* as the **Moderator Variable** and *CUSA* as the **Independent Variable** and choose the **Two-Stage** option as well as **Standardized** and **Automatic** under **Advanced Settings** (Exhibit 7.25).

When you click on **OK**, SmartPLS will include the interaction term labeled *Moderating Effect 1* in the **Modeling** window. If you like, you can right-click on this construct and select the **Rename** option to choose a different name (e.g., *CUSA * SC*) for the interaction term.

Exhibit 7.22	Indicators for Measuring Switching Costs
switch_1	It takes me a great deal of time to switch to another company.
switch_2	It costs me too much to switch to another company.
switch_3	It takes a lot of effort to get used to a new company with its specific "rules" and practices.
switch_4	In general, it would be a hassle switching to another company.

Its different color also indicates that this construct is an interaction term. Again, right-click on the interaction term and choose the menu option **Show Indicators of Selected Constructs.** The indicator

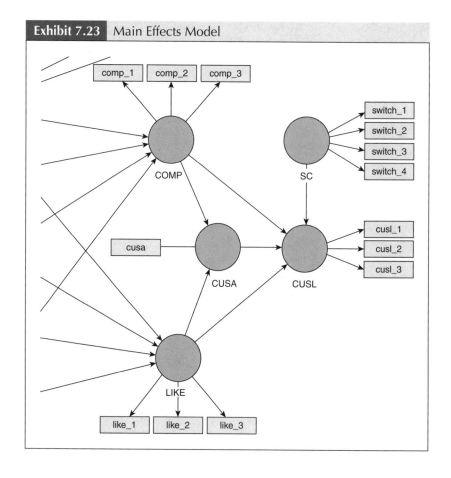

Exhibit 7.23	Main Effects Model

Exhibit 7.24	Add Moderating Effect Menu Option

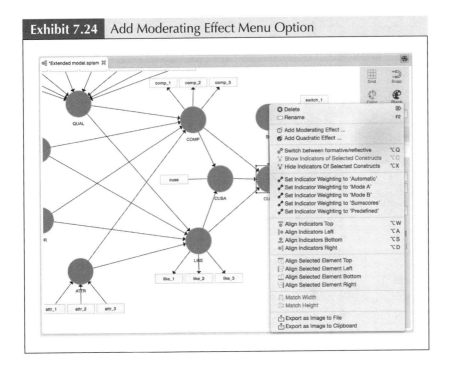

*CUSA * SC* generated in the second stage of the two-stage approach will then appear in the **Modeling** window. We can now proceed with the analysis by running the PLS-SEM algorithm (using the path weighting scheme and mean value replacement for missing values) as described in the earlier chapters. Exhibit 7.26 shows the results in the **Modeling** window.

The evaluation of the moderator variable's measurement model shows that the construct measures are reliable and valid. All indicator loadings are above 0.70, and the convergent validity assessment yields an AVE of 0.705, providing support for convergent validity of the switching cost moderator (*SC*). Cronbach's alpha and composite reliability are 0.858 and 0.905, respectively, indicating internal consistency reliability. In terms of discriminant validity, *SC* exhibits increased HTMT values only with *COMP* (0.850) and *LIKE* (0.802). A further analysis of these HTMT values using bootstrapping (no sign changes, complete bootstrapping, BCa bootstrap, two-tailed testing, and standard settings for the PLS-SEM algorithm and missing value treatment), however, shows that the bias-corrected 95% confidence intervals of *SC*'s HTMT values do not include 1. This result provides

Exhibit 7.25 Interaction Effect Dialog Box in SmartPLS

Moderating Effect

— **Basic Settings**

Dependent Variable	CUSL
Moderator Variable	SC ◇
Independent Variable	CUSA ◇

Calculation Method
- ○ Product Indicator
- ● Two Stage
- ○ Orthogonalization

— **Advanced Settings**

Product Term Generation
- ○ Unstandardized
- ○ Mean Centered
- ● Standardized

Weighing Mode
- ● Automatic
- ○ Mode A
- ○ Mode B
- ○ Sumscores
- ○ Pre Defined

Basic Settings

Dependent Variable

The selected dependent variable for which a moderating effect will be estimated.

Predictor Variable

Field to define the predictor variable for which a moderating effect will be estimated.

Moderator Variable

Field to define the moderator variable for which a moderating effect will be estimated.

Calculation Method

Selects the method of interaction term construct in PLS path modeling. There are three options:

(1) Product Indicator

This approach uses all possible pair combinations of the indicators of the latent predictor and the latent moderator variable. These product terms serve as indicators ("product indicators") of the interaction term in the structural model.

(2) Two-stage *(default)*

This approach uses the latent variable scores of the latent predictor and latent moderator variable from the main effects model (without the interaction term). These latent variable scores are saved and used to calculate the product indicator for the second stage analysis that involves the interaction term in addition to the predictor and moderator variable.

Cancel   OK

support for the measures' discriminant validity. Due to the inclusion of additional constructs in the path model (i.e., *SC* and the interaction term), the measurement properties of all other constructs in the path model will change (even though changes will likely be marginal). Reanalyzing all measurement models provides support for the measures' reliability and validity. Note that the measurement model results shown in the **Modeling** window stem from Stage 1 of the two-stage approach. The structural model results, however, stem from Stage 2 of the two-stage approach when all constructs are measured with single items.

Our next concern is with the size of the moderating effect. As can be seen in Exhibit 7.26, the interaction term has a negative effect on

Exhibit 7.26 Moderator Analysis Results in SmartPLS

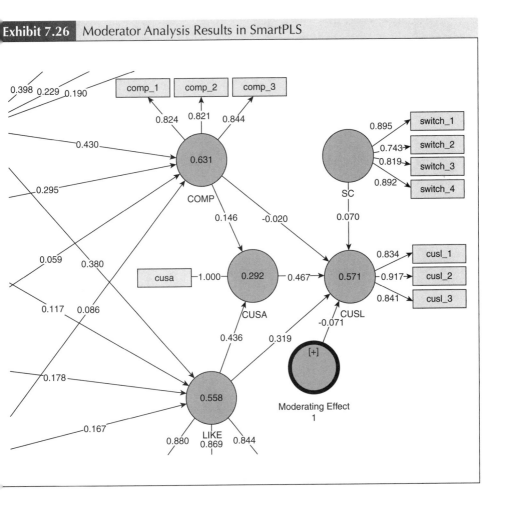

Exhibit 7.27 Simple Slope Plot in SmartPLS

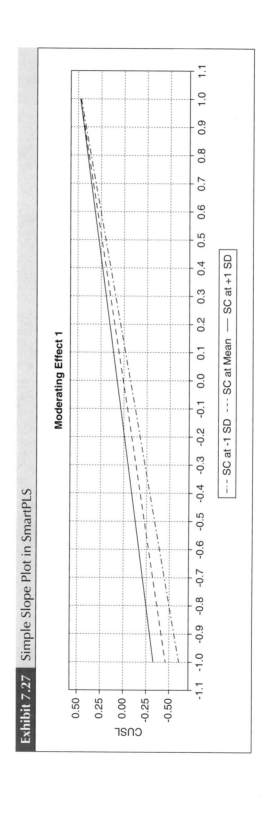

Moderating Effect 1

-- SC at -1 SD   --- SC at Mean   — SC at +1 SD

CUSL (–0.071), whereas the simple effect of CUSA on CUSL is 0.467. Jointly, these results suggest that the relationship between CUSA and CUSL is 0.467 for an average level of switching costs. For higher levels of switching costs (e.g., SC is increased by one standard deviation unit), the relationship between CUSA and CUSL decreases by the size of the interaction term (i.e., 0.467 – 0.071 = 0.396). On the contrary, for lower levels of switching costs (e.g., SC is decreased by one standard deviation point), the relationship between CUSA and CUSL becomes 0.467 + 0.071 = 0.538. To better comprehend the results of the moderator analysis, go to **Final Results → Simple Slope Analysis**. The simple slope plot that follows visualizes the two-way interaction effect (Exhibit 7.27).

The three lines shown in Exhibit 7.27 represent the relationship between CUSA (x-axis) and CUSL (y-axis). The middle line represents the relationship for an average level of the moderator variable SC. The other two lines represent the relationship between CUSA and CUSL for higher (i.e., mean value of SC plus one standard deviation unit) and lower (i.e., mean value of SC minus one standard deviation unit) levels of the moderator variable SC. As we can see, the relationship between CUSA and CUSL is positive for all three lines as indicated by their positive slope. Hence, higher levels of customer satisfaction go hand in hand with higher levels of customer loyalty.

In addition, we can analyze the moderating effect's slope in greater detail. The upper line, which represents a high level of the moderator construct SC, has a flatter slope while the lower line, which represents a low level of the moderator construct SC, has a steeper slope. This makes sense since the interaction effect is negative. As a rule of thumb and an approximation, the slope of the high level of the moderator construct SC is the simple effect (i.e., 0.467) plus the interaction effect (–0.071), while the slope of the low level of the moderator construct SC is the simple effect (i.e., 0.467) minus the interaction effect (–0.071). Hence, the simple slope plot supports our previous discussion of the negative interaction term: Higher SC levels entail a weaker relationship between CUSA and CUSL, while lower levels of SC lead to a stronger relationship between CUSA and CUSL.

Next, we assess whether the interaction term is significant. For this purpose, we run the bootstrapping procedure with 5,000 bootstrap samples, using the **No Sign Changes** option, BCa bootstrap, two-tailed testing, and the standard settings for the PLS-SEM algorithm and the missing value treatment. The analysis yields a p value of 0.027 for the

Exhibit 7.28   Bootstrapping Results of the Moderator Analysis

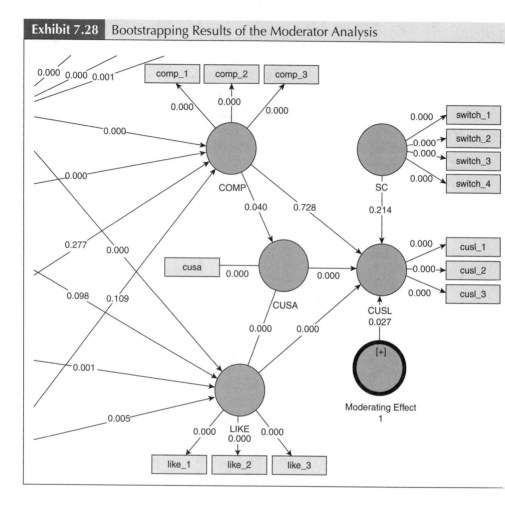

path linking the interaction term and *CUSL* (Exhibit 7.28). Similarly, the 95% bias-corrected bootstrap confidence interval of the interaction term's effect is [–0.135, –0.016]. As the confidence interval does not include zero, we conclude that the effect is significant. Again, note that these results will slightly differ from yours due to the random nature of the bootstrapping process. Overall, these results provide clear support that *SC* exerts a significant and negative effect on the relationship between *CUSA* and *CUSL*. The higher the switching costs, the weaker the relationship between customer satisfaction and customer loyalty.

For the completeness of the results representation, the final step addresses the moderator's f^2 effect size. By going to **Quality Criteria** → **f Square** in the SmartPLS algorithm results report, we learn that the interaction term's f^2 effect size has a value of 0.014. According to Kenny (2016), the value indicates a medium effect.

SUMMARY

• **Understand the basic concepts of mediation in a PLS-SEM context.** Mediation occurs when a third variable, referred to as a mediator variable, intervenes between two other related constructs. More precisely, a change in the exogenous construct results in a change in the mediator variable, which, in turn, affects the endogenous construct in the model. Analyzing the strength of the mediator variable's relationships with the other constructs enables the researcher to better understand the mechanisms that underlie the relationship between an exogenous construct and an endogenous construct. In the simplest form, the path model analysis considers only one mediator variable, but the model can involve multiple mediator variables that can be analyzed simultaneously.

• **Execute a mediation analysis using SmartPLS.** Mediating effects must be theoretically/conceptually postulated a priori. The analysis then focuses on testing such hypothesized relationships empirically. Researchers distinguish between five types of mediation and nonmediation: direct-only nonmediation, no-effect nonmediation, complementary mediation, competitive mediation, and indirect-only mediation. Testing for the type of mediation requires a series of analyses to assess whether the indirect effect and/or direct effect are significant.

• **Comprehend the basic concepts of moderation in a PLS-SEM context.** Moderation occurs when the strength or even the direction of a relationship between two constructs depends on a third variable. In other words, the nature of the relationship differs depending on the values of the third variable. Thus, the relationship is not the same for all customers but differs depending on the moderating variable, which could be, for example, customer income, age, gender, and so forth. As such, moderation can (and should) be seen as a means to account for heterogeneity in the data.

• **Use the SmartPLS software to run a moderation analysis.** Modeling moderator variables in PLS-SEM requires researchers to include an interaction term that accounts for the interrelation between the exogenous latent variable and the moderator variable. The product indicator approach, the orthogonalizing approach, and the two-stage approach are three popular approaches to model the interaction term. The product indicator and orthogonalizing approaches are restricted to setups where the exogenous latent variable and moderator variable are both measured reflectively. The two-stage approach can be used when formative measures are involved. The orthogonalizing approach proves valuable when the objective of the analysis is to minimize estimation bias of the moderating effect or to maximize prediction. However, when the objective is to identify the statistical significance of the moderator, the two-stage approach should be preferred. Generally, the two-stage approach is the most versatile approach and should generally be preferred.

REVIEW QUESTIONS

1. What does mediation mean?

2. What are the necessary conditions for substantiating an indirect-only mediation?

3. What is the difference between complementary and competitive mediation?

4. What is the most versatile approach for creating an interaction term with regard to the measurement models of the exogenous construct and the moderator variable?

5. Why should the indicators be standardized when generating an interaction term in a moderator analysis?

6. What is the interaction term and what does its value mean?

CRITICAL THINKING QUESTIONS

1. Give an example of a mediation model and establish the relevant hypotheses.

2. Why is it necessary to draw a direct relationship between the moderator and the endogenous construct?

3. Explain what the path coefficients in a moderator model mean.

4. Explain the similarities and differences between mediation and moderation.

KEY TERMS

Cascaded moderator analysis

Categorical moderator variable

Competitive mediation

Complementary mediation

Conditional indirect effect

Continuous moderator variable

Direct-only nonmediation

Full mediation

Heterogeneity

Inconsistent mediation

Index of moderated mediation

Indirect-only mediation

Interaction effect

Interaction term

Main effect

Mediating effect

Mediated moderation

Mediation

Mediation model

Mediator variable

Moderated mediation

Moderating effect

Moderation

Moderator variable

Multiple mediation analysis

No-effect nonmediation

Orthogonalizing approach

Partial mediation

Product indicator approach

Product indicators

Simple effect

Simple mediation analysis

Sobel test

Specific indirect effect

Suppressor variable

Three-way interaction

Total indirect effect

Two-stage approach

Two-way interaction

SUGGESTED READINGS

Hayes, A. F. (2013). *Introduction to mediation, moderation, and conditional process analysis: A regression-based approach.* New York, NY: Guilford.

Hayes, A. F. (2015). An index and test of linear moderated mediation. *Multivariate Behavioral Research, 50,* 1–22.

Henseler, J., & Chin, W. W. (2010). A comparison of approaches for the analysis of interaction effects between latent variables using partial least squares path modeling. *Structural Equation Modeling, 17,* 82–109.

Henseler, J., & Fassott, G. (2010). Testing moderating effects in PLS path models: An illustration of available procedures. In V. Esposito Vinzi, W. W. Chin, J. Henseler, & H. Wang (Eds.), *Handbook of partial least squares: Concepts, methods and applications in marketing and related fields* (Springer Handbooks of Computational Statistics Series, Vol. II, pp. 713–735). Berlin: Springer.

Nitzl, C., Roldán, J. L., & Cepeda, G. (in press). Mediation analyses in partial least squares structural equation modeling: Helping researchers discuss more sophisticated models. Industrial Management & Data Systems.

Preacher, K. J., & Hayes, A. F. (2008). Asymptotic and resampling strategies for assessing and comparing indirect effects in simple and multiple mediation models. *Behavior Research Methods, 40,* 879–891.

Preacher, K. J., Rucker, D. D., & Hayes, A. F. (2007). Assessing moderated mediation hypotheses: Theory, methods, and prescriptions. *Multivariate Behavioral Research, 42,* 185–227.

Rigdon, E. E., Ringle, C. M., & Sarstedt, M. (2010). Structural modeling of heterogeneous data with partial least squares. In N. K. Malhotra (Ed.), *Review of marketing research* (pp. 255–296). Armonk, NY: Sharpe.

Sarstedt, M., Henseler, J., & Ringle, C. M. (2011). Multi-group analysis in partial least squares (PLS) path modeling: Alternative methods and empirical results. *Advances in International Marketing, 22,* 195–218.

Zhao, X., Lynch, J. G., & Chen, Q. (2010). Reconsidering Baron and Kenny: Myths and truths about mediation analysis. *Journal of Consumer Research, 37,* 197–206.

CHAPTER 8

Outlook on Advanced Methods

LEARNING OUTCOMES

1. Comprehend the usefulness of a PLS-SEM importance-performance map analysis (IPMA).

2. Understand hierarchical component models (HCMs) and how to apply this concept in PLS-SEM.

3. Get to know how to assess the mode of measurement model with the confirmatory tetrad analysis in PLS-SEM (CTA-PLS).

4. Understand multigroup analysis in PLS-SEM.

5. Learn about techniques to identify and treat unobserved heterogeneity.

6. Understand measurement model invariance and its assessment in PLS-SEM.

7. Become familiar with consistent partial least squares (PLSc).

CHAPTER PREVIEW

This primer focuses on PLS-SEM's foundations. With the knowledge gained from Chapters 1 to 6, researchers have the understanding for using more advanced techniques that complement the basic PLS-SEM analyses. While Chapter 7 introduced the broadly applied mediator and moderator analysis techniques, this chapter offers a brief overview of some other useful and less frequently used advanced methods. To start with, the **importance-performance map** analysis represents a particularly valuable tool to extend the results presentation of the standard PLS-SEM estimations by contrasting the total effects of the latent variables on some target variable with their latent variable scores. The graphical representation of outcomes enables researchers to easily identify critical areas of attention and action. The next topic focuses on hierarchical component models, which enable researchers to represent constructs measured on different levels of abstraction in a PLS path model. From a conceptual perspective, using **hierarchical component models** is often more appropriate than relying on standard one-dimensional constructs. Their use typically allows reducing the number of structural model relationships, making the PLS path model more parsimonious and easier to grasp. The method that follows, confirmatory tetrad analysis, is a useful tool to empirically substantiate the mode of a latent variable's measurement model (i.e., formative or reflective). The application of **confirmatory tetrad analysis** enables researchers to avoid incorrect measurement model specification. The following sections address ways of dealing with heterogeneity in the data. We first discuss multigroup analysis, which enables testing for significant differences among path coefficients, typically between two groups. We also deal with **unobserved heterogeneity,** which, if neglected, is a threat to the validity of PLS-SEM results. We also introduce standard as well as more recently proposed latent class techniques and make recommendations regarding their use. Comparisons of PLS-SEM results across different groups are only reasonable if measurement invariance is confirmed. For this purpose, the **measurement invariance** of composite procedure provides a useful tool in PLS-SEM. Finally, we introduce consistent PLS, which applies a correction for attenuation to PLS path coefficients. When applied, PLS path models with reflectively measured latent variables estimate results that are the same as CB-SEM, while retaining many of the well-known advantages of PLS-SEM.

IMPORTANCE-PERFORMANCE MAP ANALYSIS

The **importance-performance map analysis** (IPMA; also called importance-performance matrix analysis and impact-performance map analysis) extends the standard PLS-SEM results reporting of path coefficient estimates by adding a dimension to the analysis that considers the average values of the latent variable scores (Fornell, Johnson, Anderson, Cha, & Bryant, 1996; Höck, Ringle, & Sarstedt, 2010; Kristensen, Martensen, & Grønholdt, 2000; Slack, 1994). More precisely, the IPMA contrasts structural model total effects on a specific target construct (i.e., a specific endogenous latent variable in the PLS path model such as Y_4 in Exhibit 8.1) with the average latent variable scores of this construct's predecessors (e.g., Y_1, Y_2, and Y_3 in Exhibit 8.1). The total effects represent the predecessor constructs' **importance** in shaping the target construct (Y_4), while their average latent variable scores represent their **performance**. The goal is to identify predecessors that have a relatively high importance for the target construct (i.e., those that have a strong total effect) but also a relatively low performance (i.e., low average latent variable scores). The aspects underlying these constructs represent potential areas of improvement that may receive high attention. Here, we do not explain all of the technical details of IPMA but refer the interested reader to the comprehensive explications in, for example, Höck et al. (2010) and Ringle and Sarstedt (in press).

An IPMA relies on total effects and the rescaled latent variable scores, both in an unstandardized form. **Rescaling** the latent variable scores is important to facilitate the comparison of latent variables measured on different scale levels. For example, rescaling is relevant if the indicators of one construct use an interval scale with values from 1 to 5 (e.g., Y_1) while the indicators of another construct (e.g., Y_2) use an interval scale with values from 1 to 7. Rescaling adjusts each latent variable score so that it can take on values between 0 and 100 (e.g., Höck et al., 2010; Kristensen et al., 2000). The mean values

Exhibit 8.1   IPMA Model

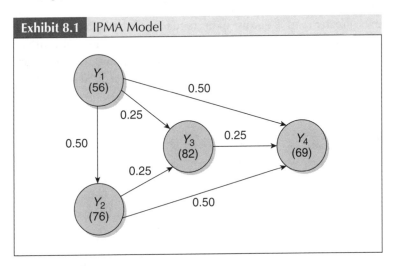

of these scores indicate the construct's performance, with 0 representing the lowest and 100 representing the highest performance. Since most researchers are familiar with interpreting percentage values, this kind of performance scale is easy to understand. In our example, Y_1 has a performance of 56, Y_2 of 76, Y_3 of 82, and Y_4 of 69. Hence, constructs Y_2 and Y_3 show a relatively high performance, while Y_4 and Y_1 have a medium and low (relative) performance, respectively.

Next, we need to determine each predecessor construct's importance in terms of its total effect on the target construct. Recall that the total effect of a relationship between two constructs is the sum of the direct and indirect effects in the structural model. For example, to determine the total effect of Y_1 on Y_4 (Exhibit 8.1), we have to consider the direct effect between these two constructs (0.50) and the following three indirect effects via Y_2 and Y_3, respectively:

$$
\begin{aligned}
Y_1 \rightarrow Y_2 \rightarrow Y_4 \quad &= 0.50 \cdot 0.50 \quad &&= 0.25, \\
Y_1 \rightarrow Y_2 \rightarrow Y_3 \rightarrow Y_4 &= 0.50 \cdot 0.25 \cdot 0.25 &&= 0.03125, \text{ and} \\
Y_1 \rightarrow Y_3 \rightarrow Y_4 \quad &= 0.25 \cdot 0.25 \quad &&= 0.0625.
\end{aligned}
$$

Adding up the individual indirect effects yields the total indirect effect of Y_1 on Y_4, which is approximately 0.34. Therefore, the total effect of Y_1 on Y_4 is 0.84 (0.50 + 0.34). This total effect expresses Y_1's importance in predicting the target construct Y_4. Exhibit 8.2 summarizes the direct, indirect, and total effects of the constructs Y_1, Y_2, and Y_3 on the target construct Y_4 as shown in Exhibit 8.1. Note that in an IPMA, the direct, indirect, and total effects (just like the latent variable scores) come in an unstandardized form and can take on values much greater than 1. The use of unstandardized total effects allows us to interpret the IPMA in the following way: A one-unit increase of the predecessor's performance increases the performance of the target construct by the size of the predecessor's unstandardized total effect, if everything else remains equal (ceteris paribus).

Exhibit 8.2	Direct, Indirect, and Total Effects in the IPMA		
Predecessor Construct	Direct Effect on Y_4	Indirect Effect on Y_4	Total Effect on Y_4
Y_1	0.50	0.34	0.84
Y_2	0.50	0.06	0.56
Y_3	0.25	—	0.25

Exhibit 8.3	Summary of the IPMA Data	
	Importance	**Performance**
Y_1	0.84	56
Y_2	0.56	76
Y_3	0.25	82

In the final step, we combine the importance and performance data, which we summarize in Exhibit 8.3.

Using the IPMA data allows us to create an **importance-performance map** as shown in Exhibit 8.4. The x-axis represents the (unstandardized) total effects of Y_1, Y_2, and Y_3 on the target construct Y_4 (i.e., their importance). The y-axis depicts the average rescaled (and unstandardized) latent variable scores of Y_1, Y_2, and Y_3 (i.e., their performance).

As can be seen, constructs in the lower right area of the importance-performance map have a high importance for the target construct but show a low performance. Hence, there is a particularly high potential for improving the performance of the constructs positioned in this area. Constructs with lower importance, relative to the other constructs in the importance-performance map, have a lower priority for

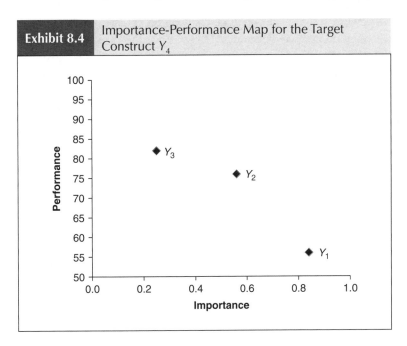

| Exhibit 8.4 | Importance-Performance Map for the Target Construct Y_4 |

performance improvements. In fact, investing into the performance improvement of a construct that has a very small importance for the target construct would not be logical, since it would have little impact in changing (improving) the target construct. In our example, Y_1 is particularly important for explaining the target construct Y_4. In a ceteris paribus situation, a one-unit increase in the performance of Y_1 increases the performance of Y_4 by the value of the total effect, which is 0.84. At the same time, the performance of Y_1 is relatively low, so there is substantial room for improvement. Consequently, in the PLS path model example, construct Y_1 is the most relevant for managerial actions.

IPMA is not limited to the construct level. We can also conduct an IPMA on the indicator level to identify relevant and even more specific areas of improvement. More precisely, we can interpret the unstandardized outer weights as the relative importance of an indicator compared with the other indicators in the measurement model, no matter whether the measurement model is reflective or formative. In our example, such an analysis would be particularly useful for the indicators of the Y_1 construct because of its strong total effect on Y_4.

Applications of the IPMA need to meet two requirements: First, all the indicator coding must have the same direction; a low value represents a negative outcome and a high value a positive outcome. Otherwise, we cannot conclude that higher latent variable values represent a better performance. If this is not the case, the indicator coding needs to be changed by reversing the scale (e.g., on a 5-point scale, 1 becomes 5 and 5 becomes 1, 2 becomes 4 and 4 becomes 2, and 3 remains unchanged). Second, no matter whether the measurement model is formative or reflective, the outer weights must not be negative. If the outer weights are positive, the performance values will be on a scale of 0 to 100. However, if outer weights are negative, the performance values will not be in this specific range but, for example, between –5 and 95. Negative weights might be a result of indicator collinearity. In this case, the researcher may carefully consider removing that indicator (see Chapter 5).

For further example IPMA applications, see Höck et al. (2010) and Kristensen et al. (2000). Other researchers have used the IPMA to better compare the group-specific outcomes of a PLS-SEM–based multigroup analysis (e.g., Rigdon et al., 2011; Schloderer et al., 2014; Völckner, Sattler, Hennig-Thurau, & Ringle, 2010).

HIERARCHICAL COMPONENT MODELS

The previous chapters dealt with first-order models, which consider a single layer of constructs. In some instances, however, the constructs that researchers wish to examine are quite complex and can also be operationalized at higher levels of abstraction. Establishing such higher-order models or **hierarchical component models (HCMs)**, as they are usually called in the context of PLS-SEM (Lohmöller, 1989), most often involves testing higher-order structures that contain two layers of constructs.

Let us consider the example of the customer satisfaction construct, which can consist of numerous more concrete constructs that capture separate attributes of satisfaction (see Chapter 2). In the context of services, these might include satisfaction with the quality of the service, the service personnel, the speed of service, or the servicescape. It is then possible to define satisfaction at two levels of abstraction. These concrete components at the first level of abstraction (i.e., first-order) form the more abstract higher-order (i.e., second-order) satisfaction component.

There are three main reasons to include an HCM in a PLS path model. First, by establishing HCMs, researchers can reduce the number of relationships in the structural model, making the PLS path model more parsimonious and easier to grasp. Second, HCMs prove valuable if the first-order constructs are highly correlated. When this situation is present, estimations of the structural model relationships may be biased as a result of collinearity issues, and discriminant validity may not be established. In situations characterized by collinearity among constructs, establishing a higher-order structure can reduce collinearity issues and may solve discriminant validity problems. Third, establishing HCMs can also prove valuable if formative indicators exhibit high levels of collinearity. Provided that theory supports this step, researchers can split the set of indicators and establish separate first-order constructs that jointly form a higher-order structure.

Exhibit 8.5 illustrates the four main types of HCMs discussed in the extant literature (Jarvis et al., 2003; Wetzels et al., 2009) and used in SEM applications (Ringle et al., 2012). HCMs have two elements: the **higher-order component (HOC)**, which captures the more abstract higher-order entity, and the **lower-order components (LOCs)**, which capture the subdimensions of the higher-order entity. Each HCM type can be characterized by different relationships between (1) the HOC and the LOCs, and (2) the constructs and their indicators. For example, the **reflective-reflective HCM** type indicates a (reflective) relationship between the HOC and the LOCs, and all first-order constructs are measured by reflective indicators. Conversely, the **reflective-formative HCM** type indicates (formative) relationships between the LOCs and the HOC, and all first-order constructs are measured by reflective indicators. Two other alternative HCMs researchers may employ are a **formative-reflective** and **formative-formative HCM.** The selection of the appropriate type of HCM is based on a priori established theoretical/conceptual considerations.

As can be seen in Exhibit 8.5, the HOCs and LOCs have a measurement model that can be either reflective or formative but does not

---

Exhibit 8.5 | Types of Hierarchical Component Models

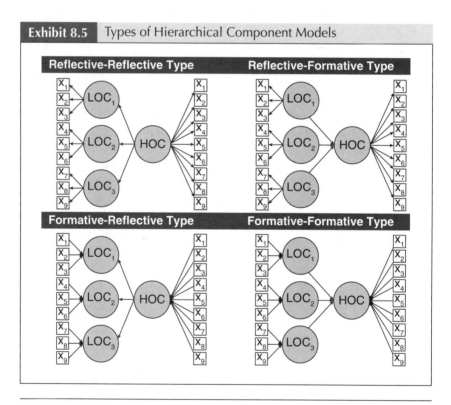

Source: Ringle, CM, Sarstedt, M and Straub, DW (2012) A Critical Look at the Use of PLS-SEM in MIS Quarterly. MIS Quarterly 36: iii–xiv.; permission conveyed through Copyright Clearance Center, Inc.

Note: LOC = lower-order component; HOC = higher-order component.

have to be the same at both levels. To represent the HOC's measurement model, researchers usually assign all the indicators from the LOCs to the HOC in the form of a **repeated indicators approach.** In the HCM examples in Exhibit 8.5, the HOC uses the indicators x_1 to x_9 of its underlying components LOC_1, LOC_2, and LOC_3 in the measurement model.

Several issues arise when modeling formative-formative and reflective-formative HCMs using the repeated indicator approach. In such settings, almost all of the HOC variance is explained by its LOCs, yielding an R^2 value of (close to) 1.0. As a result, any further path coefficients (i.e., other than those by the LOCs) for relationships pointing at the HOC will be very small (perhaps zero) and insignificant (Ringle et al., 2012). These situations require particular attention, since almost all of the HOC variance is explained by its LOCs ($R^2 \approx 1.0$). To resolve this issue, researchers should apply a combination of the repeated indicators approach and the use of latent variable scores in a **two-stage HCM analysis.** This analysis is similar to the two-stage approach in moderator analyses (Chapter 7) in PLS-SEM (Henseler & Chin, 2010). In the first stage, the repeated indicator approach is used to obtain the latent variable scores for the LOCs. In the second stage, the LOC scores serve as manifest variables in the HOC measurement model (Exhibit 8.6). The LOC scores are readily available from the SmartPLS output. When the two-stage HCM analysis is applied, the HOC is embedded in the nomological net in such a way that it allows other latent variables (not part of the HOC) as predecessors to explain some of its variance. The predecessor latent variables could be other exogenous or endogenous variables that are theoretically part of the structural model. The two-stage HCM analysis can then identify significant path relationships that may not otherwise be found.

While both approaches for modeling HCMs are relatively easy to implement, they warrant attention in at least three respects. First, the number of indicators should be similar across the LOCs; otherwise, the relationships between the HOC and LOCs may be biased by the inequality of the number of indicators per LOC (Becker et al., 2012). For example, when an HCM has two LOCs, one with two indicators (LOC_1) and another one with eight indicators (LOC_2), the repeated indicator approach (either in isolation or in the first step of the two-stage HCM analysis) requires all 10 indicators to be assigned to the HOC. A stronger relationship between LOC_2 and the HOC

| Exhibit 8.6 | Two-Stage Approach for HCM Analysis |

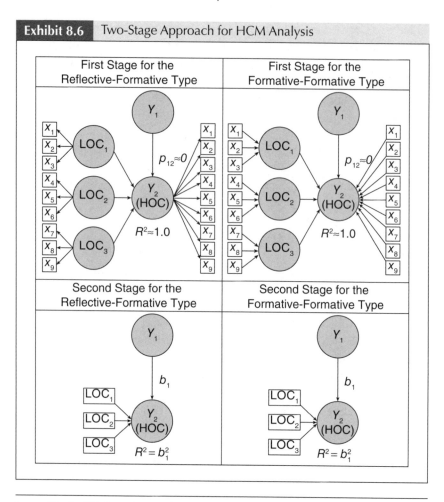

Source: Ringle, CM, Sarstedt, M and Straub, DW (2012) A Critical Look at the Use of PLS-SEM in MIS Quarterly. MIS Quarterly 36: iii–xiv.; permission conveyed through Copyright Clearance Center, Inc.

Note: LOC = lower-order component; HOC = higher-order component; Y_1 = exogenous latent variable in the structural model (its measurement model is not further specified in this illustration); Y_2 = endogenous latent variable in the structural model; p_{12} = standardized path coefficient for the structural model relationship between the latent variables Y_1 and Y_2.

automatically emerges from this kind of setup since they share a large number of indicators in the HCM. Second, not all algorithmic weighting schemes for the inner PLS path model (i.e., centroid, factor, and path; Chapter 3) apply when estimating HCMs in PLS-SEM. While the factor and path weighting schemes provide reasonable outcomes, researchers should not use the centroid weighting scheme (Hair, Sarstedt, Ringle, et al., 2012).

Apart from the above, it is important to establish HCMs on well-established theoretical/conceptual underpinnings before blindly using them in PLS path models—see Kuppelwieser and Sarstedt (2014) for an example of how to evaluate their implementation in a PLS-SEM context. The estimation, evaluation, and interpretation of HCM results require advanced knowledge and broad experience in using PLS-SEM. For instance, the research by Becker et al. (2012) provides some caveats associated with the estimation and interpretation of reflective-formative HCMs. Refer to Ringle et al. (2012) for a review of the HCM use in prior research.

CONFIRMATORY TETRAD ANALYSIS

Measurement model misspecification is a threat to the validity of SEM results (Jarvis et al., 2003). For example, modeling latent variables reflectively when the conceptualization of the measurement model, and thus the item wordings, should be a formative specification can result in biased results. The reason is that formative indicators are not necessarily correlated and are often not highly correlated. In addition, formative indicators produce lower outer loadings when represented in a reflective measurement model. Since indicators with lower outer loadings (<0.40) should always be eliminated from reflectively measured latent constructs (Chapter 4), the incorrect specification of a measurement model as reflective when it should be formative can result in deletion of indicators that should be retained. Any attempt to purify formative indicators based on correlation patterns among the indicators can have adverse consequences for the content validity of the construct. Empirically, the results in the measurement model and structural model can significantly change before and after eliminating indicators. For these reasons, researchers and practitioners must avoid measurement model misspecification to ensure the validity of their results conceptually, theoretically, and empirically.

The primary means to decide whether to specify a measurement model reflectively or formatively is by theoretical reasoning. Guidelines such as those formulated by Jarvis et al. (2003), which we summarize in Chapter 2, prove helpful in this respect. However, research has proposed a PLS-SEM–based statistical test that provides additional empirical substantiation and confirmation of the qualitative choices. More precisely, the **confirmatory tetrad analysis** in PLS-SEM (**CTA-PLS**; Gudergan et al., 2008) facilitates empirical evaluation of cause-effect relationships for latent variables and their specification of indicators in measurement models. When applied, the statistical test offers empirical information that facilitates determining a latent variable's mode of measurement model (i.e., reflective or formative) and provides support for avoiding incorrect measurement model specification.

CTA-PLS builds on the concept of **tetrads** (τ), which describe the relationship between pairs of covariances. To better understand what a tetrad is, consider a reflectively measured latent variable with four indicators. For this construct, we obtain six covariances (σ) between all possible pairs of the four indicators, as shown in Exhibit 8.7.

A tetrad is the difference of the product of one pair of covariances and the product of another pair of covariances. The six covariances of four indicator variables result in six unique pairings that form three tetrads:

$$\tau_{1234} = \sigma_{12} \cdot \sigma_{34} - \sigma_{13} \cdot \sigma_{24},$$

$$\tau_{1342} = \sigma_{13} \cdot \sigma_{42} - \sigma_{14} \cdot \sigma_{32}, \text{ and}$$

$$\tau_{1423} = \sigma_{14} \cdot \sigma_{23} - \sigma_{12} \cdot \sigma_{43}.$$

In reflective measurement models, each tetrad is expected to have a value of zero and, thereby, to vanish. The reason is that, according to the domain sampling model, reflective indicators represent one

Exhibit 8.7	Covariances of Four Indicators in a Reflective Measurement Model			
	x_1	x_2	x_3	x_4
x_1				
x_2	σ_{12}			
x_3	σ_{13}	σ_{23}		
x_4	σ_{14}	σ_{24}	σ_{34}	

specific concept or trait equally well. However, tetrads are seldom exactly zero but instead have a residual value. Therefore, if only one tetrad's residual value is significantly different from zero (i.e., it does not vanish), one can reject the reflective measurement model specification and, instead, assume the alternative formative specification. In other words, the CTA is a statistical test that considers the hypothesis H_0: $\tau = 0$ (i.e., the tetrad equals zero and vanishes) and the alternative hypothesis H_1: $\tau \neq 0$ (i.e., the tetrad does not equal zero). That is, the CTA initially assumes a reflective measurement specification. A nonsignificant test statistic supports H_0 involving consistency of the sample data, with the **vanishing tetrads** implied by a reflective measurement model. In contrast, a significant test statistic that supports H_1 casts doubt on the reflective model specification in favor of the alternative formative specification.

Bollen and Ting (2000) provide several numerical examples to illustrate the usefulness of the CTA in the context of CB-SEM. Although the procedures differ, the systematic application of CTA-PLS for assessing measurement models in PLS-SEM is similar to its CB-SEM counterpart (Bollen & Ting, 2000). CTA-PLS involves five steps.

1. Form and compute all vanishing tetrads for the measurement model of a latent variable.
2. Identify model-implied vanishing tetrads.
3. Eliminate model-implied redundant vanishing tetrads.
4. Perform a statistical significance test for each vanishing tetrad.
5. Evaluate the results for all model-implied nonredundant vanishing tetrads per measurement model.

In Step 1, all vanishing tetrads of the latent variables' measurement models are computed. A key consideration is that the tetrad construction requires at least four indicators per measurement model. Otherwise, the CTA-PLS will not produce results for the construct (Bollen & Ting, 2000, and Gudergan et al., 2008, provide some additional advice on how to deal with situations of fewer than four indicators, i.e., two and three, per measurement model). Step 2 focuses on extracting the model-implied vanishing tetrads. This step is only required when measurement models are assigned additional indicators to meet the minimum number of four indicators per measurement model for running the CTA-PLS. As a consequence, the number of model-implied vanishing tetrads may change for these adjusted measurement models as depicted in detail by Gudergan et al. (2008). In situations where measurement models meet the required number of at least four indicators, nothing changes in this step, and the generated tetrads remain unchanged. The results of Step 1 and Step 2 involve the generation of a large number of model-implied redundant vanishing tetrads. Redundancy exists whenever a selected model-implied vanishing tetrad can be represented by two other model-implied vanishing tetrads. If this happens, the tetrad is redundant and can be excluded from the analysis. Step 3 reduces the complexity of the analysis by using algebraic substitution to exclude all model-implied redundant vanishing tetrads from the analysis (Bollen & Ting, 1993). As a result, Step 3 delivers the **model-implied nonredundant vanishing tetrads.**

While the first three CTA-PLS steps deal with generating and selecting the model-implied nonredundant vanishing tetrads per measurement model, Steps 4 and 5 address their significance testing. In Step 4, the CTA-PLS draws on bootstrapping to test whether the tetrads' residual values differ significantly from zero. Independently analyzing each tetrad to make this decision involves a multiple testing problem. The greater the number of model-implied nonredundant vanishing tetrads in a particular measurement model, the higher the likelihood that a rejection of the null hypothesis (i.e., a tetrad's residual values that significantly differ from zero) will occur just by chance. For this reason, in Step 5 of CTA-PLS, the Bonferroni correction is applied to adjust for the multiple testing problem. This step calculates the Bonferroni-corrected and bias-adjusted confidence intervals of the model-implied nonredundant vanishing tetrads for a prespecified error level. A model-implied nonredundant tetrad is significantly different from zero if its confidence interval does not include the zero. In this case, we cannot reject the null hypothesis and assume a reflective measurement model specification. On the other hand, if only one of the model-implied nonredundant vanishing tetrads of a certain measurement model is significantly different from zero, one should consider a formative measurement model specification. In any case, it is important to note that if the CTA-PLS does not support a reflective measurement model, adjustments in the model must be consistent with theoretical/conceptual considerations and not just the empirical test results.

Exhibit 8.8 shows an example of two reflectively measured latent variables Y_1 and Y_2 with five and four indicators, respectively. The measurement model of Y_1 with five indicators requires analyzing five model-implied nonredundant vanishing tetrads, while the measurement model of Y_2 with four indicators requires considering two model-implied nonredundant vanishing tetrads. Exhibit 8.9 shows the vanishing tetrads and gives an example of their residual values as well as their additional bootstrapping results for 5,000 samples (bootstrap standard error and bootstrap t value for every single tetrad).

The residuals of two tetrads (i.e., τ_{1235}, τ_{1352}) are significantly different from zero. However, these results do not account for the multiple testing problem. For this reason, the last column in Exhibit 8.9 shows the 90% Bonferroni-corrected and bias-adjusted confidence intervals. Based on these results, we find that the residual of two tetrads (τ_{1235} and τ_{1352}) of Y_1 are significantly different from zero. Hence, the CTA-PLS rejects the null hypothesis of a reflective measurement model for Y_1 and provides support for the alternative formative measurement model. This result does not mean that one should mechanically switch to a formative specification. Any change of measurement perspective must be substantiated by theoretical considerations, therefore confirming measurement theory. In contrast to Y_1, all tetrads of Y_2's measurement model are not significantly different from zero, which empirically substantiates the reflective measurement model.

Gudergan et al. (2008) offer a more detailed introduction to CTA-PLS and its application. The CTA-PLS method is implemented in the SmartPLS 3 software, facilitating its straightforward use. Note

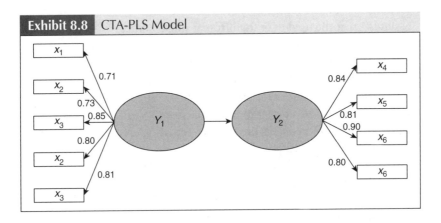

Exhibit 8.8   CTA-PLS Model

Exhibit 8.9	Example CTA-PLS Results				
Y_1	Residual Value	Bootstrap Standard Error	Bootstrap *t* Value	*p* Value	CI
τ_{1234}	0.159	0.139	1.140	0.254	[–0.165, 0.483]
τ_{1243}	0.223	0.145	1.538	0.124	[–0.116, 0.558]
τ_{1235}	0.483	0.142	3.408	0.001	[0.151, 0.811]
τ_{1352}	–0.346	0.121	2.856	0.004	[–0.626, –0.062]
τ_{1345}	–0.089	0.136	0.656	0.512	[–0.404, 0.230]
Y_2					
τ_{1234}	0.194	0.150	1.298	0.194	[–0.099, 0.488]
τ_{1243}	–0.115	0.182	0.632	0.527	[–0.469, 0.245]

that SmartPLS 3 also allows running CTA-PLS on both reflectively and formatively measured latent variables. In both cases, the null hypothesis assumes a reflective measurement model when conducting the statistical test. The CTA-PLS result either approves or disapproves the selected reflective or formative measurement model.

DEALING WITH OBSERVED AND UNOBSERVED HETEROGENEITY

Applications of PLS-SEM usually analyze the full set of data, implicitly assuming that the used data stem from a single homogeneous population. This assumption of relatively homogeneous data characteristics is often unrealistic. Individuals (e.g., in their behavior) or corporations (e.g., in their structure) are different, and pooling data across observations is likely to produce misleading results. Failure to consider such heterogeneity can be a threat to the validity of PLS-SEM results, and it can lead to incorrect conclusions (Becker, Rai, Ringle, et al., 2013; Hair, Sarstedt, Ringle, et al., 2012). For this reason, it is important to identify, assess, and, if present, treat heterogeneity in the data.

Heterogeneity can come in two forms. First, it can be **observed** in that differences between two or more groups of data relate to observable characteristics, such as gender, age, or country of origin.

Researchers can use these observable characteristics to partition the data into separate groups of observations and carry out group-specific PLS-SEM analyses. The path coefficient estimates for the separate group models are almost always numerically different. But are these differences statistically significant? To answer this question, researchers can carry out a multigroup analysis. Second, heterogeneity can be **unobserved** in that it does not depend on an a priori known observable characteristic or combinations of several characteristics. To identify and treat unobserved heterogeneity, research has proposed a multitude of approaches commonly referred to as **latent class techniques.** These techniques have proven very useful to identify unobserved heterogeneity and partition the data into corresponding groups. These groups can then be readily compared for significant differences, using a multigroup analysis. Alternatively, the latent class analysis may ascertain that the results are not influenced by unobserved heterogeneity, providing support for an analysis of a single model based on the aggregate-level data.

Multigroup Analysis

To understand the concept of multigroup analysis, consider the example in Exhibit 8.10. Here, the endogenous latent variable customer satisfaction with a product (Y_3) depends on two dimensions: perceived quality (Y_1) and perceived price (Y_2). Suppose there are two segments of similar sample sizes. Group 1 is quality conscious, whereas Group 2 is price conscious, as indicated by the different segment-specific path coefficients. More precisely, the effect of perceived quality (Y_1) on customer satisfaction (Y_3) is much stronger in Group 1 $(p_{13}^{(1)} = 0.50$; the superscript in parentheses indicates the group) than in Group 2 $(p_{13}^{(2)} = 0.10)$. In contrast, perceived price (Y_2) has a somewhat stronger influence on customer satisfaction (Y_3) in Group 2 $(p_{23}^{(1)} = 0.35)$ than in Group 1 $(p_{23}^{(2)} = 0.25)$. Importantly, when analyzing the data on an aggregate level (i.e., disregarding the grouping of data into quality and price conscious customers), perceived quality and perceived price have the same influence (0.30) on customer satisfaction. As can be seen, disregarding heterogeneous data structures in this example could easily lead to false conclusions in terms of model relationships. More important, when heterogeneity is present, significantly negative and positive group-specific effects can cancel each other out when analyzed on the aggregate data level and suggest the absence of a significant relationship.

Exhibit 8.10 Heterogeneity in PLS Path Models

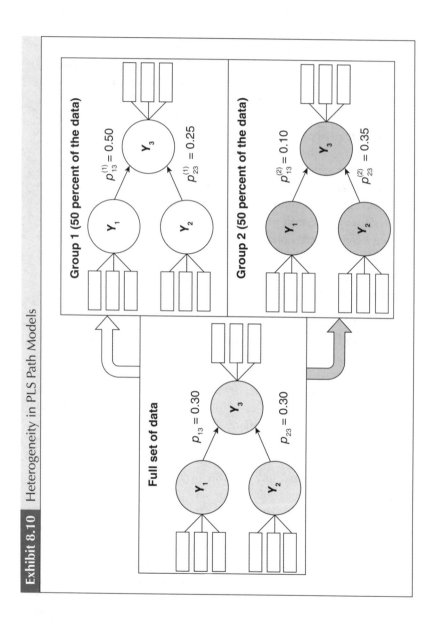

Path coefficients based on different samples are almost always numerically different, but the question is whether the differences are statistically significant. Multigroup analysis helps to answer this question. Technically, a multigroup analysis tests the null hypothesis H_0 that the path coefficients are not significantly different (e.g., $p_{13}^{(1)} = p_{13}^{(2)}$), which amounts to the same as saying that the absolute difference between the path coefficients is zero (i.e., H_0: $\left| p_{13}^{(1)} - p_{13}^{(2)} \right| = 0$). The corresponding alternative hypothesis H_1 is that the path coefficients are different (i.e., H_1: $p_{13}^{(1)} \neq p_{13}^{(2)}$ or, put differently, H_1: $\left| p_{13}^{(1)} - p_{13}^{(2)} \right| > 0$).

Research has proposed several approaches to multigroup analysis that are illustrated in Exhibit 8.11 (Sarstedt, Henseler, & Ringle, 2011). When comparing two groups of data, researchers need to distinguish between the **parametric approach** and several nonparametric approaches. The **parametric approach** (Keil et al., 2000) was the first in the field and has been widely adopted because of its ease of implementation. This approach is a modified version of a standard two independent samples t test, which relies on standard errors derived from bootstrapping. As with the standard t test, the parametric approach has two versions (Sarstedt & Mooi, 2014), depending on whether population variances can be assumed to be equal (homoskedastic) or unequal (heteroskedastic). Prior research suggests that the parametric approach is rather liberal and likely subject to Type I errors (Sarstedt, Henseler, & Ringle, 2011). Furthermore, from a

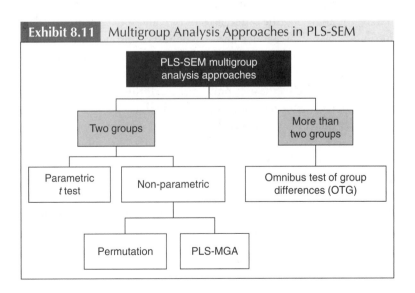

Exhibit 8.11   Multigroup Analysis Approaches in PLS-SEM

conceptual perspective, the parametric approach has limitations since it relies on distributional assumptions, which are inconsistent with PLS-SEM's nonparametric nature.

Against this background, researchers have proposed several nonparametric alternatives to multigroup analysis; see Sarstedt, Henseler, and Ringle (2011) for a review. For example, the **permutation test** randomly exchanges (i.e., permutes) observations between the groups and reestimates the model for each permutation (Chin & Dibbern, 2010; Dibbern & Chin, 2005). Computing the differences between the group-specific path coefficients per permutation enables testing whether these also differ in the population. Prior research indicates that the test performs similarly to the parametric approach but is less liberal in terms of rendering differences significant. Furthermore, its application requires the groups to be of similar size. Henseler et al. (2009) proposed another nonparametric multigroup analysis approach that builds on bootstrapping results. Their **PLS-MGA** approach compares each bootstrap estimate of one group with all other bootstrap estimates of the same parameter in the other group. By counting the number of occurrences where the bootstrap estimate of the first group is larger than those of the second group, the approach derives a probability value for a one-tailed test. PLS-MGA involves a great number of comparisons of bootstrap estimates (e.g., in a case of 5,000 bootstrap samples, there are 25,000,000 comparisons for each parameter) and reliably tests for group differences. At the same time, the test is geared toward one-sided hypothesis testing. Finally, for analyzing the differences of two and more groups of relationships, Sarstedt, Henseler, and Ringle (2011) proposed the **omnibus test of group differences (OTG)**. The OTG uses a combination of bootstrapping and permutation to derive a probability value of the variance explained by the grouping variable. If this variance is significantly different from zero, we can conclude that at least one group-specific coefficient significantly differs from the others.

Research has not yet compared the different approaches to multigroup analysis in terms of their statistical power or Type I error rates using simulated data. However, the permutation test has particularly advantageous statistical properties, and has been implemented in SmartPLS 3. We therefore recommend that researchers use it when testing the difference of parameters across two groups. In the case of more than two groups, the use of OTG is appropriate. This method has not yet been implemented in commonly used software applications for PLS-SEM, but we expect that upcoming releases of SmartPLS will include it.

Uncovering Unobserved Heterogeneity

Researchers routinely use observable characteristics to partition data into groups and estimate separate models, thereby accounting for **observed heterogeneity**. However, the sources of heterogeneity in the data can hardly be fully known a priori. Consequently, situations arise in which differences related to unobserved heterogeneity prevent the derivation of accurate results as the analysis on the aggregate data level masks group-specific effects. Failure to consider heterogeneity can be a severe threat to the validity of PLS-SEM results (Becker, Rai, Ringle, et al., 2013). If unobserved heterogeneity does not affect the results, researchers can analyze the data on the aggregate level and generalize the PLS-SEM results across groups. Hence, identifying and—if necessary—treating unobserved heterogeneity is of crucial importance when using PLS-SEM. As a result, researchers have called for the routine application of techniques that facilitate such analyses (Hair, Ringle, & Sarstedt, 2011; Hair, Sarstedt, Ringle, et al., 2012; Hair, Ringle, & Sarstedt, 2013).

Standard **cluster analysis** methods such as k-means **clustering** (Sarstedt & Mooi, 2014) only focus on the indicator data when forming groups of data. They cannot, however, account for the latent variables and their structural model relationships. Moreover, identifying different groups of data for the indicators or latent variable scores does not necessarily entail uncovering significantly different path model relationships. Hence well-known clustering methods that only focus on the indicators and latent variable scores usually fail in PLS-SEM (Sarstedt & Ringle, 2010). For this reason, research has proposed a wide array of latent class techniques (frequently referred to as **response-based segmentation techniques**), which generalize, for example, finite mixture, genetic algorithm, or hill-climbing approaches to PLS-SEM (see Sarstedt, 2008, for an early overview). Exhibit 8.12 shows the most important segment detection approaches in PLS-SEM.

The first and most prominent latent class approach is **finite mixture PLS** (**FIMIX-PLS**; Hahn, Johnson, Herrmann, & Huber, 2002; Sarstedt, Becker, Ringle, & Schwaiger, 2011). Drawing on the mixture regression concept, FIMIX-PLS simultaneously estimates the path coefficients of each observation's group membership for a predefined

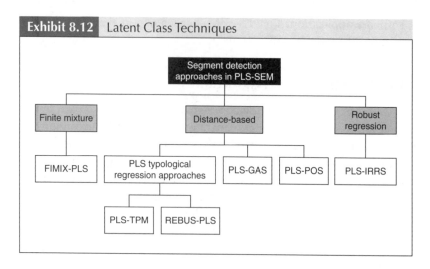

| Exhibit 8.12 | Latent Class Techniques |

number of groups. In light of the approach's performance in prior studies (e.g., Ringle, Wende, & Will, 2010; Sarstedt & Ringle, 2010) and its availability through the software SmartPLS 3, Hair, Ringle, and Sarstedt (2011) have suggested that researchers should routinely use the technique to evaluate whether PLS-SEM results are distorted by unobserved heterogeneity. However, it is important to acknowledge that FIMIX-PLS is restricted to capturing heterogeneity in the structural model. For a more detailed discussion and step-by-step illustration of the approach on empirical data, see Ringle, Sarstedt, and Mooi (2010) and Rigdon et al. (2010). Likewise, Sarstedt, Ringle, and Gudergan (in press) discuss aspects relevant to the use of FIMIX-PLS. For applications of FIMIX-PLS, see, for example, Sarstedt, Schwaiger, and Ringle (2009), Money, Hillenbrand, Henseler, and Da Camara (2012), Navarro, Acedo, Losada, and Ruzo (2011), Rigdon et al. (2011), and Wilden and Gudergan (2015).

Since the introduction of the FIMIX-PLS approach, research has proposed a range of other alternatives that assign observations to groups based on some distance criterion. Squillacciotti (2005, 2010) introduced the **PLS typological path modeling (PLS-TPM)** procedure, which Esposito Vinzi, Trinchera, Squillacciotti, and Tenenhaus (2008) advanced by presenting the **response-based procedure for detecting unit segments in PLS path modeling (REBUS-PLS)**. REBUS-PLS gradually reallocates observations from one segment to the other with the goal of minimizing the residuals. In doing so, REBUS-PLS also takes the measurement models into account but is restricted to reflectively measured constructs. Furthermore, PLS-TPM and REBUS-PLS reassign many observations per iteration and conduct a random walk without systematically advancing toward the goal criterion (Ringle, Sarstedt, Schlittgen, & Taylor, 2013; Ringle, Sarstedt, & Schlittgen, 2014). Becker, Rai, Ringle, et al. (2013) recognized these issues and presented the **prediction-oriented segmentation in PLS-SEM (PLS-POS)** approach, which is applicable to all kinds of PLS path models regardless of whether the latent variables are based on reflective or formative measurement models. Their simulation study shows that PLS-POS performs well for segmentation purposes and provides favorable outcomes compared with alternative segmentation techniques. Researchers can apply PLS-POS by using this method's implementation in SmartPLS 3. **Genetic algorithm segmentation in PLS-SEM (PLS-GAS;** Ringle et al., 2013; Ringle, Sarstedt, & Schlittgen, 2014) is another versatile approach to uncover and treat heterogeneity in measurement and structural models. This approach consists of two stages. The first stage uses a genetic algorithm with the aim of finding the partition, which minimizes the endogenous latent variables' unexplained variance. The advantage of implementing a genetic algorithm is that it has the capability to escape local optimum solutions and thereby covers a wide area of the potential search space before delivering a final best solution. In the second stage, a deterministic hill-climbing approach aims at delivering an even better solution. PLS-GAS returns excellent results that usually outperform the outcomes of alternative segmentation methods, but it has the downside that it is computationally demanding.

For the latter reason, one of the latest advances to PLS-SEM segmentation introduces the **iterative reweighted regressions segmentation method (PLS-IRRS;** Schlittgen, Ringle, Sarstedt, & Becker, 2015). PLS-IRRS builds on Schlittgen's (2011) clusterwise robust regression, which determines weights to downweight observations with extreme values and mitigates the influence of outliers in the data set. In the adaptation of this concept for PLS-SEM–based segmentation, outliers are not treated as such but as their own segment. When robust regression identifies a group of similar outliers, they may therefore become a data group of their own and represent a segment-specific PLS-SEM solution. At the same time, PLS-IRRS accentuates the impact of inhomogeneous observations in the computation of segment-specific PLS-SEM solutions. Like PLS-POS and PLS-GAS, PLS-IRRS is generally applicable to all kinds of PLS path models. Moreover, it returns excellent results in terms of parameter recovery and predictive power, which fully match those of PLS-GAS (Schlittgen et al., 2015). The key advantage of PLS-IRRS is its speed. In comparison with PLS-GAS, PLS-IRRS is more than 5,000 times faster while providing highly similar results.

Because of their existing implementation in SmartPLS 3, we suggest using a combination of FIMIX-PLS and PLS-POS. To start with, one should apply FIMIX-PLS, which provides segment retention criteria to determine the number of segments. Sarstedt, Becker, Ringle, and Schwaiger (2011) researched the performance of these segment retention criteria in depth, providing recommendations regarding their use. The FIMIX-PLS solution (i.e., the group assignment based on the probabilities of membership) then serves as a starting solution for running PLS-POS thereafter. PLS-POS improves the FIMIX-PLS solution and allows considering heterogeneity in the formative measurement models of latent variables. In addition to these explications, Becker, Rai, Ringle, et al. (2013) provide an overview and process of how to systematically uncover and explain unobserved heterogeneity.

MEASUREMENT MODEL INVARIANCE

A primary concern in multigroup analyses is ensuring **measurement invariance,** also referred to as **measurement equivalence.** By establishing measurement invariance, researchers can be confident that group differences in model estimates do not result from the distinctive content and/or meanings of the latent variables across groups. For example, variations in the structural relationships between latent variables could stem from different meanings the groups' respondents attribute to the phenomena being measured, rather than the true differences in the structural relationships. Hult et al. (2008, p. 1028) describe these concerns and conclude that "failure to establish data equivalence is a potential source of measurement error" (i.e., discrepancies between what is intended to be measured and what is actually measured). When measurement invariance is not present, it can reduce the power of statistical tests, influence the precision of estimators, and provide misleading results. In short, when measurement invariance is not demonstrated, any conclusions about model relationships are questionable. Hence, multigroup comparisons require establishing measurement invariance to ensure the validity of outcomes and conclusions.

Researchers have suggested a variety of methods to assess measurement invariance for covariance-based SEM. Multigroup confirmatory factor analysis based on the guidelines of Steenkamp and Baumgartner (1998) and Vandenberg and Lance (2000) is by far the most common approach to invariance assessment. However, the well-established measurement invariance techniques used to assess CB-SEM's **common factor models** cannot be readily transferred to PLS-SEM's composite models. For this reason, Henseler, Ringle, and Sarstedt (in press) developed the **measurement invariance of composite models (MICOM) procedure,** which involves three steps: (1) **configural invariance** (i.e., equal parameterization and way of estimation), (2) **compositional invariance** (i.e., equal indicator weights), and (3) **equality of composite mean values and variances.** The three steps are hierarchically interrelated, as displayed in Exhibit 8.13.

Step 1 addresses the establishment of configural invariance to ensure that a composite has been specified equally for all the groups and emerges as a unidimensional entity in the same nomological net across all the groups. An initial qualitative assessment of the composites' specification across all the groups must ensure the use of (1) identical

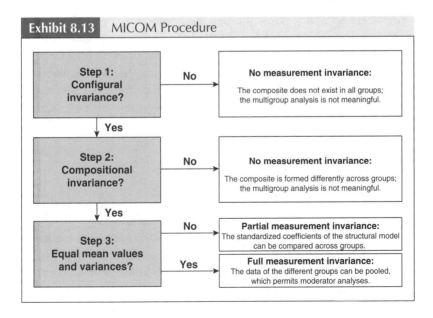

Exhibit 8.13   MICOM Procedure

indicators per measurement model, (2) identical data treatment, and (3) identical algorithm settings. Configural invariance is a precondition for compositional invariance (Step 2), which focuses on analyzing whether a composite is formed equally across the groups. When the indicator weights are estimated for each group, it is essential to ensure that—despite possible differences in the weights—the scores of a composite are the same. The MICOM procedure applies a statistical test to ensure that the composite scores do not significantly differ across groups. The measurement invariance assessment should only continue with Step 3, the equality assessment of the composites' mean values and variances, if the previous step's results support measurement invariance. In the case of equal composite mean values and variances, one can run the analyses on the pooled data level. Even though pooling the data is advantageous from a statistical power perspective, researchers must account for potential structural heterogeneity by including interaction effects that serve as moderators (Chapter 7).

In summary, running a multigroup analysis requires establishing configural (Step 1) and compositional (Step 2) invariance. If these two steps do not support measurement invariance, the results and differences of the multigroup analysis are invalid. However, if configural and compositional invariance are established, **partial measurement invariance** is confirmed, which permits comparing the path coefficient estimates across the groups. In addition, if partial measurement invariance is confirmed and the composites have equal mean values and variances across the groups, **full measurement invariance** is confirmed, which supports the pooled data analysis. Henseler, Ringle, and Sarstedt (2015) provide full details on the MICOM procedure, including simulation study results and an empirical application.

CONSISTENT PARTIAL LEAST SQUARES

In Chapter 1, we compared CB-SEM and PLS-SEM and noted that structural model relationships in PLS-SEM are generally slightly lower, and measurement model relationships are somewhat higher, compared with CB-SEM. Researchers will never obtain exactly the same results when using PLS-SEM as with CB-SEM and should not expect to. The statistical objective and the measurement philosophy of the two SEM methods are different, and thus the results will always differ. Recent research has tried to merge these two SEM techniques to maintain PLS-SEM's flexibility in terms of distributional assumptions and handling complex models, while obtaining results that are similar to those of CB-SEM. Two approaches have been proposed in recent research: the consistent and efficient **PLSe2** method (Bentler & Huang, 2014) and **consistent PLS** (**PLSc**; Dijkstra, 2014; Dijkstra & Henseler, 2015a). We discuss the latter approach, as it has been analyzed in simulation studies (e.g., Dijkstra & Henseler, 2015b) and readily implemented in SmartPLS 3. Note that we are not implying that these approaches are better than the regular PLS-SEM. Rather, they are designed specifically for situations where the research objective is to mimic CB-SEM results, which usually is not the objective when applying PLS-SEM.

PLSc's objective is to correct the correlation r_{Y_1,Y_2} between two latent variables Y_1 and Y_2 for measurement error. More precisely, PLSc corrects the original estimate to obtain the disattenuated (i.e., consistent) correlation $r^c_{Y_1,Y_2}$ by dividing the latent variable correlation r_{Y_1,Y_2} by the geometric mean of the latent variables' reliabilities. Regarding the latter, researchers can refer to Cronbach's alpha or composite reliability (see Chapter 4). Cronbach's alpha is a conservative reliability measure, since it most likely underestimates the true reliability of construct measures. On the contrary, composite reliability is generally a liberal estimate because it draws on the outer loadings, which are typically somewhat inflated. The true reliability of latent variables usually lies between Cronbach's alpha and composite reliability. As a solution to this problem and building on Dijkstra (2010), subsequent research has proposed the exact (or consistent) **reliability** ρ_A (Dijkstra, 2014; Dijkstra & Henseler, 2015b), which is defined as

$$\rho_A := (\hat{w}'\hat{w})^2 \cdot \frac{\hat{w}'(S - \mathrm{diag}(S))\hat{w}}{\hat{w}'(\hat{w}\hat{w}' - \mathrm{diag}(\hat{w}\hat{w}'))\hat{w}},$$

where $\hat{w}$ represents the outer weights estimates and S the sample covariance matrix.

PLSc follows a four-step approach (Exhibit 8.14). In Step 1, the basic PLS-SEM algorithm is run. These results are then used in Step 2 to calculate the reliability ρ_A of all reflectively measured latent variables in the PLS path model (Dijkstra, 2014; Dijkstra & Henseler, 2015b). For formatively measured constructs and single-item constructs, ρ_A is set to 1. In Step 3, the consistent reliabilities of all latent variables from Step 2 are used to correct the inconsistent correlation matrix of the latent variables obtained in Step 1. More precisely, one obtains the consistent correlation between two constructs by dividing their correlation from Step 1 by the geometric mean (i.e., the square root of the product) of their reliabilities ρ_A. This correction applies to all correlations of reflectively measured constructs. The correlation of two formative and/or single-item constructs remains unchanged. The correction for attenuation only applies when at least one reflectively measured latent variable with a consistent reliability ρ_A smaller than 1 is involved in the correlation between two constructs in the PLS path model. In Step 4, the consistent correlation matrix of the latent variables allows reestimating all model relationships yielding consistent path coefficients, corresponding R^2 values, and outer loadings. Note that significance testing in PLSc requires running an adjusted bootstrapping routine, which has also been implemented in SmartPLS 3.

To illustrate how PLSc works, consider the simple PLS path model shown in Exhibit 8.15. In the following, we will estimate this model using artificially generated data with a prespecified path coefficient of 0.30 for the structural model relationship p_{12}. Using artificially generated data has the advantage that we know the true values of the relationship in the PLS path model (i.e., 0.30) and the resulting reliabilities of the constructs. In contrast, when using empirical data, one never knows the true values of the model.

Exhibit 8.16 shows the PLS-SEM and PLSc results for 10 situations. All situations use a prespecified coefficient of 0.300 for the relationship p_{12} between the latent variables Y_1 and Y_2. The situations differ with regard to the prespecified correlation construct reliabilities ρ_A, which range between 0.950 and 0.700. The first situation starts with relatively high reliabilities ρ_A of 0.950 for both constructs. The

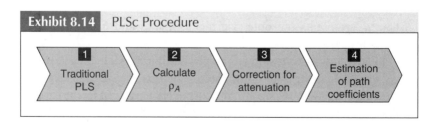

Exhibit 8.14 PLSc Procedure

1. Traditional PLS
2. Calculate ρ_A
3. Correction for attenuation
4. Estimation of path coefficients

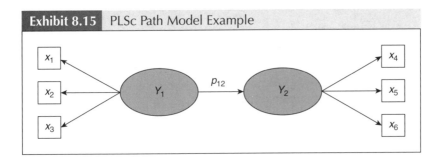

Exhibit 8.15 PLSc Path Model Example

PLS-SEM method provides an estimated p_{12} path coefficient of 0.285. This result is slightly lower than the value of 0.300 that we expected to obtain from the artificially generated set of data.

To obtain the PLSc path coefficient, one needs to divide the PLS-SEM result of p_{12} by the geometric mean of the two constructs' reliabilities ρ_A. In Situation 1, the PLS-SEM result (0.285) divided by the geometric mean of the two reliabilities (0.950) results in a consistent coefficient p_{12} of 0.300. This result matches the expected value of the artificial data generation. In the subsequent situations (2 to 10), the geometric mean of reliabilities systematically declines. In Situation 10, both reliabilities have a value of 0.700. The lower reliability levels of the constructs result in an estimated PLS-SEM coefficient of 0.210, which is clearly below the expected value of 0.300. Again, the use of the geometric mean of the reliabilities allows obtaining a consistent path coefficient of 0.300 that matches the expected value.

This illustration shows how PLSc works. In practical applications, PLSc results can be substantially influenced by low reliability levels of the constructs. As a result, the standardized PLSc path coefficients can become very high (in some situations considerably larger than 1). Moreover, in more complex PLS path models, collinearity among the latent variables has a strong negative impact on the PLSc results. In some instances, the structural model relationships become very small. Moreover, bootstrapping can produce extreme outcomes, which result in high standard errors in certain relationships, increasing the Type II error rate.

In light of these limitations, the question arises as to when researchers should use PLSc. The PLSc approach is appropriate if researchers assume **common factor models** as in confirmatory SEM analyses (Bollen, 2011; Bollen & Bauldry, 2011). In that case, they

Exhibit 8.16 Data and Results

Situation	True Value of p_{12}	PLS-SEM Result of p_{12}	Reliability ρ_A of Y_1	Reliability ρ_A of Y_2	Geometric Mean of ρ_A Reliabilities	PLSc Result of p_{12}
1	0.300	0.285	0.950	0.950	0.950	0.300
2	0.300	0.277	0.900	0.950	0.925	0.299
3	0.300	0.270	0.850	0.950	0.899	0.300
4	0.300	0.262	0.800	0.950	0.872	0.300
5	0.300	0.253	0.750	0.950	0.844	0.300
6	0.300	0.238	0.700	0.900	0.794	0.300
7	0.300	0.231	0.700	0.850	0.771	0.300
8	0.300	0.224	0.700	0.800	0.748	0.299
9	0.300	0.217	0.700	0.750	0.725	0.299
10	0.300	0.210	0.700	0.700	0.700	0.300

intend to mimic CB-SEM results by assuming that the construct represents the covariance of the underlying indicators. Simulation studies for such models reveal that CB-SEM and PLSc return almost identical results of the estimated coefficients (Dijkstra & Henseler, 2015b). While CB-SEM and PLSc have approximately the same accuracy of estimated parameters and statistical power, PLSc retains most of PLS-SEM's advantageous features (Chapter 2). Among others, PLSc does not have distributional assumptions, can handle complex models, is less affected by incorrect specifications in (subparts of) the model, and will not encounter convergence problems. PLSc and the PLSe2 algorithm by Bentler and Huang (2014), which is another approach to obtain consistent PLS results, may therefore obtain an important role in extending the capabilities offered by CB-SEM for confirmatory SEM. However, to date, the conceptual underpinnings of PLSc's approach to measurement have not been fully established, and we believe that research needs to clarify the use of composite versus common factor models before routinely applying PLSc.

Compared with PLSc, the standard PLS-SEM method assumes a different and likely more realistic view regarding measurement in that it assumes a composite model and does not require a normal distribution. Following this measurement philosophy, the latent variable (more precisely the composite) is considered a proxy for a latent concept (Rigdon, 2012). Different from factor-based models, the corresponding indicators do not need to be conceptually united and necessarily correspond to a predefined theoretical concept. Therefore, researchers have to keep in mind that, when using PLSc, they follow a fundamentally different measurement logic. Furthermore, and different from PLSc, the goal of standard PLS-SEM modeling is primarily to explain the variance of the target constructs and the outcomes of single observations, while also providing estimates of structural model relationships and measurement model parameters. In these situations, consistent and determinant latent variable scores are needed, and researchers should use the basic PLS-SEM results. In practical applications, researchers often have both goals in mind. Hence, future advances in SEM pave the way toward a combined use of PLS and PLSc in studies where both goals are emphasized.

SUMMARY

• **Comprehend the usefulness of a PLS-SEM importance-performance map analysis (IPMA).** The IPMA extends the standard PLS-SEM results reporting of path coefficient estimates by adding a dimension to the analysis that considers the average values of the latent variable scores. The analysis contrasts the total effects of latent variables on a certain target variable (impact) with their rescaled average latent variable scores (performance). The graphical representation of the outcomes enables researchers to easily identify critical areas of (managerial) attention and action (i.e., constructs with high importance but low performance). The IPMA can also be applied on an indicator data level.

• **Understand hierarchical component models (HCMs) and how to apply this concept in PLS-SEM.** HCMs are used to establish a more general HOC that represents or summarizes the information of several LOCs. Four major types of HCM represent different relationships between the HOC and the LOCs as well as the measurement models used to operationalize the constructs: reflective-reflective, reflective-formative, formative-reflective, and formative-formative. Generally, the HOC of reflective-reflective and reflective-formative HCMs represents a more general construct that simultaneously explains all the underlying LOCs (i.e., similar to reflective measurement models; Chapters 2 and 4). Conversely, in formative-reflective and formative-formative HCMs (i.e., similar to formative measurement models; Chapters 2 and 5), the HOC is formed by the LOCs. Besides this issue, each of the four HCM types must be assessed carefully. We usually expect to have the same (or comparable) number of indicators per LOC, while the relationship between reflective-formative or formative-formative HOCs and other constructs in the PLS path model that explain it requires a two-stage HCM analysis. HCMs are becoming increasingly popular in research since they offer a means of establishing more parsimonious path models.

• **Get to know how to assess the mode of measurement model with the confirmatory tetrad analysis in PLS-SEM (CTA-PLS).** CTA-PLS is a useful tool to empirically evaluate a latent variable's mode of measurement model (i.e., formative or reflective). The test requires at least four indicators per measurement model. In the case of reflective measurement, all model-implied nonredundant vanishing tetrads have a residual value that is not significantly different from zero. However, if at least one of the model-implied nonredundant vanishing tetrads is significantly different from zero, one should consider rejecting the reflective measurement model and, instead, assume a formative specification. The CTA-PLS test enables researchers to empirically evaluate measurement models, thus providing guidance that may enable researchers to avoid measurement model misspecification. When evaluating the mode of a measurement model, you must always include theoretical, conceptual, and practical considerations along with the empirical evidence provided by CTA-PLS.

- **Understand multigroup analysis in PLS-SEM.** Multigroup analysis allows testing whether differences between group-specific path coefficients are statistically significant. Researchers have proposed different approaches to multigroup analysis with the *t* test–based parametric approach being most frequently applied. Alternatives such as the permutation test and the PLS-MGA do not rely on distributional assumptions. In comparison, the permutation test has particularly advantageous statistical properties and we recommend this method when analyzing the difference of parameters across two groups. In the case of more than two groups, the use of OTG is appropriate.

- **Learn about techniques to identify and treat unobserved heterogeneity.** Unobserved heterogeneity represents a serious threat to the validity of PLS-SEM results. Research has proposed various approaches to identify and treat heterogeneity that generalize, for example, mixture regression, genetic algorithm, or hill-climbing approaches to PLS-SEM. While FIMIX-PLS constitutes the most widely used approach in the field, more recently proposed methods such as PLS-POS and PLS-GAS are more versatile and have shown superior performance. In light of the current state of implementation, researchers should use FIMIX-PLS to identify the number of segments to retain from the data and to obtain a starting partition for a subsequent PLS-POS analysis. Both methods have been implemented in SmartPLS 3.

- **Understand measurement model invariance and its assessment in PLS-SEM.** Group comparisons are valid if measurement invariance has been established. Thereby, researchers ensure that group differences in model estimates do not result from the distinctive content and/or meanings of the latent variables across groups. When measurement invariance is not demonstrated, any conclusions about model relationships are questionable. The measurement invariances of composites (MICOM) procedure represents a useful tool in PLS-SEM. The procedure comprises three steps that test different aspects of measurement invariance: (1) configural invariance (i.e., equal parameterization and way of estimation), (2) compositional invariance (i.e., equal indicator weights), and (3) equality of composite mean values and variances.

- **Become familiar with consistent partial least squares (PLSc).** PLS-SEM results generally provide somewhat higher measurement model estimates and lower structural model estimates compared with CB-SEM. When the goal of the analysis is not to maximize the endogenous latent variables' amount of explained variance but to mimic CB-SEM results in terms of parameter accuracy, PLSc permits correcting PLS path coefficients for attenuation. The PLSc results are very similar to those obtained by CB-SEM, while retaining the well-known advantages of PLS-SEM. Hence, besides using PLS-SEM for predictive modeling, researchers can use PLSc for confirmatory SEM studies that are designed to mimic the common factor model of CB-SEM. The standard PLS-SEM method assumes a different and likely more realistic view regarding measurement in that it assumes a composite model and does not require a normal distribution. When the goal of PLS-SEM modeling is primarily to explain the variance of the target constructs and the outcomes of single observations, while also providing estimates of structural model relationships and measurement model parameters, standard PLS-SEM should be used.

REVIEW QUESTIONS

1. What is the purpose of the IPMA?

2. What is an HCM? Visualize each of the four types of HCMs introduced in this chapter.

3. What is the difference between observed and unobserved heterogeneity? Why is the consideration of heterogeneity so important when analyzing PLS path models?

4. What is FIMIX-PLS?

5. Why would you run a multigroup analysis in PLS-SEM?

CRITICAL THINKING QUESTIONS

1. What kind of practical implications can you draw from IPMA results? Name an additional (third) interesting dimension of an IPMA that you would consider.

2. Why is a two-stage approach in a reflective-formative or formative-formative HCM needed if the HOC has an additional antecedent construct (other than the LOCs) in the structural model that predicts it?

3. Provide practical examples of the four major types of HCMs.

4. Critically comment on the following statement: "Measurement invariance is not an issue in PLS-SEM because of the method's focus on prediction and exploration."

5. Explain how PLSc complements and extends PLS-SEM.

KEY TERMS

Cluster analysis

Clustering

Common factor model

Compositional invariance

Configural invariance

Confirmatory tetrad analysis

Consistent PLS (PLSc)

CTA-PLS

Equality of composite mean values and variances

FIMIX-PLS

Finite mixture partial least squares (FIMIX-PLS)

Formative-formative HCM

Formative-reflective HCM

Full measurement invariance

Genetic algorithm segmentation in PLS-SEM (PLS-GAS)

HCM

Hierachical component models (HCM)

Higher-order component (HOC)

HOC

Importance

Importance-performance map

Importance-performance map analysis (IPMA)

IPMA

Iterative reweighted regressions segmentation method (PLS-IRRS)

Latent class techniques

LOC

Lower-order component (LOC)

Measurement equivalence

Measurement invariance

Measurement invariance
of composite models
(MICOM) procedure

Measurement model
misspecification

MICOM

Model-implied nonredundant
vanishing tetrads

Observed heterogeneity

Omnibus test of group
differences (OTG)

OTG

Parametric approach

Partial measurement invariance

Performance

Permutation test

PLS typological path modeling
(PLS-TPM)

PLSc

PLSe2

PLS-GAS

PLS-IRRS

PLS-MGA

PLS-POS

PLS-TPM

Prediction-oriented segmentation
in PLS-SEM (PLS-POS)

REBUS-PLS

Reflective-formative HCM

Reflective-reflective HCM

Reliability ρ_A

Repeated indicators approach
for HCM

Rescaling

Response-based procedure
for detecting unit segments
in PLS path modeling
(REBUS-PLS)

Response-based segmentation
techniques

Tetrad (τ)

Two-stage HCM analysis

Unobserved heterogeneity

Vanishing tetrad

SUGGESTED READINGS

Becker, J.-M., Klein, K., & Wetzels, M. (2012). Formative hierarchical latent variable models in PLS-SEM: Recommendations and guidelines. *Long Range Planning, 45,* 359–394.

Becker, J.-M., Rai, A., Ringle, C. M., & Völckner, F. (2013). Discovering unobserved heterogeneity in structural equation models to avert validity threats. *MIS Quarterly, 37,* 665–694.

Bollen, K. A., & Ting, K.-F. (2000). A tetrad test for causal indicators. *Psychological Methods, 5,* 3–22.

Dijkstra, T. K. (2014). PLS' Janus face—response to Professor Rigdon's "Rethinking partial least squares modeling: In praise of simple methods." *Long Range Planning, 47,* 146–153.

Dijkstra, T. K., & Henseler, J. (2015). Consistent partial least squares path modeling. *MIS Quarterly, 39,* 297–316.

Gudergan, S. P., Ringle, C. M., Wende, S., & Will, A. (2008). Confirmatory tetrad analysis in PLS path modeling. *Journal of Business Research, 61,* 1238–1249.

Hahn, C., Johnson, M. D., Herrmann, A., & Huber, F. (2002). Capturing customer heterogeneity using a finite mixture PLS approach. *Schmalenbach Business Review, 54,* 243–269.

Henseler, J., Ringle, C. M., & Sarstedt, M. (in press). Testing measurement invariance of composites using partial least squares. *International Marketing Review.*

Höck, C., Ringle, C. M., & Sarstedt, M. (2010). Management of multipurpose stadiums: Importance and performance measurement of service interfaces. *International Journal of Services Technology and Management, 14,* 188–207.

Lohmöller, J.-B. (1989). *Latent variable path modeling with partial least squares.* Heidelberg, Germany: Physica.

Ringle, C. M., Sarstedt, M., & Straub, D. W. (2012). A critical look at the use of PLS-SEM in *MIS Quarterly. MIS Quarterly, 36,* iii–xiv.

Sarstedt, M., Becker, J.-M., Ringle, C. M., & Schwaiger, M. (2011). Uncovering and treating unobserved heterogeneity with FIMIX-PLS: Which model selection criterion provides an appropriate number of segments? *Schmalenbach Business Review, 63,* 34–62.

Sarstedt, M., Henseler, J., & Ringle, C. M. (2011). Multi-group analysis in partial least squares (PLS) path modeling: Alternative methods and empirical results. *Advances in International Marketing, 22,* 195–218.

Schloderer, M. P., Sarstedt, M., & Ringle, C. M. (2014). The relevance of reputation in the nonprofit sector: The moderating effect of sociodemographic characteristics. *International Journal of Nonprofit & Voluntary Sector Marketing, 19,* 110–126.

Glossary

10 times rule: one way to determine the minimum sample size specific to the PLS path model that one needs for model estimation (i.e., 10 times the number of independent variables of the most complex OLS regression in the structural or formative measurement model). The 10 times rule should be seen only as a rough estimate of the minimum sample size. Rather, researchers should revert to recommendations such as those presented by Cohen (1992) in his "Power Primer" article or run a power analysis specific to the model at hand.

Absolute contribution: is the information an indicator variable provides about the formatively measured item, ignoring all other indicators. The absolute contribution is provided by the loading of the indicator (i.e., its bivariate correlation with the formatively measured construct).

Absolute importance: see *Absolute contribution*.

Adjusted coefficient of determination (R^2_{adj}): is a modified measure of the *coefficient of determination* that takes into account the number of predictor constructs. The statistic is useful for comparing models with different numbers of predictor constructs, different sample sizes, or both.

Algorithmic options: offer different ways to run the PLS-SEM algorithm by, for example, selecting between alternative starting values, stop values, weighting schemes, and maximum number of iterations.

Alternating extreme pole responses: is a suspicious survey response pattern where a respondent uses only the extreme poles of the scale (e.g., a 7-point scale) in an alternating order to answer the questions.

AVE: see *Average variance extracted*.

Average variance extracted: a measure of convergent validity. It is the degree to which a latent construct explains the variance of its indicators; see *Communality (construct)*.

Bias-corrected and accelerated (BCa) bootstrap confidence intervals: constitute an improvement of the *percentile method* by adjusting for biases and skewness in the bootstrap distribution. The method yields very low Type I errors but is limited in terms of statistical power.

Blindfolding: is a sample reuse technique that omits part of the data matrix and uses the model estimates to predict the omitted part. It indicates a model's out-of-sample predictive power.

Bootstrap cases: make up the number of observations drawn in every bootstrap run. The number is set equal to the number of valid observations in the original data set.

Bootstrap confidence interval: provides an estimated range of values that is likely to include an unknown population parameter. It is determined by its lower and upper bounds, which depend on a predefined probability of error and the standard error of the estimation for a given set of sample data. When zero does not fall into the confidence interval, an estimated parameter can be assumed to be significantly different from zero for the prespecified probability of error (e.g., 5%).

Bootstrap samples: are the number of samples drawn in the bootstrapping procedure. Generally, 5,000 or more samples are recommended.

Bootstrapping: is a resampling technique that draws a large number of subsamples from the original data (with replacement) and estimates models for each subsample. It is used to determine standard errors of coefficients to assess their statistical significance without relying on distributional assumptions.

Cascaded moderator analysis: is a type of moderator analysis in which the strength of a moderating effect is influenced by another variable (i.e., the moderating effect is again moderated).

Casewise deletion: an entire observation (i.e., a case or respondent) is removed from the data set because of missing data. It should be used when indicators have more than 5% missing values.

Categorical moderator variable: see *Multigroup analysis.*

Causal indicators: a type of indicator used in formative measurement models. Causal indicators do not fully form the latent variable but "cause" it. Therefore, causal indicators must correspond to a theoretical definition of the concept under investigation.

Causal links: are predictive relationships in which the constructs on the left predict the constructs to the right.

CB-SEM: see *Covariance-based structural equation modeling.*

Cluster analysis: see *Clustering.*

Clustering: is a class of methods that partition a set of objects with the goal of obtaining high similarity within the formed groups and high dissimilarity across groups.

Coding: is the assignment of numbers to scales in a manner that facilitates measurement.

Coefficient of determination (R^2): a measure of the proportion of an endogenous construct's variance that is explained by its predictor constructs.

Collinearity: arises when two variables are highly correlated.

Common factor model: assumes that each indicator in a set of observed measures is a linear function of one or more common factors. Exploratory factor analysis (EFA), confirmatory factor analysis (CFA), and CB-SEM are the three main types of analyses based on common factor models.

Communality (construct): see *Average variance extracted.*

Communality (item): see *Indicator reliability.*

Competitive mediation: a situation in mediation analysis that occurs when the indirect effect and the direct effect are both significant and point in opposite directions.

Complementary mediation: a situation in mediation analysis that occurs when the indirect effect and the direct effect are both significant and point in the same direction.

Composite indicators: a type of indicator used in formative measurement models. Composite indicators form the construct (or composite) fully by means of linear combinations. Therefore, composite indicators do not need to be conceptually united.

Composite reliability: a measure of internal consistency reliability, which, unlike Cronbach's alpha, does not assume equal indicator loadings. It should be above 0.70 (in exploratory research, 0.60 to 0.70 is considered acceptable).

Composite variable: is a linear combination of several variables.

Compositional invariance: exists when indicator weights are equal across groups.

Conditional indirect effect: see *Moderated mediation.*

Confidence interval: see *Bootstrap confidence interval.*

Configural invariance: exists when constructs are equally parameterized and estimated across groups.

Confirmatory: describes applications that aim at empirically testing theoretically developed models.

Confirmatory tetrad analysis for PLS-SEM (CTA-PLS): is a statistical procedure that allows for empirically testing the measurement model setup (i.e., whether the measures should be specified reflectively or formatively).

Consistency at large: describes an improvement of precision of PLS-SEM results when both the number of indicators per measurement model and the number of observations increase.

Consistent PLS (PLSc): a variant of the standard PLS-SEM algorithm, which provides consistent model estimates that disattenuate the correlations between pairs of latent variables, thereby mimicking CB-SEM results.

Construct-level sign change option: is the algorithmic option in bootstrapping that corrects for extreme samples drawn in the resampling runs.

Construct scores: are columns of data (vectors) for each latent variable that represent a key result of the PLS-SEM algorithm. The length of every vector equals the number of observations in the data set used.

Constructs: measure concepts that are abstract, complex, and cannot be directly observed by means of (multiple) items. Constructs are represented in path models as circles or ovals and are also referred to as *latent variables.*

Content specification: is the specification of the scope of the latent variable, that is, the domain of content the set of formative indicators is intended to capture.

Content validity: is a subjective but systematic evaluation of how well the domain content of a construct is captured by its indicators.

Continuous moderator variable: is a variable that affects the direction and/ or strength of the relation between an exogenous latent variable and an endogenous latent variable.

Convergence: is reached when the results of the PLS-SEM algorithm do not change much. In that case, the PLS-SEM algorithm stops when a prespecified stop criterion (i.e., a small number such as 0.00001) that indicates the minimal changes of PLS-SEM computations has been reached. Thus, convergence has been accomplished when the PLS-SEM algorithm stops because the prespecified stop criterion has been reached and not the maximum number of iterations.

Convergent validity: is the degree to which the formatively measured construct correlates positively with an alternative (reflective or single-item) measure of the same construct; see *Redundancy analysis*.

Covariance-based structural equation modeling (CB-SEM): is used to confirm (or reject) theories. It does this by determining how well a proposed theoretical model can estimate the covariance matrix for a sample data set.

Coverage error: occurs when the bootstrapping confidence interval of a parameter does not correspond to its empirical confidence interval.

Critical *t* value: is the cutoff or criterion on which the significance of a coefficient is determined. If the *empirical t value* is larger than the critical *t* value, the null hypothesis of no effect is rejected. Typical critical *t* values are 2.57, 1.96, and 1.65 for a significance level of 1%, 5%, and 10%, respectively (two-tailed tests).

Critical value: see *Significance testing*.

Cronbach's alpha: a measure of internal consistency reliability that assumes equal indicator loadings. In the context of PLS-SEM, composite reliability is considered a more suitable criterion of reliability. However, Cronbach's alpha still represents a conservative measure of internal consistency reliability.

Cross-loadings: an indicator's correlation with other constructs in the model.

Cross-validated communality: is used to obtain the Q^2 value based on the prediction of the data points by means of the underlying measurement model (see *Blindfolding*).

Cross-validated redundancy: is used to obtain the Q^2 value based on the prediction of the data points by means of the underlying structural model and measurement model (see *Blindfolding*).

CTA-PLS: see *Confirmatory tetrad analysis*.

Data matrix: includes the empirical data that are needed to estimate the PLS path model. The data matrix must have one column for every indicator in the PLS path model. The rows represent the observations with their responses to every indicator on the PLS path model.

Davison and Hinkley's double bootstrap: is an extension of *Shi's double bootstrap*, which introduces a bias correction based on differences between parameter estimates derived from samples and corresponding subsamples.

Degrees of freedom (*df*): is the number of values in the final calculation of the test statistic that are free to vary.

Diagonal lining: is a suspicious survey response pattern in which a respondent uses the available points on a scale (e.g., a 7-point scale) to place the answers to the different questions on a diagonal line.

Direct effect: is a relationship linking two constructs with a single arrow between the two.

Direct-only nonmediation: a situation in mediation analysis that occurs when the direct effect is significant but not the indirect effect.

Disattenuated correlation: the correlation between two constructs, if they were perfectly measured (i.e., if they were perfectly reliable).

Discriminant validity: is the extent to which a construct is truly distinct from other constructs, in terms of how much it correlates with other constructs, as well as how much indicators represent only a single construct.

Double bootstrapping: is a variant of regular bootstrapping in which further subsamples are drawn from each bootstrap sample (i.e., bootstrap the bootstrap).

Effect indicators: see *Reflective measurement*.

Empirical *t* value: is the test statistic value obtained from the data set at hand (here: the bootstrapping results). See *Significance testing*.

Endogenous constructs: see *Endogenous latent variables*.

Endogenous latent variables: serve only as dependent variables or as both independent and dependent variables in a structural model.

Equality of composite mean values and variances: is the final requirement to establish full measurement invariance.

Equidistance: is given when the distance between data points of a scale is identical.

Error terms: capture the unexplained variance in constructs and indicators when path models are estimated.

Evaluation criteria: are used to evaluate the quality of the measurement models and the structural model results in PLS-SEM based on a set of nonparametric evaluation criteria and procedures such as bootstrapping and blindfolding.

Exact fit test: a model fit test, which applies bootstrapping to derive *p* values of the (Euclidean or geodesic) distances between the observed correlations and the model-implied correlations.

Exogenous constructs: see *Exogenous latent variables*.

Exogenous latent variables: are latent variables that serve only as independent variables in a structural model.

Explained variance: see *Coefficient of determination*.

Exploratory: describes applications that focus on exploring data patterns and identifying relationships.

f^2 **effect size:** is a measure used to assess the relative impact of a predictor construct on an endogenous construct.

Factor (score) indeterminacy: means that one can compute an infinite number of sets of factor scores matching the specific requirements of a certain common factor model. In contrast to the explicit estimation in PLS-SEM, the scores of common factors are indeterminate.

FIMIX-PLS: see *Finite mixture partial least squares.*

Finite mixture partial least squares (FIMIX-PLS): is a latent class approach that allows for identifying and treating unobserved heterogeneity in PLS path models. The approach applies mixture regressions to simultaneously estimate group-specific parameters and observations' probabilities of segment membership.

First-generation techniques: are statistical methods traditionally used by researchers, such as regression and analysis of variance.

Formative-formative HCM: has formative measurement models of all constructs in the HCM and path relationships from the LOCs to the HOC (i.e., the LOCs form the HOC).

Formative measurement: is a type of measurement model setup in which the indicators fully form (see *Composite indicators*) or cause (see *Causal indicators*) the construct, and arrows point from the indicators to the construct. Also referred to as *Mode B* in PLS-SEM.

Formative measurement model: is a type of measurement model setup in which the direction of the arrows is from the indicator variables to the construct, indicating the assumption that the indicator variables cause the measurement of the construct.

Formative measures: see *Measurement models.*

Formative-reflective HCM: has formative measurement models of all constructs in the HCM and path relationships from the HOC to the LOCs (i.e., the LOCs reflect the HOC).

Fornell-Larcker criterion: a measure of discriminant validity that compares the square root of each construct's average variance extracted with its correlations with all other constructs in the model.

Full measurement invariance: is confirmed when (1) configural invariance, (2) compositional invariance, and (3) equality of composite mean values and variances are demonstrated.

Full mediation: a situation in mediation analysis that occurs when the mediated effect is significant but not the direct effect. Hence, the mediator variable fully explains the relationship between an exogenous and an endogenous latent variable. Also referred to as indirect-only mediation.

Genetic algorithm segmentation in PLS-SEM (PLS-GAS): is a distance-based segmentation method in PLS-SEM that builds on genetic segmentation results.

GoF: see *Goodness-of-fit index.*

Goodness-of-fit index (GoF): has been developed as an overall measure of model fit for PLS-SEM. However, as the GoF cannot reliably distinguish valid from invalid models and since its applicability is limited to certain model setups, researchers should avoid its use.

HCM: see *Hierarchical component model.*

Heterogeneity: occurs when the data underlie groups of data characterized by significant differences in terms of model parameters. Heterogeneity can be either observed or unobserved, depending on whether its source can be traced back to observable characteristics (e.g., demographic variables) or whether the sources of heterogeneity are not fully known.

Heterotrait-heteromethod correlations: are the correlations of the indicators across constructs measuring different constructs.

Heterotrait-monotrait ratio (HTMT): is an estimate of what the true correlation between two constructs would be, if they were perfectly measured (i.e., if they were perfectly reliable). HTMT is the mean of all correlations of indicators across constructs measuring different constructs (i.e., the heterotrait-heteromethod correlations) relative to the (geometric) mean of the average correlations of indicators measuring the same construct (i.e., the monotrait-heteromethod correlations) and can be used for discriminant validity assessment.

Hierarchical component model (HCM): is a higher-order structure (usually second-order) that contains several layers of constructs and involves a higher level of abstraction. HCMs involve a more abstract *higher-order component (HOC)*, related to two or more *lower-order components (LOCs)* in a reflective or formative way.

Higher-order component (HOC): is a general construct that represents all underlying LOCs in an HCM.

Higher-order model: see *Hierarchical component model (HCM).*

HOC: see *Higher-order component.*

HTMT: see *Heterotrait-monotrait ratio.*

Hypothesized relationships: are proposed explanations for constructs that define the path relationships in the structural model. The PLS-SEM results enable researchers to statistically test these hypotheses and thereby empirically substantiate the existence of the proposed path relationships.

Importance: is a term used in the context of *IPMA*. It is equivalent to the unstandardized total effect of some latent variable on the target variable.

Importance-performance map: is a graphical representation of the *importance-performance map analysis.*

Importance-performance map analysis (IPMA): extends the standard PLS-SEM results reporting of path coefficient estimates by adding a dimension to the analysis that considers the average values of the latent variable scores. More precisely, the IPMA contrasts structural model total effects on a specific target construct with the average latent variable scores of this construct's predecessors.

In-sample predictive power: see *Coefficient of determination.*

Inconsistent mediation: see *Competitive mediation.*

Index: is a set of formative indicators used to measure a construct.

Index of moderated mediation: quantifies the effect of a moderator on the indirect effect of an exogenous construct on an endogenous construct through a mediator.

Indicator reliability: is the square of a standardized indicator's outer loading. It represents how much of the variation in an item is explained by the construct and is referred to as the variance extracted from the item; see *Communality (item).*

Indicators: are directly measured observations (raw data), generally referred to as either *items* or *manifest variables,* represented in path models as rectangles. They are also available data (e.g., responses to survey questions or collected from company databases) used in measurement models to measure the latent variables; in SEM, indicators are often called manifest variables.

Indirect effect: represents a relationship between two latent variables via a third (e.g., mediator) construct in the PLS path model. If p_1 is the relationship between the exogenous latent variable and the mediator variable, and p_2 is the relationship between the mediator variable and the endogenous latent variable, the indirect effect is the product of path p_1 and path p_2.

Indirect-only mediation: a situation in mediation analysis that occurs when the indirect effect is significant but not the direct effect. Hence, the mediator variable fully explains the relationship between an exogenous and an endogenous latent variable. Also referred to as full mediation.

Individual-level sign change option: is an algorithmic option in bootstrapping that corrects for extreme samples drawn in the resampling runs.

Initial values: are the values for the relationships between the latent variables and the indicators in the first iteration of the PLS-SEM algorithm. Since the user usually has no information which indicators are more important and which indicators are less important per measurement model, an equal weight for every indicator in the PLS path model usually serves well for the initialization of the PLS-SEM algorithm. In accordance, all relationships in the measurement models have an initial value of +1.

Inner model: see *Structural model.*

Interaction effect: see *Moderating effect.*

Interaction term: is an auxiliary variable entered into the path model to account for the interaction of the moderator variable and the exogenous construct.

Internal consistency reliability: is a form of reliability used to judge the consistency of results across items on the same test. It determines whether the items measuring a construct are similar in their scores (i.e., if the correlations between the items are large).

Interpretational confounding: is a situation in which the empirically observed meaning between a construct and its measures differs from the theoretically implied meaning.

Interval scale: can be used to provide a rating of objects and has a constant unit of measurement so the distance between the scale points is equal.

IPMA: see *Importance-performance map analysis*.

Items: see *Indicators*.

Iterative reweighted regressions segmentation method (PLS-IRRS): is a particularly fast and high-performing distance-based segmentation method for PLS-SEM.

Kurtosis: is a measure of whether the distribution is too peaked (a very narrow distribution with most of the responses in the center).

Latent class techniques: a class of approaches that facilitates uncovering and treating unobserved heterogeneity. Different approaches have been proposed, which generalize, for example, finite mixture, genetic algorithm, or hill-climbing approaches to PLS-SEM.

Latent variables: are the (unobserved) theoretical or conceptual elements in the structural model. A latent variable that only explains other latent variables (only outgoing relationships in the structural model) is called exogenous, while latent variables with at least one incoming relationship in the structural model are called endogenous. Also see *Constructs*.

Listwise deletion: see *Casewise deletion*.

LOC: see *Lower-order component*.

Lower-order component (LOC): is a subdimension of the HOC in an HCM.

Main effect: refers to the direct effect between an exogenous and an endogenous construct in the path model without the presence of a moderating effect. After inclusion of the moderator variable, the main effect typically changes in magnitude. Therefore, it is commonly referred to as simple effect in the context of a moderator model.

Manifest variables: see *Indicators*.

Maximum number of iterations: is needed to ensure that the algorithm stops. The goal is to reach *convergence*. But if convergence cannot be reached, the algorithm should stop after a certain number of iterations. This maximum number of iterations (e.g., 300) should be sufficiently high to allow the PLS-SEM algorithm to converge.

Mean value replacement: inserts the sample mean for the missing data. Should only be used when indicators have less than 5% missing values.

Measurement: is the process of assigning numbers to a variable based on a set of rules.

Measurement equivalence: see *Measurement invariance.*

Measurement error: is the difference between the true value of a variable and the value obtained by a measurement.

Measurement invariance: deals with the comparability of responses to sets of items across groups. Among other things, measurement invariance implies that the categorical moderator variable's effect is restricted to the path coefficients and does not involve group-related differences in the measurement models.

Measurement invariance of composite models (MICOM) procedure: is a series of tests to assess invariance of measures (constructs) across multiple groups of data. The procedure comprises three steps that test different aspects of measurement invariance: (1) configural invariance (i.e., equal parameterization and way of estimation), (2) compositional invariance (i.e., equal indicator weights), and (3) equality of composite mean values and variances.

Measurement model: is an element of a path model that contains the indicators and their relationships with the constructs and is also called the *outer model* in PLS-SEM.

Measurement model misspecification: describes the use of a reflective measurement model when it is formative or the use of a formative measurement model when it is reflective. Measurement model misspecification usually yields invalid results and misleading conclusions.

Measurement scale: is a tool with a predetermined number of closed-ended responses that can be used to obtain an answer to a question.

Measurement theory: specifies how constructs should be measured with (a set of) indicators. It determines which indicators to use for construct measurement and the directional relationship between construct and indicators.

Mediated moderation: combines a moderator model with a mediation model in that the continuous moderating effect is mediated.

Mediating effect: occurs when a third variable or construct intervenes between two other related constructs.

Mediation: represents a situation in which one or more mediator variable(s) explain the processes through which an exogenous construct influences an endogenous construct.

Mediation model: see *Mediation.*

Mediator variable: see *Mediation.*

Metric data: represents data on a ratio scale and interval scale; see *Ratio scale, Interval scale.*

MICOM: see *Measurement invariance of composite models procedure.*

Minimum sample size: is the number of observations needed to represent the underlying population and to meet the technical requirements of the multivariate analysis method used. See *10 times rule.*

Missing value treatment: can employ different methods such as mean replacement, EM (expectation-maximization algorithm), and nearest neighbor to obtain values for missing data points in the set of data used for the analysis. As an alternative, researchers may consider deleting cases with missing values (i.e., casewise deletion).

Mode A: see *Reflective measurement.*

Mode B: see *Formative measurement.*

Model complexity: indicates how many latent variables, structural model relationships, and indicators in reflective and formative measurement models exist in a PLS path model. Even though PLS-SEM virtually has no limits of model complexity, knowledge about the most complex OLS regression is needed to determine the minimum sample size (*10 times rule*).

Model-implied nonredundant vanishing tetrads: are tetrads considered for significance testing in CTA-PLS.

Moderated mediation: combines a mediation model with a moderator model in that the mediator relationship is moderated by a continuous moderator variable.

Moderating effect: see *Moderation.*

Moderation: occurs when the effect of an exogenous latent variable on an endogenous latent variable depends on the values of a third variable, referred to as a moderator variable, which moderates the relationship.

Moderator effect: see *Moderation.*

Moderator variable: see *Moderation.*

Monotrait-heteromethod correlations: are the correlations of indicators measuring the same construct.

Multicollinearity: see *Collinearity.*

Multigroup analysis: is a type of moderator analysis where the moderator variable is categorical (usually with two categories) and is assumed to potentially affect all relationships in the structural model; it tests whether parameters (mostly path coefficients) differ significantly between two groups. Research has proposed a range of approaches to multigroup analysis, which rely on the bootstrapping or permutation procedure.

Multiple mediation analysis: describes a mediation analysis in which multiple mediator variables are being included in the model.

Multivariate analyses: are statistical methods that simultaneously analyze multiple variables.

No-effect nonmediation: a situation in mediation analysis that occurs when neither the direct nor the indirect effect is significant.

No sign change option: is an algorithmic option in bootstrapping that, unlike the *construct-level sign change option* and the *individual-level sign change option,* does not correct for extreme samples drawn in the resampling runs.

Nominal scale: is a measurement scale in which numbers are assigned that can be used to identify and classify objects (e.g., people, companies, products, etc.).

Observed heterogeneity: occurs when the sources of heterogeneity are known and can be traced back to observable characteristics such as demographics (e.g., gender, age, income).

Omission distance (D): determines which data points are deleted when applying the blindfolding (see *Blindfolding*) procedure. An omission distance D of 9, for example, implies that every ninth data point, and thus $1/9 = 11.11\%$ of the data in the original data set, is deleted during each blindfolding round. The omission distance should be chosen so that the number of observations used from model estimation divided by D is not an integer. Furthermore, D should be between 5 and 10.

Omnibus test of group differences (OTG): is a PLS-SEM–based multigroup analysis method that compares the parameter results of two or more groups at the same time. It corresponds to the F test in regression or ANOVA.

One-tailed test: see *Significance testing*.

Ordinal scale: is a measurement scale in which numbers are assigned that indicate relative positions of objects in an ordered series.

Orthogonalizing approach: is an approach to model the interaction term when including a moderator variable in the model. It creates an interaction term with orthogonal indicators. These orthogonal indicators are not correlated with the indicators of the independent variable and the moderator variable in the moderator model.

OTG: see *Omnibus test of group differences*.

Out-of-sample predictive power: see *Q^2 value*.

Outer loadings: are the estimated relationships in reflective measurement models (i.e., arrows from the latent variable to its indicators). They determine an item's absolute contribution to its assigned construct. Loadings are of primary interest in the evaluation of reflective measurement models but are also interpreted when formative measures are involved.

Outer models: see *Measurement model*.

Outer weights: are the results of a multiple regression of a construct on its set of indicators. Weights are the primary criterion to assess each indicator's relative importance in formative measurement models.

Outlier: is an extreme response to a particular question or extreme responses to all questions.

p value: is, in the context of structural model assessment, the probability of error for assuming that a path coefficient is significantly different from zero. In applications, researchers compare the p value of a coefficient with a significance level selected prior to the analysis to decide whether the path coefficient is statistically significant.

Pairwise deletion: uses all observations with complete responses in the calculation of the model parameters. As a result, different calculations in the analysis may be based on different sample sizes, which can bias the results. The use of pairwise deletion should generally be avoided.

Parameter settings: see *Algorithmic options.*

Parametric approach: is a multigroup variant, representing a modified version of a two independent samples *t* test.

Parsimonious models: are models with as few parameters as possible for a given quality of model estimation results.

Partial least squares structural equation modeling (PLS-SEM): is a variance-based method to estimate structural equation models. The goal is to maximize the explained variance of the endogenous latent variables.

Partial measurement invariance: is confirmed when only (1) configural invariance and (2) compositional invariance are demonstrated.

Partial mediation: occurs when a mediator variable partially explains the relationship between an exogenous and an endogenous construct. Partial mediation can come in the form of complementary and competitive mediation, depending on the relationship between the direct and indirect effects.

Path coefficients: are estimated path relationships in the structural model (i.e., between the constructs in the model). They correspond to standardized betas in a regression analysis.

Path models: are diagrams that visually display the hypotheses and variable relationships that are examined when structural equation modeling is applied.

Percentile method: is an approach for constructing bootstrap confidence intervals. Using the ordered set of parameter estimates obtained from bootstrapping, the lower and upper bounds are directly computed by excluding a certain percentage of lowest and highest values (e.g., 2.5% in the case of the 95% bootstrap confidence interval). The method has a high statistical power but may yield Type I errors.

Performance: is a term used in the context of *IPMA*. It is the mean value of the unstandardized (and rescaled) scores of a latent variable or an indicator.

Permutation test: is a multigroup analysis variant. The test randomly permutes observations between the groups and reestimates the model to derive a test statistic for the group differences.

PLS path modeling: see *Partial least squares structural equation modeling.*

PLS regression: is an analysis technique that explores the linear relationships between multiple independent variables and a single or multiple dependent variable(s). In developing the regression model, it constructs composites from both the multiple independent variables and the dependent variable(s) by means of principal component analysis.

PLS typological path modeling (PLS-TPM): is the first distance-based segmentation method developed for PLS-SEM.

PLSc: see *Consistent PLS.*

PLSe2: is a variant of the original PLS-SEM algorithm. Similar to PLSc, it makes the model estimates consistent in a common factor model sense.

PLS-GAS: see *Genetic algorithm segmentation in PLS-SEM.*

PLS-IRRS: see *Iterative reweighted regressions segmentation method.*

PLS-MGA: is a bootstrap-based multigroup analysis technique that further improves Henseler's MGA.

PLS-POS: see *Prediction-oriented segmentation approach in PLS-SEM.*

PLS-SEM: see *Partial least squares structural equation modeling.*

PLS-SEM algorithm: is the heart of the method. Based on the PLS path model and the indicator data available, the algorithm estimates the scores of all latent variables in the model, which in turn serve for estimating all path model relationships.

PLS-SEM bias: refers to PLS-SEM's property that structural model relationships are slightly underestimated and relationships in the measurement models are slightly overestimated compared with CB-SEM. This difference can be attributed to the methods' different handling of the latent variables in the model estimation but is negligible in most settings typically encountered in empirical research.

PLS-TPM: see *PLS typological path modeling segmentation.*

Prediction: is the primary goal of the PLS-SEM method. The higher the R^2 value (R^2 *values*) of endogenous constructs (*latent variables*), the better their prediction by the PLS path model.

Prediction error: measures the difference between the prediction of a data point and its original value in the sample.

Prediction-oriented segmentation in PLS-SEM (PLS-POS): is a distance-based segmentation method for PLS-SEM.

Predictive relevance (Q^2): is a measure of a model's predictive power. It examines whether a model accurately predicts data not used in the estimation of model parameters. This characteristic makes Q^2 a measure of out-of-sample predictive power (i.e., predictive relevance).

Product indicator approach: is an approach to model the interaction term when including a moderator variable in the model. It involves multiplying the indicators of the moderator with the indicators of the exogenous latent variable to establish a measurement model of the interaction term. The approach is only applicable when both moderator and exogenous latent variables are operationalized reflectively.

Product indicators: are indicators of an interaction term, generated by multiplication of each indicator of the exogenous construct with each indicator of the moderator variable. See *Product indicator approach.*

q^2 effect size: is a measure to assess the relative predictive relevance of a predictor construct on an endogenous construct.

Q^2 value: is a measure of a model's predictive power. The computation of Q^2 draws on the *blindfolding* technique, which uses a subset of the available data to estimate model parameters and then predicts the omitted data. Q^2 examines whether a model accurately predicts data not used in the estimation of model parameters (i.e., *out-of-sample predictive power* or *predictive relevance*).

R^2_{adj} value: see *Adjusted coefficient of determination.*

R^2 **values:** are the amount of explained variance of endogenous *latent variables* in the *structural model*. The higher the R^2 values, the better the construct is explained by the latent variables in the structural model that point at it via structural model path relationships. High R^2 values also indicate that the values of the construct can be well predicted via the PLS path model. See *Coefficient of determination*.

Ratio scales: are the highest level of measurement because they have a constant unit of measurement and an absolute zero point; a ratio can be calculated using the scale points.

Raw data: are the unstandardized observations in the *data matrix* that is used for the PLS path model estimation.

REBUS-PLS: see *Response-based procedure for detecting unit segments in PLS path modeling*.

Redundancy analysis: is a measure of a formative construct's *convergent validity*. It tests whether a formatively measured construct is highly correlated with a reflective measure of the same construct.

Reflective-formative HCM: has reflective measurement models of all constructs in the HCM and path relationships from the LOCs to the HOC (i.e., the LOCs form the HOC).

Reflective measure: see *Reflective measurement*.

Reflective measurement: is a type of measurement model setup in which measures represent the effects (or manifestations) of an underlying construct. Causality is from the construct to its measures (indicators). Also referred to as *Mode A* in PLS-SEM.

Reflective measurement model: *See Reflective measurement*

Reflective-reflective HCM: has reflective measurement models of all constructs in the HCM and path relationships from the HOC to the LOCs (i.e., the LOCs reflect the HOC).

Relative contribution: is the unique importance of each indicator by partializing the variance of the formatively measured construct that is predicted by the other indicators. An item's relative contribution is provided by its weight.

Relevance of significant relationships: compares the relative importance of predictor constructs to explain endogenous latent constructs in the structural model. Significance is a prerequisite for the relevance, but not all constructs and their significant path coefficients are highly relevant to explain a selected target construct.

Reliability: is the consistency of a measure. A measure is reliable (in the sense of test-retest reliability) when it produces consistent outcomes under consistent conditions. The most commonly used measure of reliability is the *internal consistency reliability*.

Reliability ρ_A: is the exact reliability of common factor models.

Repeated indicators approach for HCM: is a type of measurement model setup in HCM that uses the indicators of the LOCs as indicators of the HOC to create an HCM in PLS-SEM.

Rescaling: changes the values of a variable's scale to fit a predefined range (e.g., 0 to 100).

Response-based procedure for detecting unit segments in PLS path modeling (REBUS-PLS): is a distance-based segmentation method for PLS-SEM that builds on PLS-TPM.

Response-based segmentation techniques: see *Latent class techniques.*

RMS$_{theta}$: see *Root mean square residual covariance.*

Root mean square residual covariance (RMS$_{theta}$): is a model fit measure, which is based on the (root mean square) discrepancy between the observed covariance and the model-implied correlations. In CB-SEM, an SRMR value indicates good fit, but no threshold value has been introduced in a PLS-SEM context yet. Initial simulation results suggest a (conservative) threshold value for RMS$_{theta}$ of 0.12. That is, RMS$_{theta}$ values below 0.12 indicate a well-fitting model, whereas higher values indicate a lack of fit.

Sample: is the selection of individuals that represents the underlying population.

Scale: is a set of reflective indicators used to measure a construct.

Second-generation techniques: overcome the limitations of first-generation techniques, for example, in terms of accounting for measurement error. SEM is the most prominent second-generation data analysis technique.

SEM: see *Structural equation modeling.*

Shi's double bootstrap: translates the percentile method to double bootstrapping, accounting for coverage errors. The method has proven to be accurate in various data constellations but is also computationally demanding.

Sign indeterminacy: is a characteristic of PLS-SEM that causes arbitrary sign changes in the bootstrap estimates of path coefficients, loadings, and weights compared with the estimates obtained from the original sample.

Significance testing: is the process of testing whether a certain result likely has occurred by chance. In the context of structural model evaluation, it involves testing whether a path coefficient is truly different from zero in the population. Assuming a specified significance level, we reject the null hypothesis of no effect (i.e., the path coefficient is zero in the population) if the empirical t value (as provided by the data) is larger than the critical value. Commonly used critical values for two-tailed tests (derived from the normal distribution) are 2.57, 1.96, and 1.65 for significance levels of 1%, 5%, and 10%, respectively. For these significance levels and one-tailed tests, the critical values are 2.33, 1.65, and 1.28, respectively.

Simple effect: is a cause-effect relationship in a moderator model. The parameter estimate represents the size of the relationship between the exogenous and endogenous latent variable when the moderator variable is included in the model. For this reason, the main effect and the simple effect usually have different sizes.

Simple mediation analysis: describes a mediation analysis in which only one mediator variable is being included in the model.

Single-item construct: a construct that has only a single item measuring it. Since the construct is equal to its measure, the indicator loading is 1.00, making conventional reliability and convergent validity assessments inappropriate.

Singular data matrix: occurs when a variable in a measurement model is a linear combination of another variable in the same measurement model or when a variable has identical values for all observations. In this case, the variable has no variance and the PLS-SEM approach cannot estimate the PLS path model.

Skewness: is the extent to which a variable's distribution is symmetrical around its mean value.

Sobel test: is a test that has been proposed to assess the significance of the indirect effect in a mediation model. Due to its parametric nature and reliance on unstandardized path coefficients, the test is not applicable in a PLS-SEM context.

Specific indirect effect: describes an indirect effect via one single mediator in a multiple mediation model.

SRMR: see *Standardized root mean square residual.*

Standard error: is the standard deviation of the sampling distribution of a given statistic. Standard errors are important to show how much sampling fluctuation a statistic has.

Standardized data: have a mean value of 0 and a standard deviation of 1 (*z*-standardization). The PLS-SEM method usually uses standardized *raw data*. Most software tools automatically standardize the raw data when running the PLS-SEM algorithm.

Standardized root mean square residual (SRMR): is a model fit measure, which is defined as the root mean square discrepancy between the observed correlations and the model-implied correlations. In CB-SEM, an SRMR value below 0.08 indicates good fit, but no threshold value has been introduced in a PLS-SEM context yet.

Standardized values: indicate how many standard deviations an observation is above or below the mean.

Statistical power: the probability to detect a significant relationship when the relationship is in fact significant in the population.

Stop criterion: see *Convergence.*

Straight lining: describes a situation in which a respondent marks the same response for a high proportion of the questions.

Structural equation modeling (SEM): is used to measure relationships between latent variables.

Structural model: represents the theoretical or conceptual element of the path model. The structural model (also called inner model in PLS-SEM) includes the latent variables and their path relationships.

Structural theory: specifies how the latent variables are related to each other. That is, it shows the constructs and the paths between them.

Studentized bootstrap method: computes confidence intervals similarly to a confidence interval based on the t distribution, except that the standard error is derived from the bootstrapping results. Its performance parallels that of the *percentile method*.

Sum scores: represent a naive way to determine the latent variable scores. Instead of estimating the relationships in the measurement models, sum scores use the same weight for each indicator per measurement model (equal weights) to determine the latent variable scores.

Suppressor variable: describes the mediator variable in competitive mediation, which absorbs a significant share of or the entire direct effect, thereby substantially decreasing the magnitude of the total effect.

Tetrad (τ): is the difference of the product of a pair of covariances and the product of another pair of covariances. In reflective measurement models, this difference is assumed to be zero or at least close to zero; that is, they are expected to vanish. Nonvanishing tetrads in a latent variable's measurement model cast doubt on its reflective specification, suggesting a formative specification.

Theoretical t value: see *Critical t value*.

Theory: is a set of systematically related hypotheses developed following the scientific method that can be used to explain and predict outcomes and can be tested empirically.

Three-way interaction: is an extension of two-way interaction where the moderator effect is again moderated by another moderator variable.

TOL: see *Variance inflation factor*.

Tolerance: see *Variance inflation factor*.

Total effect: is the sum of the direct effect and the indirect effect between an exogenous and an endogenous latent variable in the path model.

Total indirect effect: is the sum of all specific indirect effects in a multiple mediation model.

Two-stage approach: is an approach to model the interaction term when including a moderator variable in the model. The approach can be used when the exogenous construct and/or the moderator variable are measured formatively.

Two-stage HCM analysis: is an approach to modeling and estimating an HCM in PLS-SEM. It is needed to estimate path relationships between an exogenous latent variable and a *reflective-formative HCM* or a *formative-formative HCM* in PLS-SEM.

Two-tailed test: see *Significance testing*.

Two-way interaction: is the standard approach to moderator analysis where the moderator variable interacts with one other exogenous latent variable.

Unobserved heterogeneity: occurs when the sources of heterogeneous data structures are not (fully) known.

Validity: is the extent to which a construct's indicators jointly measure what they are supposed to measure.

Vanishing tetrad: see *Tetrad*.

Variance-based SEM: see *Partial least squares structural equation modeling*.

Variance inflation factor (VIF): quantifies the severity of collinearity among the indicators in a formative measurement model. The VIF is directly related to the tolerance value ($VIF_i = 1/tolerance_i$).

Variate: see *Composite variable*.

VIF: see *Variance inflation factor*.

Weighting scheme: describes a particular method to determine the relationships in the *structural model* when running the *PLS-SEM algorithm*. Standard options are the centroid, factor, and path weighting schemes. The final results do not differ much, and one should use the path weighting scheme as a default option since it maximizes the R^2 *values* of the PLS path model estimation.

References

Aguinis, H., Beaty, J. C., Boik, R. J., & Pierce, C. A. (2005). Effect size and power in assessing moderating effects of categorical variables using multiple regression: A 30-year review. *Journal of Applied Psychology, 90,* 94–107.

Albers, S. (2010). PLS and success factor studies in marketing. In V. Esposito Vinzi, W. W. Chin, J. Henseler, & H. Wang (Eds.), *Handbook of partial least squares: Concepts, methods and applications in marketing and related fields* (Springer Handbooks of Computational Statistics Series, Vol. II, pp. 409–425). Berlin: Springer.

Apel, H. & Wold, H. O. A. (1982). Soft modeling with latent variables in two or more dimensions: PLS estimation and testing for predictive relevance. In K. G. Jöreskog & H. Wold (Eds.), *Systems under indirect observa Part II* (pp. 209–247). Amsterdam: North-Holland.

Bagozzi, R. P. (2007). On the meaning of formative measurement and how it differs from reflective measurement: Comment on Howell, Breivik, and Wilcox (2007). *Psychological Methods, 12,* 229–237.

Bagozzi, R. P., Yi, Y., & Philipps, L. W. (1991). Assessing construct validity in organizational research. *Administrative Science Quarterly, 36,* 421–458.

Barclay, D. W., Higgins, C. A., & Thompson, R. (1995). The partial least squares approach to causal modeling: Personal computer adoption and use as illustration. *Technology Studies, 2,* 285–309.

Baron, R. M., & Kenny, D. A. (1986). The moderator-mediator variable distinction in social psychological research: Conceptual, strategic and statistical considerations. *Journal of Personality and Social Psychology, 51,* 1173–1182.

Bearden, W. O., Netemeyer, R. G., & Haws, K. L. (2011). *Handbook of marketing scales: Multi-item measures of marketing and consumer behavior research.* Thousand Oaks, CA: Sage.

Becker, J.-M., Klein, K., & Wetzels, M. (2012). Formative hierarchical latent variable models in PLS-SEM: Recommendations and guidelines. *Long Range Planning, 45,* 359–394.

Becker, J.-M., Rai, A., & Rigdon, E. E. (2013). Predictive validity and formative measurement in structural equation modeling: Embracing practical relevance. In *Proceedings of the 34th International Conference on Information Systems,* Milan, Italy.

Becker, J.-M., Rai, A., Ringle, C. M., & Völckner, F. (2013). Discovering unobserved heterogeneity in structural equation models to avert validity threats. *MIS Quarterly, 37,* 665–694.

Bentler, P. M., & Huang, W. (2014). On components, latent variables, PLS and simple methods: Reactions to Rigdon's rethinking of PLS. *Long Range Planning, 47,* 136–145.

Binz Astrachan, C., Patel, V. K., & Wanzenried, G. (2014). A comparative study of CB-SEM and PLS-SEM for theory development in family firm research. *Journal of Family Business Strategy, 5,* 116–128.

Bollen, K. A. (2011). Evaluating effect, composite, and causal indicators in structural equation models. *MIS Quarterly, 35,* 359–372.

Bollen, K. A., & Bauldry, S. (2011). Three Cs in measurement models: Causal indicators, composite indicators, and covariates. *Psychological Methods, 16,* 265–284.

Bollen, K. A., & Lennox, R. (1991). Conventional wisdom on measurement: A structural equation perspective. *Psychological Bulletin, 110,* 305–314.

Bollen, K. A., & Ting, K.-F. (1993). Confirmatory tetrad analysis. In P. V. Marsden (Ed.), *Sociological methodology* (pp. 147–175). Washington, DC: American Sociological Association.

Bollen, K. A., & Ting, K.-F. (2000). A tetrad test for causal indicators. *Psychological Methods, 5,* 3–22.

Bruner, G. C., James, K. E., & Hensel, P. J. (2001). *Marketing scales handbook: A compilation of multi-item measures.* Oxford, UK: Butterworth-Heinemann.

Cadogan, J. W., & Lee, N. (2013). Improper use of endogenous formative variables. *Journal of Business Research, 66,* 233–241.

Cassel, C., Hackl, P., & Westlund, A. H. (1999). Robustness of partial least squares method for estimating latent variable quality structures. *Journal of Applied Statistics, 26,* 435–446.

Cenfetelli, R. T., & Bassellier, G. (2009). Interpretation of formative measurement in information systems research. *MIS Quarterly, 33,* 689–708.

Chernick, M. R. (2008). *Bootstrap methods: A guide for practitioners and researchers* (2nd ed.). Newton, PA: Wiley.

Chin, W. W. (1998). The partial least squares approach to structural equation modeling. In G. A. Marcoulides (Ed.), *Modern methods for business research* (pp. 295–358). Mahwah, NJ: Lawrence Erlbaum.

Chin, W. W. (2003). *PLS Graph 3.0.* Houston, TX: Soft Modeling, Inc.

Chin, W. W. (2010). How to write up and report PLS analyses. In V. Esposito Vinzi, W. W. Chin, J. Henseler, & H. Wang (Eds.), *Handbook of partial least squares: Concepts, methods and applications in marketing and related fields* (Springer Handbooks of Computational Statistics Series, Vol. II, pp. 655–690). Berlin: Springer.

Chin, W. W., & Dibbern, J. (2010). A permutation based procedure for multi-group PLS analysis: Results of tests of differences on simulated data and a cross cultural analysis of the sourcing of information system services between Germany and the USA. In V. Esposito Vinzi, W. W. Chin, J. Henseler, & H. Wang (Eds.), *Handbook of partial least squares: Concepts, methods and applications in marketing and related fields* (Springer Handbooks of Computational Statistics Series, Vol. II, pp. 171–193). Berlin: Springer.

Chin, W. W., Kim, Y. J., & Lee, G. (2013). Testing the differential impact of structural paths in PLS analysis: A bootstrapping approach. In H. Abdi, W. W. Chin, V. Esposito Vinzi, G. Russolillo, & L. Trinchera (Eds.), *New perspectives in partial least squares and related methods* (pp. 221–229). New York: Springer.

Chin, W. W., Marcolin, B. L., & Newsted, P. R. (2003). A partial least squares latent variable modeling approach for measuring interaction effects: Results from a Monte Carlo simulation study and an electronic-mail emotion/adoption study. *Information Systems Research, 14*, 189–217.

Chin, W. W., & Newsted, P. R. (1999). Structural equation modeling analysis with small samples using partial least squares. In R. H. Hoyle (Ed.), *Statistical strategies for small sample research* (pp. 307–341). Thousand Oaks, CA: Sage.

Coelho, P. S., & Henseler, J. (2012). Creating customer loyalty through service customization. *European Journal of Marketing, 46*, 331–356.

Cohen, J. (1988). *Statistical power analysis for the behavioral sciences.* Mahwah, NJ: Lawrence Erlbaum.

Cohen, J. (1992). A power primer. *Psychological Bulletin, 112*, 155–159.

Davis, F. D. (1989). Perceived usefulness, perceived ease of use, and user acceptance of information technology. *MIS Quarterly, 13*, 319–340.

Davison, A. C., & Hinkley, D. V. (1997). *Bootstrap methods and their application.* Cambridge, UK: Cambridge University Press.

DeVellis, R. F. (2011). *Scale development.* Thousand Oaks, CA: Sage.

Diamantopoulos, A. (2006). The error term in formative measurement models: Interpretation and modeling implications. *Journal of Modelling in Management, 1*, 7–17.

Diamantopoulos, A. (2011). Incorporating formative measures into covariance-based structural equation models. *MIS Quarterly, 35*, 335–358.

Diamantopoulos, A., & Riefler, P. (2011). Using formative measures in international marketing models: A cautionary tale using consumer animosity as an example. *Advances in International Marketing, 10*, 11–30.

Diamantopoulos, A., Riefler, P., & Roth, K. P. (2008). Advancing formative measurement models. *Journal of Business Research, 61*, 1203–1218.

Diamantopoulos, A., Sarstedt, M., Fuchs, C., Kaiser, S., & Wilczynski, P. (2012). Guidelines for choosing between multi-item and single-item scales for construct measurement: A predictive validity perspective. *Journal of the Academy of Marketing Science, 40*, 434–449.

Diamantopoulos, A., & Siguaw, J. A. (2006). Formative vs. reflective indicators in measure development: Does the choice of indicators matter? *British Journal of Management, 13*, 263–282.

Diamantopoulos, A., & Winklhofer, H. M. (2001). Index construction with formative indicators: An alternative to scale development. *Journal of Marketing Research, 38*, 269–277.

Dibbern, J., & Chin, W. W. (2005). Multi-group comparison: Testing a PLS model on the sourcing of application software services across Germany and the USA using a permutation based algorithm. In F. W. Bliemel, A. Eggert, G. Fassott, & J. Henseler (Eds.), *Handbuch PLS-Pfadmodellierung: Methode, Anwendung, Praxisbeispiele* [Handbook of partial least squares modeling: Methods, applications, practical examples] (pp. 135–160). Stuttgart, Germany: Schäffer-Poeschel.

Dijkstra, T. K. (2010). Latent variables and indices: Herman Wold's basic design and partial least squares. In V. Esposito Vinzi, W. W. Chin, J. Henseler, & H. Wang (Eds.), *Handbook of partial least squares: Concepts, methods and applications* (Springer Handbooks of Computational Statistics Series, Vol. II, pp. 23–46). Berlin: Springer.

Dijkstra, T. K. (2014). PLS' Janus face—response to Professor Rigdon's "Rethinking partial least squares modeling: In praise of simple methods." *Long Range Planning, 47,* 146–153.

Dijkstra, T. K., & Henseler, J. (2015a). Consistent and asymptotically normal PLS estimators for linear structural equations. *Computational Statistics & Data Analysis, 81,* 10–23.

Dijkstra, T. K., & Henseler, J. (2015b). Consistent partial least squares path modeling. *MIS Quarterly, 39,* 297–316.

do Valle, P. O., & Assaker, G. (in press). Using partial least squares structural equation modeling in tourism research: A review of past research and recommendations for future applications. *Journal of Travel Research.*

Drolet, A. L., & Morrison, D. G. (2001). Do we really need multiple-item measures in service research? *Journal of Service Research, 3,* 196–204.

Eberl, M. (2010). An application of PLS in multi-group analysis: The need for differentiated corporate-level marketing in the mobile communications industry. In V. Esposito Vinzi, W. W. Chin, J. Henseler, & H. Wang (Eds.), *Handbook of partial least squares: Concepts, methods and applications in marketing and related fields* (Springer Handbooks of Computational Statistics Series, Vol. II, pp. 487–514). Berlin: Springer.

Eberl, M., & Schwaiger, M. (2005). Corporate reputation: Disentangling the effects on financial performance. *European Journal of Marketing, 39,* 838–854.

Edwards, J. R., & Bagozzi, R. P. (2000). On the nature and direction of relationships between constructs and measures. *Psychological Methods, 5,* 155–174.

Efron, B. (1987). Better bootstrap confidence intervals. *Journal of the American Statistical Association, 82,* 171–185.

Efron, B., & Tibshirani, R. (1986). Bootstrap methods for standard errors, confidence intervals, and other measures of statistical accuracy. *Statistical Science, 1,* 54–75.

Esposito Vinzi, V., Chin, W. W., Henseler, J., & Wang, H. (Eds.). (2010). *Handbook of partial least squares: Concepts, methods and applications* (Springer Handbooks of Computational Statistics Series, Vol. II). Berlin: Springer.

Esposito Vinzi, V., Trinchera, L., & Amato, S. (2010). PLS path modeling: From foundations to recent developments and open issues for model assessment and improvement. In V. Esposito Vinzi, W. W. Chin, J. Henseler, & H. Wang (Eds.), *Handbook of partial least squares: Concepts, methods and applications* (Springer Handbooks of Computational Statistics Series, Vol. II, pp. 47–82). Berlin: Springer.

Esposito Vinzi, V., Trinchera, L., Squillacciotti, S., & Tenenhaus, M. (2008). REBUS-PLS: A response-based procedure for detecting unit segments in PLS path modelling. *Applied Stochastic Models in Business and Industry, 24,* 439–458.

Falk, R. F., & Miller, N. B. (1992). *A primer for soft modeling.* Akron, OH: University of Akron Press.

Festinger, L. (1957). *A theory of cognitive dissonance.* Stanford, CA: Stanford University Press.

Fornell, C. G. (1982). A second generation of multivariate analysis: An overview. In C. Fornell (Ed.), *A second generation of multivariate analysis* (pp. 1–21). New York: Praeger.

Fornell, C. G. (1987). A second generation of multivariate analysis: Classification of methods and implications for marketing research. In M. J. Houston (Ed.), *Review of marketing* (pp. 407–450). Chicago: American Marketing Association.

Fornell, C. G., & Bookstein, F. L. (1982). Two structural equation models: LISREL and PLS applied to consumer exit-voice theory. *Journal of Marketing Research, 19,* 440–452.

Fornell, C. G., Johnson, M. D., Anderson, E. W., Cha, J., & Bryant, B. E. (1996). The American Customer Satisfaction Index: Nature, purpose, and findings. *Journal of Marketing, 60,* 7–18.

Fu, J.-R. (2006). VisualPLS—An enhanced GUI for LVPLS (PLS 1.8 PC) version 1.04 [Computer software]. Retrieved from http://www2.kuas .edu.tw/prof/fred/vpls/

Fuchs, C., & Diamantopoulos, A. (2009). Using single-item measures for construct measurement in management research: Conceptual issues and application guidelines. *Die Betriebswirtschaft, 69,* 197–212.

Garson, G. D. (2014). *Partial least squares: Regression and structural equation models.* Asheboro, NC: Statistical Associates Publishers.

Gefen, D., Rigdon, E. E., & Straub, D. W. (2011). Editor's comment: An update and extension to SEM guidelines for administrative and social science research. *MIS Quarterly, 35,* iii–xiv.

Gefen, D., Straub, D. W., & Boudreau, M. C. (2000). Structural equation modeling techniques and regression: Guidelines for research practice. *Communications of the AIS, 1,* 1–78.

Geisser, S. (1974). A predictive approach to the random effects model. *Biometrika, 61,* 101–107.

Goodhue, D. L., Lewis, W., & Thompson, R. (2012). Does PLS have advantages for small sample size or non-normal data? *MIS Quarterly, 36,* 891–1001.

Götz, O., Liehr-Gobbers, K., & Krafft, M. (2010). Evaluation of structural equation models using the partial least squares (PLS) approach. In V. Esposito Vinzi, W. W. Chin, J. Henseler, & H. Wang (Eds.), *Handbook of partial least squares: Concepts, methods and applications in marketing and related fields* (Springer Handbooks of Computational Statistics Series, Vol. II, pp. 691–711). Berlin: Springer.

Gudergan, S. P., Ringle, C. M., Wende, S., & Will, A. (2008). Confirmatory tetrad analysis in PLS path modeling. *Journal of Business Research, 61,* 1238–1249.

Haenlein, M., & Kaplan, A. M. (2004). A beginner's guide to partial least squares analysis. *Understanding Statistics, 3,* 283–297.

Hahn, C., Johnson, M. D., Herrmann, A., & Huber, F. (2002). Capturing customer heterogeneity using a finite mixture PLS approach. *Schmalenbach Business Review, 54,* 243–269.

Hair, J. F., Black, W. C., Babin, B. J., & Anderson, R. E. (2010). *Multivariate data analysis.* Englewood Cliffs, NJ: Prentice Hall.

Hair, J. F., Ringle, C. M., & Sarstedt, M. (2011). PLS-SEM: Indeed a silver bullet. *Journal of Marketing Theory and Practice, 19,* 139–151.

Hair, J. F., Ringle, C. M., & Sarstedt, M. (2012). Partial least squares: The better approach to structural equation modeling? *Long Range Planning, 45*(5–6), 312–319.

Hair, J. F., Ringle, C. M., & Sarstedt, M. (2013). Partial least squares structural equation modeling: Rigorous applications, better results and higher acceptance. *Long Range Planning, 46,* 1–12.

Hair, J. F., Sarstedt, M., Pieper, T., & Ringle, C. M. (2012). The use of partial least squares structural equation modeling in strategic management research: A review of past practices and recommendations for future applications. *Long Range Planning, 45,* 320–340.

Hair, J. F., Sarstedt, M., Ringle, C. M., & Mena, J. A. (2012). An assessment of the use of partial least squares structural equation modeling in marketing research. *Journal of the Academy of Marketing Science, 40,* 414–433.

Hair, J. F., Celsi, M., Money, A. H., Samouel, P., & Page, M. J. (2016). *Essentials of business research methods* (3rd ed.). Armonk, NY: Sharpe.

Hayduk, L. A., & Littvay, L. (2012). Should researchers use single indicators, best indicators, or multiple indicators in structural equation models? *BMC Medical Research Methodology, 12*(159), 12–159.

Hayes, A. F. (2013). *Introduction to mediation, moderation, and conditional process analysis: A regression-based approach.* New York: Guilford.

Hayes, A. F. (2015). An index and test of linear moderated mediation. *Multivariate Behavioral Research, 50,* 1–22.

Helm, S., Eggert, A., & Garnefeld, I. (2010). Modelling the impact of corporate reputation on customer satisfaction and loyalty using PLS. In V. Esposito Vinzi, W. W. Chin, J. Henseler, & H. Wang (Eds.), *Handbook of partial least squares: Concepts, methods and applications in marketing and related fields* (Springer Handbooks of Computational Statistics Series, Vol. II, pp. 515–534). Berlin: Springer.

Henseler, J. (2010). On the convergence of the partial least squares path modeling algorithm. *Computational Statistics, 25,* 107–120.

Henseler, J., & Chin, W. W. (2010). A comparison of approaches for the analysis of interaction effects between latent variables using partial least squares path modeling. *Structural Equation Modeling, 17,* 82–109.

Henseler, J., & Dijkstra, T. K. (2015). ADANCO 1.1 [Computer software]. Retrieved from http://www.compositemodeling.com

Henseler, J., Dijkstra, T. K., Sarstedt, M., Ringle, C. M., Diamantopoulos, A., Straub, D. W., et al. (2014). Common beliefs and reality about partial least squares: Comments on Rönkkö & Evermann (2013). *Organizational Research Methods, 17,* 182–209.

Henseler, J., & Fassott, G. (2010). Testing moderating effects in PLS path models: An illustration of available procedures. In V. Esposito Vinzi, W. W. Chin, J. Henseler, & H. Wang (Eds.), *Handbook of partial least squares: Concepts, methods and applications in marketing and related fields* (Springer Handbooks of Computational Statistics Series, Vol. II, pp. 713–735). Berlin: Springer.

Henseler, J., Ringle, C. M., & Sarstedt, M. (2012). Using partial least squares path modeling in international advertising research: Basic concepts and recent issues. In S. Okazaki (Ed.), *Handbook of research in international advertising* (pp. 252–276). Cheltenham, UK: Edward Elgar.

Henseler, J., Ringle, C. M., & Sarstedt, M. (2015). A new criterion for assessing discriminant validity in variance-based structural equation modeling. *Journal of the Academy of Marketing Science, 43,* 115–135.

Henseler, J., Ringle, C. M., & Sarstedt, M. (in press). Testing measurement invariance of composites using partial least squares. *International Marketing Review.*

Henseler, J., Ringle, C. M., & Sinkovics, R. R. (2009). The use of partial least squares path modeling in international marketing. *Advances in International Marketing, 20,* 277–320.

Henseler, J., & Sarstedt, M. (2013). Goodness-of-fit indices for partial least squares path modeling. *Computational Statistics, 28,* 565–580.

Höck, C., Ringle, C. M., & Sarstedt, M. (2010). Management of multi-purpose stadiums: Importance and performance measurement of service interfaces. *International Journal of Services Technology and Management, 14,* 188–207.

Homburg, C., & Giering, A. (2001). Personal characteristics as moderators of the relationship between customer satisfaction and loyalty—an empirical analysis. *Psychology and Marketing, 18,* 43–66.

Hu, L.-T., & Bentler, P. M. (1998). Fit indices in covariance structure modeling: Sensitivity to underparameterized model misspecification. *Psychological Methods, 3,* 424–453.

Hubona, G. (2015). PLS-GUI [Software program]. Retrieved from http://www.pls-gui.com

Hui, B. S., & Wold, H. O. A. (1982). Consistency and consistency at large of partial least squares estimates. In K. G. Jöreskog & H. O. A. Wold (Eds.), *Systems under indirect observation, Part II* (pp. 119–130). Amsterdam: North-Holland.

Hulland, J. (1999). Use of partial least squares (PLS) in strategic management research: A review of four recent studies. *Strategic Management Journal, 20,* 195–204.

Hult, G. T. M., Ketchen, D. J., Griffith, D. A., Finnegan, C. A., Gonzalez-Padron, T., Harmancioglu, N., et al. (2008). Data equivalence in cross-cultural international business research: Assessment and guidelines. *Journal of International Business Studies, 39,* 1027–1044.

Jarvis, C. B., MacKenzie, S. B., & Podsakoff, P. M. (2003). A critical review of construct indicators and measurement model misspecification in marketing and consumer research. *Journal of Consumer Research, 30,* 199–218.

Jones, M. A., Mothersbaugh, D. L., & Beatty, S. E. (2000). Switching barriers and repurchase intentions in services. *Journal of Retailing, 76,* 259–274.

Jöreskog, K. G., & Wold, H. (1982). The ML and PLS techniques for modeling with latent variables: Historical and comparative aspects. In H. Wold & K. G. Jöreskog (Eds.), *Systems under indirect observation, Part I* (pp. 263–270). Amsterdam: North-Holland.

Kamakura, W. A. (2015). Measure twice and cut once: The carpenter's rule still applies. *Marketing Letters, 26,* 237–243.

Keil, M., Saarinen, T., Tan, B. C. Y., Tuunainen, V., Wassenaar, A., & Wei, K.-K. (2000). A cross-cultural study on escalation of commitment behavior in software projects. *MIS Quarterly, 24,* 299–325.

Kenny, D. A. (2016). Moderation. Retrieved from http://davidakenny.net/cm/moderation.htm

Kim, G., Shin, B., & Grover, V. (2010). Investigating two contradictory views of formative measurement in information systems research. *MIS Quarterly, 34,* 345–365.

Klarner, P., Sarstedt, M., Höck, M., & Ringle, C. M. (2013). Disentangling the effects of team competences, team adaptability, and client communication on the performance of management consulting teams. *Long Range Planning, 46,* 258–286.

Kock, N. (2015). *WarpPLS 5.0 user manual.* Laredo, TX: ScriptWarp Systems.

Kocyigit, O., & Ringle, C. M. (2011). The impact of brand confusion on sustainable brand satisfaction and private label proneness: A subtle decay of brand equity. *Journal of Brand Management, 19,* 195–212.

Kristensen, K., Martensen, A., & Grønholdt, L. (2000). Customer satisfaction measurement at Post Denmark: Results of application of the European Customer Satisfaction Index Methodology. *Total Quality Management, 11,* 1007–1015.

Kuppelwieser, V., & Sarstedt, M. (2014). Applying the future time perspective scale to advertising research. *International Journal of Advertising, 33,* 113–136.

Lee, L., Petter, S., Fayard, D., & Robinson, S. (2011). On the Use of Partial Least Squares Path Modeling in Accounting Research. *International Journal of Accounting Information Systems, 12,* 305–328.

Little, R. J. A., & Rubin, D. B. (2002). *Statistical analysis with missing data.* New York: John Wiley.

Little, T. D., Bovaird, J. A., & Widaman, K. F. (2006). On the merits of orthogonalizing powered powered and product terms: Implications for modeling interaction terms among latent variables. *Structural Equation Modeling, 13,* 497–519.

Lohmöller, J.-B. (1987). LVPLS 1.8 [Computer software]. Cologne, Germany: Zentralarchiv für Empirische Sozialforschung.

Lohmöller, J.-B. (1989). *Latent variable path modeling with partial least squares.* Heidelberg, Germany: Physica.

Loo, R. (2002). A caveat on using single-item versus multiple-item scales. *Journal of Managerial Psychology, 17,* 68–75.

MacKenzie, S. B., Podsakoff, P. M., & Podsakoff, N. P. (2011). Construct measurement and validation procedures in MIS and behavioral research: Integrating new and existing techniques. *MIS Quarterly, 35,* 293–295.

MacKinnon, D. P., Krull, J. L., & Lockwood, C. M. (2000). Equivalence of the mediation, confounding and suppression effect. *Prevention Science, 1,* 173–181.

Marcoulides, G. A., & Chin, W. W. (2013). You write but others read: Common methodological misunderstandings in PLS and related methods. In H. Abdi, W. W. Chin, V. Esposito Vinzi, G. Russolillo, & L. Trinchera (Eds.), *New perspectives in partial least squares and related methods* (pp. 31–64). New York: Springer.

Marcoulides, G. A., & Saunders, C. (2006). PLS: A silver bullet? *MIS Quarterly, 30,* iii–ix.

Mateos-Aparicio, G. (2011). Partial least squares (PLS) methods: Origins, evolution, and application to social sciences. *Communications in Statistics–Theory and Methods, 40,* 2305–2317.

Monecke, A., & Leisch, F. (2012). semPLS: Structural equation modeling using partial least squares. *Journal of Statistical Software, 48.* Retrieved from http://www.jstatsoft.org/v48/i03/paper

Money, K. G., Hillenbrand, C., Henseler, J., & Da Camara, N. (2012). Exploring unanticipated consequences of strategy amongst stakeholder segments: The case of a European revenue service. *Long Range Planning, 45,* 395–423.

Muller, D., Judd, C. M., & Yzerbyt, V. Y. (2005). When mediation is moderated and moderation is mediated. *Journal of Personality and Social Psychology, 89,* 852–863.

Navarro, A., Acedo, F. J., Losada, F., & Ruzo, E. (2011). Integrated model of export activity: Analysis of heterogeneity in managers' orientations and perceptions on strategic marketing management in foreign markets. *Journal of Marketing Theory and Practice, 19,* 187–204.

Nitzl, C. (in press). The use of partial least squares structural equation modelling (PLS-SEM) in management accounting research: Directions for future theory development. *Journal of Accounting Literature.*

Nitzl, C., Roldán, J. L., & Cepeda, G. (in press). Mediation analyses in partial least squares structural equation modeling: Helping researchers discuss more sophisticated models. Industrial Management & Data Systems.

Nunnally, J. C., & Bernstein, I. (1994). *Psychometric theory.* New York: McGraw-Hill.

Peng, D. X., & Lai, F. (2012). Using Partial Least Squares in Operations Management Research: A Practical Guideline and Summary of Past Research. *Journal of Operations Management, 30,* 467–480.

Preacher, K. J., & Hayes, A. F. (2004). SPSS and SAS procedures for estimating indirect effects in simple mediation models. *Behavior Research Methods, Instruments, and Computers, 36,* 717–731.

Preacher, K. J., & Hayes, A. F. (2008a). Asymptotic and resampling strategies for assessing and comparing indirect effects in simple and multiple mediator models. *Behavior Research Methods, 40,* 879–891.

Preacher, K. J., & Hayes, A. F. (2008b). Contemporary approaches to assessing mediation in communication research. In A. F. Hayes, M. D. Slater, & L. B. Snyder (Eds.), *The SAGE sourcebook of advanced data analysis methods for communication research* (pp. 13–54). Thousand Oaks, CA: Sage.

Preacher, K. J., Rucker, D. D., & Hayes, A. F. (2007). Assessing moderated mediation hypotheses: Theory, methods, and prescriptions. *Multivariate Behavioral Research, 42,* 185–227.

Raithel, S., & Schwaiger, M. (2015). The effects of corporate reputation perceptions of the general public on shareholder value. *Strategic Management Journal, 36,* 945–956.

Raithel, S., Wilczynski, P., Schloderer, M. P., & Schwaiger, M. (2010). The value-relevance of corporate reputation during the financial crisis. *Journal of Product and Brand Management, 19,* 389–400.

Ramirez, E., David, M. E., & Brusco, M. J. (2013). Marketing's SEM based nomological network: Constructs and research streams in 1987–1997 and in 1998–2008. *Journal of Business Research, 66,* 1255–1269.

Reinartz, W., Haenlein, M., & Henseler, J. (2009). An empirical comparison of the efficacy of covariance-based and variance-based SEM. *International Journal of Research in Marketing, 26,* 332–344.

Richter, N. F., Sinkovics, R. R., Ringle, C. M., & Schlägel, C. (in press). A critical look at the use of SEM in International Business Research. *International Marketing Review.*

Rigdon, E. E. (2005). Structural equation modeling: Nontraditional alternatives. In B. Everitt & D. Howell (Eds.), *Encyclopedia of statistics in behavioral science* (pp. 1934–1941). New York: Wiley.

Rigdon, E. E. (2013). Partial least squares path modeling. In G. R. Hancock & R. D. Mueller (Eds.), *Structural equation modeling: A second course* (2nd ed., pp. 81–116). Charlotte, NC: Information Age.

Rigdon, E. E. (2012). Rethinking partial least squares path modeling: In praise of simple methods. *Long Range Planning, 45,* 341–358.

Rigdon, E. E. (2014a). Comment on "Improper use of endogenous formative variables." *Journal of Business Research, 67,* 2800–2802.

Rigdon, E. E. (2014b). Rethinking partial least squares path modeling: Breaking chains and forging ahead. *Long Range Planning, 47,* 161–167.

Rigdon, E. E., Becker, J.-M., Rai, A., Ringle, C. M., Diamantopoulos, A., Karahanna, E., et al. (2014). Conflating antecedents and formative indicators: A comment on Aguirre-Urreta and Marakas. *Information Systems Research, 25,* 780–784.

Ringle, C. M., Götz, O., Wetzels, M., & Wilson, B. (2009). *On the use of formative measurement specifications in structural equation modeling:*

A Monte Carlo simulation study to compare covariance-based and partial least squares model estimation methodologies (METEOR Research Memoranda RM/09/014). Maastricht, the Netherlands: Maastricht University.

Rigdon, E. E., Ringle, C. M., & Sarstedt, M. (2010). Structural modeling of heterogeneous data with partial least squares. In N. K. Malhotra (Ed.), *Review of marketing research* (pp. 255–296). Armonk, NY: Sharpe.

Rigdon, E. E., Ringle, C. M., Sarstedt, M., & Gudergan, S. P. (2011). Assessing heterogeneity in customer satisfaction studies: Across industry similarities and within industry differences. *Advances in International Marketing, 22,* 169–194.

Ringle, C. M., Sarstedt, M., & Mooi, E. A. (2010). Response-based segmentation using finite mixture partial least squares: Theoretical foundations and an application to American customer satisfaction index data. *Annals of Information Systems, 8,* 19–49.

Ringle, C. M., Sarstedt, M., & Schlittgen, R. (2014). Genetic algorithm segmentation in partial least squares structural equation modeling. *OR Spectrum, 36,* 251–276.

Ringle, C. M., Sarstedt, M., Schlittgen, R., & Taylor, C. R. (2013). PLS path modeling and evolutionary segmentation. *Journal of Business Research, 66,* 1318–1324.

Ringle, C. M., Sarstedt, M., & Straub, D. W. (2012). A critical look at the use of PLS-SEM in *MIS Quarterly. MIS Quarterly, 36,* iii–xiv.

Ringle, C. M., Sarstedt, M., & Zimmermann, L. (2011). Customer satisfaction with commercial airlines: The role of perceived safety and purpose of travel. *Journal of Marketing Theory and Practice, 19,* 459–472.

Ringle, C. M., Wende, S., & Becker, J.-M. (2015). SmartPLS 3 [Computer software]. Retrieved from http://www.smartpls.com

Ringle, C. M., Wende, S., & Will, A. (2005). SmartPLS 2 [Computer software]. Retrieved from http://www.smartpls.com

Ringle, C. M., Wende, S., & Will, A. (2010). Finite mixture partial least squares analysis: Methodology and numerical examples. In V. Esposito Vinzi, W. W. Chin, J. Henseler, & H. Wang (Eds.), *Handbook of partial least squares: Concepts, methods and applications in marketing and related fields* (Springer Handbooks of Computational Statistics Series, Vol. II, pp. 195–218). Berlin: Springer.

Ringle, C. M., & Sarstedt, M. (in press). Gain more insight from your PLS-SEM results: The importance-performance map analysis. Industrial Management & Data Systems.

Roldán, J. L., & Sánchez-Franco, M. J. (2012). Variance-based structural equation modeling: Guidelines for using partial least squares in information systems research. In M. Mora, O. Gelman, A. L. Steenkamp, & M. Raisinghani (Eds.), *Research methodologies, innovations and philosophies in software systems engineering and information systems* (pp. 193–221). Hershey, PA: IGI Global.

Rönkkö, M., & Evermann, J. (2013). A critical examination of common beliefs about partial least squares path modeling. *Organizational Research Methods, 16*(3), 425–448.

Rossiter, J. R. (2002). The C-OAR-SE procedure for scale development in marketing. *International Journal of Research in Marketing, 19,* 305–335.

Rossiter, J. R. (2011). *Measurement for the social sciences: The C-OAR-SE method and why it must replace psychometrics.* Berlin: Springer.

Sánchez, G., Trinchera, L., & Russolillo, G. (2015). R Package plspm: Tools for Partial Least Squares Path Modeling (PLS-PM) version 0.4.7 [Computer software]. Retrieved from http://cran.r-project.org/web/packages/plspm/

Sarstedt, M. (2008). A review of recent approaches for capturing heterogeneity in partial least squares path modelling. *Journal of Modelling in Management, 3,* 140–161.

Sarstedt, M., Becker, J.-M., Ringle, C. M., & Schwaiger, M. (2011). Uncovering and treating unobserved heterogeneity with FIMIX-PLS: Which model selection criterion provides an appropriate number of segments? *Schmalenbach Business Review, 63,* 34–62.

Sarstedt, M., Diamantopoulos, A., Salzberger, T., & Baumgartner, P. (in press). Selecting single items to measure doubly-concrete constructs: A cautionary tale. *Journal of Business Research.*

Sarstedt, M., Henseler, J., & Ringle, C. M. (2011). Multi-group analysis in partial least squares (PLS) path modeling: Alternative methods and empirical results. *Advances in International Marketing, 22,* 195–218.

Sarstedt, M., & Mooi, E. A. (2014). *A concise guide to market research: The process, data, and methods using IBM SPSS statistics* (2nd ed.). Berlin: Springer.

Sarstedt, M., & Ringle, C. M. (2010). Treating unobserved heterogeneity in PLS path modelling: A comparison of FIMIX-PLS with different data analysis strategies. *Journal of Applied Statistics, 37,* 1299–1318.

Sarstedt, M., Ringle, C. M., & Gudergan, S. P. (in press). Guidelines for treating unobserved heterogeneity in tourism research: A comment on Marques and Reis (2015). *Annals of Tourism Research.*

Sarstedt, M., Ringle, C. M., Henseler, J., & Hair, J. F. (2014). On the emancipation of PLS-SEM: A commentary on Rigdon (2012). *Long Range Planning, 47,* 154–160.

Sarstedt, M., Ringle, C. M., Smith, D., Reams, R., & Hair, J. F. (2014). Partial least squares structural equation modeling (PLS-SEM): A useful tool for family business researchers. *Journal of Family Business Strategy, 5,* 105–115.

Sarstedt, M., & Schloderer, M. P. (2010). Developing a measurement approach for reputation of non-profit organizations. *International Journal of Nonprofit & Voluntary Sector Marketing, 15,* 276–299.

Sarstedt, M., Schwaiger, M., & Ringle, C. M. (2009). Do we fully understand the critical success factors of customer satisfaction with industrial goods? Extending Festge and Schwaiger's model to account for unobserved heterogeneity. *Journal of Business Market Management, 3,* 185–206.

Sarstedt, M., & Wilczynski, P. (2009). More for less? A comparison of single-item and multi-item measures. *Business Administration Review, 69,* 211–227.

Sarstedt, M., Wilczynski, P., & Melewar, T. (2013). Measuring reputation in global markets: A comparison of reputation measures' convergent and criterion validities. *Journal of World Business, 48*, 329–339.

Sattler, H., Völckner, F., Riediger, C., & Ringle, C. (2010). The impact of brand extension success factors on brand extension price premium. *International Journal of Research in Marketing, 27*, 319–328.

Schafer, J. L., & Graham, J. L. (2002). Missing data: Our view of the state of the art. *Psychological Methods, 7*, 147–177.

Schlittgen, R. (2011). A weighted least-squares approach to clusterwise regression. *Advances in Statistical Analysis, 95*, 205–217.

Schlittgen, R., Ringle, C. M., Sarstedt, M., & Becker, J.-M. (2015). Segmentation of PLS path models by iterative reweighted regressions. In J. Henseler, C. M. Ringle, J. L. Roldán, & G. Cepeda (Eds.), *2nd International Symposium on Partial Least Squares Path Modeling: The conference for PLS users*. Seville, Spain.

Schloderer, M. P., Sarstedt, M., & Ringle, C. M. (2014). The relevance of reputation in the nonprofit sector: The moderating effect of socio-demographic characteristics. *International Journal of Nonprofit & Voluntary Sector Marketing, 19*, 110–126.

Schwaiger, M. (2004). Components and parameters of corporate reputation: An empirical study. *Schmalenbach Business Review, 56*, 46–71.

Schwaiger, M., Raithel, S., & Schloderer, M. P. (2009). Recognition or rejection: How a company's reputation influences stakeholder behavior. In J. Klewes & R. Wreschniok (Eds.), *Reputation capital: Building and maintaining trust in the 21st century* (pp. 39–55). Berlin: Springer.

Schwaiger, M., Sarstedt, M., & Taylor, C. R. (2010). Art for the sake of the corporation: Audi, BMW Group, DaimlerChrysler, Montblanc, Siemens, and Volkswagen help explore the effect of sponsorship on corporate reputations. *Journal of Advertising Research, 50*, 77–90.

Shi, S. G. (1992). Accurate and efficient double-bootstrap confidence limit method. *Computational Statistics & Data Analysis, 13*, 21–32.

Shmueli, G. (2010). To explain or to predict? *Statistical Science, 25*, 289–310.

Slack, N. (1994). The importance-performance matrix as a determinant of improvement priority. *International Journal of Operations and Production Management, 44*, 59–75.

Sobel, M. E. (1982). Asymptotic confidence intervals for indirect effects in structural equation models. *Sociological Methodology, 13*, 290–312.

Squillacciotti, S. (2005). Prediction-oriented classification in PLS path modeling. In T. Aluja, J. Casanovas, V. Esposito Vinzi, & M. Tenenhaus (Eds.), *PLS & marketing: Proceedings of the 4th international symposium on PLS and related methods* (pp. 499–506). Paris: DECISIA.

Squillacciotti, S. (2010). Prediction-oriented classification in PLS path modeling. In V. Esposito Vinzi, W. W. Chin, J. Henseler, & H. Wang (Eds.), *Handbook of partial least squares: Concepts, methods and applications in marketing and related fields* (Springer Handbooks of Computational Statistics Series, Vol. II, pp. 219–233). Berlin: Springer.

Steenkamp, J. B. E. M., & Baumgartner, H. (1998). Assessing measurement invariance in cross national consumer research. *Journal of Consumer Research, 25*, 78–107.

Stone, M. (1974). Cross-validatory choice and assessment of statistical predictions. *Journal of the Royal Statistical Society, 36*, 111–147.

Temme, D., Kreis, H., & Hildebrandt, L. (2010). A comparison of current PLS path modeling software: Features, ease-of-use, and performance. In V. Esposito Vinzi, W. W. Chin, J. Henseler, & H. Wang (Eds.), *Handbook of partial least squares: Concepts, methods and applications* (Springer Handbooks of Computational Statistics Series, Vol. II, pp. 737–756). Berlin: Springer.

Tenenhaus, M., Amato, S., & Esposito Vinzi, V. (2004). A global goodness-of-fit index for PLS structural equation modeling. In *Proceedings of the XLII SIS Scientific Meeting* (pp. 739–742). Padova, Italy: CLEUP.

Tenenhaus, M., Esposito Vinzi, V., Chatelin, Y.-M., & Lauro, C. (2005). PLS path modeling. *Computational Statistics & Data Analysis, 48*, 159–205.

Test&Go (2006). SPAD-PLS version 6.0.0 [Computer software]. Paris: Author.

Thiele, K. O., Sarstedt, M., & Ringle, C. M. (2015). A comparative evaluation of new and established methods for structural equation modeling. In A. G. Close & D. L. Haytko (Eds.), *Proceedings of the 2015 Academy of Marketing Science Annual Conference*. Denver, CO: Academy of Marketing Science.

Vandenberg, R. J., & Lance, C. E. (2000). A review and synthesis of the measurement invariance literature: Suggestions, practices, and recommendations for organizational research. *Organizational Research Methods, 3*, 4–70.

Vilares, M. J., Almeida, M. H., & Coelho, P. S. (2010). Comparison of likelihood and PLS estimators for structural equation modeling: A simulation with customer satisfaction data. In V. Esposito Vinzi, W. W. Chin, J. Henseler, & H. Wang (Eds.), *Handbook of partial least squares: Concepts, methods and applications* (Springer Handbooks of Computational Statistics Series, Vol. II, pp. 289–305). Berlin: Springer.

Völckner, F., Sattler, H., Hennig-Thurau, T., & Ringle, C. M. (2010). The role of parent brand quality for service brand extension success. *Journal of Service Research, 13*, 359–361.

Voorhees, C. M., Brady, M. K., Calantone, R., & Ramirez, E. (2016). Discriminant validity testing in marketing: An analysis, causes for concern, and proposed remedies. *Journal of the Academy of Marketing Science, 44*, 119–134.

Walsh, G., Mitchell, V.-W., Jackson, P. R., & Beatty, E. (2009). Examining the antecedents and consequences of corporate reputation: A customer perspective. *British Journal of Management, 20*, 187–203.

Wanous, J. P., Reichers, A., & Hudy, M. J. (1997). Overall job satisfaction: How good are single-item measures? *Journal of Applied Psychology, 82*, 247–252.

Wetzels, M., Odekerken-Schroder, G., & van Oppen, C. (2009). Using PLS path modeling for assessing hierarchical construct models: Guidelines and empirical illustration. *MIS Quarterly, 33*, 177–195.

Wilden, R., & Gudergan, S. (2015). The impact of dynamic capabilities on operational marketing and technological capabilities: Investigating the role of environmental turbulence. *Journal of the Academy of Marketing Science, 43,* 181–199.

Wilson, B., Callaghan, W., Ringle, C. M., & Henseler, J. (2007). Exploring causal path directionality for a marketing model using Cohen's path method. In H. Martens, T. Næs, & M. Martens (Eds.), *Causalities explored by indirect observation: Proceedings of the 5th International Symposium on PLS and Related Methods (PLS'07)* (pp. 57–61). Åas, Norway: MATFORSK.

Wold, H. O. A. (1966). Estimation of principal components and related models by iterative least squares. In P. R. Krishnaiaah (Ed.), *Multivariate Analysis* (pp. 391–420). New York: Academic Press.

Wold, H. O. A. (1975). Path models with latent variables: The NIPALS approach. In H. M. Blalock, A. Aganbegian, F. M. Borodkin, R. Boudon, & V. Capecchi (Eds.), *Quantitative sociology: International perspectives on mathematical and statistical modeling* (pp. 307–357). New York: Academic Press.

Wold, H. O. A. (1982). Soft modeling: The basic design and some extensions. In K. G. Jöreskog & H. Wold (Eds.), *Systems under indirect observations: Part II* (pp. 1–54). Amsterdam: North-Holland.

Wold, H. O. A. (1985). Partial least squares. In S. Kotz & N. L. Johnson (Eds.), *Encyclopedia of statistical sciences* (pp. 581–591). New York: John Wiley.

Zhang, Y., & Schwaiger, M. (2009). An empirical research of corporate reputation in China. *Communicative Business, 1,* 80–104.

Zhao, X., Lynch, J. G., & Chen, Q. (2010). Reconsidering Baron and Kenny: Myths and truths about mediation analysis. *Journal of Consumer Research, 37,* 197–206.

Author Index

Italicized pages refer to Exhibits

Subject Index